Forgotten Justice

Forgotten Justice

The Forms of Justice in the History of Legal and Political Theory

Allan Beever

UNIVERSITY PRESS

Great Clarendon Street, Oxford, OX2 6DP,
United Kingdom

Oxford University Press is a department of the University of Oxford.
It furthers the University's objective of excellence in research, scholarship,
and education by publishing worldwide. Oxford is a registered trade mark of
Oxford University Press in the UK and in certain other countries

© A. Beever, 2013

The moral rights of the authors have been asserted

First Edition published in 2013

Impression: 1

All rights reserved. No part of this publication may be reproduced, stored in
a retrieval system, or transmitted, in any form or by any means, without the
prior permission in writing of Oxford University Press, or as expressly permitted
by law, by licence or under terms agreed with the appropriate reprographics
rights organization. Enquiries concerning reproduction outside the scope of the
above should be sent to the Rights Department, Oxford University Press, at the
address above

You must not circulate this work in any other form
and you must impose this same condition on any acquirer

Crown copyright material is reproduced under Class Licence
Number C01P0000148 with the permission of OPSI
and the Queen's Printer for Scotland

British Library Cataloguing in Publication Data

Data available

ISBN 978–0–19–967548–7

Printed and bound in Great Britain by
CPI Group (UK) Ltd, Croydon, CR0 4YY

Links to third party websites are provided by Oxford in good faith and
for information only. Oxford disclaims any responsibility for the materials
contained in any third party website referenced in this work.

To Beth

Acknowledgements

I would like first to thank the School of Law at the University of Southampton for allowing me the leave during which I wrote much of this book. It is with considerable regret that personal circumstances meant that I was unable, in even a small way, to repay that debt. Thanks and apologies are in order.

Thanks also to the Leverhulme Trust for the Major Research Fellowship that facilitated the writing of this book. The break from teaching was very much appreciated. On that note, thanks also to the Alexander von Humboldt Foundation for the von Humboldt Research Fellowship and to the Max-Planck-Institut für ausländisches und internationales Privatrecht, Hamburg, and Professor Reinhard Zimmermann in particular, for hosting me during the period in which, through confrontation with Kant's work, I formulated the basic thesis of this book.

I would also like to express my appreciation for the help given to me by Alex Flach and Natasha Flemming, and others at OUP, in the preparation of this book. Thanks also to the two anonymous reviewers who forced me to confront some important matters.

Finally, I would like to express my gratitude to my family. To Tana, Piri, and Ineawa for putting up with a father whose mind is not always on the mundane and for reminding me that that is, after all, where the fun is. And to Cathryn for her unfailing support and love, without which it would all be pointless.

And to my mother, who has given me so much and whose only real failing is a lack of a sense of her own rightful honour.

Contents

Figures	xi
Introduction	1
The Modern Conception of Political Philosophy and Law	13
Part I: Discovery	**35**
Plato: A Beginning	37
Plato: A New Beginning	54
Aristotle	61
Cicero	89
Part II: Establishment	**95**
Aquinas	99
Pufendorf	118
Kant	150
Part III: Forgetting	**171**
Hobbes	175
Locke	207
The Utilitarians	227
Part IV: Implications	**241**
Legal Analysis	243
Political Philosophy	278
Conclusion	308
Bibliography	311
Index	321

Figures

The Basic Structure of Political Morality

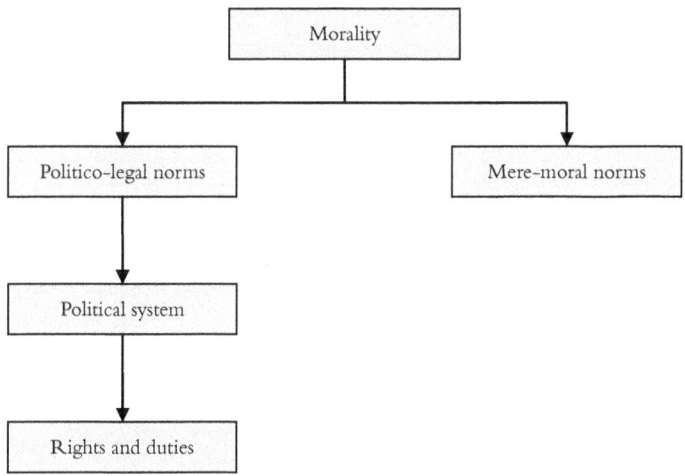

M1 The Modern View

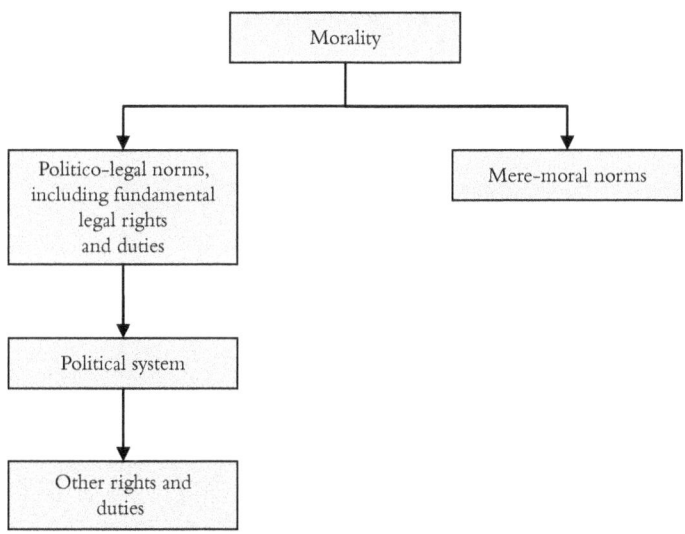

T1 The Traditional View

Justice and Rights

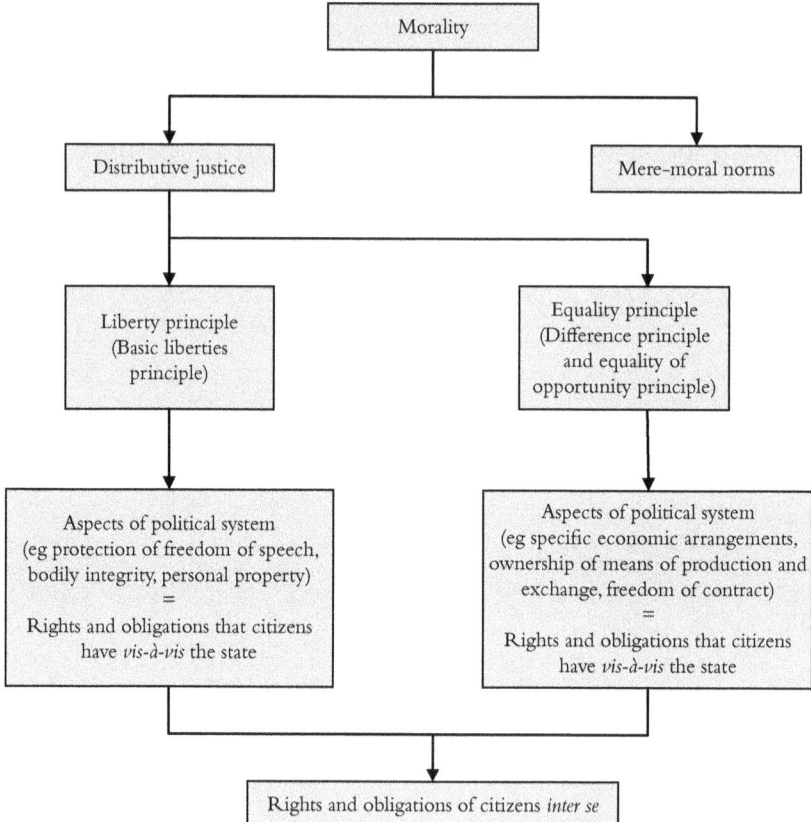

M2 The Modern View (Based on Rawls)

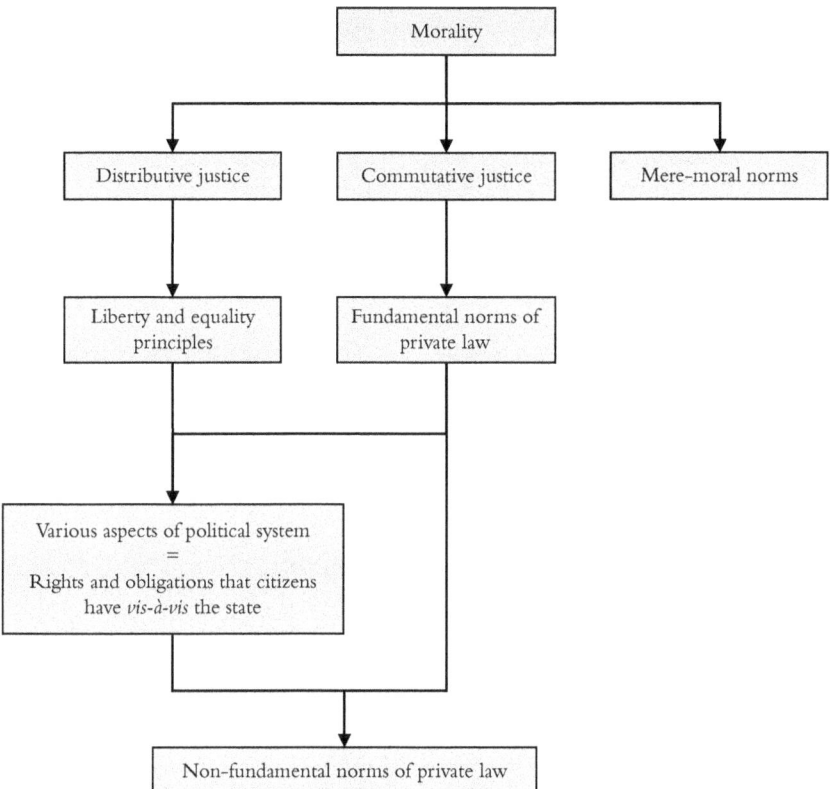

T2 The Traditional View

xiv FIGURES

Justice and Law

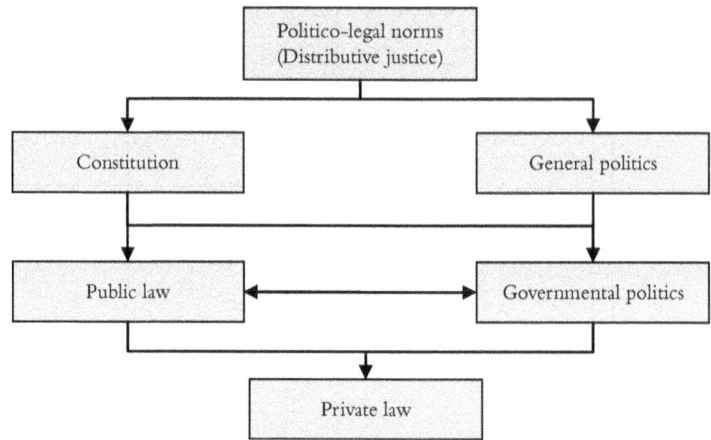

M3 The Modern View

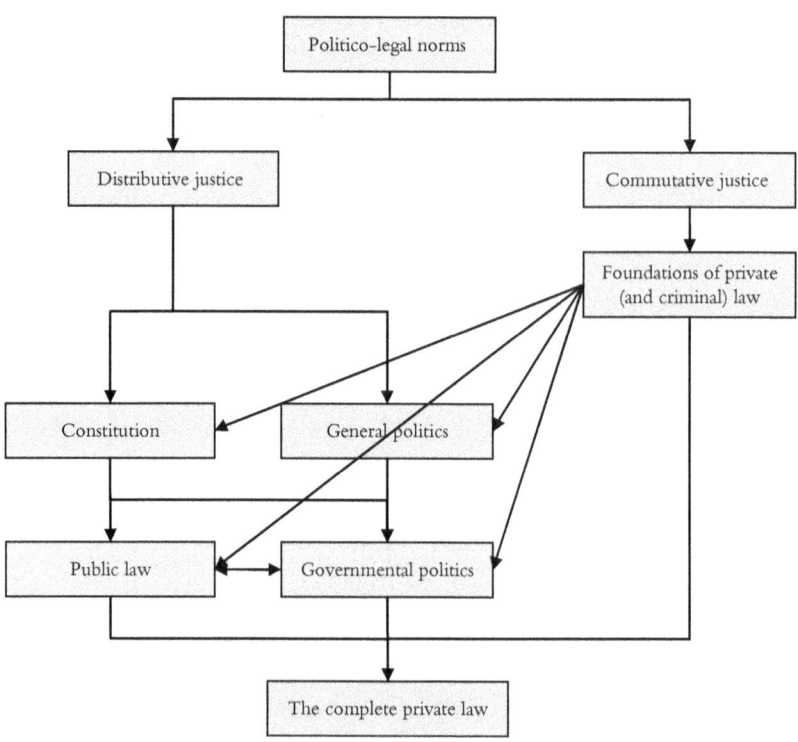

T3 The Traditional View

The Forms of Justice

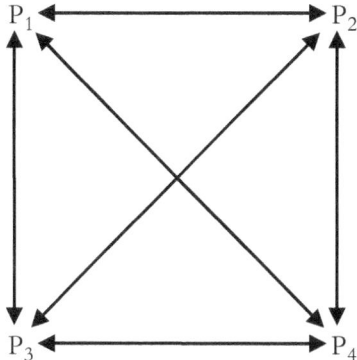

J1: Distributive Justice

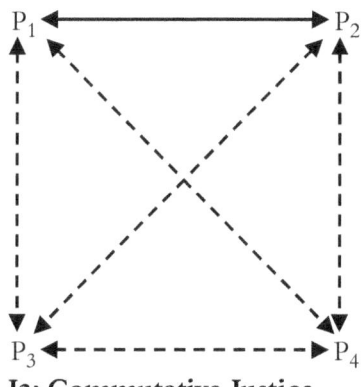

J2: Commutative Justice

Introduction

1. The Story of Political and Legal Philosophy

This book is prompted by the uncomfortable conviction that there is something very wrong with the modern conception of political and legal theory. The conviction, to which I have reluctantly and only gradually come, is that we do not understand the most basic features of our political or legal obligations to one another. This is because modern theorists have adopted an understanding of the political and the legal that is fundamentally wrong.

It is not easy to capture this mistake or to present it in simple terms. This is in part because the mistake infects the terminology that we use to describe the political and legal realms. In fact, it infects the terms 'political' and 'legal' themselves. Because of this, while one could well say that the problem with the modern view is that it wrongly thinks that the political is exhausted by politics and that the legal is exhausted by the law, this will not make much sense to the reader, at least not until she has finished reading this book.

It is possible, however, immediately to give the reader a glimpse of the error. This is because the mistake lies in wrongly insisting on the adoption of one particular point of view from which the political and the legal are to be analysed. What is that point of view? In short, it is the state.

Writing on social, political, or legal philosophy today is all but exclusively concerned with the state and with the issues that emanate from that concern. For all the diversity of this material, the state is its modern obsession.[1] For instance, political philosophers argue about the demands of distributive justice, ie how the state ought to distribute benefits and burdens; political and legal philosophers debate the justification of 'constitutional' rights thought to be beyond legislative encroachment; social theorists dispute the character of the modern state, whether it is, for example, as disciplinarian as Foucault maintains; and legal positivists analyse law from the perspective of the 'officials'. All of this analysis is state oriented. It gets its point of view from the state, from the society taken as a unit, and from distributive justice.

The aim of this book is not to challenge any specific modern theory. Moreover, though it calls into question some parts of some of those theories, the majority is left untouched. Rather, the point of the book is to reject the idea—so ubiquitous that it has become unconscious—that this is *the* point of view from which to understand the political, the social, and the legal. Certainly, the state's point of view is a valid one, but it is only one of two relevant points of view. What is more, the second, the one we have forgotten, is by far the most fundamental.

The goal of the first two parts of this book is to present that point of view. But let me now provide a glimpse of it.

Even very young children know that they should not hit each other or take each other's toys. Whether this is learnt or innate need not concern us.[2] But the sense of injustice burning on a toddler's face when he is hit or when a toy is grabbed out of his hands can be palpable. What is this sense? When the toddler feels it, what is he feeling?

To put it simply, the toddler feels that he has been wronged. Now, of course, that does not mean that the toddler is remotely able to articulate that feeling, let alone justify it. But nor would it be right to say that the toddler is merely reacting to an unwanted event. It is plain that the toddler can see that something happened to him that should not have happened.

Just as obviously, the toddler does not have this feeling because he possesses some dim awareness that his playmate is distributing burdens throughout society unjustly or because he has a right in accordance with just distribution that has been violated. Nor is it because the

---

[1] As Skinner, 'The Idea of the State: A Genealogy' highlights, relying on the development of transnational bodies, some modern theorists have predicted the decline of the state. However, as Skinner argues, as this view ignores the fact that the state is the major player in international relations, this view is 'inattentive'. What is more, a theory of the decline of the state is of course deeply concerned with the state.

[2] For an interesting discussion of like issues, see Bloom, 'The Moral Life of Babies'.

toddler has some grasp of the fact that the state or society has prohibited behaviour of the kind in question. Rather, the toddler feels wronged by his playmate without any conception of society at all.

And while it is tempting to say that children learn these responses from the behaviour of their parents, it is also telling that—unless the parents are legal or political philosophers, and probably not even then—they did not have these social ideas in mind either. As I write, my one-year-old son has developed a habit of whacking his three-year-old brother, a habit we are trying to cure. But though I recognize the social aspects of this behaviour, the main and most important reason I want him to stop is that I regard his actions as wrongful toward his brother. I can also see that idea written very powerfully on his brother's face.

Certainly, the modern philosopher will be untroubled by these observations. Perhaps her reply will be that the entitlements and obligations referred to above are neither political nor legal but moral or ethical. The toddler, then, may have some sense of his moral entitlements (through nature or nurture), but has no understanding of the political or legal.

But what does it mean to say that an entitlement or obligation is moral *rather than* political or legal? The answer to this question is likely to beg all of the questions that prompted the writing of this book. It will have the form, 'Political and legal obligations emanate in some way from the state or society, but moral obligations are or can be independent thereof.' That, I think, is the wrong answer, but it will be of more use now specifically to consider the nature of moral obligation.

It is often said that moral obligations are about the agent, about the individual. Kant's moral theory is traditionally understood in this fashion. It is thought to be a theory about what constitutes a good person. On this view, then, morality demands that people not hit each other because doing so is inconsistent with being a good person. That formulation might sound too solipsistic to be plausible. It appears to suggest that a person concerned about morality is interested only in her own moral integrity. But the idea need not be understood in that fashion. Part of being a good person is having the right attitudes and feelings towards others, and so the moral person could not be self-obsessed. Nevertheless, the idea is that morality is focused on individuals as such.

But the thing to notice is that this point of view does not match the one encountered above. It is certainly true that my youngest son will not grow up to be a good person if he keeps hitting people, but I do not see that thought reflected on his brother's face after he has been hit and, though I am cognizant of it, it is not at the front of my mind either.

Two points are relevant here. First, the norm in question is not merely moral in the sense used above. The fundamental reason my youngest son should not hit his brother is the same reason I should not hit my wife, and it would be odd to think that this reason was moral rather than political. Moreover, the feeling is not about my youngest son. If our interest were solely in the agent, then the fact that my son hits *his brother* would be merely a detail. The idea is that he acts immorally (or would do so were he older) because he acts as a good person would not have done *by hitting his brother*. As it were, 'his brother' is a placeholder, a variable, that could in principle be replaced by someone else: 'his mother', 'his sister', 'his cousin', 'his other brother', etc. But again, that is not the thought I see burning on his brother's face. *He* felt wronged. What is more, I agree. I feel that my son wronged *his brother*. In other words, the feeling to which I am drawing attention is not about my youngest son. It is about both of my sons.

Now, modern philosophers have thought that this move involves a shift from morality or ethics, with its focus on the good individual, to the political, with its emphasis on the state and society. But that is surely a step too far. My oldest son feels that he is being wronged by his brother, but that is not because he thinks that his brother is breaching some kind of social convention or the like. It is because of the immediate experience he is having. He feels the pain, sees that his brother has caused it intentionally, and feels that to be wrongful (he feels quite differently about accidents). He does all this without any reference to the social at all. His feeling is based entirely on the interpersonal, on the interaction between his brother and himself. It is also noteworthy that I am sure my wife would feel the same way were I to hit her. Her response would not be of the kind: 'Stop distributing burdens unfairly' or 'Don't you realize I have a right not to be hit because the existence of that right is a necessary condition for fair distribution?'[3]

My son's feeling is about him and his brother. My wife's would be about her and me. The feelings are not about anyone else. And

---

[3] In case this sounds too implausible to be taken seriously, the position that these rights are based on distributive justice is advanced in, for example, Cane, 'Distributive Justice and Tort Law', 415. It is the standard position taken in modern legal analysis.

though I interfere to prevent my son hitting his brother, I do not do so because I feel that I am somehow being wronged, that the wrong committed encompasses me or any such thing. I interfere because, as a parent of the two boys, I feel a responsibility to prevent them wronging each other. The norm in question is of concern to me, but it does not involve me.

Now, this leads to the second possible way in which the modern philosopher might choose to deal with these cases. She might maintain that, though the feelings in question have the character I have described, the actual norms involved can be justified only in accordance with distributive justice or the like. That might turn out to be the case, but it ought to strike us as odd. If children can understand that they should not wrong each other and yet have no idea of the state or society, then it is natural to think that the first thought does not rely on the second. The argument of this book is that this is right.

This is something that we all knew as children. But when we became theorists, we were taught to forget it. I suppose it is meant to be unsophisticated and childish. But my contention is that the children are right and the (modern) philosophers are wrong. In short, a theory that cannot accommodate the thoughts enunciated above, having to translate them into social concerns or arguments of distributive justice, is seriously deficient. It has forgotten one of the most fundamental elements of our moral lives.

It is also worth noting that many of our so-called moral utterances have the double nature encountered above: they are about being a good person and about behaving rightly with respect to others; they are about the personal and the interpersonal. If I see my son grabbing a toy from his younger brother, I might tell him to stop being selfish. My concern with his selfishness is in part a concern with his character, but it is also in part a concern with the interaction between him and his brother. I feel that his brother should have the toy quite independently of either of my sons' moral characters. Moreover, that feeling has nothing to do with distributive justice. Similarly, the golden rule in part reflects an idea about what constitutes personal goodness, but it also suggests how others should be treated independently of the moral character of either party.

If the children are right, if interpersonal moral norms exist that rightly govern our behaviour, then it is natural to think that those norms lie at the basis of our political and legal obligations. That, no doubt, will sound strange to many. But, as I show in this book, it was accepted by a great many of our leading political philosophers and until comparatively recently was accepted as a piece of common sense.

This book tells a story: the story of the discovery, establishment, and decline of the view glimpsed above—what I call the traditional view.[4] It first attempts to enable the modern reader to see the political world through the eyes of the traditional theorists. This is no small task. The modern view places a veil over all our thought that is very hard to lift. I try to do so by examining the issues that led the traditional thinkers to their views. The idea is to follow them down the paths that they took and thereby, with luck, learn to see the vistas that they saw open before them. It then explores the decline of the traditional view after the convulsion set off by Hobbes and the English Civil War. As is stressed, this decline was not the result of a confrontation between the traditional and the modern view won by the latter. It was rather because of a 'paradigm shift' in the way that people thought about politics, effected by historical and intellectual events. The result is that the traditional view has been not defeated, but simply forgotten. This book is an attempt to remember.

A second theme of this book concerns the relationship between politics and law. To the modern mind, that seems unconnected with the material discussed above. But as we will see, these issues are thoroughly intertwined. To the modern thinker, 'law is the offspring of politics',[5] and so the study of law is necessarily conceptually posterior to the study of the political. But the traditional theorists did not share this view. For them, it is rather that politics is the offspring of law. It is law, then, that has conceptual priority.

Now, the claim is, of course, not that *all* law is prior to politics. Much law is the product of political institutions. But the traditionalist holds that far from being such a product, some law provides the basis for those institutions. And what is perhaps even more remarkable, this law is *private*, not public, law. Accordingly, in the following I place much

---

[4] I do not mean to imply that there is only one line of thought that could be described as traditional. Nor do I claim that the history of the ideas I label traditional and modern is linear in this regard. In fact, it is clear that it is not. The decline happened twice, the first time during the renaissance. See Tuck, *Natural Rights Theories*, ch 2. This, then, is an appropriate subject to test the reversal of Marx's maxim: 'Hegel remarks somewhere that all great, world-historical facts and personages occur, as it were, twice. He has forgotten to add: the first time as [farce], the second as [tragedy]' (Marx, 'The Eighteenth Brumaire', 594).

[5] Waldron, 'Kant's Legal Positivism', 1538.

emphasis on the place of private law in the theories of the thinkers examined. Most modern political philosophers have no theory of private law at all; a fact that is generally regarded as insignificant, even natural. But the traditional theorists began their discussions of politics with an analysis of that law and built their political theories on it. Our task is to understand why this was and what this difference reveals about the wider differences between traditionalists and moderns.

2. The Structure of this Book

The first chapter of this book describes something with which we are familiar but, due to its ubiquity, seldom contemplate: the modern conception of the nature of political and legal theory. It examines the general structure of this conception in order to contrast it with the traditional view developed in later chapters.

The argument of the book begins in earnest in Part I. This part explores the origins of the traditional view in the writings of Plato, Aristotle, and Cicero. Part II examines the traditional view in the fully developed forms found in the theories of Aquinas, Pufendorf, and Kant. Part III then discusses the decline of the traditional view and its replacement with the modern, paying particular attention to the theories of Hobbes, Locke, and the utilitarians. Part IV explores some of the important differences, not already examined in previous chapters, between the traditional and modern views and discusses the way in which the modern conception has affected our understanding of political and legal reality.

As indicated above, this book is intended to present the story of the birth, development, and death of an idea. Because of this, the book does not examine the theories it considers in great detail. It is not, for instance, a comprehensive account of Plato's *The Republic* or Aristotle's *The Politics*. Obviously, it would have been impossible to present comprehensive accounts of all the works examined here. For this reason also, though I have been much influenced by the wealth of secondary literature covering these thinkers, I mention very little of it.

Moreover, while I hope to convince the reader that the traditional view is attractive and has much to recommend it, I have not attempted to provide a rigorous philosophical defence of that view. Likewise, while I suggest difficulties with the modern view, I present no knockdown argument against it. I wanted to write a story that was engaging enough to be read, that opened up for the reader a new (or rather an old) way of thinking about political and legal reality and that led her to ponder whether the deep questions of political and legal thought might be answered in different ways. If I have succeeded at all in this, it is because of my focus on the general and thematic, rather than on detail and rigorous proof. The latter is needed, of course, but must be provided elsewhere.

I feel it also important to say that, in the interests of (relative) brevity and ease of exposition, I have ignored some thinkers who must be regarded as central to the traditional view: Gratian, Cajetan, Grotius, Fichte, and Hegel amongst others. I assure the reader that I have done so only after giving the matter much thought (Grotius, for instance, is too unclear about the foundations of his view and Fichte and Hegel are already a little too obsessed with the state). I have also bypassed thinkers important to the third part of this study: Hume, Rousseau, Burke, and Paine, for example. My neglect of those thinkers implies only that I wanted to keep the book short enough to be read.

Also worth stressing is that, though I claim that the traditional view is forgotten today, I do not mean that it is *entirely* so. On the contrary, some thinkers hold a version of the traditional. Not coincidentally, these thinkers are strongly attached to the philosophers examined in Part II of this book. The most important include John Finnis (Aquinas) and Ernest Weinrib (Kant). It is in no small part because they espouse versions of the traditional view that their theories are often met with considerable miscomprehension.[6]

3. The Nature of the Modern Conception and Traditional View

A crucial point that needs to be stressed from the outset is that neither the modern conception nor the traditional view is to be understood as a theory. On the contrary, modern and traditional thinkers propound

---

[6] Other thinkers are also important. One can discern the influence of the traditional view on authors such as Peter Benson, John CP Goldberg, James Gordley, Stephen R Perry, Arthur Ripstein, Robert Stevens, Martin Stone, Richard W Wright, and Benjamin C Zipursky, for instance.

distinct and often contrasting theories. What holds the modern and the traditional views together is that they share not a theory, but an outlook on the nature of politico-legal theorizing.

For all their differences, modern thinkers hold that the point of view from which to analyse the politico-legal is the state. And for all their differences, the traditional thinkers disagree. Thus, to put this another way, the fundamental difference between the traditional and the modern views lies in their conception of the central questions of political philosophy and how those questions relate to each other and to other politico-legal issues. For the modern, for instance, the state comes first and the law last; for the traditional, it is the other way around.

4. Terminology

When attempting to understand the views of those who lie on the other side of a paradigm shift, one of the greatest problems concerns terminology. The problem is that the paradigm shift not only produces a new understanding of a subject matter, but also entails that words are used with different meaning. Part of the difficulty, of course, is that this difference in meaning is usually not immediately apparent.

With respect to the issues examined in this book, the chief difficulty is with the use of the term 'law'. This, as we see, is no coincidence. The shift between the traditional and the modern view is primarily a shift in the understanding of the nature of law. Though I do not concentrate on this aspect of the issue, it is noteworthy that the shift has produced an understanding of law conducive to legal positivism.

A paradigm example of this confusion is found in HLA Hart's interpretation of Augustine's maxim, '*Lex iniusta non est lex*' as implying 'a twofold contention: first, that there are certain principles of true morality or justice…; secondly, that man-made laws which conflict with these principles are not valid law'.[7] Hart rejects this view on the ground that many unjust laws, Nazi laws for instance, were valid laws.

Augustine's maxim means that an unjust law is not a law. But when Augustine made this statement, he meant by 'law' what he

---

[7] Hart, *The Concept of Law*, 156.

meant by 'law'.[8] But, as positivists are unfortunately inclined to do, Hart insists on reading 'law' his way. In effect, Hart forces Augustine to 'say' that those things that we moderns call laws that are also unjust are not valid examples of those things that we moderns call laws. Hart has no difficulty dismissing that view.

The traditional theorists did not share the modern understanding of law. Nor did they all agree with each other about the nature of law. But they did all agree that law is in its essence concerned with legitimate coercion.[9] In particular, all held that coercion is legitimate only when it is justified by law. Note that this does not mean, as we are inclined to read it, that coercion is just only if it is sanctioned by a body with sovereign authority. That position is impossible because sovereign authority is itself coercive and we need to know what justifies it. For the traditional thinkers, the law—the natural law, that is—justifies the sovereign. And that means that the law is prior to the state. The law is what gives the sovereign his authority to govern. It also gives the sovereign the authority to make new laws—positive laws—that also must be obeyed.

Another difficult term is 'politics'. If, as the tradition holds, sovereign authority is based on law, then it is possible to think of this law as part of politics. This is how some in the tradition thought of it. But we are now tied up in knots. We are asked to think of law as grounding politics and as being part of politics.

In order to avoid this confusion, it is necessary to adopt definitions of 'law' and 'politics' that prevent equivocation. I begin with the latter.

The *Oxford English Dictionary* defines the relevant sense of 'politics' as: 'The theory or practice of government or administration…The science or study of government and the state.' That is the sense adopted here. As we might say, politics is concerned with the direction of the community.

In the light of what has gone above, this raises the question: does politics exhaust the realm of legitimate coercion? In other words, is the only possible justification for coercion political? As we will see, the modern answer to this position is basically 'yes', but the traditional

---

[8] For a developed analysis of this point, see Orrego, 'Classical Natural Law Theory', 299–302.

[9] Hence, Augustine's motto means something more like: 'A purported piece of legitimate coercion that is unjust is not really a piece of legitimate coercion.'

is 'no'. For the traditionalist, some justified coercion is warranted by politics, but some is warranted by another area of moral concern.

Because of this, we require a term to refer to all norms that relate to justified coercion. Because the modern thinker holds that justified coercion is exhausted by the political, she needs no term other than 'politics' itself. But because the traditionalist thinks otherwise, a new term is required. But what could it be?

On the face of it, 'natural law' suggests itself. In fact, however, it is not at all appropriate. We are looking for an umbrella term to refer to all norms concerned with legitimate coercion. Now, certainly, the thinkers examined in the second part of this book hold that all legitimate coercion is ultimately justified by the natural law. But any norm that legitimately coerces is a norm of the kind in question, not only those norms that ultimately justify coercion. Thus, a legitimate positive law falls under the umbrella.

As noted above, the term actually used by the thinkers examined in this book is 'law'. However, as we moderns tend to use that term to refer only to the positive law, and as I will generally use that term in that way in this book, the term will not do here. No term suggests itself. I have considered using foreign expressions—*ius*, *droit*, *Recht*, etc—but that strategy is beset with obvious problems. Instead, I am forced to use the neologism: 'politico-legal'. Any norm that relates to justified coercion is politico-legal.

A final point of terminology concerns the contrary of the term 'state of nature'. Different authors use different terms. For convenience, I use only one: the term Kant adopts—'civil condition'.

1

The Modern Conception of Political Philosophy and Law

This is a book about the way in which modern political and legal philosophy differs from its ancestors. I am not interested in the differences that others have noted—the kinds of differences that fill introductory texts in political philosophy and that are routinely drawn to the attention of undergraduate students in courses on the history of the subject. Rather, I am interested in the fundamental conception of political philosophy; in understandings of the deep structure of our subject matter.

Because of this, it is useful to examine the modern view before we begin our investigation of the past. Though we are of course familiar with the modern view, this familiarity need not be, and usually is not, fully articulate. On the contrary, the modern view is so ingrained that many of its features are noticed only with difficulty. It is, as it were, the glasses through which we look at the world, forgetting that we are wearing them. My task in this chapter is to draw attention to those glasses.

The modern conception of political theory is examined in the first section of the chapter. The following section enunciates the modern view of the relationship between politics and law, in particular the private law. The third section ends the chapter by suggesting that, despite the fact that the modern conception is ours, reflection reveals it to be deeply counterintuitive.

1. The Modern Conception of the Structure of Political Morality

Because the modern conception is generally transparent to us, it is impossible to find an explicit statement of it. It is not treated as a premise in our political arguments. It is not presented in even cursory terms on the first pages of our political treatises. It rather provides the invisible intellectual background for contemporary discussion of politics and the place of law within it—a phrase that, as we will see, itself exhibits the modern conception. As a result, we must piece together our picture of this conception by forcing ourselves to notice this background. We must become aware of the assumptions made by theorists, even though few today are disposed to question them.

This chapter focuses primarily on the political theory presented by John Rawls in *A Theory of Justice*. I choose this work for two reasons. First, it is unquestionably the most influential political treatise of the latter twentieth century. Of course, this is not to say that the position it advances is universally accepted. It is not. But our focus is not on the controversial conclusions it reaches but on the assumptions from which it begins. These assumptions are shared by almost all of Rawls' friends and foes. If they were not, then his theory could not have had anything like the influence that it has had.

The second reason for choosing Rawls as our example is found in his style of argumentation. As he makes clear, his task is to provide a theory that fits as closely as possible our intuitions regarding politics and justice.[1] Because of this, Rawls quite consciously builds his theory on assumptions that are widely shared, at least by those who are raised in Western liberal democracies. Again, this indicates that, despite disagreements with Rawls, his assumptions are widely accepted.

Conveniently, Rawls provides a diagram to express his understanding of the constellation of political philosophy (see Figure 1.1 at the end of the chapter).[2] Although it is not intended to be complete and though it would be wrong to place great emphasis on it,[3] it suffices to explain the most general features of Rawls' conception.

This diagram presents the following picture. At the apex stands practical reason, ie the part of reason that deals with action (as opposed

---

[1] Rawls, *A Theory of Justice*, xi–xii, xvii–xviii, 40–46.
[2] Ibid, 94.
[3] Ibid, 93.

to theoretical reason that concerns knowledge and belief). Practical reason can then be divided into three 'sub-disciplines' that relate to the concepts of value, moral worth, and right. The distinction between the second and third concerns that between what one ought to do in order to be a good person (moral worth) and what one ought and can appropriately be compelled to do (right). Politics and law, of course, belong to the latter, and that is the only topic with which we or Rawls are concerned.

Right can then be divided into three areas: that which defines appropriate social systems and institutions, that which determines how individuals should and can be coerced to behave, and that which identifies an appropriate law of nations. Rawls then divides these further.

Though we will return to some of the ideas captured in this diagram later, we need go no further now. For us, the crucial point is indicated by the roman numerals and Rawls' intention in using them. As he explains, they 'express the order in which the various sorts of principles are to be acknowledged in the original position. Thus, the principles for the basic structure of society are to be agreed to first, principles for individuals next, followed by those for the law of nations.'[4] This, of course, relies on Rawls' social contract argument, to be outlined shortly, but the key point concerns the conceptual hierarchy Rawls envisages.

At the top of this hierarchy stands the concept of right: ie the concept of how human beings ought to and can be compelled to behave. This concept first generates an account of the social systems and institutions that a society ought in justice to possess. From that account can in turn be generated an understanding of how individuals are and can be obliged to behave with respect to each other. Importantly, these include the so-called natural duties, examined further below, which demand inter alia that individuals refrain from harming each other.

Clear, then, is Rawls' view that individuals' rights and obligations vis-à-vis one another are a product of social institutions. More fully, justice demands that individuals possess rights and obligations *inter se*, but it does not demand this directly. Rather, it first demands the creation of certain social institutions and then, as a result of those institutions, demands that such rights be upheld. We can summarize this by saying that, for Rawls, the origin of our private rights and obligations is social.

[4] Ibid.

This view is also evidenced in the claim, made in the very first paragraph of *A Theory of Justice*, that the basic structure of society is the 'primary subject of justice'.[5] Witness also the claim that natural conflict between human beings means that: 'A set of principles is required for choosing among the various social arrangements which determine this division of advantages and for underwriting an agreement on the proper distributive shares. These principles are the principles of social justice: they provide a way of assigning rights and duties in the basic institutions of society and they define the appropriate distribution of the benefits and burdens of social cooperation.'[6] In itself, this statement is unremarkable. But it is revealed to be significant when it is realized that, for Rawls, *all* rights and duties are to be understood as benefits and burdens to be assigned in accordance with the principles of justice to which he refers.[7] For Rawls, then, all rights and duties are essentially social. They are a creation of society. This is nicely captured in the following passage.

For us the primary subject of justice is the basic structure of society, or more exactly, the way in which the major social institutions distribute fundamental rights and duties and determine the division of advantages from social cooperation. By major institutions I understand the political constitution and the principal economic and social arrangements. Thus the legal protection of freedom of thought and liberty of conscience, competitive markets, private property in the means of production, and the monogamous family are examples of major social institutions. Taken together as one scheme, the major institutions define men's rights and duties and influence their life prospects, what they can expect to be and how well they can hope to do.[8]

The view to which I am drawing attention is also captured in Rawls' version of the social contract argument. In brief, Rawls builds his account by conducting a thought experiment. He imagines a group of people whose task it is to construct a society. When they come together, they are confronted with a *tabula rasa*. That is, they do

---

[5] Ibid, 3.
[6] Ibid, 4.
[7] Ibid, 5. I was reluctant to attribute this view to Rawls in Beever, *Rediscovering the Law of Negligence*, 64. The reason for my reluctance is examined below. As we see there, Rawls is in fact ambivalent in this regard.
[8] Rawls, *A Theory of Justice*, 6–7.

not bring with them the laws or political decisions of any existing communities but are tasked with creating a new society from a blank canvas. Rawls labels the situation in which these people find themselves the 'original position' and identifies it with the state of nature in traditional social contract thinking.[9]

The first task set for these people is to choose principles of justice that will govern their future interactions. In order to ensure that they choose impartially, Rawls insists that they do so behind a 'veil of ignorance'. That is, it is stipulated that they are unaware of the positions that they will hold, the kind of lives they will wish to lead, etc, in the new society.

This is how Rawls describes his project, here presented in the most general terms:

> the guiding idea is that the principles of justice for the basic structure of society are the object of the original agreement. They are the principles that free and rational persons concerned to further their own interests would accept in an initial position of equality as defining the fundamental terms of their association. These principles are to regulate all further agreements; they specify the kinds of social cooperation that can be entered into and the forms of government that can be established...
>
> Thus we are to imagine that those who engage in social cooperation choose together, in one joint act, the principles which are to assign basic rights and duties and to determine the division of social benefits. Men are to decide in advance how they are to regulate their claims against one another and what is to be the foundation charter of their society...[A] group of persons must decide once and for all what is to count among them as just and unjust. The choice which rational men would make in this hypothetical situation of equal liberty, assuming for the present that this choice problem has a solution, determines the principles of justice.[10]

Clear in this picture is the idea that, before the principles of justice are chosen, no politico-legal norms exist. Those norms in their entirety are created by this process.

Of course, the idea of the social contract is merely a thought experiment. Rawls does not think that people actually did or should get together in this way. He does not believe that there was a time, or will

---
[9] Ibid, 11.
[10] Ibid, 10–11.

be one, in which people possess no rights and duties but create them in an original position. Rather, the experiment is meant to reveal our commitment to the principles of justice that Rawls enunciates. Nevertheless, the experiment makes sense only on the assumption that all rights and duties are social, so that *if* an original position were to be obtained, then no rights or duties would exist within it.

The crux of Rawls' argument is his claim that people in the original position would choose the following principles of justice.

Each person is to have an equal right to the most extensive total system of equal basic liberties compatible with a similar system of liberty for all. [And] Social and economic inequalities are to be arranged so that they are both: (a) to the greatest benefit of the least advantaged, consistent with the just savings principle, and (b) attached to offices and positions open to all under conditions of fair equality of opportunity.[11]

The first principle is known as the basic liberties principle. The second is in turn divided into two and labelled (a) the difference principle; and (b) the equality of opportunity principle. These principles are lexically or serially ordered, so that violations of the first principle cannot be justified in order to realize the second. In other words, the first principle trumps the second.

We need not examine why Rawls thinks that these principles would be chosen in the original position. Suffice it to say that, in Rawls' view, following these principles will ensure that individuals are afforded a 'fair go' in life, where fairness is determined by comparing the positions of individuals with those of all others in society. Thus, we can see that these principles belong to *distributive* justice; they are concerned with the distribution of benefits and burdens amongst individuals throughout a society as a whole.

With reference to the first principle, Rawls provides a list of basic liberties. Though the list is not intended to be complete, it comprises of:

political liberty (the right to vote and to hold public office) and freedom of speech and assembly; liberty of conscience and freedom of thought; freedom of the person, which includes freedom from psychological oppression

---

[11] Ibid, 266.

and physical assault and dismemberment (integrity of the person); the right to hold personal property and freedom from arbitrary arrest and seizure as defined by the concept of the rule of law.[12]

Of most interest to us is the inclusion of bodily integrity and personal property on this list. I examine them in turn.

Again, it is unremarkable to suggest that bodily integrity is a basic liberty. But crucial for us is that, for Rawls, bodily integrity is a basic liberty because people are afforded a fair go in life vis-à-vis others in society only if their bodily integrity is protected. The origin of the right, then, is social and is found in distributive justice.

Property is more complicated. The first thing to notice is that personal property for Rawls does not equate with the legal concept, ie movable and intangible property as opposed to real property or land. Rather, Rawls includes only that property required in order to provide individuals with 'a sufficient material basis for personal independence and a sense of self-respect'.[13] Specifically excluded is ownership of the means of production and exchange.[14] This does not mean that Rawls conceives of such as unjust. It means rather that such ownership is justified if and only if it meets the demands of the second principle of justice.

Some property rights, then, are justified because no one without them could have a fair go in life. Others are justified because, taking into account the property holdings of others, the demand to be given a fair go calls for them. Either way, on this view property rights have a social foundation. As we are told, property rights are derived from the social contract. They too are based in distributive justice.[15]

As we have seen, Rawls imagines a group of people in the original position tasked with determining principles of justice. He further maintains that, after such principles have been discovered, the next task is to undertake a 'constitutional convention' in which a political system is defined in accordance with the principles of justice already outlined.[16] The product of this convention is a constitution (which could in principle be unwritten), which is to be the primary legal

---

[12] Ibid, 53.
[13] Rawls, *Justice as Fairness: A Restatement*, 114.
[14] Rawls, *A Theory of Justice*, 54.
[15] Rawls, *Justice as Fairness: A Restatement*, 114.
[16] Rawls, *A Theory of Justice*, 12, 172.

instrument of the new state, defining the constitutional powers of government and the basic rights of citizens.[17]

Rawls also imagines a further stage. This is the fully political, legislative stage, in which more specific rights and duties are created in accordance with both the constitution and the principles of justice.[18] It is at this stage that the private law is said to arise.[19]

None of the above is intended to be controversial. It is certainly not intended as a critique of Rawls. On the contrary, it is expected that the reader will find Rawls' views on the structure of political philosophy intuitive. Our task has been merely to call attention to that view.

In that regard, it will be useful to present Rawls' view in relation to the diagrams contained at the beginning of this book. As we see, Rawls' theory is neatly captured by all of the diagrams representing the modern position.

The first diagram, M1, represents the modern understanding of the general structure of the nature of morality and politics. At its apex stands morality, an umbrella term for all categorically binding norms. This is then divided into politico-legal and mere-moral norms, ie norms that can and cannot rightly be enforced, respectively. Politico-legal norms then generate a political system, which in turn, in the light of the politico-legal norms, generates the rights and duties of citizens. We have seen that Rawls' theory fits into this basic structure. But this structure is also shared by the theories of most of his critics.

The second diagram, M2, describes the modern view of the relationship between justice and rights. Again, morality stands at the apex of the diagram. This time it is divided into distributive justice and mere-moral norms. In conjunction with M1, this reflects the fact that fundamental politico-legal norms are held to belong to distributive justice. At least ordinarily, distributive justice then generates two types of principles: principles dealing with liberty and principles dealing with equality.

For the purposes of illustration, M2 contains Rawls' terms in parenthesis at this level. But that is for illustration only. What is important is that distributive justice is seen to generate a concern for liberty and/or a concern for equality. Whether that concern takes Rawls' form is not significant here. It is also important to say that some do

---

[17] Ibid, 172–174.
[18] Ibid, 174–176.
[19] For the best analysis of this of which I am aware, see Ripstein, 'The Division of Responsibility and the Law of Tort'.

not recognize the existence of one of these principles. Libertarians, for instance, insist that distributive justice generates no entitlement to equality.[20] Others maintain that liberty and equality cannot be separated.[21] Again, however, these debates need not detain us. The precise way in which a philosopher navigates from the third to the fourth level of the diagram is not our concern.

What is significant is that the principles of liberty and/or equality generated are then seen to govern the political system. Here again, I have presented Rawls' view in parenthesis. For him, the basic liberties principle governs some aspects of political life, while other aspects are directed by the difference or equal opportunity principles. And finally we get to the bottom of the diagram, to the rights and obligations that individuals hold against each other as individuals.

Diagram M3 presents the modern understanding of the relationship between politics and law. Though Rawls does not discuss law in any detail, it is clear that it falls into the final, legislative, stage of the development of the state. Accordingly, we begin with the politico-legal norms upon which a society is founded—its basic conceptions of distributive justice. These norms are reflected in the political viewpoints of the members of that society, though there will naturally be disagreements as to how those norms relate to other norms, such as religious values, and how they should be realized in practice. That is general politics. The basic politico-legal norms underlie the constitution of the society, which is framed in accordance with, or revised to reflect, those norms. Then things become more complicated. First, the constitution defines the powers of government. In accordance with this, the government governs. But the government (here used widely to include the legislature, etc) also creates other norms of public law that determines how it governs. Moreover, in democratic societies especially, the government governs with an eye on general politics. The precise nature of these interactions need not concern us. Crucial here is that private law is, on this model, seen as a product of the interaction between public law and governmental politics. This is most clearly the case when the legislature passes a statute that relates to the private law, but the model is also meant to apply to judge-made law.

That, then, is the modern conception of the nature of political philosophy that will be contrasted with more traditional views in the

---

[20] Eg Nozick, *Anarchy, State, and Utopia*.
[21] Eg Dworkin, 'What is Equality? Part III: The Place of Liberty', 7–10.

following chapters. Again, it should be stressed that none of this is intended to be controversial or critical. On the contrary, it is suggested that the general layout of these ideas is so familiar to us that we are unlikely to regard it as remarkable.

2. The Modern Conception of the Relationship between Politics and Private Law

In the following, I examine three central topics: the laws of property, tort, and contract. The aim here is to show, if it is not already obvious, that these are generally understood in terms of the picture sketched above.

2.1 Property

It goes almost without saying that it is generally thought that the basis of the law of property is social and is found in distributive justice. This is certainly the view of philosophers. We have already seen that both of these ideas are reflected in Rawls' theory, where property is a consequence of the social contract and is supported by (depending on its nature) the basic liberties or difference and equality of opportunities principles. Of course, not all agree with Rawls' conclusions in this regard. The debate over the legitimacy of private property is well known. But that debate today is about the demands of distributive justice. Generally agreed on is the idea that *if* private property is justified, then it is justified in terms of distributive justice, and if it is so justified, then the contours of property law should reflect the demands of that form of justice.

2.2 Tort Law

Tort law is more difficult and more interesting. For one thing, the nature of tort law has been much discussed in recent times. As a result, tort lawyers are generally ready to express their views on the foundations of tort law. What is interesting, however, is that despite their readiness to elucidate these foundations, they almost never actually do this. Though this is what they claim to be doing, what they in fact do is something quite different.

It is standard for textbooks in this area to begin with a chapter examining the law's purported functions. For instance, *Markesinis and*

Deakin's Tort Law, one of English law's leading textbooks, lists punishment, deterrence, compensation, and loss spreading as functions frequently thought to be at the heart of the law.[22] For reasons we need not explore, the authors of this book discuss in detail only deterrence and compensation. Along with loss spreading, today these are widely held to be the chief functions of the law.

Though the authors accept that some torts have an important deterrent function, they reject the idea that deterrence is a central function of the law in general. It is worth briefly examining their reasons for this view. First, they argue that, largely due to the impact of insurance, the deterrent force of tort law is weak at best. If driving negligently will cost me directly, then I have much incentive to be careful. But if the cost will be borne by my insurance company, then things are different. Secondly, it is argued that deterrence cannot explain cases where liability frequently follows understandable error rather than genuine fault, such as in areas of strict liability. As they ask,

empirical studies carried out by the US Department of Transportation in the early 1970s...suggested that in Washington the average good driver...commits approximately nine driving errors of four different kinds during every five minutes of driving! In such cases, how can it be said that the threat of a tort action will deter a potential tortfeasor when it appears humanly unavoidable to continue making such errors...?[23]

Though these arguments have been quite influential, particularly in the Commonwealth, they are not persuasive. The first has the following structure:

(premise)	The function of tort law is to deter wrongdoing.
(observation)	But the deterrent effect of tort law is weak at best.
(conclusion)	Therefore, the premise must be false. Deterrence is not the function of tort law.

It must be clear that the conclusion does not follow. The most natural conclusion is simply that tort law does not perform its function.[24]

---

[22] Deakin, Johnston, and Markesinis, *Markesinis and Deakin's Tort Law*, 49.

[23] Ibid, 51 (citation omitted).

[24] A quite different argument has the following form: (premise) the function of tort law is to deter wrongdoing; (observation) tort law is frequently quite unconcerned with wrongdoing; (conclusion) therefore the premise is false. For an argument of that kind, see Beever, *Rediscovering the Law of Negligence*, 22.

It is quite possible for tort law to be a system that attempts to achieve something that, due to the influence of insurance and the like, it does not achieve.

No more compelling is the second argument. If we cannot avoid committing errors that impose risks on others, then it is irrational to attempt to avoid those errors. But that does not justify the conclusion actually reached. To take the example we are provided, if a good driver commits nine driving errors every four minutes, then it is silly to think that tort law could make anyone a perfect driver; but it does not follow from this that liability for traffic accidents cannot be justified in terms of deterrence. The issue is whether liability would make people more careful than they would otherwise be.

For our purposes, however, these arguments are not important in themselves. What is significant is that the authors of *Markesinis and Deakin's Tort Law* feel the need to engage in them when it must be clear that the position they are attacking is really an irrelevance. The issue, remember, is meant to be the function of tort law. Deterrence is presented as a purported function. But deterrence *simpliciter* could not possibly be the function of anything.

We are offered a theory: tort law is concerned to deter. But *what* is it concerned to deter and *why*? The answer, no doubt, would be that the function of tort law is to deter wrongdoing or unwanted behaviour. But what exactly is wrongdoing in this context and what kinds of behaviour are unwanted? Until we have answers to these questions, the claim that tort law is a system of deterrence is *entirely empty*. It is no better than being told that the function of tort law is promotion.

In that light, it is instructive to observe the way in which the authors of *Markesinis and Deakin's Tort Law* deal with compensation, their preferred account of the primary function of (most of) tort law. This is what we are told: 'The need to compensate victims of modern accidents is obvious.'[25] This claim is curious. For a start, why the reference to *modern* accidents? Do we think that the victims of accidents in the past were any less deserving of help? And how does the purported need to compensate explain the point of tort law? We are not told.

In any case, again what is crucial is what is missing: an account of why compensation is necessary or valuable. Though compensation is often presented as the, or at least a, goal of tort law, it cannot in itself

---

[25] Deakin, Johnston, and Markesinis, *Markesinis and Deakin's Tort Law*, 52.

be a goal at all. The idea surely cannot be that tort law compensates people for the sake of compensating them. It cannot be rational to compensate for its own sake. To express this in other language, compensation is not an end in itself; it can only be a means to an end. If we are to understand the function of tort law (assuming it has one), we need to comprehend its ends, not merely the means by which it achieves its ends.

Consequently, the claim that compensation is the function of tort law tells us precisely nothing about the nature of that law. Of course, tort law (often) compensates. But unless we know what purpose is served by the kind of compensation that tort law offers, we cannot comprehend tort law's function.

Some of this might strike the reader as nit-picking. But it is intended seriously. In general, theorists commit errors of this kind when their concepts are inadequate to deal with the phenomenon they are describing and when they possess some awareness of this. In other words, the error is usually the result of floundering. We return to this issue in Chapter 12.

In particular, the lacuna that has just been identified is serious, but it should not surprise us. The authors of *Markesinis and Deakin's Tort Law* do not confront it because they hold that the justification for compensation is obvious. It seems obvious to them and to many others because it is suggested by the modern conception of the structure of political morality. In short, the idea is that compensation is demanded by distributive justice. And while that might not be strictly obvious—ie it is not self-evident—it is at least highly plausible.

But the question is not only whether distributive justice demands compensation, but also whether the compensation offered by the law of tort is best explained in terms of distributive justice. The general assumption is that a positive answer should be given to both of those questions, but that is only an assumption.

It is important to note that the assumption is shared by many, even by those who consider themselves opponents of the view advanced in works like *Markesinis and Deakin's Tort Law*. This is perhaps most illustratively revealed in Nicholas McBride and Roderick Bagshaw's textbook, *Tort Law*. Under the heading 'The tort wars', McBride and Bagshaw explain that modern tort scholarship can be divided into two camps. The first camp consists of those who believe that 'tort law is…the law on compensation—it tells us when one person will be held liable to compensate another for some loss that he or she has caused that other to suffer'.[26] In the other camp are 'a significant minority of tort academics' who hold that:

> in tort cases, the courts determine whether A has committed a wrong in relation to B, and if he has, they determine what remedies will be available to B. To put it another—exactly equivalent—way, in tort cases, the courts determine whether A has violated B's rights in acting as he did, and if he has, they determine what remedies will be available to B.[27]

The authors of *Markesinis and Deakin's Tort Law* belong to the first camp, McBride and Bagshaw to the second.

I do not wish to deny that there is significance to this debate,[28] but as far as legal theory is concerned—that is, to the extent that we are trying to understand what the law is doing and why—the debate comes to nothing. If this is what the tort war is about, then the war is phoney.

How do 'courts determine whether A has committed a wrong in relation to B'? For McBride and Bagshaw, at least one answer is clear: the courts refer to public policy. Without this, they maintain, it would be impossible to determine whether a person's rights had been violated.

> If B wants to argue that A violated her rights in acting in some way, it seems to us that one has to take into account considerations of public policy in determining whether B had a right that A not act in the way he did. For example, suppose that B argues: 'A said something offensive to me and that upset me a great deal. I have an ongoing right that A not do anything that might offend me, so A violated my rights in acting as he did'. In determining whether B has such a right against A, it seems to us obvious that one has to take into account the impact on freedom of speech that recognising the existence of such a right would have, and that the adverse effect that recognising a 'right not to be offended' would have on freedom of speech is one of the most obvious reasons why no such right is recognised in English law.[29]

---

[26] McBride and Bagshaw, *Tort Law*, xiii.
[27] Ibid, xiv.
[28] As McBride and Bagshaw note (ibid, xiv n 7), I belong to the 'significant minority'. This is because, as I argue especially in Beever, *Rediscovering the Law of Negligence*, the causes of action in tort law (or at least the law of negligence) are better analysed in this fashion.
[29] McBride and Bagshaw, *Tort Law*, xix (citation omitted).

For McBride and Bagshaw, then, it is obvious that rights must have their origin in public policy. This is the same obviousness to which the authors of *Markesinis and Deakin's Tort Law* appeal. It is found in the modern conception of the structure of political morality, specifically the idea that all rights and duties are ultimately based on distributive justice.

McBride and Bagshaw's second argument is that public policy is needed to explain why the law orders remedies for wrongs.

Let's assume that A has violated B's rights and B has suffered some kind of loss as a result. B is allowed to sue A in tort for compensation for the loss that she has suffered....[I]t seems to us that the reason why the law allows B to sue A for compensation in this case is because it is in the public interest that wrongs should be remedied. In the words of Lord Bingham, 'the rule of public policy that has first claim on the loyalty of the law [is] that wrongs should be remedied.'[30]

Again we see the modern view of political morality reflected here. At the end of the day, the justification for awarding a remedy could only be distributive justice.

Because of this, the 'war' identified above is phoney. For the majority, the law compensates when it does and does not compensate when it does not in order to realize the demands of distributive justice. For writers such as McBride and Bagshaw, on the other hand, the law compensates only when the defendant has violated the plaintiff's rights. But those rights are defined in terms of distributive justice. In the end, then, the 'war' is over which is the best of two ways of doing the same thing. For all, the basic conception of law is reflected in Figures M1–M3.

2.3 Contract

Three general accounts of the law of contract are most prominent today: promissory theory, reliance theory, and efficiency theory.[31] The last, according to which contract law is justified because it is economically efficient, is clearly a theory that fits the patterns noted above.

---

[30] Ibid; quoting *D v East Berkshire Community Health NHS Trust* 2005 UKHL 23, [2005] 2 AC 373 (HL), [24]–[25].

[31] These and others are usefully summarized in Chen-Wishart, *Contract Law*, 20–33. For a detailed discussion, see Smith, *Contract Theory*.

This is not so obvious with respect to promissory or reliance theory. In part, this is because these notions need not be wedded to the modern view of political morality. In fact, as we see below, these approaches had their origin within views of a quite different kind. Nevertheless, it is possible to reveal that, in the hands of modern theorists, these approaches too share the assumptions outlined earlier. This can be shown by examining some of the arguments raised in favour of and against these views.

In a nutshell, the promissory theory holds that contracts are binding because they are promises. Of course, this assumes that promises are binding. We examine some of the traditional attempts to justify an assumption of this kind in later chapters. But it is clear that most modern thinkers believe or at least tacitly assume that the answer must be a social one and must therefore lie in distributive justice. If this were not so, then it would be impossible to explain the influence of the objection to the position raised by Lon Fuller and William Perdue in their seminal article on the subject,[32] here nicely summarized by Mindy Chen-Wishart.

[T]o enforce a promise is essentially to compel the promisor to benefit the promisee. Fuller and Perdue famously observed that expectation damages represents a 'queer kind of compensation' since it gives the promisee something he never had. As such, it seems to contradict the foundational principle of modern liberalism, the 'harm principle', according to which the state should only interfere with individual liberty to *prevent harm* to another.[33]

Now, I have no idea why lawyers think that the harm principle is the foundational principle of modern liberalism. It is certainly an influential principle, though it was presented by a man who was, philosophically rather than politically speaking, a utilitarian rather than a liberal.[34] But the principle is not supported by many of liberalism's leading theorists, including Rawls. It should also be obvious to the lawyer that the law routinely imposes liability for reasons other than the prevention of harm. The laws of taxation and unjust enrichment are two examples.

Again, however, our interest is not so much in these arguments but in the assumptions that underlie them. And the point here is that only

---

[32] Fuller and Perdue, 'The Reliance Interest in Contract Damages'.
[33] Chen-Wishart, *Contract Law*, 22
[34] Mill, 'On Liberty'.

one who shared the modern assumptions about the nature of political morality would find Fuller and Perdue's argument even relevant. If the foundations of contract law were not social, if they did not ultimately lie in distributive justice, then one could respond to the argument by saying, simply, 'My position does not correspond to the fundamental principle of liberalism and therefore of distributive justice? True. So what?'

On the other hand, it is thought to be a strength of the reliance view that it is consistent with the harm principle. If you rely on my promise to your detriment and I break that promise, then I harm you. But again, this argument has appeal only if one accepts the assumptions described above.

At this point, it is also useful to deal with Fuller and Perdue's claim that reliance theory is to be preferred because, as it maintains that judges award damages only to compensate for harms, it holds that judges enforce corrective rather than distributive justice, while the promissory view asserts the contrary view.[35] Apparently, this reveals that Fuller and Perdue do not share the modern assumptions after all.

However, a more careful analysis will show that this is not the case. Fuller and Perdue's claim is that judges should not *directly* enforce distributive justice, that being outside their remit. For instance, it is not part of the proper role of judging to implement schemes designed to achieve a fair distribution of wealth. Instead, in the main at least, judges should confine themselves to healing harms; ie corrective justice. But the point of this healing—the point of corrective justice according to Fuller and Perdue—is ultimately to achieve distributive justice. The argument is aimed at the social good.

In these areas then, we can see that the assumptions made by modern political philosophers are very much shared by legal theorists. Of course, this is entirely unsurprising. The modern view is the modern view. As I now suggest, however, there is good reason to doubt that the modern view is right.

3. Questioning the Modern View

Let us explore Rawls' thought experiment. Imagine that you and I are together with a group of others, about to deliberate in the original

---

[35] Fuller and Perdue, 'The Reliance Interest in Contract Damages', 56–57.

position. As we have seen, Rawls insists that we are all equal and that we must deliberate from behind a veil of ignorance. Why is this? The answer, as we have also seen, is a moral one. According to Rawls' diagram, Figure 1.1 (at the end of the chapter), the concept of right demands that persons be considered equal and that they not favour themselves in determining principles of justice. We can call these the principles of equality and impartiality.

The first question we need to ask ourselves relates to Figure M1. Where do the principles of equality and impartiality belong on this diagram? Do they belong at the first level of the diagram to morality in general, or do they belong at the second level, specifically to politico-legal morality? It seems that the answer must be the former. It is a demand of all morality, whether merely moral or politico-legal, that people be considered equal and that people deliberate impartially. This means that these principles are not and cannot be *products* of the social contract. They exist before that contract and govern the way in which it is drawn up. To put this another way, the principles of equality and impartiality are prior to the social. Accordingly, they are not demanded *by* distributive justice. On the contrary, they are prior to distributive justice and require distributive justice to have a certain character—ie one that respects equality and impartiality.

On the face of it, perhaps, this is a point of small importance. Perhaps the issue seems to be merely one of classification. But consider Rawls, description of the principle of equality:

the parties in the original position are equal. That is, all have the same rights in the procedure for choosing principles; each can make proposals, submit reasons for their acceptance, and so on...The basis of equality is taken to be similarity in these two respects. Systems of ends are not ranked in value; and each man is presumed to have the requisite ability to understand and to act upon whatever principles are adopted.[36]

It is easy to accept that the principle of equality has these consequences. What is not so easy to accept is the implicit view that these are the *only* consequences of that principle.

Consider this hypothetical. Imagine that as we sit down to deliberate in the original position, I punch you in the back of the head.

---

[36] Rawls, *A Theory of Justice*, 17.

Now, of course, Rawls maintains that this action violates binding mere-moral norms. But if his theory of justice is to be believed, then we must conclude that my action violates a politico-legal norm only if it prevents you having a fair say in the convention. And, I suggest, this is a conclusion that we should be very reluctant to reach.

Recall that the distinction between mere-moral and politico-legal norms—what Rawls relates to the concepts of moral worth and the good on the one hand and right on the other—lies in the fact that only the latter norms justify coercion. Given this, Rawls' position must be that coercion to prevent me from punching you in the back of the head, or to prevent me from doing it again, cannot be justified before the social contract. But that is surely wrong. Surely, the principle of equality immediately generates an entitlement in you not to be struck by me, an entitlement that generates an entitlement in you and others to prevent me striking you. And this is to say that these entitlements belong to right and not (or not only) to the good or to moral worth. They are politico-legal and not mere-moral norms.

In other words, the equality (and impartiality) upon which the original position is predicated generates more than that position. It also generates other rights and duties of a politico-legal nature. Before we even begin to debate principles of distributive justice in the original position, a politico-legal norm exists that demands I refrain from striking you. And this demand cannot be social and it cannot belong to distributive justice, as the social contract is yet to be closed. If this is right, then diagrams M1–M3 exhibit a mistaken view.

In fact, Rawls exhibits a remarkable, though partial, awareness of precisely this point. Under the heading of 'natural duties', Rawls lists as examples the duty of beneficence, the duty not to cause unnecessary suffering, and, crucially, the duty not to harm others. What makes these duties distinctive, Rawls argues, is that 'they apply to us without regard to our voluntary acts. Moreover, they have no necessary connection with institutions or social practices; their content is not, in general, defined by the rules of these arrangements.'[37] The implication seems clear: the natural duties are not products of the social contract and they do not owe their justification to the principles of distributive justice.

However, when Rawls returns to discuss the natural duties in depth, he paints a rather different picture.

---

[37] Ibid, 98.

In an earlier chapter...I described briefly the principles of natural duty and obligation that apply to individuals. We must now consider why these principles would be chosen in the original position. They are an essential part of a conception of right: they define our institutional ties and how we become bound to one another.[38]

In fact, despite the apparent tension here, Rawls does not contradict himself. In the later passage, he tells us that the principles of natural duty would be chosen in the original position. He does not say that they are duties *because* they are so chosen.

The question, however, is that if the natural duties are duties whether or not they are chosen, why does it matter whether they are chosen in the original position? The answer to this question is suggested by the first examples Rawls employs to elucidate the natural duties: 'we have a natural duty not to be cruel, and a duty to help another whether or not we have committed ourselves to these actions. It is no defense or excuse to say that we have made no promise not to be cruel or vindictive.'[39] The duty not to be cruel is, itself, a mere-moral norm. Though some forms of cruelty, eg torture, violate politico-legal norms, cruelty is itself a mere-moral concept. Hence, if a prohibition on cruelty, or on some forms of cruelty, is to become politico-legal, then that prohibition needs to be chosen in the original position or to flow in some way from the principles of justice, institutions, etc, chosen there.

But as we have seen, this position is much less convincing with respect to the duty not to harm others, which seems a politico-legal norm from the outset. Consider Rawls' own claim, intended to illustrate the idea that the natural duties do not rely on agreement, that 'a promise not to kill...is normally ludicrously redundant, and the suggestion that it establishes a moral requirement where none already existed is mistaken'.[40] This, of course, is correct. But by the same token, agreeing in the original position that killing will be prohibited when that position is defined in terms of equality is also ludicrously redundant, and not merely because killing someone would prevent her having her say in the deliberations. In that light, it is telling that in his

---

[38] Ibid, 293.
[39] Ibid, 98.
[40] Ibid.

detailed analysis of the natural duties, where he focuses on distributive justice, Rawls neglects to consider the duty not to harm others.

This criticism can be summarized in the following manner. Rawls certainly presents a plausible account of the content of distributive justice and its connection with social institutions. As such, he demonstrates the source of many of the politico-legal norms that are binding on us. But in presenting this picture he makes one general and crucial assumption: that *all* politico-legal norms have the same general origin. And it is telling that he presents no argument whatsoever to support that, on reflection, unintuitive view.

The ideas we have examined and criticized are the modern theorist's glasses. In conjunction with the next chapter, in which we investigate a prototype of these glasses, we will be in a position to notice them. But we have as yet no idea what the world would look like without them. But many theorists in the past did not wear these glasses. As long as we open our eyes then, their theories are able to provide us with vistas few today imagine.

34 THE MODERN CONCEPTION OF POLITICAL PHILOSOPHY AND LAW

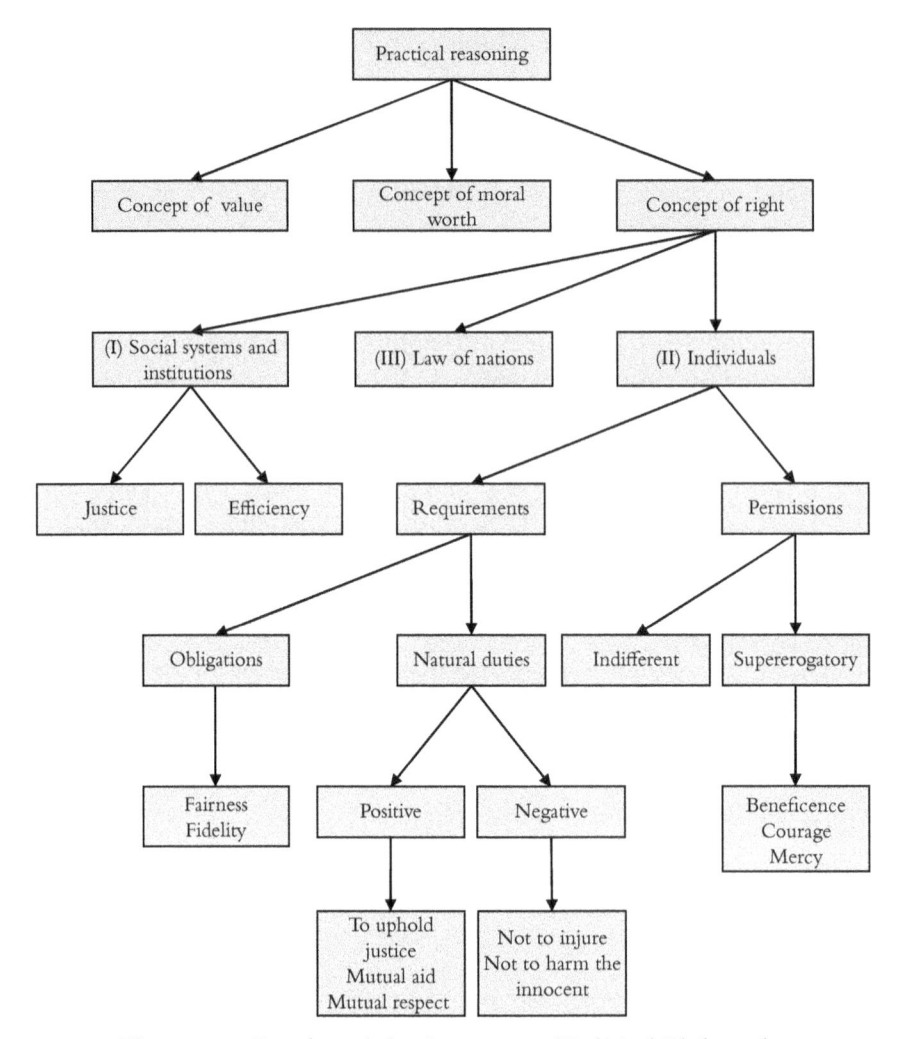

Figure 1.1 Rawls and the Structure of Political Philosophy.

PART I:
Discovery

Chapter 1 examined and began to question the modern conception of the political and the legal. The following four chapters begin to present the alternative view. They start, however, with an antecedent of the modern view, found in Plato's *The Republic* and *The Laws*. This material is important because it enables us to see how the traditional view developed in opposition to the account provided there.

2

Plato: A Beginning

We begin our investigation of the past, as is fitting, with the West's first great philosopher, Plato, and with his two major works of political philosophy, *The Republic* and *The Laws*. Though other works such as the relatively early *Apology*, *Crito,* and *Gorgias* and the later *The Statesman* are also significant, I concentrate on the major dialogues here. Because it helps us to understand Plato's motivations, I begin by providing a brief biographical sketch.

1. Biographical Background

Plato was born in Athens or Aegina between 429 and 423 BC. Though much about his life is unclear, it is known that he was born into a politically powerful family. According to one tradition, Plato's father was descended from Codrus, the last king of Athens (r ca 1089–1068). His mother was also associated with the lawmaker and lyric poet Solon and, through her future husband, with the Athenian leader Pericles.

At the time of Plato's birth, Athens was at the height of its power and influence. It had been the major player in the Delian League founded in 478–477, which had been successful in resisting invasion from Persia, and had established an empire. As a result of this, Athenians were naturally proud of their city, and this pride extended to Athens' democratic political system.

Shortly before Plato's birth, however, all this began to change. The first great event was the outbreak of the Peloponnesian war between Athens, Sparta, and their allies. This war, or series of wars, broke out in 431 and lasted until Athens' surrender to the Spartan general Lysander in 404. This defeat saw Athens lose its pre-eminence to Sparta and also resulted in a general decline in the Greek world south of Macedonia.

One consequence of the defeat was the collapse of the Athenian democracy. Sparta installed a sympathetic oligarchy, the Thirty, in power, which severely restricted the rights of Athenians and began a purge of the previous leadership. Hundreds of people were sentenced to death by drinking hemlock and thousands were exiled.

This reign of terror was eventually defeated as a result of Thrasybulus' Phyle campaign, a revolt that began when Thrasybulus seized the now ungarrisoned Athenian border fort of Phyle. Though the Spartans defeated the revolt, they agreed to a restoration of the Athenian democracy.

This may have been a welcome development for most Athenians, but the new regime soon exhausted what little credit it had with the already sceptical Plato when, fearful of dissent, it sentenced to death Plato's teacher, mentor, and friend, Socrates, in 399 for encouraging the youth of Athens to question democracy and the status quo.

The Republic was written around 375; *The Laws* around 350. Despite the fact that they are written in dialogue form, they are very recognizably works of political philosophy. They are more than this, however. As any informed reader of the dialogues can see, they are also reactions to the events narrated above.

The war between Athens and Sparta pitted two very different political systems against each other. Athens, as has been noted, was a democracy. Sparta was something quite different. It is difficult to summarize the political structure of that city adequately, but perhaps best is to say that it was—to our eyes, at least—a nightmarish hybrid of dual monarchy and military dictatorship. Plato generally characterizes it as a monarchy. In both *The Republic* and *The Laws*, most explicitly in the latter,[1] Plato blames the disasters of the prior decades on the inadequate political systems of these cities. His aim, therefore, is to seek for a system that will not lead to catastrophes of the kind that he had experienced. What is more, his strategy is to search for a not merely preferable but ideal alternative.

That is the first task of *The Republic* and *The Laws*. But it is not its only one. As well as discussing political systems, these dialogues also examine the way in which those brought to power in such systems should govern. This second feature of these works is infinitely more

---

[1] Plato, *The Laws*, 693c–702e.

developed in *The Laws* than in *The Republic*, but the description fits both works.

We can summarize all this by saying that *The Republic* and *The Laws* raise a fundamental question: how should society be governed? We now begin to explore Plato's answer to this question.

2. *The Republic*

2.1 Political Theory

Because of features of Plato's theory to be examined below, Karl Popper, having fled Austria to New Zealand during the Second World War, famously wrote that behind the totalitarian movements haunting the world of his day lay Plato's disastrous *Republic*. According to Popper, that work's chief failing is that, due to its apparent persuasiveness and power of vision, it gives the impression that it is not only possible to develop a political regime whose justice relies on the virtue of its rulers, but such reliance is in fact the only way in which justice can be achieved. This, Popper insisted, ignores the lesson so clear to us moderns: that power corrupts.[2] Simply, we cannot rely on the powerful to be virtuous.

Like many other claims that attribute naivety to our ancestors, this too is mistaken. Plato was wrong about many things, but not about this, and he was seldom naïve. In fact, he was well aware that power corrupts. He saw first-hand the corruption of the powerful in Athens. It appears to have entirely disgusted him and partly to have motivated his philosophical endeavours. More importantly for us, the fact that power corrupts is a point that he recognizes explicitly in *The Republic*. And, contra Popper, this recognition produces the political system advanced in that work.

In his discussion of justice in the state, Plato claims that the state needs 'guardians' to protect it from external attack.[3] This, Plato notes, is problematic, because the guardians will be a danger to the citizens in general.[4] Guardians (or at least those guardians who are soldiers) must be trained to be 'high spirited' (*thumos*) so that they fight well in defence

---

[2] Popper, *The Open Society and its Enemies*, vol 1, 145.
[3] Plato, *The Republic*, 375d–e.
[4] Ibid, 375b–c.

of the state, but this makes them naturally aggressive towards the citizens. The point, of course, is that the guardians have de facto power because of their physical dominance, and power corrupts. The question, then, is how to protect society from the 'aggression' of the guardians.

The modern response is to ensure that the 'guardians' are subject to the control of the citizens. The armed forces, for instance, are commanded by a civilian authority that is elected by and accountable to citizens. Plato was not unaware of this possibility. It is, allowing for the differences in social structure, the system that existed in his own city. But as we have seen, Plato had no truck with this system. His answer to our question, then, is profoundly different to ours.

It can be presented in a single word: education. For Plato, the way to prevent the guardians acting 'aggressively' to the citizens is to ensure that they are properly educated so that they do not possess the desire to act in such a way.[5] The majority of *The Republic*, roughly 300 pages in English translation, elucidates the content of this education.

Plato first addresses the place of literature in society.[6] Though this focus may seem odd today, it was natural for an ancient Greek. This is because, for the Greek male, reading literature formed a crucial part of his education. Greek schooling was divided into three parts: (i) reading and writing; (ii) physical education; and (iii) literary education. In consequence, the ancient Greek was educated in the ways of the world by reading literature, most importantly the works of the great Greek poets.

Plato thought that the content of this literature meant that this education was extremely problematic. There were two major difficulties. First, Greek literature portrays gods and heroes—ie 'role models'—behaving wickedly and thus encouraged vice. Secondly, as a result of the first difficulty, Greek literature was blasphemous. Hence, Plato maintained that all such poetry—including works then and now regarded as preeminent, such as Homer's *Iliad* and the tragedies of Aeschylus, Sophocles, and Euripides—must be banned. For Plato, the entire focus of education ought to be the production of virtuous citizens. Only in that way, he thought, can we hope for a just society.

Furthermore, Plato maintains that the guardians must be divided into two groups: soldiers and rulers.[7] The first are, of course, those

---

[5] Ibid, 376a–c.
[6] Ibid, 375c–403c.
[7] Ibid, 412b–415d.

adept in the arts of warfare. The latter are those who show an aptitude in the skills required for leadership—as we see below, these are not what one would think. Plato also insists that people should be chosen as soldiers or rulers entirely according to merit. It is worth noting in particular that he maintains that women be admitted to these classes and that they receive the same education as men.[8]

Crucial to Plato's political theory is the demand that rulers be educated to govern with disinterest and impartiality. But he clearly recognizes that education alone is not enough to ensure a disinterested and impartial ruling class. This must have been readily apparent to anyone who had lived through the reign of the Thirty in Athens, as it must have been plain that a primary cause of the terror was the clash between the interests of the oligarchs, particularly their interest in maintaining their power and wealth, and the interests of the citizens. Accordingly, Plato realized that, in addition to education, it is necessary to ensure that rulers pursue a lifestyle of a kind that harmonizes with the interests of the citizens.

For Plato, two sources of disharmony were particularly important. Again, this can be illustrated by reference to the Thirty. As indicated above, these were oligarchs. They held and distributed to others political power based on wealth. It is not difficult to imagine, then, that their interests in their own wealth came into conflict with the proprietary interests of the citizens. Similar problems are (or ought to be) a particular concern today. Moreover, in an effort to maintain power, the Thirty were naturally inclined to favour likeminded individuals. For instance, they restricted the right to participate in legal functions, something that had previously been open to all citizens, to 500 people. It is also easy to envisage a strong tendency for the rulers to favour members of their own family in this regard.

Plato's solution to these problems is to regulate the lifestyle of the rulers so that such conflicts of interest cannot arise. It is as radical as we might now expect. He stipulates that the guardians are to hold no private property and are to have no families.[9]

With regard to the latter idea, the rule is not that guardians are prohibited from procreating. It is that they are not entitled to have spouses or to act as parents. Instead, they are to copulate during state-run mating festivals and their children are to be raised by a state-run

---

[8] Ibid, 449a–457b.
[9] Ibid, 415d–421c.

organization in ignorance of their biological parents.[10] Moreover, as Plato holds that physical and moral traits are hereditary, he maintains that the state must adopt a programme of eugenics.[11]

Plato also argues that the rulers must have a certain character: they must be philosophers.[12] This is Plato's famous notion of the Philosopher King. Through our modern eyes, this claim is easy to misunderstand. If a modern philosopher were to make such a claim, it would mean that she and her colleagues should be given political power. But Plato is not making a similar claim. There were no philosophy departments in universities in Socrates' day and he had no colleagues.

A philosopher is, quite literally, a lover of wisdom—from *philos* (loving) and *sophia* (wisdom). A philosopher, then, is anyone who loves wisdom.[13] Plato's claim, then, is not that political power should be in the hands of a particular predefined group of people, a sort of aristocracy. It is rather that power should be given to those whose focus in life is to discover the truth, rather than pursue their self-interest in terms of wealth or pleasure.[14]

Again, this surprises us. Why would one want to be governed by some mad, esoteric philosophers who have no interest in the everyday running of the world? Plato's answer to this question is not to deny this description of the philosopher. He accepts that contemporary philosophers were crazy and even dangerous.[15] He even accentuates their unconcern with the everyday world with his also famous simile of the cave.[16] But his point relates to the one made above: in order to prevent power corrupting the rulers, it is necessary to ensure that the rulers are disinterested. Philosophers who would rather be philosophizing than ruling—but who are prepared to dedicate much of their time to ruling out of a sense of duty—are most likely to rule in a disinterested manner. Hence, Plato supports the by now perhaps common-sense notion that the only people who deserve power are those who do not want it.

Furthermore, Plato maintains that the state must be governed justly, and the only people who have even a hope of discovering

[10] Ibid, 457b–461e.
[11] Ibid.
[12] Ibid, 473d–e.
[13] Ibid, 474b–483e.
[14] Ibid, 483e–487a.
[15] Ibid, 487b–497a.
[16] Ibid, 513e–521b.

what justice is are philosophers—in Plato's terms, those focused on the form of the good.[17]

We have seen enough to know that Popper's criticism of *The Republic* is misplaced. Plato is not unaware of the problem that power corrupts; far from it. But we are surely entitled to doubt the wisdom of Plato's response to the problem.[18] Today, it can be seen that Plato's response is unacceptably authoritarian. Censorship, the abolition (for the guardians) of private property, of the family, eugenics, and the (admittedly purportedly meritocratic) authoritarian rule of the Philosopher Kings is too much for even the most utopian modern thinker to stomach.

In fact, not only is Plato's position authoritarian, it is recognizably totalitarian, as Popper sensed (though not for his reasons). This is because running through the whole of *The Republic* is the idea that the individual is merely a means to the community's ends. For instance, Plato claims that the goal of medicine is not to help those individuals who are ill lead better lives per se; rather, it is to benefit the community (usually by helping ill individuals). This is revealed by his consideration of the following case. Imagine a person who has a terminal illness and, in consequence of that illness, is of no benefit to society. Imagine also that this illness can be cured so that the person need not die, but that even if cured of the disease the person will remain handicapped and no longer of use to the community. In these circumstances, Plato insists that this person be left to die, because even if cured he would be 'useless'.[19]

Plato's authoritarianism is not unmotivated, however. It is the product of his view—never properly elucidated or explicitly argued for, in part because it was an element of the Greek world view—that the well-being of the individual is very tightly connected to that of the *polis*. Because of this view, Plato would reject the allegation that he is interested in the well-being of the *polis* rather than that of the individual, or even that he is prepared to sacrifice the well-being of one individual for that of other individuals. For him, these ideas cannot be separated. That helps to explain Plato's position, but of course it just gives us another reason for disagreeing with him.

---

[17] Ibid, 502c–521b.
[18] According to Gerhardt, 'Refusing Sovereign Power', Kant was the first systematically to do so. Gerhard's article provides an extremely interesting analysis of the issue.
[19] Plato, *The Republic*, 405a–408b.

2.2 Private Law

The above is a summary of Plato's political theory. For reasons yet to be fully revealed, it is also important to examine the connection between that account and the concerns of private law. The first thing that must be said in this context is that Plato draws no connection in this regard whatsoever. The closest we get to any discussion of private law in *The Republic* is found in the claim that the guardians must ensure that citizens' property holdings are relatively equal in order to prevent social strife.[20] There are two things that must in turn be said about this.

The first is that, to my knowledge, no one has ever regarded the fact that *The Republic* ignores the private law as surprising or remarkable. In fact, I know of no work that even acknowledges this omission. On the contrary, it is thought quite natural that Plato pays no heed to the laws of tort, contract, or property. It is thought that these are issues that can be left to the Philosopher Kings to determine once the state has been created. *The Republic*, it is believed, is concerned with more fundamental matters.

The second point is this: if Plato says nothing about the private law in *The Republic*, then why am I examining Plato's views in this book? As I indicated in the Introduction, one of my tasks is to examine the relationship between politics and private law. Given that Plato does not even mention private law, is *The Republic* not then irrelevant to my task?

Not at all. *The Republic* is most relevant. The best way to show this is to respond to the first point. Against the received view, I hold that the omission of the private law and its concerns from *The Republic* is most remarkable. It is, of course, entirely unsurprising to us, given the nature of political philosophy as we understand it. But that it is unsurprising does not mean that it is unremarkable.

Plato's omission was a mistake. It was an epic blunder. Epic, because it was an oversight that is in part responsible for our inadequate understanding of political philosophy, justice, and law today. In combination with other blunders, it has meant that we understand only part of political philosophy, only half of justice, completely misconstrue the relationship between politics and law, and totally misunderstand the content of law. In other words, Figures M1–M3 are wrong. Or so I shall argue.

---

[20] Ibid, 421c–427c.

3. *The Republic* and Modern Philosophy

Despite its brilliance, we have seen that *The Republic* contains a political theory that is soundly rejected by modern thinkers. My next claim, then, must come as a surprise. Modern political philosophy is fundamentally platonic. Let me explain.

Of course, I do not mean that *The Republic* shares much by way of *content* with modern political philosophies. We have no time for Plato's massive regulation of social life, for instance. But the *structure* of Plato's theory corresponds exactly with that of modern philosophy. I do not intend this claim to be controversial. To the contrary, it ought to appear trivial. It is simply that both Plato and the modern philosopher share the view that justice is concerned with the relationship between every individual in a community (as well, possibly, as outside that community).

There are two respects in which this is so. First, Plato holds that, morally speaking, every person counts equally. This is somewhat hidden by Plato's elitism and acceptance of slavery. To deal with these in reverse order, Plato's view is that justice is equally concerned with the interests of all *citizens*, though it is naturally unconcerned with slaves. This is, of course, because Plato regarded, or was prepared to treat, slaves as non-persons. My claim, then, is not that Plato's theory gives equal regard to all human beings. It gives equal regard only to those considered by Plato to be persons (ie citizens). Turning now to the second point, this does not mean that Plato thought that all people were equal in a modern sense. As we have seen, the Philosopher Kings are thought uniquely qualified to rule. But it is central to Plato's view that they rule in the interests of others. The Philosopher Kings have *unique power*, but they are not given *special consideration*. The state is structured so that everyone's interests are served. We can summarize this by saying that, for Plato, all citizens count and everyone who counts counts equally.

This feature of Plato's theory is very important and all too often overlooked, but it is not our concern here. We are interested in another feature of Plato's position. For Plato, justice is concerned with everybody (who counts) *taken as a whole*. We can express this by saying that justice has a *sphere*, and that the sphere of justice for Plato is the entire community. In other words, justice for Plato is distributive justice. This fits the pattern captured in Figure J1 presented at the beginning of this book. In this diagram, which represents a four-person society, justice is determined by considering the relationship between all members of that society. So, for instance, justice between P_1 and P_2 is determined by considering the relationship between P_1 and P_2, but also all other relationships with respect to P_3 and P_4. The form of justice is social.

It is also clear that we can see at least the origins of M1 and M2 in the theory we have examined. Moreover, the theory advanced in *The Republic* is structurally identical with modern positions in another important way as well. Again, the point is so obvious that it is usually unnoticed. Plato and the modern philosophers share their understanding of the relationship between morality, politics, and law.

As we have seen, in *The Republic* Plato argues that justice demands the creation of a particular kind of political system; ie one that, in Plato's mind, is likely to govern appropriately. In that work, very little emphasis is given to the policies by which the rulers are to govern beyond those needed to ensure that the rulers will rule appropriately. In other words, almost the only policies pursued by Plato are those that relate to the education and lifestyle of the Philosopher Kings, because the appropriate education and lifestyle is necessary and sufficient to guarantee that the Kings will govern justly. If that is achieved, then the Kings will naturally pass laws that are just.

Again, our focus now is not on the content but on the structure of these thoughts. Modern thinkers are certain that Plato places too much trust in the Philosopher Kings' sense of justice. Nevertheless, they share Plato's view of the structure of political argument. That structure is the following. At the most abstract, we begin with a moral argument; in Plato's case an argument about justice. This argument is then applied to the political sphere in order to generate a political system. It is then thought that this political system, when functioning appropriately, will produce laws. No doubt, unlike Plato, the modern thinker holds that even perfectly just systems can produce unjust laws, but the crucial point is that the theory of law is seen to be *consequent* to the theory of the political system. Hence, Plato's view can be seen as the origin of the one found in Figure M3.[21]

---

[21] Rawls, *Political Liberalism*, lectures 4–5, maintains that the account of justice on which a modern liberal society should be founded is 'political' rather than 'comprehensive'. By this, Rawls intends that the appropriate political system is generated, not by examining morality as it is in fact, but by developing an 'overlapping consensus' among the views that people actually have. On the face of it, this suggests that the structure of Rawls' theory differs from Plato's.

In fact, however, that is not the case. For Rawls, the reason for adopting an overlapping consensus rather than a comprehensive view is a moral one. It is prompted by the ideas that

4. The Laws

The first thing that must be said about *The Laws* is that it presents a theory quite unlike the one found in *The Republic*. The reasons for and the exact nature of this difference are much disputed. Because the difference is of central importance to our investigation, we will need to examine it in the following chapter. But it suffices to say here that *The Laws* is in some ways a continuation of the themes we have already examined and in other ways a new beginning. The continuation is examined here; the new beginning is explored in the following chapter. In particular, we focus now on the discussion in *The Laws* of issues that relate to private law.

Above, we saw that *The Republic* does not examine these matters. *The Laws*, however, is different. As its title suggests, it is more focused on specific laws than *The Republic*. What is more, many of the laws Plato examines belong to what we would recognize as private law. For instance, the work contains sections examining marriage, trade, wounding (ie battery), assault, property, commercial law, and family law.

It is also significant that Plato explicitly recognizes what we would call the private law action and distinguishes it from public law.

Cases may be brought before the other courts for two reasons: one private person may charge another with having done him wrong, and bring him to court so that the issue can be decided; or someone may believe that one of the citizens is acting against the public interests, and wish to come to the community's assistance.[22]

This distinction is also reflected in his theory of punishment.

[W]e should not simply call it 'just' when one man bestows some object on [ie benefits] another, nor simply 'unjust' when correspondingly he takes

---

everyone's views are entitled to respect and, most obviously, that it is desirable that we live in societies that can be accepted as just. Again, there is no doubt that the content of Rawls' theory differs from Plato's, but the structure is the same.

In any case, in this book we are most interested in the place of law in this schema, and it is plain that Rawls' would not demur from our analysis at this point. Law as such is almost entirely ignored by Rawls, surely because he thought that law was a product of politics.

[22] Plato, *The Laws*, 767b–c.

it from him [ie causes loss]. The description 'Just' is applicable only to the benefit conferred or injury inflicted by someone with a just character and outlook. This is the point the lawgiver has to watch; he must keep his eyes on these two things, injustice and injury. He must use the law to exact damages for damage done, as far as he can; he must restore losses, and if anyone has knocked something down, put it back upright again; in place of anything killed or wounded, he must substitute something in a sound condition. And when atonement has been made by compensation, he must try by his laws to make the criminal and the victim, in each separate case of injury, friends instead of enemies...[W]hen anyone commits an act of injustice, serious or trivial, the law will combine instruction and constraint, so that in the future either the criminal will never again dare to commit such a crime voluntarily, or he will do it a very great deal less often; and in addition, he will pay compensation for the damage he has done.[23]

Here we see Plato identifying two possible legal responses to wrongdoing. If A destroys B's property, then A can be made to pay B for his loss and A can be punished for his unjust act.

The purpose of the second of these actions is much discussed in *The Laws* and in a number of Plato's other dialogues. It is one of (the many of) Plato's seminal contributions to political philosophy. Plato maintains that the aim of punishment is not retribution or deterrence in the modern sense, but reform of the criminal for the criminal's own sake.[24] Hence, he tells us:

When one man harms another by theft or violence and the damage is extensive, the indemnity he pays to the injured party should be large, but smaller if the damage is comparatively trivial. The cardinal rule should be that in every case the sum is to vary in proportion to the damage done, so that the loss is made good. And each offender is to pay an additional penalty appropriate to his crime, to encourage him to reform.[25]

This enables us to understand Plato's discussion of various individual laws. For instance, he examines the appropriate legal response to intentional invasions of property and maintains that in these cases

---

[23] Ibid, 862b–d.
[24] Ibid, 861e–863a, 863e–864c, 933e–934c.
[25] Ibid, 933e–934a.

offenders should pay victims three times the damage that they cause.[26] For instance, if I enter your property and break a window that costs £50 to replace, I should have to pay £150: £50 to compensate you for your loss; £100 'by way of cure for such uncivilised and inconsiderate behaviour'.[27] The latter is a 'lesson' from which I am meant to learn that it is not appropriate to act in this kind of way. It is worth noting that the whole £150 is paid to you.

There is considerable similarity here between Plato's theory and modern practice. We would call my action a trespass and we distinguish between its tortious and criminal aspects. In the example above, I will have to compensate you for the damage that I caused and may also face criminal prosecution and punishment, which is likely to be a fine. There are differences here also, however. First, today the appropriateness and quantum of a criminal penalty will be determined, not in relation to the amount of damage caused per se, but in proportion to my culpability, a position Plato explicitly rejects (though the exact nature of the rejection is not entirely clear).[28] Secondly, if I am fined, the fine goes not to you but to the state. Interestingly, these differences relate to the criminal or public law aspect of the example, not to the private.

There is, however, one apparently serious gap in Plato's account as it relates to what we would call private law. This is that he provides no account of the basis of the relevant action. Consider, for instance, the distinction drawn above between the two possible legal responses to trespass. As we saw, if *A* intentionally trespasses on *B*'s land causing damage, *A* must pay *B* three times the damage caused. We saw that this was to compensate *B* and to reform *A*. We also noted that Plato presents a sophisticated and influential theory of the latter. It is very notable, then, that Plato presents no account of the former whatsoever. Similarly, Plato claims that if one person voluntarily wounds another, then the normal response will be that the first person must compensate the latter and must be banished.[29] The reason for the latter is examined; the reason for the former receives no attention at all. Plato also tells us that if a contract is breached, then 'an action for such an unfulfilled agreement should be brought in the tribal courts',[30] but he

---

[26] Ibid, 843c–d.
[27] Ibid.
[28] Ibid, 857a–864c.
[29] Ibid, 877a–b.
[30] Ibid, 920d.

does nothing to explain why this should occur, or even what the legal response should be. Likewise, he presents a theory of prescription and limitation, but presents no justification for these laws.[31] As a result, one must wonder if there is any real *theory* here at all.

In fact, however, a theory is present, though it is only implicit in Plato's general approach. When we understand this theory, we will see that though the above points to a lacuna in Plato's account, that lacuna is a great deal smaller than it first appears. I examine this issue now.

The central conceit of the dialogue is that one of the interlocutors, Cleinias, has been tasked along with others from his city to set up a new colony on Crete. He is told that this colony ought to be governed in accordance with the best laws that can be devised. The three characters in the dialogue then set about describing such a society.

This reveals that Plato's general approach to political philosophy remains as it was in *The Republic*. His focus is on how a society should be set up. Moreover, the point of imagining the foundation of a new colony is that the interlocutors are able to envisage the state as a blank slate upon which just laws can be written. What is more, though in the dialogue the speakers intend actually to create such a state, this is of course merely a conceit, a narrative device. It is in reality a mere thought experiment. Again, then, we see the close connection between Plato's and the modern approaches to political philosophy, especially with respect to Rawls' original position.

In this light, we can see what Plato's answers to our questions above would have been. Why does a trespasser have to pay compensation for the damage that he causes? Because that is in the public interest. A state in which wrongly caused harm is compensated for is a better ordered state than an alternative. We are not told exactly why this is, but that need not concern us here. Again, our chief concern is with the structure rather than the content of Plato's theory. And the crucial point is that what we consider to be elements of private law are justified in the way in which everything in *The Republic* and *The Laws* is justified: in terms of the public interest. Hence, for Plato, the kind of justice that applies to the private law is the kind of justice that applies in general. This picture is the origin of the ideas captured in Figure M3. It is also to be noted that the lacunas, and the solutions to those lacunas, in Plato's theory match exactly those found in modern works,

---

[31] Ibid, 954c–e.

such as in *Markesinis and Deakin's Tort Law* examined in the previous chapter.

This observation enables us to understand Plato's otherwise perplexing discussion of what we would call the conversion or theft of fruit. Plato argues for the following rule.

Anyone who consumes any part of the coarse crop of grapes or figs [ie the fruit for making wine], whether on his own land or another', before the rising of Arcturus ushers in the vintage [ie before the autumn equinox],

must owe

(a) fifty drachmas, to be presented to Dionysus, if he takes the fruit from his own trees,
(b) 100 if from his neighbour's, and
(c) sixty-six and two-thirds drachmas if from anyone else's trees.

If a man wants to gather in the 'dessert' grapes or figs (as they are called nowadays) [ie fruit for immediate consumption], he may do so whenever and however he likes, provided they come from his own trees...[32]

The first thing to be noticed about this is that the public interest overrides the private. One is entitled to take dessert fruit from one's own trees whenever one wants, because that fruit is of comparatively little public importance. But, as it is used to make wine, the coarse fruit is of considerable public interest. Hence, it is an offence to pick even one's own fruit early.

Moreover, notice the, to our eyes odd, difference in treatment between the person who takes his neighbour's fruit and the one who takes another's. The reason for this rule is presumably that disputes between neighbours are more socially disruptive than others, and so need to be more strongly discouraged.[33]

Another example of this can be seen in the rule that, at harvest time, crops can be brought in by any means whatever, as long as triple damages are paid to anyone adversely affected.[34] This means, for instance, that if it is convenient for *A* to bring in his crops over the land of *B*, then he is entitled to do so, as long as he pays thrice for any damage

---

[32] Ibid, 844d–e.
[33] It is a moot point how this fits with Plato's theory of punishment, however.
[34] Plato, *The Laws*, 845e–846c.

he causes. The reason for *A*'s privilege is clear: it is the social importance of securing the harvest. The reason for the ability of *B* to claim compensation is not clear, but it must be that Plato holds that the public interest is likewise served:

Consider also Plato's theory of property. In this regard, it is important to introduce a much overlooked distinction that will be crucial when we turn to examine Aristotle's theory in Chapter 4. Theories of property can be designed to answer one or both of the following two questions:

(1) What is the justification for the existence of property rights?
(2) How should property holdings be distributed?

For reasons we will examine later, there is a very strong tendency to confound these two questions. But they must be kept separate. Of course, an answer to (1) is likely to at least point in the direction in which (2) must be answered and vice versa. But it is clear that the questions are different. One can present an account that is intended to justify the existence of property rights without taking a stand on how those rights ought to be distributed, and one can provide a theory of how property ought to be distributed simply on the *assumption* that it ought to exist.

In the following, I refer to theories that attempt to answer the first question as theories of property and to theories that respond to the second question as theories of property distribution.

In *The Laws*, Plato presents only a theory of property distribution. He argues that the unattainable ideal is complete communal ownership,[35] that in practice land should be distributed as evenly as possible between families,[36] and that land holdings be inalienable.[37] He also imposes considerable restrictions on the holdings and use of money and other possessions.[38] Again, all this is justified in the name of the public interest.

He presents no theory of property, however. But it is not too difficult to provide one for him. It seems that Plato assumes that property is required in order to provide for a sufficient level of material

---

[35] Ibid, 739b–e.
[36] Ibid, 737c–d.
[37] Ibid, 741a–e.
[38] Ibid, 741e–772c.

well-being so that the citizens of the state are able to lead worthwhile lives.

What we see, then, is that the laws, whether related to private or public law, are determined in accordance with the interests of the public. In our imaginary four-person society, the position is arrived at by considering the interests of P_1, P_2, P_3, and P_4 *together*. As noted, this is just Plato's general approach to political philosophy. Again, then, we can say that Plato's account in *The Laws* is the ancestor of the approach taken by most modern legal theorists.

5. Conclusion

It is worth stressing again that the above has been intended to draw attention to the structural similarities of the views of Plato and modern views. It in no way attributes the content of Plato's theory to those views. And it is certainly not criticism. That Plato's theory is problematic and that the modern approaches share a structure with that view does not show that the modern approaches must also be problematic. The difficulties with Plato's account may lie solely in its peculiar content. Nor is this discussion intended to be controversial. It is meant to elucidate claims that can easily be accepted. As it is meant to be uncontroversial, the discussion is not even intended to be genuinely interesting. Not yet.

3
Plato: A New Beginning

This chapter discusses a single issue: the relationship between *The Republic* and *The Laws*. For our purposes, the issue requires only a small discussion, but is of great significance nevertheless. In the previous chapter, we saw that the structure of Plato's view in *The Republic* and also in much of *The Laws* is mirrored in the works of modern theorists. As we see here, however, on another level *The Laws* also presents a very different kind of theory; one importantly distinct from both modern ideas and the account Plato presented in *The Republic*.

As we have already seen, one difference between *The Republic* and *The Laws* is that only the latter explores specific laws, such as the laws dealing with trespass and the harvest. This may appear to suggest that *The Laws* is intended as an application of the theory presented in *The Republic*. The thought behind this idea is that one must produce a political theory before determining the content of individual laws, a thought we have represented in Figure M1. That Plato himself presented this thought in *The Republic* appears to support this idea. The notion, then, is that *The Republic* concentrates on the first two levels of M1, while *The Laws* focuses on the final two.

In fact, however, that is not the case. As is widely recognized, *The Laws* is no mere application of *The Republic*. On the contrary, it presents a different theory that, most notably, has no place for the Philosopher Kings and does not hold that society should be governed by a group of enlightened and disinterested people with absolute power. A first issue to confront, then, is the reason for this difference. Two general explanations have been suggested. Before I examine those explanations, it will help to present a little more of Plato's biography.

In 388 BC, Plato was invited to visit the court of Dionysius I, ruler of Syracuse. The invitation was issued due to the prodding of Dionysius' brother-in-law, Dion, an admirer of Plato's teaching, who hoped that Plato's ideas would influence Dionysius. Though Plato advised Dionysius to engage in reform, this advice seems to have been almost entirely ignored and Plato returned to Athens. In 367 Dionysus I died and was succeeded by Dionysus II, who Dion believed would be more amenable and so encouraged Plato to return. Dionysus II, however, was no more receptive than his predecessor, became suspicious of Dion and by extension Plato and forced Dion to leave Syracuse, prompting Plato to return again to Athens. Plato was persuaded to return to Syracuse again in 361, when Dionysius promised to consult Plato in regard to Dion, but this promise was not kept and Plato, with extreme difficulty, returned to Athens once more. In 357 Dion managed to expel Dionysius, but was assassinated in turn in 354 by Calippus, another disciple of Plato's. In short, then, the experience in Syracuse was an unmitigated disaster. What, if any, was the effect of this on Plato's political philosophy?

First is the idea that Plato's political theory became less utopian and more realistic as he matured. On this view, as Plato's experience of the world grew, he came to appreciate that the society described in *The Republic* was unrealizable. Accordingly, *The Laws* presents an alternative and less utopian vision of the political.

This view receives no support from Plato himself. But many have found it attractive. As Trevor Saunders explains: 'What makes this explanation so irresistible is of course the way in which the alleged doctrinal development matches the chronological sequence of the dialogues concerned: we feel in our bones that realism must come later than idealism.'[1] And, we might add, his adventure in Syracuse surely taught Plato circumspection.

However, Saunders argues, the interpretation is ultimately untenable.

[T]his charmingly simple account of the development of Plato's political theory really will not do, because it confuses *attainable* ideals with *unattainable* ideals. Only if we take the *Republic* as an attainable ideal does it make sense to argue that Plato abandoned it in favour of something more

---

[1] Saunders, 'Introduction', xxxii–xxxiii.

realistic; but to suppose that Plato ever thought that the *Republic* was attainable would be to suppose him capable not merely of optimism or idealism but of sheer political *naïveté*. It makes much better sense to think of the *Republic* as an extreme statement, designed to shock, of the consequences of an uncompromising application of certain political principles—in fact, as an unattainable ideal—and to suppose that even when Plato wrote the *Republic*, he had some realistic practical programme, which may well have been more or less what we find in the *Laws*.[2]

In Saunders' view,

Plato could perfectly well have written the *Laws* when he wrote the *Republic* and the *Republic* when he wrote the *Laws*, for they are the opposite sides of the same coin. The *Republic* presents merely the *theoretical* ideal, and... explicitly and emphatically allows for some diminution in rigour if it were to be put into practice. The *Laws* describes, in effect, the *Republic* modified and realized in the conditions of this world.[3]

In my view, however, we should accept neither of these interpretations. Though both contain elements of the truth, neither gets to the heart of the difference between *The Republic* and *The Laws*.

First, both readings rely on the idea that *The Laws* is significantly less idealistic than *The Republic*. This, however, is not the case. Both works are highly utopian. For instance, in *The Laws* Plato imagines the creation of a society that from the outset or soon after foundation possesses a set of laws so flawless that they require only very occasional fine tuning from the Nocturnal Council.[4] In this regard, *The Laws* is appreciably more utopian than *The Republic*. In general, it cannot be said that one work is more utopian than the other. As we saw in the previous chapter, *The Republic* realistically recognizes the challenge posed by the corrupting force of political power, but it presents a highly utopian answer to this challenge based on education. In comparison, *The Laws* realistically recognizes the limits of education (at least implicitly) and so is more realistic than *The Republic* in recognizing the challenge that the rulers pose to the realization of justice. But the response to this challenge is the also highly utopian

---

[2] Ibid, xxxiii.
[3] Ibid (footnote omitted). See also Lewis, 'Reason Striving', 85–6.
[4] Plato, *The Laws*, 960b–968e.

postulation of a near-perfect system of laws, a form of utopianism absent from *The Republic*. *The Republic* and *The Laws* are simply utopian in different ways.

Accordingly, the first interpretation is wrong to claim that Plato became less utopian as he aged. But Saunders is also wrong to allege that *The Laws* is Plato's realistic alternative to the utopian vision of *The Republic*. Plato almost certainly did learn something from his adventures in Syracuse, but that something was not a rejection of utopianism.

Secondly, we cannot explain the difference between *The Republic* and *The Laws* by claiming that the first is a work of ideal political philosophy while the latter is focused on the attainable, because the distinction between the ideal and the realizable is present in both works.[5] In *The Laws*, Plato describes both an ideal state and one that is practically realizable, but the first state is not the one characterized in *The Republic*.

Thirdly, and most importantly, the explanations provided by both of the views examined above are unable to account for the fundamental difference between *The Republic* and *The Laws*. It will help to think of this issue in relation to Figure M1.

Both interpretations imply that Plato presents two different theories that fit the pattern drawn in M1. The theories differ either because Plato changes his mind (the first view) or because Plato presents theories about two different things, the ideal and the realizable (the second view). But this is wrong. The position presented in *The Laws* does not match M1 at all. Hence, the fault line that separates *The Republic* and *The Laws* is not one between the ideal and the realizable. It is rather, as we are about to see, between two competing understandings of the fundamental structure of political philosophy.

In *The Republic*, Plato imagines a state run by Philosopher Kings. Not much is said about the precise mechanism of their government, but it is easy to imagine them laying down rules for conduct—laws, in other words. In *The Republic*, then, the rulers are front and centre; the rules are in the background.

But, as the title of the work suggests, this is reversed in *The Laws*. The crucial passage in this regard is the following:

we maintain that laws which are not established for the good of the whole state are bogus laws, and when they favour particular sections of the

---

[5] See, eg ibid, 739b–e.

community, their authors are not citizens but party-men; and people who say those laws have a claim to be obeyed are wasting their breath. We've said all this because in your new state we aren't going to appoint a man to office because of his wealth or some other claim like that, say strength or stature or birth. We insist that the highest office in the service of the gods must be allocated to the man *who is best at obeying the established laws* and wins *that* sort of victory in the state; the man who wins the second prize must be given second rank in that service, and so on, the remaining posts being allocated in order on the same system. Such people are usually referred to as 'rulers', and if I have called them '*servants of the laws*' it's not because I want to mint a new expression but because I believe that the success or failure of a state hinges on this point more than on anything else. Where the law is subject to some other authority and has none of its own, the collapse of the state, in my view, is not far off; but if *law is the master of the government and the government is its slave*, then the situation is full of promise and men enjoy all the blessings that the gods shower on a state. That's the way I see it.[6]

Here we see Plato confronting the challenge mentioned above: the near certainty that the rulers will rule unjustly if left to their own devices. In *The Republic*, the solution to this problem was to ensure that the rulers be educated in a certain way. There is no suggestion of that here, however. Plato's position in *The Laws* is that states should be governed by a set of almost immutable rules to be set up before or early in a state's existence,[7] and that the rulers be those who prove themselves to be most law-abiding. In *The Republic*, the rulers were the masters of the law. In *The Laws*, the law is the master of the rulers. As Plato puts it, the law is the master and 'the government is its slave'.[8]

To be sure, Plato does not deny that legal reform may be necessary. But this reform, undertaken by the Nocturnal Council, is a relatively insignificant fine tuning of what already exists, and the unimportance of the Council is indicated by the fact that it is examined only in the last section of the dialogue.[9] In *The Laws*, then, the rules are front and centre; the rulers are in the background.

---

[6] Ibid, 716a–d (all but the second emphasis added).
[7] Ibid, 772a–d.
[8] Also of significance here is the claim that the laws of the states of the Athenian's interlocutors have divine, ie non-human, origin. Ibid, 631b–d.
[9] Ibid, 734e–747e, 960b–968e.

It is this feature that prompts Aristotle's complaint that 'In the *Laws* there is hardly anything but laws; not much is said about the constitution.'[10] We can see, however, that the complaint is unjustified. Aristotle finds no constitution in *The Laws* because he understands a constitution to elucidate the way in which the rulers govern. But in *The Laws* the rulers do not govern. The laws govern. Hence, that 'there is hardly anything but laws' in *The Laws* does not mean that there is no constitution there. Of course, Plato's position may be objectionable, but it is not objectionable for the reasons enunciated by Aristotle.

We can state the difference between *The Republic* and *The Laws* baldly. The former is an account of the rule of man; the latter is an account of the rule of law. *The Laws* is the first such discussion in Western philosophy.

As the significance of this distinction may be opaque, it is important to expand on it now. The rule of law can be given two general interpretations: a thick and a thin. According to the thin view, often associated with 'positivistic' views of law, a system operates in accordance with the rule of law if its rulers govern through law. On this view, what is decisive is the *method* by which the rulers rule. If they govern by personal fiat, then we have the rule of man. If they govern by setting down general rules, then we have the rule of law. According to the thick version, however, the rule of law means what it appears to mean: the rule of law exists only if the law rules. Different theorists disagree over precisely what this means, but on the thick understanding of the rule of law, that notion is a substantive political ideal that holds that law is not merely the medium through which government ought to be carried out, but constrains the way that government ought to govern. It is the thick notion, an extremely thick notion, to which *The Laws* is committed.

It will help to capture this difference in diagrammatic form, presented for the moment as simplifications of the diagrams presented at the beginning of this book.

Moral argument —generates→ Political system —generates→ Laws

Figure 3.1 Politics and Law in *The Republic*

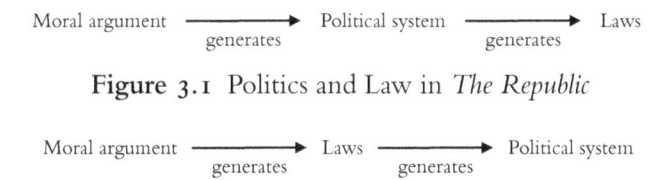

Moral argument —generates→ Laws —generates→ Political system

Figure 3.2 Politics and Law in *The Laws*

---

[10] Aristotle, '*The Politics*', 1265a.

Here we can see that the difference is crucial. According to Figure 3.1, law is the offspring of politics. According to Figure 3.2, however, politics is the offspring of law. On this view, as Plato tells us though in different words, the study of the fundaments of politics is the study of the laws through which just government is possible.[11]

This picture ought to give us pause. To most modern thinkers, the position captured by Figure 3.1 is so obviously true that not only do we fail to consider alternative views, that position is so deeply burnt into our brains that we fail to see that alternatives were advanced by others.

I am far from suggesting that the position advanced in *The Laws* is attractive or plausible. The idea of even nearly immutable laws and the excessively strong understanding of the rule of law are beyond the pale.[12] But more credible views are examined in the following.

And it is worth pausing to consider the consequence if something like Figure 3.2 were right. It would be very significant indeed. It would be that the modern understanding of the relationship between law and politics, and of politics itself, is fundamentally defective.

---

[11] Plato, *The Laws*, 714b–715e.
[12] The first idea, however, possessed a strong attraction for the ancient Greeks. See Tuck, *Natural Rights Theories*, 8.

4

Aristotle

This chapter examines the second great thinker in the history of Western philosophy: Aristotle. His theory is pivotal. Unfortunately, the surviving material on most of the issues that concern us is so scanty that it is often impossible to be sure of Aristotle's precise views. Nevertheless, as we will see, it is quite clear that they are in strong contrast to modern conceptions of the nature of politics and its connection to law. Again, I begin with a brief examination of Aristotle's biography.

1. Biographical Background

Aristotle was born in 384 BC in Stagira, Macedonia. He was educated as a Macedonian aristocrat and his family, particularly his father, was associated with the Macedonian kings. In 367, he travelled to Athens to attend Plato's academy. He stayed in Athens until Plato died in 347. He then moved around the Greek world, eventually returning to Macedonia, where in 343 he was invited by Philip II to become tutor to his son, the future Alexander the Great. He was also appointed head of the royal academy of Macedonia and gave lessons to Ptolemy and Cassander. In 334 he returned to Athens to found his own school, the Lyceum. It is during this period that he is thought to have written his major works. In 332 Alexander died, an event that triggered a rise of anti-Macedonian feeling in Athens. Fearing that he would share Socrates' fate, Aristotle departed Athens for Chalcis, where he died in 332.

This period witnessed significant tensions between Athens and Macedonia that culminated in the Battle of Chaeronea in 338, in which forces under Philip defeated a combined Athenian and Theban army. The result was what is now known as the League of Corinth: an alliance of Greek states, with the exception of Sparta, under the command of Philip and then Alexander.

This was never a comfortable alliance. The Athenians recalled their former imperial power and resented the domination of Macedonia. Moreover, though the Macedonians fervently wished to be considered Greeks, their state lay outside what might be called the core of the ancient Greek world and many Athenians regarded them as barbarians. Given Aristotle's origin and connection to the Macedonian rulers, then, it was natural for these tensions to affect his life in Athens.

It would also be natural to think that this tension would be reflected in Aristotle's philosophical writings, particularly in his politics. To an extent this is true, but the way in which this tension plays out is rather surprising.

First, despite his connection with Philip and Alexander, Aristotle does not support the Macedonian desire to found a united Greek empire. To the contrary, Aristotle claims that the *polis*, the traditional Greek city state, is the ideal. But nor does Aristotle use his works actively to oppose Macedonian ambitions. He simply describes what he regards as the ideal state and explains why that state is ideal. It just turns out that this places him offside with the ambitions of the Macedonian kings.

Moreover, in comparison with Plato, Aristotle is much more focused on existing political realities. For instance, one of the tasks he undertook at the Lyceum was to collect 158 actual constitutions. The point of this was to learn how states are governed in order better to decide how they should be. This focus on empirical research contrasts with Plato's more '*a priori*' approach.

This, of course, is in line with the familiar contrast of Plato's and Aristotle's methodologies, beautifully captured in Raphael's the *School of Athens*. Plato and Aristotle are the central figures in this painting and are presented interacting, perhaps even disputing, with each other. Plato holds a copy of his *Timeaus* and points upwards towards the heavens. Aristotle carries a copy of his *Nicomachean Ethics* and holds his hand out in front of him, palm down, in a gesture that suggests both rejection of his teacher's views and a pointing towards the terrestrial. This is thought to symbolize the general approaches of the two men.

The *Timeaus* is perhaps Plato's most 'metaphysical', most unworldly, work. It is a dialogue that examines the transcendental realm of the forms. Hence, Plato points up to the transcendent, away from the world of experience. The *Nicomachean Ethics*, however, is a work deeply engaged in the practical realities of human life and Aristotle rebuffs Plato's invitation to turn away from this reality, indicating that the truth lies in front of them.

No doubt, there is much truth in this picture. But it is not the whole truth. Plato's philosophy is more 'metaphysical' than Aristotle's. Plato is more likely to engage in abstract philosophical thought unconnected with the everyday than Aristotle. But it is also true that Plato is much more concerned than Aristotle with contemporary events. If you like, his strategy is to provide 'metaphysical' solutions to today's problems. Aristotle's strategy, on the other hand, is to provide practical solutions, but not to today's problems. Of course, for instance, Aristotle knew about the tensions between Athens and Macedonia, but he does not structure his discussion around them, overtly or covertly. He simply collects his data, analyses it, and describes what he takes it to show. If the result happens to be in tension with the aims of his political masters, so be it. In this way, then, Aristotle's theory is more removed from concrete reality than Plato's.

The significance of this for us is that, despite the volatility of the contemporary political situation, Aristotle's political theory is not driven in the way that Plato's is. As a result, Aristotle is able to notice and dwell on features of the political landscape that one more driven would tend to overlook. I examine the most important of these features here.

2. Distributive and Corrective Justice

An investigation of Aristotle's political philosophy must begin with his celebrated distinction between distributive and corrective justice.[1] As we see, despite its fame, it is not an easy distinction to understand.

---

[1] In the translation from which I work, Terence Irwin prefers 'rectificatory justice' to 'corrective justice'. However, I have chosen to replace 'rectificatory' with 'corrective' for two reasons. First, I wish to reserve 'rectificatory justice' for an aspect of corrective justice as defined by Aristotle. Secondly, 'corrective justice' is the term most widely used in legal circles.

Moreover, as is stressed later in this section and in subsequent chapters, it is now very frequently misunderstood.

Aristotle first distinguishes between what he calls general and special justice.[2] As he explains, the first of these is a synonym for complete goodness or virtue. As we might say, in this sense 'just' simply means good. But there is another sense of justice, which enables us to say that a man is wicked in some regard and yet acts justly.[3] It is this special sense on which Aristotle's discussion focuses, a sense he defines in contradistinction from overreaching, ie attempting to gain more of the good or to accept less of the bad than one should.[4] Aristotle then claims that justice, ie special justice, comes in two forms: the distributive and the corrective.[5] I examine these in turn.

2.1 Distributive Justice

Aristotle begins with distributive justice. He maintains that it is concerned with individuals' shares of good and bad things.[6] As we would say, distributive justice is focused on the distribution of benefits and burdens. Because of this, he claims that distributive justice 'requires four things at least; the people for whom it is just are two, and the [equal] things involved are two'.[7] This leads him to the observation that distributive justice operates in accordance with 'geometrical' proportion.[8] This claim is not at all easy to understand, but unpacking it will put us in a good position to comprehend Aristotle's idea of justice in general.

A key to understanding the assertion is the notion that distributive justice depends on a conception of worth.

[A]ll agree that the just in distributions must accord with some sort of worth, but what they call worth is not the same; supporters of democracy say it is free citizenship, some supporters of oligarchy say it is wealth, others good birth, while supporters of aristocracy say it is virtue.[9]

---

[2] Aristotle, *Nicomachean Ethics*, 1129b–1130a.
[3] Ibid, 1128b.
[4] Ibid, 1129a–b.
[5] Ibid, 1130b–1131a.
[6] Ibid, 1131a.
[7] Ibid. See also ibid, 1131a–b (the addition is the translator's).
[8] Ibid, 1131b.
[9] Ibid, 1131a.

Distributive justice is concerned with the distribution of benefits and burdens. It demands that these be distributed fairly. But people disagree over the appropriate criterion of fairness. Some think that everyone should possess equal amounts of the good. Others maintain that some individuals or groups should have more than others. Aristotle tells us that underlying these disputes is a disagreement about the nature of worth.

The democrat defines worth in accordance with free citizenship. Accordingly, she holds that all free citizens are of equal worth and so are entitled to the same consideration in terms of distributive justice. However, some oligarchs define worth in terms of wealth. They maintain that the wealthy are worth more than the poor and accordingly deserve special consideration. And so on.

This last touched on feature of Aristotle's theory needs to be stressed. The concern is not with distributions per se, but with the degree of consideration to which individuals are entitled. Accordingly, the issue upon which Aristotle focuses is not reflected in modern debates over the nature of distributive justice. This is despite the fact that we too disagree over the justice of particular distributions. For instance, the modern strict egalitarian demands that property be distributed equally, the liberal egalitarian holds that it may be distributed unequally but only so that the overall distribution advantages everybody,[10] while the libertarian maintains that property be distributed in accordance with the free market.[11] These are genuine disagreements, of course, but they are not about the worth of persons or about the entitlement to consideration. The strict egalitarian, the liberal egalitarian, and the libertarian agree that all individuals are of equal worth and deserve equal consideration. They disagree on what scheme of distribution follows from this.

This, of course, is because we live in a 'democratic age' where, at least in the West, the notion that all humans are of equal moral worth can be taken for granted. But Aristotle did not live in such an age. For him, then, what we take for granted was a matter for debate. Accordingly, the disagreements he discusses are not about the appropriate scheme of distribution—though those disagreements certainly have an impact on that issue. Rather, his analysis focuses on the level of consideration particular individuals or groups deserve. For the

---

[10] Eg Rawls, *A Theory of Justice*, 65–73.
[11] Eg Nozick, *Anarchy, State, and Utopia*.

democrat, all free citizens deserve equal consideration, but those who are not free citizens such as children, women, and slaves, deserve less or none. Similarly, for oligarchs, the wealthy deserve more consideration than the poor. And so on.

This is one of the reasons Aristotle's claim that distributive justice is geometrical can be hard to understand. Because we take for granted the idea that people are of equal worth, the issue that prompts Aristotle's remark does not arise for us. But that does not mean that Aristotle's position is any less pertinent now that it was. It is just as true now as it was in ancient Greece that distributive justice relies on a conception of worth, it just turns out that we moderns generally share the same conception.

Because the content of distributive justice is dependent on an account of worth, issues of distributive justice cannot be determined merely by comparing people's holdings. It is also necessary to consider their worth. So, for instance, if I were to claim that you have too much and I too little, I can make out this claim only by pointing both to our holdings and to our worth. In a two-person society, then, distributive justice operates in relation to four variables: A's wealth and A's worth, and B's wealth and B's worth. For this reason, Aristotle describes distributive justice as geometrical.

It is noteworthy that, though Aristotle discusses the attitudes of others to worth in the *Nicomachean Ethics*, he says nothing about his own view there. That discussion must await the *Politics*.

Before we finish our examination of distributive justice, it is important to say something about Aristotle's use of the term 'equality' in relation to this notion. He tells us that:

Since the equal involves at least two things [equal to each other], it follows that the just must be intermediate and equal, and related to something, and for some people. Insofar as it is intermediate, it must be between too much and too little; insofar as it is equal, it involves two things; and insofar as it is just, it is just for some people.[12]

At first glance, this may appear to imply that distributive justice calls for people (or at least people of equal worth) to have equal holdings. But the second sentence of this passage reveals that this is not Aristotle's intention. As far as distributive justice is concerned, equality

---

[12] Aristotle, *Nicomachean Ethics*, 1131a (the addition is the translator's).

is about having neither too much nor too little. It is about having as much as one deserves. Hence, *A* and *B* are in a position of equality if they have what they deserve, even if their holdings are different.

To translate this into modern terms, a strict egalitarian holds that people are in a position of equality only if they have equal resources. But a liberal egalitarian maintains that the rich and the poor are in a position of equality as long as the wealth of the rich advantages everyone. For the libertarian, moreover, people are in a position of equality, no matter how vastly different their wealth, as long as their positions were a product of the free market. With this notion of equality in mind, we can turn to the second form of justice.

2.2 Corrective Justice

Aristotle's Terminology Unfortunately, Aristotle's account of corrective justice is beset with terminological difficulties, difficulties that, as we will see, have resulted in serious misunderstandings. In order to deal with this problem, I first exhibit Aristotle's theory as it is presented in the *Nicomachean Ethics* before identifying the areas of terminological difficulty and responding to them.

The first thing that Aristotle says about corrective justice is that it is 'found in transactions' that can be voluntary or involuntary.[13] He further claims that, like distributive justice, corrective justice is concerned with proportionality. However, the proportionality relevant to corrective justice is arithmetical, rather than geometrical.[14] It is also a proportionality that ignores the worth of the parties, being interested only in the causing and suffering of harm.[15] Aristotle maintains that the law focuses on this harm, and that the people whose job it is to enforce corrective justice—ie judges—try to 'restore this unjust situation to equality' by subtracting from the offender's profit to compensate for the victim's loss.[16] Aristotle does not define the sphere of corrective justice—he does not tell us to which actions this form of justice does and does not apply—but in the course of his discussion he reveals that corrective justice is relevant, inter alia, to theft, adultery, battery (wounding and killing), and buying and selling.

---

[13] Ibid, 1131b.
[14] Ibid, 1132a.
[15] Ibid.
[16] Ibid, 1132a–b.

As presented, there are numerous problems with this position. First, it seems clear that in the cases Aristotle imagines offenders do not necessarily make profits and victims do not necessarily suffer losses. For instance, if *A* strikes and wounds *B*, then *B* suffers a loss, but *A* need not make any profit. Moreover, if *C* steals *D*'s property and uses it, but then returns it without damaging it, then while it seems right to say that *C* has made a profit, *D* may have suffered no loss. What is more, in this case *C* appears to have caused no harm to *D*, despite the fact that Aristotle insists that corrective justice is concerned with the causing and suffering of harm. Also, the claim that corrective justice is 'found in transactions' sits uncomfortably with his examples. If I punch you in the back of the head when you are not looking, that is a wounding; but it is odd to think of it as a transaction. There are other problems also, though they are more hidden. We discuss them below.

In fact, Aristotle is well aware of these problems. With respect to his use of 'profit' and 'loss', he says 'we speak of profit for the attacker who wounded his victim, for instance, even if that is not the proper word for some cases; and we speak of loss for the victim who suffers the wound.'[17] Moreover, he tells us that 'These names "loss" and "profit" are derived from voluntary exchange. For having more than one's own share is called making a profit, and having less than what one had at the beginning is called suffering a loss.'[18] Hence, Aristotle explicitly gives these terms a wider meaning than they ordinarily have. For instance, as Aristotle uses the term, 'profit' does not mean profit; it means having more than one ought to have. Why does Aristotle do this?

It is important to remember that Aristotle's work in this area, as in many others, was revolutionary. He either substantially reformed or invented outright a great many scholarly disciplines. Because of this, he must frequently have needed to communicate concepts for which no extant words were adequate. This presented him with a choice. He could either invent a neologism for the concept or he could extend the meaning of an existing term to cover that concept. Sometimes he did the former. But doing so as a matter of course is at best an uncomfortable strategy, as it is likely to render one's position unintelligible. Consequently, Aristotle often adopted the latter strategy; a strategy with its own pitfalls but which is often the least bad option.

[17] Ibid, 1132a.
[18] Ibid, 1131b.

Accordingly, Aristotle adopted the Greek equivalents of 'profit' and 'loss' because they were the terms closest in meaning to his intention that he could find.

The same must be said of Aristotle's use of 'transactions'. We do not transact when I punch you in the back of the head, but Aristotle should not be read to claim otherwise. Similarly, a person whose property is taken but who suffers no loss is not literally harmed, but she is 'harmed' in the sense in which Aristotle uses this term.

Though we are not told specifically, it is clear what Aristotle means by 'transactions'. The claim is that corrective justice is concerned with cases in which an offender affects a victim by 'harming' that victim, so that the offender gains a 'profit' and the victim suffers a 'loss'. In that light, 'interactions' seems better than 'transactions'.

Unfortunately, Aristotle does not tell us enough to know what he means by 'profit', 'loss', or 'harm'. We are left to guess. But I will not do that here. As with Plato, we are interested not so much in the content but in the structure of Aristotle's view and so these issues need not be solved now (if they ever can be). For us, more pressing issues must be faced. These are the relationship between corrective and distributive justice and the scope of the former. I deal with these in turn.

The Independence of Corrective from Distributive Justice It is common to think that corrective justice must somehow be grounded in distributive justice. For instance, James Gordley claims that writers in the Aristotelian tradition (which I suppose includes Aristotle himself) maintain that 'commutative [ie corrective[19]] justice depended on distributive justice'.[20] Moreover, Gordley alleges that these writers

distinguished two fundamental concepts of justice on which the law ultimately rests: distributive and commutative justice. The object of distributive justice is to ensure that each person has the resources he requires. The object of commutative justice is to enable him to obtain them without unfairly diminishing others' ability to do so.[21]

According to Gordley, then, the role of corrective justice is to protect distributive justice. Its role, therefore, is secondary.

---

[19] The relationship between these terms is discussed below.
[20] Gordley, *Foundations of Private Law: Property, Tort, Contract, Unjust Enrichment*, 11; see also 12, 32.
[21] Ibid, 8.

Other writers, some of whom are examined later in this book, think that the link between corrective and distributive justice is more indirect. The idea, especially prominent in legal circles, is that an injustice in the eyes of corrective justice is committed when a person's rights are violated, and those rights are a creation of distributive justice.[22] For instance, a battery is a wrong relevant to corrective justice because a battery violates the victim's right to bodily integrity. But the victim has the right because of distributive, not corrective, justice.

Our assessment of these views will be aided if we think of them in the light of the following example. Imagine that A, B, C, and D live in a perfectly just, four-person society and that A wilfully damages B's property, causing a £1,000 loss to B. Aristotle's idea is that corrective justice sees A's action as an injustice and demands that A pay £1,000 to B.[23] But why is A's act an injustice?

According to Gordley, it is because A unfairly diminished B's ability to acquire (and retain) the resources he requires in order to live his life. According to others, it is because A violated a rule created in accordance with distributive justice. But these answers are not Aristotle's.

First, it is important to see that A's action need not have resulted in distributive injustice. This is so even though the *status quo ante* was perfectly distributively just. Though B is made worse off, he may not be made worse off to an extent that he is in a position of inequality with respect to the other members of his society. To take liberal egalitarianism as an example, it may be the case that the resulting distribution remains to the advantage of all and thus remains perfectly distributively just.

Moreover, if we change our example and imagine that B originally had more than that to which distributive justice entitled him, it may follow that A's action resulted in a more distributively just society than previously existed. In that sense, distributive justice would applaud at least the outcome of A's action. But there is no suggestion in Aristotle that this would affect what corrective justice has to say about this case.

Secondly, it must be remembered that, though in our initial example the *status quo ante* was perfectly just, it cannot be restored. Certainly, requiring A to pay £1,000 to B returns B to the position that he was in before, but it does so by altering A's position, and it is not evident

---

[22] See most explicitly Cane, 'Distributive Justice and Tort Law'.
[23] Aristotle, *Nicomachean Ethics*, 1132a.

that the result will be a just distribution. It is not unlikely that distributive justice will call for *A*, *C*, and *D* to surrender some of their resources to *B*. In fact, it is possible that, though *A* harmed *B*, distributive justice will call for only *C* and *D* to surrender their resources in order to compensate *B* for his loss.

To avoid these relatively obvious points, the theorist who holds that corrective justice is dependent on distributive justice maintains that in practice this dependence is somewhat indirect. For instance, she might maintain that the reason *A* must pay *B* £1,000 in our example is not in order to restore a distributively just *status quo ante*, but because a rule against wilful damage (or whatever) coupled with the demand that those who violate that rule must compensate their victims tends to distributive justice in the long run. I will have more to say about this position in later chapters. The point now is that on reflection this is quite clearly not Aristotle's view.

For a start, the idea that corrective justice is dependent on distributive justice is inconsistent with Aristotle's assertion that distributive and corrective justice are the two forms of justice, and in particular that corrective justice 'belongs to a different species from' distributive justice.[24] On the view under examination, however, corrective justice is not a form of justice in its own right, but only a method for promoting distributive justice in certain contexts. One way to bring this out is to say that, on the view under examination, a complete account of distributive justice—abstract and applied—will already include an account of corrective justice, but the reverse is not the case. On this view, 'corrective justice' would refer to a subset of the norms required in order to realize distributive justice. Those norms are themselves, on this view, a subset of the norms of distributive justice. It is precisely this that Aristotle is concerned to reject by maintaining that distributive and corrective justice are the two forms of justice.

Moreover, in his account of corrective justice, Aristotle makes no mention of the idea that this form of justice is concerned with the ability of individuals to obtain resources 'without unfairly diminishing others' ability to do so'.[25] As we see now, the distributive element in this definition is absent from Aristotle's account.[26]

---

[24] Ibid, 1131b.
[25] Gordley, *Foundations of Private Law: Property, Tort, Contract, Unjust Enrichment*, 8.
[26] An anonymous reviewer invited me to consider the following argument: 'to say that the purpose of the circulatory system is to deliver the nutrients that the digestive system

72 ARISTOTLE

After defining corrective justice as that 'found in transactions' and telling us that it is unconcerned with issues relevant to distributive justice,[27] Aristotle claims that:

> the law looks only at differences in the harm [inflicted], and treats the people involved as equals, if one does injustice while the other suffers it, and one has done the harm while the other has suffered it.
>
> And so the judge tries to restore this unjust situation to equality, since it is unequal. For [not only when one steals from another but] also when one is wounded and the other wounds him, or one kills and the other is killed, the action and the suffering are unequally divided [with profit for the offender and loss for the victim]; and the judge tries to restore the [profit and] loss to a position of equality, by subtraction from [the offender's] profit.[28]

The first thing to notice about this passage is the exclusion of distributive concerns. First, Aristotle's claim is not that corrective justice

---

provides does not imply the digestive system is superior. It implies only that each system has a function in relation to the other, and that each function promotes the welfare of the organism. That idea seems to be implicit in Aristotle's teleological analysis of the state, and a passage the author quotes in which Aquinas says that distributive justice concerns the order of the whole to the parts and commutative justice the order of the parts to each other.'

My reply is the following. The analogy with biology is inapt. The circulatory and digestive systems are physical entities that have an existence quite apart from the values that (on a teleological view of nature) apply to them. Thus, even if the sole purpose of the circulatory system was to provide nutrients supplied by the digestive system (which of course it is not), then the systems remain independent entities. But there is no equivalent with respect to the forms of justice. Corrective justice is a norm. If it can be derived from distributive justice because the point of corrective justice is to realize distributive justice, then corrective justice is a mere aspect of distributive justice in a way in which the circulatory system could never be a mere aspect of the digestive system.

Moreover, the analogy with biology is inapt in another way also. The analogy is meant to block the inference from the idea (1) that corrective justice has the purpose of protecting the distribution of resources to the conclusion; (2) that distributive justice is superior to commutative justice. This is why the claim that the circulatory and digestive systems are interdependent, neither being superior to the other, is relevant—the claim is analogous to the converse of (2). But the analogy could be fitting only if the point of the circulatory system was to realize/fulfil/protect (or whatever word is appropriate) the digestive system, as that is the analogous claim to (1). But that is not true. In fact, the circulatory and digestive systems are interdependent, neither being superior to the other, both 'designed' to promote the welfare of the organism. Accordingly, then, this is precisely analogous to my claim regarding corrective and distributive justice. Neither of these forms of justice have the point of realizing/protecting (or whatever) the other, but are designed to promote, in their separate ways, the welfare of the whole. And, as this book attempts to show, that welfare is a matter of distributive and commutative justice.

[27] Aristotle, *Nicomachean Ethics*, 1131b–1132a.
[28] Ibid, 1132a (the additions are the translator's).

ought to be done in order to realize some distributive end. The claim is rather that corrective justice ought to be done because corrective justice demands it. That is what it means for corrective justice to be a form of justice. Secondly, Aristotle insists that corrective justice operates by reference to its own concerns—examined immediately below—ignoring entirely those of distributive justice. Certainly, that view is in itself consistent with the idea that distributive justice is the ultimate aim of corrective justice. But it is just as clear that the idea is not entailed or even suggested by anything that Aristotle says and, moreover, the idea is quite incompatible with Aristotle's insistence on the separation of the two forms of justice.

Aristotle's conception is the following. When one person wrongs another, she ends up with more than she ought to have and her victim ends up with less than she should have. Moreover, as Aristotle stresses by utilizing the metaphor of an inappropriately divided line,[29] the offender has more than she should have vis-à-vis the victim and the victim has less than she should have vis-à-vis the offender. Aristotle describes this having more or less as inequality and maintains that the task of the judge is to restore equality by taking from the offender and giving to the victim. Because the offender has more than she should have vis-à-vis the victim and the victim has less than she should have vis-à-vis the offender, the appropriate response is to take from the offender in order to give to the victim.

This aspect of corrective justice is absolutely central. In corrective justice, the focus is on the *relationship between* the parties. It is not on the parties as solitary individuals or as members of a wider community. It is interested in the offender only because he 'harmed' the victim and it is interested in the victim only because he was 'harmed' by the offender. Hence, the reasons for holding the offender liable are the same reasons for finding that liability is owed to the victim. In corrective justice, the relationship between the parties forms a conceptual unity. Again, this is captured by Aristotle's notion that corrective justice can be represented by the metaphor of a single line and by his claim that proportionality in corrective justice is arithmetic.

Let us return to our example in which *A* damages *B*'s property. For corrective justice, there is an injustice here because *A* harmed *B*. The fact that *B* suffered a loss as a result is the reason that *A* must compensate *B*. We cannot give content to this idea without knowing

[29] Ibid, 1132a–b.

what 'harm' means in this context, but what is crucial is that C and D are irrelevant to this equation, a fact which is again indicated by the metaphor of the single line and the insistence that proportionality in corrective justice is arithmetic rather than geometric.

This helps to distinguish corrective from distributive justice. Inequality in the eyes of distributive justice occurs when a person has less or more than he should have vis-à-vis all others in society. For corrective justice, however, inequality occurs when one person has less than she should have vis-à-vis another individual, because the second person harmed the first.

In summary, then, for Aristotle corrective justice is independent of distributive justice. These are two autonomous forms of justice. Each has its own understanding of the just and the unjust and each responds to the just and the unjust in its own way. These ideas are examined in greater detail in following chapters.

The Scope of Corrective Justice As indicated above, Aristotle clearly enunciates the separation of distributive and corrective justice.[30] Why, then, is it so common to attribute to him the view that the latter is dependent on the former? The answer is that, to the modern mind, it seems all but axiomatic that corrective justice can have no content unless it is at least indirectly based on distributive justice, and so it seems clear that corrective justice must be based on the distributive.

In order to examine this position, it will be useful to make the following distinction. As we saw in section 2.1, in conjunction with a conception of equality, distributive justice generates certain norms. Let us call these 'primary norms'. These norms tell us the way that society ought to be. Hence, in a distributively ideal society, the primary norms will be fully realized. But imagine now that this distribution is disturbed. In these circumstances, 'secondary norms' would come into play, which would determine the appropriate way in which to respond to the disruption. The secondary norms are secondary in that their point is to respond to the violation of the primary norms.

For instance, imagine that distributive justice demanded that the difference in wealth between the rich and the poor not exceed the ratio 10:1. That is a primary norm of distributive justice. And imagine that in some society P_1 gained 20 times the wealth of P_2. In these circumstances, a norm would come into effect determining, say, that

[30] Ibid, 1131b–1132a.

some of P_1's wealth be redistributed to P_2. That is a secondary norm because it does not belong to distributive justice as such. In a perfectly just society, there would be no norm according to which P_1's wealth must be redistributed to P_2.

The view under discussion here is that corrective justice can generate only secondary norms. Because of this, it is thought that corrective justice can have content only in the presence of primary norms, upon which it is to operate. Moreover, it of course follows that these primary norms cannot be provided by corrective justice.

Despite its popularity, the argument for this position is flawed. It is the following. Corrective justice is about correcting injustice. It tells us how to rectify circumstances when one person has committed an injustice against another. But because it tells us only how to correct injustices, it cannot inform us about injustice itself. That must, therefore, be the task of distributive justice. For instance, if A has damaged B's property, corrective justice can tell us how this injustice should be corrected, but it cannot tell us why, or even that, A's action was unjust. Those issues can be settled only by distributive justice.[31]

This argument is dreadful, because its pivotal and missing premise holds that the content of corrective justice is necessarily captured by the meaning of the word 'corrective'. It commits the all-too-frequent mistake of holding that a concept is to be understood in terms of the meaning of the words that constitute its name. This is never appropriate. Distributive justice is not approached by insisting that it be comprehended through analysis of the dictionary meaning of 'distributive'. Nor do we think that an appropriate way to learn about nuclear physics is to look up 'atom' in the dictionary. Names must not be confused with the concepts to which they refer.

Moreover, the error is particularly egregious given that Aristotle was writing, not in modern English, but in ancient Greek. He did not refer to 'corrective' justice at all. Now, due to our lack of knowledge of the ancient world, we often cannot be certain how Aristotle's terms are best understood. Furthermore, as we have seen, Aristotle was forced frequently to use terms in ways that did not correspond to their exact contemporary meaning. We have seen that his use of (the Greek equivalents of) 'profit', 'loss', 'harm', and 'transactions' are examples. Accordingly, it is quite wrong to place great emphasis on

---

[31] For an historical analysis of the growth of this misunderstanding, see Tuck, *Natural Rights Theories*, 45.

the meanings of the modern English terms into which his translators have chosen to render his language.

To understand Aristotle's idea of corrective justice, it is entirely inappropriate to fixate on the words 'corrective' and 'justice'. Instead, in order to discern his meaning, we must examine the way in which he employs the concept. I do that now.

At first, Aristotle's examination of corrective justice appears to lend support to the view I have rejected. Very early in his discussion, he examines the way in which courts should respond to instances of wrongdoing. And as we have seen, Aristotle tells us that 'the law looks only at differences in the harm [inflicted], and treats the people involved as equals... And so the judge tries to restore this unjust situation to equality, since it is unequal.'[32] It is perhaps natural, then, to think that in Aristotle's mind corrective justice is only corrective in this way.

But this thought comes too quickly. Aristotle tells us that corrective justice is concerned with correcting injustices. That is clearly so. But it does not follow from this that corrective justice is thereby exhausted. Aristotle talks about the way in which courts respond to injustice, because his audience would have been familiar with this—especially given the role of citizens as jurors in ancient Athens. It was therefore a useful illustration of the concept under discussion; but it is only one good example.

At the end of the discussion devoted to the concept of corrective justice, Aristotle claims that in buying and selling,

> when people get neither more nor less, but precisely what belongs to them, they say they have their own share and make neither a loss nor a profit. Hence the just is intermediate between a certain kind of loss and profit, since it is having the equal amount both before and after [the transaction].[33]

As we discuss in the following, the meaning of this passage is not entirely transparent. But it is immediately obvious that it is inconsistent with the view under examination. Aristotle claims that if one enters a transaction that preserves equality, then the outcome is just. That is very clearly a primary, not a secondary, norm. Here, corrective justice is telling us what is just, not merely how to respond to the violation of a norm determined by distributive justice or some other notion.

---

[32] Aristotle, *Nicomachean Ethics*, 1132a (the additions are the translator's).
[33] Ibid, 1132b (the addition is the translator's).

However, the most obvious meaning of this passage is not intended by Aristotle. He appears to claim that a transaction such as a sale is just only if the wealth of each party is preserved. That, however, ignores what Aristotle means by equality. To understand his view in this regard, it is necessary to comprehend his rejection of a rival theory, associated with Pythagoras, that justice is reciprocity.[34] Aristotle's response to this theory is to argue that justice cannot be understood as reciprocity, as morally significant reciprocity gets its content from justice and not vice versa. To use his example, imagine that a builder gives a shoemaker a house and that, in return, the shoemaker gives the builder a shoe. Strictly literally, there is reciprocity here. It is clear, however, that the builder would not so regard the shoemaker's actions, houses being much more valuable than shoes. Accordingly, Aristotle maintains that genuine reciprocity can exist only if houses and shoes are 'equalized'.[35]

This does not mean that houses and shoes must somehow be made to have the same value. It means that a method must be discovered to enable people to compare the value of houses and the value of shoes, so that a morally meaningful act of reciprocity can be made. For instance, if a house is worth 12,793 shoes, then the builder can give 12,793 shoes in return for the house and his act can be understood to be genuinely reciprocal. Aristotle maintains that money was invented (at least in part) to facilitate this.[36] He also says that the ultimate measure of value in this regard is need.[37] We would say rather want or preference.

Aristotle ends this part of his discussion by saying that:

Reciprocity will be secured, then, when things are equalized, so that the shoemaker's product is to the farmer's as the farmer is to the shoemaker. However, they must be introduced into the figure of proportion not when they have already exchanged and one extreme has both excesses, but when they still have their own; in that way they will be equals and members of a community, because this sort of equality can be produced in them.[38]

There are two ways of taking these claims and their connection with justice. First, expressing these ideas in terms of sale and purchase, one

---

[34] Ibid, 1132b–1133b.
[35] Ibid, 1133a.
[36] Ibid.
[37] Ibid.
[38] Ibid, 1133a–b.

could maintain that a particular transaction is just if it reflects the value placed on the items bought and sold *by the parties* to the transaction. This view aligns with the general approach of the common law, which permits the parties freedom of contract subject only to unconscionability. Secondly, one could maintain that equality in exchange is determined—in some way about which Aristotle is not explicit—*by the market price*. This connects with the civil law and its concept of *laesio enormis*—the idea that justice sometimes requires the setting aside (or voidability) of contracts for sale because the price, though freely agreed to, is unfair.[39] In fact, Reinhard Zimmermann traces the ideas that gave rise to the *laesio enormis* in the *ius commune* precisely to the passages quoted above.[40] The second view appears to be Aristotle's, though it is impossible to be sure.

In any case, the crucial point for us is the one noted above. Aristotle holds that corrective justice demands equality in transactions.[41] This is despite the fact that Aristotle illustrates his points by referring to cases with 'four terms', which recalls the claim examined above that distributive justice must refer to four things. That distributive justice must refer to four things does not show that whenever justice refers to four things that justice must be distributive justice. Moreover, it is clear that the discussion of justice in exchange is connected to the last paragraph of Aristotle's examination of corrective justice. In fact, the former is an application of the latter.[42] Finally, in his illustrations of justice in exchange, Aristotle ignores the central problem of distributive justice and the reason why applications of distributive justice must refer to four terms: the relevance of the worth of the parties. It is impossible, then, to regard this discussion as concerning distributive justice.

Corrective justice does not merely tell us how to correct injustice. It identifies equality and inequality in transitions. '[T]he just is intermediate between a certain kind of loss and profit, since it is having the equal amount both before and after [the transaction].'[43]

---

[39] For this reason, Finnis' claim that Aquinas' allegiance to Aristotle's account of corrective justice was fake (see Finnis, *Natural Law and Natural Rights*, 179) is unlikely to be correct. It is more likely that Aquinas interpreted Aristotle's account in the light of these ideas, as it reflects important aspects of Aquinas' own view. See Aquinas, *Summa theologica*, SS Q77 A1. See also Chapter 6.

[40] Zimmermann, *The Law of Obligations*, 266.

[41] Aristotle, *Nicomachean Ethics*, 1132b.

[42] It is also important to note that the headings of the various sections are not Aristotle's, and so the apparent changes of topic suggested by those headings may be merely apparent.

[43] Aristotle, *Nicomachean Ethics*, 1132b (the addition is the translator's).

Note that this does not mean that corrective justice is unconcerned with correction. It is concerned with both primary and secondary norms. Corrective justice determines what our (primary) rights are and determines how violations of those rights should be corrected (ie it determines secondary rights). Applying this idea to law, corrective justice tells us what a tort is and how the law should respond to tortious wrongdoing; it tells us how contracts are formed and why they are binding, as well as how the law should respond to breach of contract; and it tells us what an unjust enrichment is and also how unjust enrichments should be remedied. It establishes our rights and directs remedial action when those rights are violated.

In the light of this discussion, we can see that the concept of corrective justice is today frequently misunderstood. Though the term is often used, it is usually understood to refer to a concept that is dependent on distributive justice in the ways examined above. That is not corrective justice as Aristotle understood it. As a result, the vast majority of modern thinkers have in reality a concept only of distributive justice and they use 'corrective justice' to refer to a part of it—ie to a subset of the secondary norms generated by distributive justice. Today, corrective justice is virtually unknown. It is the forgotten justice.[44]

Labelling Aristotle's Corrective Justice As we have seen, it is likely that Aristotle used his term because no better was available. We, however, need not use 'corrective'. Given the level of misunderstanding, it is desirable to find another term. Unfortunately, none is ideal.

When Aristotle's works were translated into Latin, his term was rendered as '*commutativo*'. This term was picked up by Aristotle's followers from Aquinas on. Hence, we have our not quite archaic 'commutative justice'. In some ways, this term is better than 'corrective justice', but it is not perfect. According to the *Oxford English Dictionary*, 'commutative' means 'Pertaining to exchange or mutual dealings'. This presents the same problem as 'transactions' noted above. But here the near-archaism of 'commutative' comes to the rescue. Because the term has fallen out of use, its meaning is now unfamiliar. Consequently, it can be used as a quasi-neologism. Its meaning as used here can be defined, and it is reasonable to hope that readers will understand the term in

---

[44] Of course, again, there are exceptions. See section 3 of the Introduction to this book.

the light of that definition, as is perhaps too hopeful regarding 'corrective'. In the following, then, I use 'commutative justice' to refer to the concept identified by Aristotle in Book V of the *Nicomachean Ethics* and examined above. That concept is greatly developed in the material that follows.

It is also convenient to have a term to refer specifically to the corrective element of corrective or commutative justice. 'Corrective justice' obviously suggests itself, but it will not do. The term is now too confusing and using it will no doubt suggest to some readers tensions with other positions (including ones advanced earlier by myself) that do not in reality exist. Accordingly, I will use the term 'rectificatory justice'.

At this point, it is useful to examine the diagrammatic presentation of commutative justice in Figure J2 at the beginning of this book. The first point to notice is the presence of solid and dotted lines in the diagram. This indicates two things. First, the focus of commutative justice can only be on two individuals (that is, two individuals in the eyes of the commutative justice, though these individuals can in fact be constituted by a plurality of natural persons; for instance, one individual can be the state and another an association). In the diagram, the focus is solely on P_1 and P_2. Secondly, commutative justice is relevant to all and treats all equally. So whatever it says about P_1 and P_2, it will also say about P_1 and P_3, P_1 and P_4, P_2 and P_3, P_2 and P_4, and P_3 and P_4 when those persons are identically situated in the relevant way. Hence, in ruling for one, commutative justice lays down rules for all. But this does not mean that it lays down rules *by considering* all. In other words, that commutative justice creates rules for everyone—as we might loosely say, that it 'distributes' rules—does not mean that it is distributive justice. In particular, if a court (or anyone) decides an issue between P_1 and P_2 in terms of commutative justice, then it produces a decision of significance to all relationships in society, but it does so by considering only the position of P_1 and P_2. As Aristotle indicated, this is appropriate if the way in which the issue is determined abstracts from the particularities of P_1 and P_2 so that it applies with equal justice to P_3 and P_4 etc.[45]

For commutative justice, then, the investigation is into the relationship between two people. It examines their interaction and it takes those two people as a unit. It does not seek to compare their positions with those of others, external to the interaction. It is an interpersonal justice.

---

[45] Aristotle, *Nicomachean Ethics*, 1132a.

3. Politics and Law

We now turn to Aristotle's political theory proper. This is set out in *The Politics*, which presents an analysis of, amongst other things, the best constitution. We need not examine the content of this analysis in great detail. The following sketch will suffice.

First, Aristotle maintains that the goal of politics is to create conditions that encourage virtue.[46] This is because citizens are unlikely to live good lives unless they possess virtue. As we would say, this is a concern with the public interest. Secondly, though Aristotle argues that aristocracy, ie the rule of the virtuous, is the ideal form of government, he also insists that it is unlikely to be realizable in practice.[47] This is because aristocracy depends on the ability to determine and promote to power the truly virtuous and because it supposes that there will be agreement on such. Because this is unrealistic, Aristotle settles for polity, a combination of democracy and oligarchy in which decision-making is distributed through the citizenry so that all have a say, though an unequal one.

To modern eyes, the shape of Aristotle's theory appears clear. The fundamental truths of morality are discussed in Aristotle's ethical works: the *Nicomachean Ethics*, the *Eudemian Ethics*, and, perhaps, the *Magna Moralia*. These are applied to the political sphere in *The Politics*. The result is a constitution of a kind outlined above. When that constitution is in place, the government will pass laws in accordance with the constitution itself and in the light of justice as examined in the *Nicomachean Ethics*. As Aristotle tells us, the law follows the constitution.[48]

This reading attributes to Aristotle two crucial views: first, that Aristotle's understanding of the relationship between morality, politics, and law is the same as Plato's in *The Republic*; secondly, that Aristotle's theory is based on distributive, rather than commutative, justice. This is supported by the notion that politics is concerned with the public interest. Though Aristotle either wrote too little or insufficient material survives to determine Aristotle's position with certainty, I argue now there is good reason to believe that this interpretation seriously distorts Aristotle's views.

---

[46] Ibid, 1179a–1180a.
[47] Aristotle, '*The Politics*', see especially Bk VI.
[48] Ibid, 1282b, 1310a.

It is true that Aristotle maintains that the law must follow the constitution, but this does not imply the acceptance of the view outlined above. As he also tells us, 'laws, when good, should be supreme'.[49] Though modern readers are inclined to interpret this claim in a weak fashion, as we see shortly it means what it says: that the law rules the government and not vice versa. Aristotle also says that 'The legislator should always include the middle class in his government'[50] and insists that the legislator should come from the middle class.[51] On the face of it, these claims are odd given that he also maintains that the structure of government should combine democracy and oligarchy but does not intend the first two claims as repetitions of the third.

The key to solving these apparent difficulties is to see that, for Aristotle, the legislator is not part of government. On the contrary, he is a single person—Aristotle refers to the legislator, not to legislators—separate from government, who gives the state its constitution and laws.

To us, this seems an extraordinary idea, but to Aristotle and his audience it was commonplace. In Athens, the rulers—whether kings, the democratic assembly, or oligarchs—were not legislators. The legislators were appointed officials who were given the sole task of writing laws. Most of them were indeed members of the middle class and were chosen because they had a reputation for impartiality. To protect this impartiality, convention insisted that political outsiders, not members of the government, be chosen as legislators. The most famous legislator was Solon, to whom Aristotle refers in *The Politics*.[52]

Accordingly, *The Politics* is not a discussion of politics as we understand it. It is rather advice given to the legislator on how to write the constitution. Moreover, a constitution for Aristotle was not what we understand by a constitution. According to the *Oxford English Dictionary*, the relevant meaning of 'constitution' is 'The system or body of fundamental principles according to which a nation, state, or body politic is constituted and governed.' This is too wide to capture Aristotle's notion. For him, a constitution concerns only the legal means by which a state is ruled. As we would say, though we must be especially wary of anachronism at this point, the constitution explored in *The Politics* is an examination only of the appropriate legal form through which *executive power* should be expressed.

---

[49] Ibid, 1282b.
[50] Ibid, 1296b.
[51] Ibid, 1296a.
[52] Ibid.

It is no coincidence that this understanding is reflected in all but the most modern uses of the term 'democracy'. Today, the term is most closely associated with the election of legislators by popular vote and the accountability of the executive either to the legislature or to a directly elected official. But this is not what the term used to mean. Kant, for instance, uses 'republic' for at least something like what we call democracy. And for him, a democracy is a state in which the people have direct executive power.[53] This understanding of 'democracy' is much closer to the original, Greek notion than ours. 'Democracy' was about rulers, not lawmakers.

These considerations reveal that the picture painted above misdescribes Aristotle's views. His claim that the law must be accommodated to the constitution does not mean that those given power by the constitution have the power to make law and should do so in a certain way. It means that the legislator must make law in a consistent fashion, and so having made the constitution one way must continue to make other laws in that same way. If, for instance, the legislator had written an oligarchic constitution, then he should make sure that his laws fit that kind of constitution. And Aristotle's assertion that law should be supreme means that the laws made by the legislator should govern; that the rulers must rule through these laws. Finally, though he holds that moral argument generates the political system, the idea that the political system generates the law is entirely foreign to his outlook. On the contrary, Aristotle maintains that politics occurs only after the legislator has created the law, hopefully doing so in a way that sets up a political system based on the concept of polity. For Aristotle as for the Plato of *The Laws*, law is not the offspring of politics; rather, politics is the offspring of law.

Aristotle's view can be represented as in Figure 4.1.

Moral argument —generates→ Political system that includes a constitution and laws —allows for and governs→ Politics

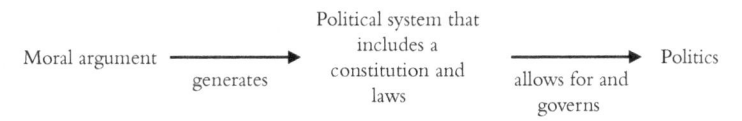

Figure 4.1 Politics and Law in Aristotle

---

[53] Kant, 'Toward Perpetual Peace', 8:8:352–353.

84 ARISTOTLE

There are also other suggestions in Aristotle's writings that support this picture. Unfortunately, they are contained in his writing on rhetoric, which, for reasons examined below, means that they must be approached with caution.

Aristotle distinguishes between 'particular' and 'general' law.[54] Particular laws are those that are written down, while general laws are 'those unwritten laws which are held to be agreed by all men'.[55] He later identifies general laws with the law of nature, and insists that this is rightly called law.[56]

The position is complicated by the fact that he also says that only written laws are compulsory,[57] that jurors should follow the written law,[58] and that citizens and jurors should not always follow the written law.[59] This apparent inconsistency is easily resolved, however, when it is noticed that these claims occur during Aristotle's discussion of the role of rhetoric in law. He is not here elucidating what he takes to be the truth, but discussing the way in which lawyers are able to argue cases. These claims, then, can be put aside. The claims concerning the distinction between particular and general law, however, are not made in this context and so must be taken to present Aristotle's view.

As we have seen, then, the general law has two properties. It is natural law and is (therefore?) law about which all men agree, at least in principle. As this law must be based on justice, this strongly suggests that the general law is based on commutative rather than distributive justice. This is because, as we saw above, distributive justice is by nature controversial, as it can be given content only in accordance with contentious views of worth. Commutative justice, however, is not controversial in this way. Of course, this does not mean that all of the commands of commutative justice are uncontroversial; the claim is only that if general law exists, if there is law about which all agree, then that law must have its moral basis in commutative justice. If this is right, then the general law is evidently pre-political in a double sense. As we saw earlier in this section, like all law general law is prior to the operations of day-to-day politics. But, as it is natural law, the general law is prior even to the lawgiving of the legislator. Again, this

---

[54] Aristotle, *The Art of Rhetoric*, 1386b.
[55] Ibid.
[56] Ibid, 1373b.
[57] Ibid, 1375a.
[58] Ibid, 1135b.
[59] Ibid.

supports the notion that Aristotle rejected the modern view of the connection between politics and law in favour of that contained in the diagram above.[60]

4. The Private Law

4.1 Commutative Justice and the Private Law

Aristotle's exploration of rhetoric also presents the following intriguing passage:

[J]ustice in relation to the person is defined in two ways. For it is defined either in relation to the community or to one of its members what one should or should not do. Accordingly, it is possible to perform just and unjust acts in two ways, either towards a defined individual or towards the community. The adulterer and mugger wrongs one of the individuals, the draft-dodger the community.[61]

The second sentence of this passage recalls the distinction between distributive and commutative justice. Laws that command 'in relation to the community' are based on distributive justice, while those that command 'in relation to...one of its members' are founded in commutative justice. According to the third sentence, when one violates a law of the first kind, one commits an injustice towards one's community; when one breaks a law of the second kind, one commits an injustice towards an individual.

Even if we forget the distinction between general and particular law, even if we imagine that a command can be a law only if written by the legislator, it follows that the legislator is required to make law

---

[60] Against this, however, one may point out that in the *Nicomachean Ethics* Aristotle maintains that politics is the master science (Aristotle, *Nicomachean Ethics*, 1094a–b). This seems to be inconsistent with the claim that law is prior to the political. But as Aristotle also makes clear, 'politics' in the sense in which he uses the term in the *Nicomachean Ethics* is not restricted to politics in our sense (ibid, 1094b). 'Politics', for Aristotle, is about the determination of what is good for individuals and communities. He explicitly includes ethics in this (ibid). Given what is said about corrective justice later in the *Nicomachean Ethics*, law must be included too. In other words, for Aristotle 'politics' is not the master of law; law is part of 'politics'. Hence, the claim that 'politics' is the master science does not mean that 'politics' is the master of law.

[61] Aristotle, *The Art of Rhetoric*, 1373b.

in accordance with commutative justice. As it is made by the apolitical legislator, the law is itself apolitical. Moreover, it is natural to think, and Aristotle's argument indicates, that this law must be private law. For example, there must be a law that requires that A not strike B (a demand of commutative justice) and a law that allows B to take appropriate action if that law is violated (a demand of the rectificatory aspect of commutative justice). It is also likely, though we cannot be sure, that Aristotle would have regarded this as a 'constitutional' norm in our sense of the term, ie as a foundation of, rather than a consequence of, the political system. For Aristotle, citizenship is central to the constitution and, as Aristotle's contemporary, Demosthenes argued, (they were born and died in the same years) the distinction between a citizen and a slave lies in the fact that the body of a free man is sacrosanct, even if convicted of wrongdoing.[62] The sanctity of a citizen's body is recognized only if citizens possess rights to bodily integrity, and so citizenship itself requires the recognition of that right. On this view, then, norms generated by commutative justice are foundational and they appear to include the most fundamental norm of private law: bodily integrity.

4.2 Commutative Justice, Private Law, and Crime

The passage quoted immediately above distinguishes between the two possible kinds of injustice: injustice to the community as a whole and injustice to an individual. Aristotle then gives the following illustrations of these forms of injustice. In relation to the latter, he mentions adultery and mugging and with respect to the former he refers to draft-dodging.

There is no difficulty seeing the second of these as an injustice only to the community as a whole. If I refuse to comply with the (just) demands of my community to contribute to its defence, then I wrong everyone and no one in particular. It is also easy to understand the idea that acts of adultery and mugging also wrong one person in particular. To concentrate on mugging, if I mug you, then I wrong you in a way that I wrong no one else. But to the modern mind, it seems also that I commit a wrong against society as a whole. For this reason, my action is regarded by modern law as a tort and a crime.

---

[62] Demosthenes, *Against Androtion*, 22.55–56.

In an earlier work, my response to this difficulty was to conclude that Aristotle simply misunderstood the nature of wrongdoing. He failed to see that one action could be wrong in two ways, the idea never having occurred to him.[63] Given what little we know about Aristotle's views in this regard, this position may indeed be correct. However, I now think it likely to be mistaken. It seems impossible to think that it would never have crossed so great a mind that one action can be wrong in two ways. It is also significant to note that Aristotle thinks that adultery, mugging, and draft-dodging are all crimes,[64] though he is aware that not all injustices are crimes.

With this in mind, we can begin to piece together Aristotle's view. I do so by presenting an account of the development of law that would be accepted by most modern historians and comparing it with what I take to be Aristotle's own view.

In its early days, Athens had no official laws. Instead, people lived according to customs established over generations. One of these was that a wronged person or his family had a moral obligation to avenge the wrong. For instance, if a man was killed, then it fell to his sons to avenge his murder by killing the killer, or at least by obtaining compensation in the form of a blood price. As a consequence of these customs, families often engaged in long-lasting blood feuds. In about 620 BC, however, Draco, the legislator, passed a series of laws including a law requiring the banishment of murderers. This law was retained by Solon when he drafted his laws in about 594. The question is why Draco did as he did. What was the point?

According to the modern mind, the answer is that it came to be recognized that the state had an interest in preventing murder and blood feuds that required the state to take action. Generally, the idea is that the state passed laws against wrongdoing because it saw that wrongdoing as a violation of the public interest. This, however, is clearly not Aristotle's view. He maintains that the state becomes involved for the sake of the private interests of the parties.

I suggest that the modern picture of the development of the law is wrong. It is deeply wrong. The reason the state became involved in preventing murder and blood feuds is not that it felt that it had an interest in so doing, but because it recognized that individuals had such an interest and that that interest was not adequately protected by

---

[63] Beever, 'Justice and Punishment in Tort', 259.
[64] Aristotle, *The Art of Rhetoric*, 1373b.

the extant customs. In other words, if the state were to speak in order to explain its law, it would say not 'We prohibit these acts because when they are committed they wrong all of us' but 'We prohibit these acts because they wrong an individual when they are committed.' To put this another way, these actions were made crimes because they offended against commutative, not distributive, justice.

On this view, at least part of the Greek criminal law is best understood as a strengthening of private law, an idea to which we will return in later chapters.

5. Conclusion

The chapter has introduced three key ideas: first, that there are two forms of justice—distributive and commutative—and that each is independent of the other; secondly, that at least some law is prior to politics; and thirdly that the private law is based directly on commutative justice. Also important is the notion that there is at least a strong link between the criminal law and the private law. These ideas are developed in the chapters to come.

5

Cicero

The contrast between the material bequeathed to us by the ancient Greeks and Romans could not be starker. The Greeks left us a wealth of philosophical writings on all subjects, including law. However, they left us little in the way of individual laws. This, of course, is not because the Greeks were without sophisticated legal systems. It is because the documents recording these laws have generally not survived. As a result, much of what we know about Greek law comes second hand, from commentaries on those laws by philosophers or literary writers. The Romans present almost the opposite picture. Though much has been lost, the most important of their legal materials has survived, including the *Institutes* of Gaius and Justinian and Justinian's *Digest*. This is unquestionably the most influential body of legal writing ever produced. About half of today's legal systems are derived from it. But Roman philosophy is quite different. Though Roman philosophers existed, they pale in comparison to their Greek counterparts, as many of them were well aware.

In consequence of the dominance of Greek philosophy, the Roman bares many of the hallmarks of the Greek. The themes explored by Greek writers were often simply transplanted to Roman soil. Most of this, then, is of no interest to us. However, the writings of perhaps the most important Roman political philosopher, Cicero, are significant. His most important works in this area are entitled *The Republic* and *The Laws*, indicating the unmistakable influence of Plato on his thought. But as we will also see, there are important differences between Cicero's theories and Plato's, differences that may be due to the influence of Aristotle or, perhaps, to the shape of the Roman law. We also see that, as in Aristotle's thought, the private law has a special place in Cicero's political theory, a place not at all consonant with Plato's or modern conceptions. These issues are explored in this chapter.

1. Biographical Background

Like the philosophers we have examined earlier, Cicero (106–43 BC) lived during a time of great political turmoil. Much of his life can be described as the failed attempt to prevent the destruction of the Roman Republic and its replacement by what became the Empire.

Cicero was a writer and a lawyer, but was also actively engaged in Roman politics. Notably, he served as consul in 63, when he defeated the Cataline conspiracy to overthrow the Republic. Partly as a result of his behaviour at the conclusion of this conspiracy, when the political tide turned against him in 61 he was forced into exile. He was recalled 14 months later, however. In part, this was due to the influence of Pompey, with whom and with other members of the senatorial aristocracy he developed a close relationship. He then came to see his role as defending the traditional position of the Senate and its members in the Roman state.

His association with Pompey soon became an embarrassment, however, when it became clear that Pompey was no friend of the Republic. In fact, it became known that Pompey was plotting with Julius Caesar to overthrow the Republic, and he eventually joined Caesar and Crassus in the First Triumvirate. As a result, Cicero felt that his position had become impossible and he turned from public life to writing.

This did not mean retirement from all political activity. On the contrary, some of his writings have, given their context, a clear political aim. Most significantly, one of the goals of *The Republic* is to present the case for republican government against alternative systems, including the one represented by the Triumvirate and the eventual dictatorship under Caesar.

It seemed that Cicero's political career had been resurrected when conspirators assassinated Caesar in 44. Though Cicero was not involved in the conspiracy, he could hardly have received a more pressing invitation from the conspirators to return to public life. Lifting the dagger with which he had stabbed Caesar, still dripping with Caesar's blood, Brutus called upon Cicero to 'restore the Republic'.

This, however, brought Cicero into conflict with Mark Antony, the chief representative of the Caesarean faction. This led Cicero to hatch a rather unlikely plan. When Octavian, Caesar's adopted son and heir (and the future Augustus) arrived in Rome, Cicero tried to use him against Antony in order to save the Republic. As we know, however, despite some initial successes, this strategy spectacularly failed. Eventually, Antony and Octavian were reconciled and with Lepidus formed the Second Triumvirate. Cicero was proscribed and his death ordered. Apparently, his last words, uttered to the soldier who had come to kill him, were: 'There is nothing proper about what you are doing, soldier, but do try to kill me properly.' He leaned out of the litter upon which he was being carried, barred his neck and throat to the soldier, who killed him and then cut off his head.

For our purposes, the most important feature of Cicero's background is that his writings on political philosophy are motivated to preserve a relatively liberal regime (at least in the eyes of the aristocratic senators) from an authoritarian one. Cicero is not unique in this regard. As we see in Chapter 10, John Locke found himself in a similar position. Because of this, it is instructive to compare the natures of Cicero's and Locke's views. As we will see, though they argue for similar goals, their arguments are remarkably different. In summary, one could say with only slight exaggeration that while Locke's appeal is to politics as we understand it, Cicero's is to law.

2. The Rule of Law

The concept of the rule of law features strongly in both *The Republic* and *The Laws*. Cicero's understanding of the nature and significance of this concept is distinct from, though related to, the dispute that was to rise to the forefront of Roman politics under the Emperors. This dispute is most famously presented by two leading figures in the political and legal life of Rome: Seneca and Ulpian. First is Seneca's famous, though futile, admonition to the Emperor Nero to act as if he were answerable to his own laws.[1] Opposed to this is Ulpian's ominous principle that 'The emperor is not bound by statutes.'[2] It was, perhaps unsurprisingly, the latter that triumphed.

[1] Seneca, *De clementia*, 1.4.
[2] Waston (ed), *The Digest of Justinian*, 1.3.31.

Though it is relevant to this dispute, Cicero's focus is more abstract. He is concerned with the connection between the concept of law and the concept of the state. Early in *The Republic*, he claims rather obscurely that a republic is the property of the public and, more transparently, that a republic is a group of people 'brought together by legal consent and community of interest'.[3]

For us, the crucial element in these ideas is the claim regarding 'legal consent'. On the face of it, it appears to mean that the consent of the governed must not be obtained wrongly or that when the consent is given it has legal consequences. But these rather bland claims are not intended by Cicero. Rather, these assertions, made at the beginning of *The Republic*, are a kind of Trojan horse or bomb timed to go off later in the dialogue. That occurs in Book III.

There, Cicero argues that, because a republic is the property of the public, a genuine republic must possess justice. Consequently, tyranny, oligarchy, and democracy (in the sense defined in Chapter 4) cannot be republics in the proper sense.[4] Clearly, in tyrannies and oligarchies the state does not belong to the people. It seems odd to say this of democracy, however. After all, if the public rules, then it seems that the state is the property of the public. We are certainly accustomed to thinking this way. The response, however, is emphatic.

> Actually there is no state to which I should be quicker to refuse the name of republic than the one which is totally in the power of the masses. If we decided that there was no republic in Syracuse or Agrigentum or Athens when tyrants held sway, or here in the regime of the Ten, I don't see how there is any stronger case for applying the name of republic to a state enslaved by the mob. In the first place, for me there is no public except when it is held together by a legal agreement... That rabble is just as tyrannical as one man, and all the more repellent in that there is nothing more monstrous than a creature which masquerades as a public and usurps its name. It is quite inconsistent that, when the property of the insane is placed by law in the hands of male relatives because the former are no longer capable of managing it themselves, the property of the public should be left in the hands of an insane mob.[5]

---

[3] Cicero, '*The Republic*', 1.39.
[4] Ibid, 42–48.
[5] Ibid, 45.

What democracy is missing, then, is the rule of law. A mob might agree with its own rule, but its agreement is not a legal one. The point is not that the agreement does not receive the recognition of the law or that it does not have legal effects. The point is that the agreement does not give rise to rule through law. Hence, as Cicero points out in *The Laws*, law is part of his *definition* of a state, so that 'lawless state' is an oxymoron.[6]

Cicero, then, as the Greeks before him, supports the distinction between executive and legislative power and holds that the latter is not a proper part of government. For Cicero, legislative power is not part of government; rather, legislation is required in order to have legitimate government. This separation of government and legislation is so strong that Cicero echoes Plato's claim in his *The Laws* that the laws should never be altered.[7] We might express this idea by saying that, for Cicero, law has a constitutional status.

This indicates, as we are about to see in more detail, that the rule of law for Cicero is more than a merely formal notion. If the law should never be altered, then it obviously matters what the law is. The rule of law, then, is an idea that calls for the law to have certain content.

This idea is both a partial product of and supported by Cicero's commitment to natural law theory,[8] an idea that generates his view that a law must be just in order to be a genuine law.[9] The consequence of this notion is that a society governed inconsistently with the natural law would not be a state in the proper sense. The rulers of this society may be able to compel obedience by force and threat, of course, but they lack moral authority. In the language of later thinkers, these conditions are correctly classified as states of nature.

For Cicero then, as for Aristotle and sometimes for Plato, politics—ie genuine, real politics, rather than mere coercion—is the offspring of law and not vice versa. Law, we are saying, has a constitutional status: it sets up and governs the political system. It is not merely the way in which political rulers govern or govern appropriately. Also of significance is that Cicero includes in law that has constitutional status private law, which he says is given by God.[10] Hence, we can see that Cicero rejects

---

[6] Except, of course, in the sense of the *condition* of lawlessness. Cicero, '*The Laws*', 2.12, 3.5.
[7] Ibid, 2.14.
[8] Ibid, 1, 2.7–17.
[9] Ibid, 2.13.
[10] Ibid, 2.9–10. This could be regarded as somewhat controversial, depending on one's conception of the Roman delict. I cannot examine that issue here.

the modern view captured in Figures M1–M3. Moreover, we can see that Cicero's understanding of the place of law mirrors Aristotle's.

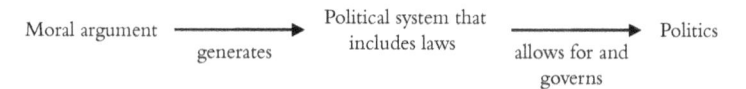

Moral argument —generates→ Political system that includes laws —allows for and governs→ Politics

Figure 5.1 Politics and Law in Cicero

Here, we can see that law, and specifically private law, has a constitutional status. We have also seen that this status is a product of Cicero's natural law theory. But the precise connection between that theory and the private law is not explained by Cicero, at least not in the extant materials. He tells us that the law is God-given, but not why God gives it. Answers to that and to equivalent questions must be sought from later thinkers.

PART II:
Establishment

In the following three chapters, we examine the establishment of the traditional view by considering three key figures: Aquinas, Pufendorf, and Kant. Naturally, these theorists were not the only representatives of the traditional view. Nor is the following intended as a comprehensive survey of that view. Rather, the task is to present the general structure of the traditional understanding of law and politics by examining three of the tradition's leading proponents.

In that regard, Pufendorf and Kant are especially significant for us. This is not only because the traditional view reaches a high level of perfection in their works, but also because they were writing after the decline of that view had begun. As we see in Chapter 9, the central figure in the decline is Hobbes, whose most important book, *Leviathan*, was published in 1651. Pufendorf's greatest work in this regard, *The Law of Nature and Nations*, was published in 1688 and is heavily influenced by Hobbes' thought. Kant's most significant works in this context were published roughly 150 years after *Leviathan*, and though Kant is less exercised by Hobbes than was Pufendorf, it is also plain that he was influenced by him.[1] Because of this, Pufendorf and Kant were reacting to the development of the modern conception. They were reasserting the traditional view against it. For that reason, this view is more clearly evident in their works that in that of their predecessors.

This is also a convenient point to remind the reader that the claim is not that Aquinas, Pufendorf, and Kant hold the same theory. They do not. The claim is that they share an outlook, an understanding of

---

[1] See especially Kant, 'Common Saying', 8:8:289.

the way in which the theory of the politico-legal ought to be pursued. That outlook is what I am calling the traditional view.

In Part I of this book, I presented short biographical sketches of the thinkers examined. I do the same in Part III. But I omit these here. This is because the biographies of these philosophers are not illuminating for our purposes. Aquinas, Pufendorf, and Kant led very different lives. But the differences between those lives do not tell us much about what is crucial in their theories. What is of more significance is something that they shared, something that their lives had in common. I examine this here.

The key fact in this regard is that all three thinkers lived at a time, at least in the region in which they lived, where the state was not the dominant force that it was in ancient Greece or Rome or that it was to become (more slowly than convention has it) after the Peace of Westphalia in 1648. In fact, the lives of all three thinkers were heavily influenced by the Holy Roman Empire. (Pufendorf wrote a seminal analysis of the Empire's constitution.[2]) It is not easy to summarize the nature of this political entity, nor is it easy for the modern mind to comprehend even detailed accounts. But in order to understand the outlook shared by Aquinas, Pufendorf, and Kant, it important that we make some attempt to do so.

The Holy Roman Empire received its first Emperor, Otto I, in 962. It lasted until 1806 when the last Emperor, Francis II, abdicated after defeat at the hand of Napoleon's armies. It was replaced in 1815 by the not entirely dissimilar German Confederation, in turn replaced in 1866 by the Prussian-dominated North German Confederation, which became the German Empire in 1871. As one might expect, the territory of the Empire was fluid, but it incorporated the majority of central Europe, including at least much of the modern territories of the Netherlands, Germany, Poland, Switzerland, the Czech Republic, Austria, eastern France, the upper Balkans, and northern Italy.

For our purposes, the most important and most difficult to understand feature of the Empire was its political structure. It was, as has been implied, governed by an emperor. But the emperor had nothing like absolute sovereign control over its territory. On the contrary, the Empire was made up of a great number of distinct territories, or *Kleinstaaten* (about 300 at the time of the Peace of Westphalia), each with its own system. The territories were usually divided into three

---

[2] Pufendorf, *De statu imperii Germanici*.

categories: those governed by a hereditary noble such as a king, prince, archduke, duke, or count; those governed by a clerical dignitary, such as an archbishop, bishop, or abbot; and free imperial cities subject only to the emperor. Some of the rulers of these territories, the Electors, had the authority to elect new emperors.

To use modern terminology, the power of the territories' rulers, or *Fürsten*, was not delegated by the Emperor. Rather, the jurisdiction of each *Fürst* depended on a number of factors, most significantly traditional and historical. We can, then, understand the Empire as a federation, but it is a federation much looser than modern examples such as Australia, the USA, or even the European Union. The Empire was perhaps most like the United Nations, but again there are serious disanalogies, perhaps the most important of which is the following.

Today, citizens generally recognize strong obligations to their states and weaker ones to the UN. But the inhabitants of the Holy Roman Empire did not necessarily feel a strong allegiance to their territories or to the Empire. They frequently felt no great attachment to either. This was in part because of the physical and psychological distance of the Emperor and his rule on the one hand and the nature of the rule of the *Fürsten* on the other. In short, the citizens of a territory often had a weak allegiance to that territory because the allegiance of the *Fürst* was weak also. The context in which Kant lived can be used to illustrate this point. This context is particularly revealing because Kant lived at the end of this period when the *Fürstens* (in his case, the Prussian King's) rule over their territory was near its strongest.

Kant was born in 1724 and lived his whole life in Königsberg. In the recent past, Königsberg had been the capital of the territory known as Ducal Prussia. This was not the Prussia of Kant's day, the state ruled from Berlin. It was rather a Polish fief located in what is now northern Poland and the lower Baltic states. In 1618, Ducal Prussia had been inherited by the Elector John Sigismund of Brandenburg (whose capital was Berlin). But this inheritance did not merge Brandenburg and Prussia. Rather, it meant that the Duchy of Prussia was in personal union with the Margraviate of Brandenburg. To cut a long story short, John Sigismund and his successors had greater authority over Brandenburg than they had over Ducal Prussia because, while they were the rulers of that territory, the overlord of the territory remained the King of Poland. Hence, the state ruled by John Sigismund and his successors was referred to as Brandenburg-Prussia.

Over time, the power of the Brandenburg electors increased over Prussia until the territory was effectively annexed, forming the state of Prussia with its capital in Berlin. Even so, the state's first king, Frederick I, much to the amusement of Europe's other monarchs, was entitled to call himself only King *in* (not of) Prussia, because the official overlord of Ducal Prussia remained the King of Poland. What is more, during Kant's lifetime, Königsberg was occupied by the Russians for over four years.[3]

The picture that develops, then, is of a political world of loose allegiances and great fluidity. In this world, the chief constants were not the state (not death *and taxes* as we are fond of saying), but family and social life, religion and, crucially for us, law. When John Sigismund inherited Ducal Prussia, he inherited a territory with pre-existing laws. And those laws survived the change in ruler. In fact, what made Ducal Prussia the same territory (in the legal, moral, or political, rather than physical sense) before and after the inheritance was the stability in its laws.

Through the eyes of a person living in this world, it was natural to think that law makes the state. Though the state also makes laws, of course, Hobbes' assertion that all law is constituted by 'those rules, which the commonwealth hath commanded [the citizen], by word, writing, or other sufficient sign of the will, to make use of for the distinction of right, and wrong' would have seemed bizarre.[4]

The central point is this. For thinkers of this period, it was by no means obvious that the politico-legal realm was concerned primarily with the state. Though the centrality of the state seems beyond question to us, that very idea would have seemed highly questionable, if not strange, to many of our predecessors. Moreover, in a world in which political and state power was in flux and one of the few constants was law, it would have seemed quite unnatural to seek the foundations of law in politics. Precisely where, then, should they be sought? That is the question answered in the next three chapters.

---

[3] For a brilliant, and wonderfully readable, account of this period, see Clark, *Iron Kingdom*.
[4] Hobbes, *Leviathan*, XXVI 3.

6

Aquinas

Aquinas is unquestionably one of the world's great philosophers. His influence on the late medieval world in particular is difficult to overestimate. But his theory is widely misunderstood by non-specialists today, particularly by lawyers. As his theory is linked with the movement known as scholasticism, it has been tainted by the notion that it presents, in the famous words of William James, merely common sense made pedantic; a largely pointless philosophy, obsessed with meaningless questions such as 'How many angels can dance on the head of a pin?' It is also frequently thought that Aquinas is an essentially Catholic philosopher, meaning that his is a philosophy only for Catholics. This is partly because it is thought that he asks many questions of interest only to Catholics and because the answers he gives to these and other questions rely on an acceptance of Catholicism. It is also probably due to the unfortunate fact that almost all of those who promote his theories today, particularly in legal circles, happen to be Catholic and often wear their Catholicism on their sleeves.[1]

But these criticisms are misguided. While scholasticism can be dry and, to the modern mind, sometimes irrelevant, James' criticism is wide of the mark with respect to the movement in general and frankly bizarre when applied to Aquinas. Nor is Aquinas an essentially Catholic thinker in the sense outlined above. Though his theory is rooted in the teachings of that church (to the extent that one can separate those teachings from Aquinas' own), he insists that the basic principles of

---

[1] I am, of course, thinking primarily of John Finnis. See Finnis, *Natural Law and Natural Rights*; Finnis, *Aquinas*.

morality are accessible to human reason quite independently of faith or revelation.[2] His theory therefore ought to be of interest to all.

Another difficulty concerns Aquinas' commitment to natural law theory (also thought by some to be essentially religious). This is problematic, because many today regard that theory as having been refuted. (In fact, I am aware of courses in the philosophy of law that use Aquinas—or rather, a caricature of Aquinas—as a cross between a running joke and the bogeyman; a spectre to be raised whenever students stray across the boundaries of the 'acceptable'.) Though we are not concerned with Aquinas' natural law theory per se, this seemingly remains a problem for us: we are interested in Aquinas' views regarding the foundation of politico-legal norms, and his label for this foundation is natural law.

Despite this, we need take no stand on the viability of Aquinas' natural law theory here. The positivist attack on Aquinas' view proceeds on two fronts. It argues that Aquinas is wrong to think that what he calls natural law is law proper and it alleges that positive law (ie 'real law') is not constrained by natural law in the way Aquinas purportedly maintains. In my view, this criticism is entirely misguided, but even if it were sound it need not delay us further. We are focused on Aquinas' understanding of the foundations of politico-legal norms, not on his label for that foundation. I examine that understanding now.

1. Morality, the Good, and the Nature of Harm

According to Aquinas, 'the whole [moral] Law is comprised in this one commandment, "Thou shalt love thy neighbor as thyself," as expressing the end of all [more specific] commandments'.[3] This account of morality generates Aquinas' theory of sin, according to which a sin is an act contrary to eternal law.[4] Aquinas also maintains that this general principle implies the more specific notion that one is prohibited from inflicting harm or evil on others.[5] It is this notion upon which we focus here.

---

[2] Aquinas, *Summa theologica*, FS 100 a; 108.2 r1.
[3] Ibid, FS 99.1 r2; see also 100.3 r1; 11 a.
[4] Ibid, FS 71.6.
[5] Ibid, FS 100.3 a.

In order to understand Aquinas' account, we must answer two central questions. First, what is meant by harm or evil in this context? Secondly, what is the nature of the wrong of inflicting harm or evil? Though the answers to these questions are tightly linked, I address them in turn.

The first point that must be stressed is that not all unwanted effects are harms. For instance, if you thwart my attempt to do something sinful, then the effect of your action was unwanted by me, but it may nevertheless benefit rather than harm me.[6] For Aquinas, a harm is an effect that robs a person of the good. As he explains, 'Evil . . . is the privation of good.'[7] For our purposes, the key concept here is that evil is that which 'occurs by the subtraction of the form, or of any part required for the integrity of the thing, as blindness is an evil, as also it is an evil to be wanting in any member of the body'.[8] On this view, then, physically injuring someone harms her, not because it deprives her of something that is useful or wanted, but because it deprives her of the good. In other words, the issue is not whether the victim has suffered some quantifiable loss but whether she has been divested of the good.

This enables us to answer the second question: the wrongdoing is complex. It can consist in the sin committed by the perpetrator. But it can also consist in the harm suffered by the victim. Imagine, for instance, that I intentionally strike you, injuring your arm. In this case, I violate the law and hence sin. But I also deprive you of the good by injuring you, and that is an evil quite apart from the fact that I sinned. That evil would be present had I injured you innocently or had your injury been the result of natural causes. As we see below, these points are of considerable importance.

2. Justice and Law

Aquinas' account of justice begins by adopting Aristotle's distinction between what we are calling commutative and distributive justice. As Aquinas tells us:

justice is directed to the private individual, who is compared to the community as a part to the whole. Now a twofold order may be considered in

---

[6] Ibid, FF 21.2 r2.
[7] Ibid, FF 48.5 a.
[8] Ibid.

relation to a part. In the first place there is the order of one part to another, to which corresponds the order of one private individual to another. This order is directed by commutative justice, which is concerned about the mutual dealings between two persons. In the second place there is the order of the whole towards the parts, to which corresponds the order of that which belongs to the community in relation to each single person. This order is directed by distributive justice, which distributes common goods proportionately. Hence there are two species of justice, distributive and commutative.[9]

Moreover, it is clear in Aquinas that commutative justice is not solely a 'corrective' or 'reparative' notion. It is and generates both primary and secondary norms.[10] Hence, while commutative justice governs responses to violations of rights, it also grounds (primary) rights themselves. As Aquinas tells us, commutative justice is concerned with 'the order' that regulates interactions between individuals. It is concerned with the just and unjust within that sphere. Accordingly, it discloses which actions are just and which are unjust, as well as how to respond to actions of the latter kind. Hence, Aquinas claims that a person who performs an obligation founded on a just contract acts in accordance with commutative justice—a primary norm. His position is not that this person merely does not bring commutative justice into play, which he would have done (on this hypothesis) only had he violated the contract—a secondary norm.[11]

For Aquinas, commutative justice is concerned with interactions between individuals. It can therefore be divided into two parts. The first part determines how interactions ought to proceed. These norms are primary.[12] The second part of commutative justice governs the appropriate responses to the violation of primary norms. These norms are secondary. Aquinas labels this part of commutative justice 'restitutionary'. Hence, restitution is that aspect of commutative justice that deals with correcting commutative injustices.[13] In short, restitutionary justice is a subset, not the whole, of commutative justice.

---

[9] Ibid, SS 61.1 a.
[10] See section 2.2 of Chapter 4.
[11] Aquinas, *Summa theologica*, SS 61.2 a.
[12] See also ibid, SS 64–66.
[13] Ibid, SS 62.

Unfortunately, however, Aquinas does not tell us much about the content of commutative (or distributive) justice. Though he discusses its form, he does not present any general theory of its content. Accordingly, we are forced to fill out the notion by examining Aquinas' applications of commutative justice. In the following three sections, I do so by examining three key concerns: bodily integrity, responses to violations of rights, and property.

Before turning to those issues, however, it is first necessary to discuss Aquinas' account of the relationship between law and justice. His central claim in this regard is that law is directed to the common good. As he puts it,

> the law belongs to that which is a principle of human acts, because it is their rule and measure. Now as reason is a principle of human acts, so in reason itself there is something which is the principle in respect of all the rest: wherefore to this principle chiefly and mainly law must needs be referred. Now the first principle in practical matters, which are the object of the practical reason, is the last end: and the last end of human life is bliss or happiness... Consequently the law must needs regard principally the relationship to happiness.[14]

Given the dominance of the modern conception, this appears to be a sufficient invitation to conclude that Aquinas held that law is based on and is designed to produce distributive justice. But that would be too quick. Aquinas maintains that law is directed to the common good. But what is the common good?

The modern understanding of the term has been heavily influenced by utilitarianism. Because of this, it is useful now to explore the broad outlines of that theory, examined in more detail in Chapter 11.

Classical utilitarianism is characterized by two views: that right action is that which maximizes utility for all and that utility is pleasure. According to this view, then, the common good is simply the pleasure of all, and the injunction to realize the common good is simply the command to maximize the pleasure of all. On this view, then, the concept of the common good is essentially tied to distributive justice.

This understanding has been so influential that even opponents of utilitarianism often use the term 'common good' in the utilitarian sense. As this can lead to misunderstanding, it is important to pause for a moment to consider this terminology.

[14] Ibid, FS 90.2 a.

Take an example. Imagine a debate between two lawyers over the purpose of a particular law. According to the first lawyer, the point of the law is to realize the common good. According to the second, the law's aim is not to realize the common good but to do justice to individuals. Debates of this kind are frequent, but what is to be made of the second lawyer's position?

Dan Dobbs once claimed that the fundamental question facing modern analysis of tort law is: 'Should judges decide cases on the basis of corrective justice with a view to righting wrongs and doing justice between the parties? Or should they decide cases according to what is good for society as a whole?'[15] This can be a felicitous way of putting the issue, but it can also seriously mislead. The person who thinks that judges should decide cases in accordance with corrective/commutative justice need not deny that doing so is good for society as a whole. She may well think that judges do what is good for society as a whole only if they so decide cases. Clearly, then, when theorists of this kind insist that the point of the law is not the realization of the common good, they do not mean to deny that the law is intended to realize something that it actually ought to realize. They do not deny that the law, if it is justified, is in accordance with what is actually in the common good. What they deny is that the law's purpose is captured by what is commonly meant by the term 'the common good'. Typically, their aim is to deny that the point of the law is found in utilitarian considerations or concerns of distributive justice.

Similarly, when a lawyer denies that a law is designed to serve public policy or the public interest, he does not mean to deny that that law is concerned with public policy or the public interest as they actually are. He denies only that the law is indifferent to those concerns usually identified by the terms 'public policy' and 'public interest'.

Hence, a lawyer who denies that an area of law should serve the public interest typically claims in fact that it would not be in what *really is* the public interest for that area of the law to be managed in accordance with concerns of a kind *generally perceived to* relate to the public interest.[16] Accordingly, the argument could be presented, not

---

[15] Dobbs, *Torts and Compensation*, 840–841.
[16] It is important to stress that the focus is on kinds of concerns, not on the veracity of individual claims. For instance, a libertarian might deny that relative wealth is a concern that

as one about the *role* of the public interest in that area of the law, but about the *content* of the public interest.

However, we have not found it convenient to express ourselves in that fashion. To us, it would seem odd to argue that it is not in the public interest to consider the interests of all the public or that the common good calls for us to ignore the good of most of society. In other words, we take terms such as 'common good', 'public interest', and 'public policy' to refer to their utilitarian referents, and rather than arguing over the referents of the terms, those who reject utilitarianism reject the moral relevance of those referents.

As we have seen, then, when we use terms such as 'common good', we take ourselves to be referring to the good of all; in other words, to distributive justice. But, of course, that we use the term in this fashion does not warrant the assumption that Aquinas did also. On the contrary, reflection reveals quite clearly that he did not. For Aquinas, the good at which the law aims is justice.[17] In particular, the law is concerned to instil in individuals respect for the rights of others.[18] This is important because, as justice is divided into the commutative and the distributive, so is the common good.

Imagine, then, a dispute between *A* and *B* that ought to be settled in keeping with commutative justice. Aquinas tells us that we must settle this dispute in accordance with the common good. But that does not mean that we should do so by considering the interests of all. On the contrary, the command to realize the common good is the command to do justice. And as, *per hypothesis*, this case raises concerns only of commutative justice, only the interests of *A* and *B* ought to be considered. Similarly, as we have seen, though it would be confusing to do so, modern proponents of the traditional view could claim that the common good, public policy, the public interest, and so on as they really are demand that courts frequently ignore the common good, public policy, the public interest, and so on as they are thought to be.

With this in mind, we can turn to the three more specific issues mentioned above.

---

relates to the common good. But she would nevertheless recognize that it is a concern of a kind that so relates.

[17] Aquinas, *Summa theologica*, SS 57.1.
[18] Ibid, SS 58.1.

3. Bodily Integrity

Though he appears to possess the concept,[19] Aquinas does not examine what we would call the right to bodily integrity.[20] Instead, he explores various kinds of wrongdoing that we recognize as violations of that right: killing ('murder'), injury (the 'mutilation of members'), striking 'blows', and imprisonment.[21] This approach is familiar from the Roman law and the modern common law, neither of which contains an explicit area of the law detailing the rights of individuals, both of which list a catalogue of wrongs that violate such implicit rights. We must therefore focus our investigation on these wrongs.

Our task is made immediately difficult because Aquinas begins his discussion with what appears to be a mistake. His introduction to this part of his investigation declares that he will consider 'vices opposed to commutative justice' and states that he will divide these into '(1) those sins that are committed in relation to involuntary commutations; [and] (2) those that are committed with regard to voluntary commutations'.[22] But this does not seem to be what he does. He examines *actions*, not vices, that oppose commutative justice. The problem is that wrongful actions can be performed by those who lack the corresponding vice. As Aquinas elsewhere realizes,[23] one does this when one acts wrongly out of character. Hence, his discussion does not address vices opposed to commutative justice at all.

This problem is a consequence of Aquinas' attempt to fit his theory into the mould of Aristotle's virtue ethics. It may be that an adequate response to the difficulty can be discovered in Aquinas writings. We need not attempt to discover it here, however. Suffice it to say that Aquinas' theory is in fact concerned with actions opposed to commutative justice.

The second part of that formulation needs to be stressed now: the discussion is of actions opposed to *commutative* justice. For Aquinas, then, killing, injury, striking, and imprisonment are violations of commutative justice or, to put it in reverse, our right to be free of these

---

[19] Ibid, SS 104.5 a.
[20] Moreover, it is unclear whether Aquinas possesses the concept of a subjective right. See Tuck, *Natural Rights Theories*, 19. I ignore this issue in the following.
[21] Aquinas, *Summa theologica*, SS 64–65.
[22] Ibid, SS 64.
[23] Ibid, FS 74.1, esp r1.

actions, our right to bodily integrity, is founded in commutative, not distributive, justice.

However, this should not, I think, be understood to imply that these actions are not also inconsistent with distributive justice. They may frequently be so. But the idea is that these actions *most fundamentally* violate norms of commutative justice. I take an example to illustrate and explain this point.

Imagine that A kills B (without justification). This, as we have seen, is wrongful in two chief senses. First, A sins. A breaches eternal law. Secondly, A harms B, depriving B of the good. But there is a third wrong here, the result of A's harming the community as a whole. This harm is the result of A's violation of the community's laws (about which more in a moment) and his depriving the community of the benefit of B's membership in it. The wrong specifically to B is a commutative injustice, the wrong to the community as a whole is a distributive injustice. No sound theory could ignore the latter. But I take this not to be Aquinas' point in claiming that murder is a sin opposed to commutative justice. Rather, his point is that the harm to B is both more important than and, as I am about to show, more conceptually fundamental than, the harm to the community at large.

The harm to the community occurs only because the community exists. This must be distinguished from the idea that the harm *to the members* of the community relies on the existence of the community. That claim is false. But the first claim is true. Let me explain.

Imagine that A's action harms not only B but also C and D, B's children. Obviously, that harm does not rely on the existence of the community. But nor is there reason to think that the harm is a violation of distributive justice. It might be, but that could be so only if there is a community and that harm—ie the harm that relates to the violation of distributive justice—will be relatively trivial.

The crucial theoretical point is fundamental and needs to be emphasized. Imagine our four-person society pictured in Figures J1 and J2. Imagine that P_1 performs an action that wrongs P_2, P_3, and P_4. What form of justice is implicated? It is tempting to think that, as P_1 wrongs everyone in his society, the answer must be distributive justice. But that is wrong. P_1's action may be a commutative injustice against P_2, a commutative injustice against P_3, and a commutative injustice against P_4. His action is a commutative injustice as between himself and the others if the reason it is wrongful is that it violates the norms that govern his interactions with them. It is a distributive injustice only if the reason it is wrongful is that it results in an unfair distribution of benefits and burdens amongst the community or because it violates norms that arise from that consideration. This is a product of the fact that commutative and distributive justice are *forms* of justice. Distributive justice is not simply an aggregation of commutative justices. Distributive justice is not just big commutative justice. The terms refer to different kinds of justice.

In the example currently under discussion, it does not follow from the fact that C and D are harmed that the killing of B was an act of distributive injustice. It may be a violation of commutative justice as between A and C and A and D. For instance, if the harm we have in mind is the deprivation of their father's love, and if we think that C and D have an entitlement to that love that they hold independently of the community, then we think that the entitlement is grounded in commutative justice. But if the harm we have in mind is that C and D no longer have the financial recourses to afford go to university, and if we think that they have an entitlement to go to university, then that will be because of features of the community in which C and D live—eg the cost of going to university, the importance of a university education, etc—and we will then think that the entitlement is grounded in distributive justice.

For this reason, murder is more fundamentally a violation of commutative than of distributive justice. It violates distributive justice only in the civil condition. It violates the community's laws and/or results in an unfair distribution of benefits and burdens only in that condition. But it would violate commutative justice even in the state of nature. As I suggested in Chapter 4, these insights were shared by our predecessors, but they are largely lost today.

For Aquinas, then, killings, injuries, strikings, and imprisonments harm and therefore wrong the victim(s) quite independently of the existence of any community or state. To put this another way, individuals have a right to their bodily integrity that is conceptually prior to the state. It is based on commutative, not distributive, justice, and it exists even in the state of nature. It is time now to explore the consequences of the violation of this and other rights based on commutative justice.

4. Responses to Violations of Commutative Justice

Aquinas maintains that 'it is an act of commutative injustice to take away what belongs to another. Therefore to restore it is an act of that justice which directs commutations.'[24] Hence, commutative justice not only affords individuals rights, it also dictates that restitution be made when those rights are violated.

Moreover, Aquinas explains why commutative justice has this character. 'To restore is seemingly the same as to reinstate a person in the possession or dominion of his thing, so that in restitution we consider the equality of justice attending the payment of one thing for another, and this belongs to commutative justice.'[25] In the eyes of commutative justice, a wrong consists of one person taking away something to which another is entitled. Accordingly, the appropriate response to that wrong is for the first person to restore it, or to provide an equivalent, to the second person. When this is done, the commutative injustice no longer exists, as the first person no longer has more than he should have vis-à-vis the second (as least as far as commutative justice is concerned).

It is important to underline these features of commutative justice. If I take something of yours in a way that violates eternal law, I commit a sin. That is an event. But that, as we have seen, is not the commutative injustice. The commutative injustice is that I have more than I should vis-à-vis you and you have less than you should vis-à-vis me. That is a state of affairs and not an event. The state of affairs remains in force until I return the object to you or—the second point that must be stressed—give you something (eg money) so that I no longer have more than I should vis-à-vis you, etc. The reparation is not an attempt to correct something that happened in the past, and there is no reason why, in principle, it cannot be done with a money payment.

Again, the requirement to make restitution is conceptually prior to the existence of the state. If I wrongly injure you, then the reason I must make recompense is because I violated a right that you held against me, a right whose violation entails a duty to compensate. It is not because the state has told me that I must or because distributive justice requires it (if it does). Of course, if the state tells me or distributive justice commands that I must compensate you, then that gives me other reasons to do so,[26] but that is a different matter. My immediate obligation to compensate you is independent of bodies such as courts of law. For this reason, Aquinas insists that, though courts are entitled

---

[24] Ibid, SS 62.1 c.
[25] Ibid, SS 62.1 a.
[26] See ibid, SS 62.3 a.

to exercise discretion in acting in what we would regard as their criminal capacity—eg they are entitled to exercise leniency with a view to the public good—courts have not the power but the duty to order defendants to make full reparation.[27] Accordingly, in the relevant area of law, a court that denied a plaintiff's claim on the ground that it was not in the public interest would commit an act of injustice.[28] It would remove the plaintiff's rights in the name of the public interest, thereby using the plaintiff as a means to other's ends in violation of the fundamental principle of morality.[29]

5. Property

Aquinas' account of property is more difficult to understand. There are three reasons for this. First, Aquinas simply says too little for us to derive a comprehensive theory of property from his writings. Secondly, as in the *Summa* in general, Aquinas presents his views as answers to certain questions, and these questions are often not the ones that we would want to ask him. Thirdly, and by no means of least importance, Aquinas makes some claims that appear to fit with the modern conception of political philosophy, inclining modern readers so to pigeonhole them.

With respect to the last point, the chief difficulty here is Aquinas' repetition of Aristotle's discussion of the benefits of private, rather than communal, property. According to Aquinas, private property

is necessary to human life for three reasons. First because every man is more careful to procure what is for himself alone than that which is common to many or to all: since each one would shirk the labor and leave to another that which concerns the community, as happens where there is a great number of servants. Secondly, because human affairs are conducted in more orderly fashion if each man is charged with taking care of some particular thing himself, whereas there would be confusion if everyone had to look after any one thing indeterminately. Thirdly, because a more peaceful state is ensured to man if each one is contented with his own. Hence it is to be

---

[27] Ibid, SS 67.4 a.
[28] Ibid. The idea that the court cannot commit an injustice in this sense as it is not bound by the commutative justice relevant to the parties is examined in section 6 below.
[29] For a discussion of these ideas, see Finnis, *Aquinas*, 170–6.

observed that quarrels arise more frequently where there is no division of the things possessed.[30]

On the face of it, this passage argues that the moral basis for private property is found in distributive justice. In the following, however, I argue that this view is mistaken.

The first thing that must be said is that this passage is not presented as a justification for private property, but as a response to the question: 'Whether it is lawful for a man to possess a thing as his own?'[31] On the face of it, this point is of little significance, as the answer to that question seems to provide a moral justification for property. And so it does, but there is more than one way of providing such a justification. Let me explain.

In the passage quoted above, Aquinas maintains that private property is *advantageous*. He maintains that it is a good means to the realization of distributive justice. If successful, that argument would provide a moral justification for private property. But that argument does not preclude an argument of a different kind: an argument to show that private property is *good*, ie an end in itself and not merely a good means to an end good in itself. And in the section *preceding* the one from which the quotation is taken, Aquinas makes just such a claim.

In that context, his assertion is that private property is *natural*, here meaning that it is good. Under the heading 'Whether it is natural for man to possess external things?', Aquinas writes:

External things can be considered in two ways. First, as regards their nature, and this is not subject to the power of man, but only to the power of God Whose mere will all things obey. Secondly, as regards their use, and in this way, man has a natural dominion over external things, because, by his reason and will, he is able to use them for his own profit, as they were made on his account: for the imperfect is always for the sake of the perfect...It is by this argument that the Philosopher proves that the possession of external things is natural to man.[32]

Note that this discussion is not concerned merely with the *use* of external things. The section is focused on possession, dominion, things

---

[30] Aquinas, *Summa theologica*, SS 66.2 a.
[31] Ibid, SS 66.2.
[32] Ibid, SS 66.1 a.

that are 'his own', subjection, and belonging. The focus, in other words, is property.

On this view, our right to property is not based on distributive justice. Rather, it is derived from our entitlement to use objects and our dominion over them, an entitlement dependant on the notion that they were made for the benefit of human beings. The result is a justification, not merely of use, but of possession in the moral and legal, rather than merely physical, sense of that term.[33]

What, then, is the point of the passage examining the advantageousness of private property? It is twofold. First, it is designed to defeat a number of objections, most importantly the objection that private property gives wealth to some by robbing it from others.[34] Secondly, it supports the institution of private property by revealing its advantageous effects. This is why the passage begins with the following: 'Two things are competent to man in respect of exterior things. One is the power to procure and dispense them, and in this regard it is lawful for man to possess property. Moreover this is necessary to human life for three reasons' (Aquinas then argues that property is advantageous, as quoted above).[35] Hence, the section begins with a reminder of the claim made in the previous section—that property is natural and lawful—and then goes on to add *additional* considerations.

The significance of this point can be expressed in this way, taking into account the natural law context in which they are made. The claim that private property is good (natural) entails that private property exists unless abolished by positive law. But the claim that private property is advantageous does not have this consequence. That claim establishes only that, (i) if it did not exist already, the institution of private property should be created by positive law; and (ii) if the institution does exist, then it should not be abolished. This means that the foundations of property are found in the argument that property is natural or good; the argument that property is advantageous provides only support.

One difficulty with this interpretation is that it seems to clash with the following claim.

Community of goods is ascribed to the natural law, not that the natural law dictates that all things should be possessed in common and that nothing

---

[33] See n 37 below.
[34] Aquinas, *Summa theologica*, 66.2 o2.
[35] Ibid, SS 66.2 a.

should be possessed as one's own: but because the division of possessions is not according to the natural law, but rather arose from human agreement which belongs to positive law, as stated above.[36]

The reference to positive law appears to undercut my suggestion that Aquinas argues that property law is good and therefore that the existence of property does not depend on positive law.

But it is important to remember that this material is intended as an answer to the question: 'Whether it is lawful for a man to possess a thing as his own?' The question, then, is not, or not exclusively, about the existence of the institution of private property. It is rather about particular holdings. In this passage, Aquinas' claim is that a particular property holding is not a matter of the natural law alone, but requires positive law. This is because there is nothing in the natural law that determines that any particular thing belongs to any particular person.

The point is more obvious when made with regard to contract law. Though Aquinas does not explore the issue directly, it seems fair to say that the basic principles of contract law belong to the natural law. These principles generate the norm that when one person promises to sell his horse to another for £1,000, he is bound to do so. But they do not establish that any particular person must sell his horse. Now, if A promises to sell his horse to B for £1,000 (and B accepts, etc), then the principles determine that A is bound, but that is because A's promise (and B's acceptance, etc) coupled with those principles brings into existence a new law that dictates, inter alia, that A is bound. And that specific law is positive law.[37]

The positive law upon which property relies is of this kind. It is law created in accordance with general principles so that those principles are instantiated in actual instances. And note that this positive law, in both the property and contract cases, is created, not by the state, but by individuals as such.

This means that property is the result, not of the state, but of interactions between human beings (and things). And that entails that it belongs to commutative, not distributive, justice. As Aquinas tells us, 'Distributive and commutative justice differ not only in respect of unity and multitude, but also in respect of different kinds of due: because

---

[36] Ibid, SS 66.2 r1.
[37] Ibid, SS 57.2.

common property is due to an individual in one way, and his personal property in another way.'[38]

It is also important to stress that the origin of private property in commutative justice and the consequence of this idea, that property is prior to the state, does not imply that property rights are inviolable or mean that the state is incapable of adjusting property holdings for the sake of the common good. Aquinas specifically holds that circumstances of necessity justify the use of another's property. In fact, he asserts that in these circumstances all property becomes common.[39] Moreover, he maintains that if property is accumulated in a way inconsistent with the common good, then (in our language) that property must be redistributed.[40] These claims are perfectly consistent with the reading presented here. Our focus has been on the origins and nature of the relevant rights, not on their normative strength vis-à-vis other concerns.

6. The State

Following Aristotle, Aquinas claims that the state is natural. As John Finnis explains, 'the *civitas* could be called "natural" if participation in it *(a)* instantiates in itself a basic human good, or *(b)* is a rationally required component in, or indispensable means to instantiating, one or more basic human goods'.[41] As Finnis maintains, Aquinas' view is the latter.

What, then, are the basic human goods for which we need the state? Again, Finnis puts the point well. Without the state, individuals and groups lack the means 'to secure themselves *well* against violence (including invasion), theft, and fraud, and ... to maintain a fair and stable system of distributing, exploiting, and exchanging the natural resources ... That is to say, individuals and families cannot well secure and maintain the elements which make up the *public good* of justice and peace.'[42]

---

[38] Ibid, SS 61.1 r5. Note also that this suggestion is inconsistent with the possible appearance that by possession in the passages examined above, Aquinas intended only physical possession.
[39] Ibid, SS 32.7; 66.7.
[40] Ibid, SS 66.2 r2.
[41] Finnis, *Aquinas*, 246.
[42] Ibid, 247 (citations omitted).

Accordingly, the justification for the state lies in part in the need for the state to secure the rights we possess in virtue of commutative justice: our bodily integrity and our property most significantly. The justification also lies in the need for the state to promote other ends, in particular ones of distributive justice.

With this in mind, we are able to resolve a difficulty left over from the discussion in section 4. Imagine that A wrongly harms B, inflicting a loss on B of £1,000. As we saw, Aquinas insists that a court must award B £1,000 in compensation, regardless of any contrary public interest. But one might wonder how that could be so. If commutative justice in this context operates as between A and B, then it cannot be violated by the court, as it does not operate as between A and the court or B and the court. In fact, it seems that commutative justice as between A and B must be irrelevant to the court as it is, in that sense, a third party.

But that phrase points to the solution to this difficulty. In our case, we might regard C, a bystander who was not injured in any way in the accident, as a third party and hence as having no legitimate interest in the case. But that is not how we think of courts. They are not third parties to a dispute with an interest in resolving it. What are they then?

They are the parts of the state whose role it is in these contexts to do justice. And according to Aquinas, they have this role because that is part of the reason for which the state exists. Recall Finnis' claim that, absent the state, individuals 'cannot well secure and maintain the elements which make up the *public good* of justice and peace'.[43] It is because of this that the state is created. It, therefore, has the task of ensuring respect for the public good of justice and peace, including commutative justice.

As it were, then, the parties to a dispute over commutative justice are entitled to respond to any third party who attempts to intervene by saying 'Mind your own business, this does not concern you.' But they are not entitled to say this to a court, because the court is not just another party. It is rather, inter alia, the part of the state set up to ensure that commutative justice is done between citizens. A commutative injustice is therefore the courts' business.

---

[43] Ibid (citations omitted).

A court's duty to intervene in these cases and to do justice is a matter of distributive, not commutative, justice. The courts are set up in order to realize the public good of justice for everyone, as that is an important benefit to be shared by all. But that does not mean that the court does only distributive justice. Let us return to our example.

Imagine that *A v B* goes to court and that commutative justice demands, as between *A* and *B*, that *B* succeed. The court has an obligation to hear the case and in these circumstances to rule in favour of *B*. Those obligations belong to distributive justice. That is, the obligations binding on the court are ones of distributive justice. But that does not mean that the obligations as between *A* and *B* are of distributive justice. They are not. Nor does it mean that the obligations binding on the court exist entirely because of distributive justice. On the contrary, the court has an obligation of distributive justice to rule in favour of *B* because (i) commutative justice demands that, as between *A* and *B*, *B* must succeed; and (ii) the court has been set up in part in order to ensure respect for commutative justice. Here, it is commutative justice that is primary, and that gives content to distributive justice.

It is also worth saying, though this idea is not found in Aquinas, that if the court orders *A* to pay reparation to *B*, *A* now has two reasons to pay. He must pay because he owes the money to *B* as a matter of commutative justice. And he must pay because he has come under an obligation to the court—or better to society as a whole—to obey the command of a body set up in order to protect the public good of justice, a benefit to be shared by all. Again, the fundamental obligation is the first. The second is derived from commutative justice.[44]

7. Conclusion

What I am calling the traditional view was glimpsed in the writers examined in Chapters 3–5, but it is present front and centre in Aquinas. For Aquinas, our rights and duties are not all derived from politics, as Figure M1 contends. Rather, as T1 has it, some are directly

---

[44] Note that the claim is not that the second obligation is derived from the first. One can have an obligation to pay compensation to someone who one did not, in fact, wrongly injure. This happens when a court incorrectly rules that one must pay. In this case, the obligation to pay is purely of distributive justice. But even here it exists because of the need to have courts in order to enforce commutative justice.

derived from morality, and the justification for the state is partly based on these. Secondly, our rights are not all derived from distributive justice, but many have their origin in commutative justice, a form of justice independent of the distributive. This reflects T2 rather than M2. Thirdly, the foundations of private law are not found in public law and politics, but directly in (commutative) justice and those foundations impact on the political sphere: T3, not M3. Though these ideas are not fully developed in Aquinas—in part because his interests lay elsewhere—the foundations of that view are fully formed. Those foundations were built upon by the writers we examine in the remainder of this part of the book.

7

Pufendorf

1. Justice

Like Aristotle and Aquinas before him, Pufendorf centres his theory on an account of justice. It is here, then, that our analysis must begin. But that presents an immediate difficulty. As we will see, Pufendorf's explicit account of justice is deficient. The main problem is that Pufendorf provides definitions of the forms of justice but then operates with a conception of justice that does not fit the offered definitions.

This occurs in part because of the influence on Pufendorf of Hobbes, the leading figure in the destruction of the traditional view. And it helps to explain the ease with which many of Pufendorf's interpreters have overlooked his commitment to that view. Nevertheless, as I show below, Pufendorf is committed to the traditional view, and his theory remains one of the most powerful expressions of it.

1.1 Pufendorf's Definitions of Justice

Pufendorf begins by distinguishing between universal and particular justice in a way that mirrors Aristotle's distinction between general and special justice examined in section 2 of Chapter 4. For Pufendorf, universal justice concerns the goodness of all other-regarding actions, while particular justice is concerned only with those other-regarding actions about which rights and duties apply.[1] We are interested only in the latter.

---

[1] Pufendorf, *Of the Law of Nature and Nations*, I VII 8.

Like Aristotle and Aquinas, Pufendorf also divides particular justice into the distributive and the commutative.[2] However, his definitions of these terms differ from Aristotle's and Aquinas'.

Let us start with the term 'distributive justice'. This poses the least difficulty. Pufendorf defines it in accordance with his version of the famous social contract argument, examined in section 7 below. As he tells us, 'Distributive justice rests on an agreement between society and its members about pro rata sharing in loss and gain.'[3] This means that the social contract gives content and moral force to distributive justice. To express this more precisely, x is distributively just if it is required by the social contract and people are obligated to realize x in those circumstances because the social contract so requires.

For whenever a person is received into a society an express or tacit agreement is entered into between the society and the member to be received, by which the society undertakes to give him a *pro rata* share of the goods which belong to the society as such, and the member, on his part, promises to undertake to bear his just share of the burdens which make for the preservation of the society as such.[4]

Though the language is different, these are concepts with which we are familiar. In particular, there is only a relatively short step from this view to the account provided by John Rawls examined in Chapter 1.

Pufendorf's account of commutative justice is more problematic, however. He tells us that 'Commutative justice...rests on a bilateral contract particularly concerned with things and actions relevant to commerce'[5] and that 'whatever be done that is owed by virtue of a mutual agreement, in cases concerning things and arts connected with business, that is called commutative justice'.[6]

The first thing to notice about this is that Pufendorf's definition focuses on contracting, commerce, and agreements. As we saw in Chapter 4, this use accords with the strict meaning of 'commutative'. The second thing to notice is that Pufendorf maintains that commutative justice 'rests on' bilateral contracts. Hence, as distributive justice

---

[2] Ibid, I VII 9–10; Pufendorf, *On the Duty of Man and Citizen*, I II 14.
[3] Pufendorf, *On the Duty of Man and Citizen*, I 2 14.
[4] Pufendorf, *Of the Law of Nature and Nations*, I VII 9.
[5] Pufendorf, *On the Duty of Man and Citizen*, I 2 14.
[6] Pufendorf, *Of the Law of Nature and Nations*, I VII 10.

is derived from the social contract, so commutative justice is derived from bilateral contracts. We capture these two points by saying that, for Pufendorf, commutative justice is contractual rather than general and derivative rather than freestanding.

This is important because, as I have argued, commutative justice for Aristotle and Aquinas was general and freestanding. Hence, if the view so far expressed is correct, Pufendorf cannot belong to the tradition as I have described it.

As I now argue, however, this cannot be right, as Pufendorf is committed to the existence of a non-distributive, general, and freestanding form of justice, even though his definitions of justice allow no place for it.

1.2 *Pufendorf's Commitment to Commutative Justice*

We have seen that particular justice is concerned with rights and duties. Pufendorf divides these into two kinds: absolute and hypothetical. Hypothetical rights and duties are those that 'presuppose some state or institution'.[7] Hence, these do not exist in the state of nature, but must be created by institutions in societies. On the other hand, absolute rights and duties are those that 'obligate all men, in whatever state they be, and without regard to any institution formed or accepted by men'.[8]

The claim that absolute rights and duties are independent of 'any institution formed or accepted by men' has two crucial consequences. First, the rights cannot depend on bilateral (ie ordinary) contract. Secondly, they cannot depend on the social contract and hence they are independent of distributive justice. This follows as a matter of definition because, as we saw above, distributive justice is given content by the social contract. Accordingly, Pufendorf defines absolute rights and duties in such a way that they arise independently of bilateral contract or the social contract, and hence are independent of contract and distributive justice. But as, given Pufendorf's general theory, these rights and duties must be based on justice (ie particular justice), this means that they can have no place within his schema.

That would be fine if Pufendorf thought that no absolute rights and duties existed, but the truth is quite the reverse. Not only does

---

[7] Ibid, II III 24.
[8] Ibid.

he assert that they exist, they are afforded pride of place. They are the building blocks of his theory.[9]

Similarly, Pufendorf argues against Hobbes' claim that all rights arise from agreement, asserting that some arise from nature. Given Pufendorf's general theory, that must imply that those rights are demanded by justice.[10] But the form of justice in question cannot be distributive justice, because that arises from the social contract and thus from agreement. Hence, Pufendorf again implies the existence of a sphere of justice that is non-contractual and non-distributive. And that could only be commutative justice as we have been using the term. It is a form of justice that governs interactions between individuals that does not rely on the state or on distributive justice (and hence it holds in the state of nature).

The difficulty, then, is fundamental. Pufendorf defines justice in a way that is inconsistent with the rest of his theory. Our task now is to ask why this happened.[11]

1.3 Pufendorf's Influences

The first answer to our question is that Pufendorf misunderstands Aristotle. His first mistake in this regard is to attribute to Aristotle the view that justice has three parts: the distributive, the corrective, and the 'retaliatory'.[12] Secondly, he interprets corrective justice to refer only to 'the righting of private transactions'.[13] This is close to the view criticized in Chapter 4: that corrective justice must be concerned only with correcting injustices. In fact, however, unlike most modern commentators, Pufendorf recognizes that Aristotle's account is not purely rectificatory, which leads Pufendorf to postulate that Aristotle referred also to what Pufendorf rather unhelpfully calls 'retaliatory' justice. But, thirdly, Pufendorf interprets this third form of justice too narrowly, to concern only 'the manner in which men exchange things among themselves',[14] specifically to the equalization that must be carried out

---

[9] See especially ibid, III I 1.
[10] Ibid, I VII 7.
[11] The issue cannot be solved by claiming that Pufendorf recognizes commutative justice, as that term has been defined here, but simply presents no label for it. This is because he defines perfect rights and duties in accordance with his definitions of distributive and commutative justice. Eg ibid, I VII 9.
[12] Ibid, I VII 12.
[13] Ibid.
[14] Ibid.

to ensure that transactions are fair (see the discussion of shoes and houses in section 2.2 of Chapter 4). Though this definition is too narrow, it nevertheless recognizes Aristotle's commitment to a right-generating form of justice other than the distributive.

But that recognition comes to little in the end, as Pufendorf replaces Aristotle's account with his own. The idea that distributive justice is concerned with the allocation of honour, wealth, and the like in accordance with a political account of equality is replaced with the notion that distributive justice is based on the social contract. The idea that corrective or commutative justice governs interactions between individuals is replaced with the notion that commutative justice is based on bilateral contracts.

It is not difficult to locate the source of this change. It is Hobbes. As we see in Chapter 9, though there are differences even at this point, these ideas are elements of Hobbes' theory. In particular, Hobbes maintains that 'To speak properly, commutative justice, is the justice of a contractor; that is, a performance of covenant, in buying, and selling; hiring, and letting to hire; lending, and borrowing; exchanging, bartering, and other acts of contract.'[15] It is this view that Pufendorf acquires.

But it is also, for the reasons we have seen, inconsistent with Pufendorf's theory. The problem can be expressed shortly. Pufendorf attempts to provide a traditional politico-legal theory based on a modern account of justice. No such attempt can succeed. Though Pufendorf's account of justice has no place for commutative justice as we have been using that term, his analysis of politico-legal norms utilizes that concept routinely. The question now is what to do about this.

1.4 Reconciling the Terminology

As we are interested in Pufendorf's general theory and not in his account of justice for its own sake, it is clear that we must abandon that account. But how are we to do this? For the purposes of exposition, we are faced with a choice. We could use 'commutative justice' as Pufendorf defines the term and find another label for the area of justice Pufendorf relies on but cannot account for. Or we could continue to use 'commutative justice' as it was defined in Chapter 4,

---

[15] Hobbes, *Leviathan*, XV 14. As always, the claim is not that Hobbes was the first or only thinker to advance this view.

noting that this use does not correspond to Pufendorf's. Because it is far more convenient, I have chosen the second option. Thankfully, this causes few problems, as Pufendorf's discussion of the issues examined below does not rely heavily on his terminology. That, of course, is no surprise. As Pufendorf's definitions of justice are inconsistent with his general theory, it is no wonder that he normally ignores those definitions.

2. Justice and Law

As noted above, Pufendorf presents a social contract argument for the authority of the state. The most familiar version of this argument is, of course, the one presented by Hobbes. We examine it in Chapter 9. But at least the outlines of that account are well known. Hobbes maintains that before the state existed, ie in the state of nature, there were no laws and no public authorities with the power to enforce the peace. Because of this, people in that condition were condemned to lives that were 'solitary, poor, nasty, brutish, and short'.[16] In consequence, Hobbes maintains, people in the state of nature do or would agree to enter a compact that sets up a sovereign with such authority, whose first task is to create laws that ensure peace.

Though Pufendorf was greatly influenced by Hobbes, as we have already seen and as is evidenced by his acceptance of the social contract methodology, he emphatically rejects Hobbes' version of that argument.[17] First, Pufendorf denies that the state of nature is void of law. Hence, he rejects Hobbes' claim that all law is the creation of the sovereign. Secondly, while Pufendorf accepts Hobbes' claim that the state of nature is problematic and so must be transcended, his analysis of the problem and its transcendence is radically different. For Pufendorf, the issue is not that the state of nature lacks law. The problem is that the state of nature lacks an enforcement mechanism for the laws it contains. It is therefore 'a poor custodian of man's safety'.[18] As discussed in section 7, the impetus to leave the state of nature for the civil condition arises primarily from the need to institute bodies capable of enforcing these laws.

[16] Ibid, XIII 9.
[17] Pufendorf, *Of the Law of Nature and Nations*, I II 3.
[18] Ibid, II II 12.

The question for us now is: what is the basis of the laws said to exist in the state of nature? If they are not made by the sovereign (there is no sovereign), then by what are they made? The answer, of course, is justice.[19] But what form of justice is in operation here?

To modern eyes, the answer may appear obvious. Pufendorf tells us that the law is based on the need for human society and welfare.[20] This, it seems, is a reference to distributive justice. But it is quite plain that this must be wrong. If legal norms exist in the state of nature, then they cannot be based on distributive justice, because, as Pufendorf tells us, distributive justice arises *out of* the social contract,[21] and it is definitive of the state of nature that it contains no such contract. The norms, Pufendorf says, are 'obligation[s] of natural law, by which all men are bound, in so far as they are endowed with reason, and which does not owe its original introduction to any convention of men'.[22]

Moreover, it is important to interpret Pufendorf's references to human society and welfare through his, not our, eyes. As discussed in Chapter 6, due to the influence of utilitarianism, these terms today immediately call to mind issues of utility and distributive justice. But they need not and traditionally were not understood in that way. A well-functioning human society is one in which justice is realized, both commutative and distributive. Similarly, human welfare is achieved when human lives go well, and on the whole they will go well only when human beings are treated justly, both commutatively and distributively. Pufendorf's references, then, are not exclusively to distributive justice.

Also significant is that, though Pufendorf insists that law in the state of nature is founded on justice,[23] he does not name the form of justice involved. This is at first surprising, but its explanation is contained in the analysis above. As we have seen, Pufendorf divides justice into the distributive and the contractual ('commutative'). But the justice in question cannot be distributive, as it precedes the social contract. Nor is the justice under examination contractual. In Pufendorf's sense, this means that it is not 'commutative'. The sphere of justice in question, then, is the sphere for which Pufendorf's theory of justice has no place.

[19] Ibid, I VII 7.
[20] Ibid, I I 3–5; I VII 7; II I 5, 8.
[21] Pufendorf, *On the Duty of Man and Citizen*, I 2 14; Pufendorf, *Of the Law of Nature and Nations*, I VII 9.
[22] Pufendorf, *Of the Law of Nature and Nations*, II II 11.
[23] Ibid, I VII 7.

But as we have noted, that is what we are calling (non-contractual) commutative justice. Hence, Pufendorf's position is that the law that exists in the state of nature is based on commutative justice as we have defined that term. As we see below, this idea provides the foundation of Pufendorf's account of our natural rights.

3. Bodily Integrity

The first aspect of the substantive law that Pufendorf discusses is the law '*No one should hurt another*'.[24] Why does this law exist?

First, Pufendorf tells us that this law 'obligate[s] all men even before the formation of any human institution'[25] and that it '[d]erive[s its] force from that common relationship which nature established among all men even before any act was exchanged between them'.[26] In other words, the law exists in the state of nature. It is no mere command of the sovereign. For the reasons examined in the previous section, this means that the basis for the law must be commutative, not distributive, justice.

Why, then, does commutative justice demand the existence of this law? According to Pufendorf, the law is given to us by 'nature herself'.[27] By this, Pufendorf intends that the existence of the law is required in order for people to live good lives. That in turn is because a person whose bodily integrity was not respected would lack the freedom essential to the good life.[28]

Note that this claim is different to, though compatible with, the notion that a person whose bodily integrity was not respected would not receive a fair go vis-à-vis others in society. Pufendorf separately recognizes the force of this notion when he states that 'this duty is of the greatest necessity, since without it the social life of men could in no way exist' and when he asks 'how can I live at peace with him who does me injury, since nature has bred into each man so tender a love for himself and his own possessions that he cannot help using all possible means to ward off the man who is about to do him harm'?[29]

---

[24] Ibid, III I 1. See also Pufendorf, *On the Duty of Man and Citizen*, I 6.
[25] Pufendorf, *Of the Law of Nature and Nations*, III I 1.
[26] Ibid, III IV 1.
[27] Ibid, III I 1.
[28] Ibid.
[29] Ibid.

But this does not mean, nor does Pufendorf intend, that the right to bodily integrity has its origin in such concerns. Here, mirroring the discussion of property in the previous chapter, Pufendorf first argues that the right is absolute—ie that it is grounded in the law of nature prior to the social contract—and then argues that it is also advantageous because it furthers distributive justice. On this view, the basis of the right lies in the fact that it is demanded by commutative justice, though the recognition of the right is also distributively just.

It is also worth noting that Pufendorf includes in the list of rights 'which nature herself has immediately granted us', not only bodily integrity ('life, our body, our limbs'), but also 'our virtue, our plain reputation, [and] our liberty'.[30] All of these rights exist in the state of nature and are based on commutative justice.

4. Responses to Violations of Commutative Justice

Immediately after discussing the origin of these rights, Pufendorf remarks that a 'further consequence of this command is: *If any one has done another some hurt, and has caused him in any way some loss, which can properly be imputed to the aggressor, the aggressor must, so far as he can, make good the loss.*'[31]

The first thing to be said in this context is that, despite Pufendorf's references to hurt and loss here, these terms are not to be understood in the sense given to them by the modern law, ie as involving any factual deprivation. On the contrary, Pufendorf maintains that

> it must be observed...that, inasmuch as a thing may be owed us in two ways, either by a perfect, or by an imperfect obligation, to which a perfect and an imperfect right correspond respectively, damage which another is bound to restore can be done us only in things owed under the first category, but not in things owed us under the second category.[32]

In other words, an injury in this context is not defined as a factual deprivation but as a violation of a person's legal rights. Hence, the

---

[30] Ibid.
[31] Ibid, III I 2.
[32] Ibid, III I 3. See also Pufendorf, *On the Duty of Man and Citizen*, I 6 5.

term 'hurt' in the principle 'No man should be hurt'[33] and the terms 'loss' in the principle '*If he has caused another a loss, he should make it good*'[34] are to be given legal/moral rather than factual interpretations. To put this another way, a person is 'hurt' and suffers 'loss' only if her legal rights have been violated, not merely if she suffers some sort of factual detriment such as the happening of an unwanted event or the failure to realize a hoped for gain. In themselves, such issues are legally irrelevant. The significance of this issue is examined in Chapter 12.

The issue now is the reason for the existence of the rule under examination. Why must a person who has injured another make good the loss?

It is not because of any social benefit thought to accrue from such actions—remember that there is as yet no society to benefit (more strictly, the duty to repair is conceptually prior to society). Rather, Pufendorf argues:

For it is surely a vain thing to have given orders that a person receive no hurt, if, when such hurt befalls him, he must accept the loss at his own cost, while the man who offered him the hurt may enjoy the fruit of his injury in peace and without making restitution.[35]

This is the familiar thought that a right without effect is meaningless. The idea is echoed in Holt CJ's famous judgment in *Ashby v White*,[36] written 15 years after the publication of Pufendorf's great treatise.

If the plaintiff has a right, he must of necessity have a means to vindicate and maintain it, and a remedy if he is injured in the exercise or enjoyment of it; and indeed it is a vain thing to imagine a right without a remedy; for want of right and want of remedy are reciprocal.[37]

The argument will not quite do, however. Even if want of right and want of remedy were reciprocal, it would not follow from this

---

[33] Pufendorf, *Of the Law of Nature and Nations*, III I. See also Pufendorf, *On the Duty of Man and Citizen*, I 6.
[34] Pufendorf, *Of the Law of Nature and Nations*, III I 1.
[35] Ibid, III I 2. See also Pufendorf, *On the Duty of Man and Citizen*, I 6 4.
[36] (1703) 2 Ld Raym 938, 92 ER 126, 136.
[37] Ibid.

alone that the remedy for the violation of a right must be reparation. Moreover, though Pufendorf goes on to argue that 'men are so depraved that they will never refrain from hurting each other, unless they are forced to make restitution, nor will it be easy for a man who has suffered some loss to make up his mind to live at peace with another, so long as he has not received proper restitution',[38] these remarks cannot be utilized at this stage of the argument. They cannot be used to establish a duty that 'obligate[s] all men even before the formation of any human institution'[39] and 'which nature herself has immediately granted us'.[40] These duties hold even in the state of nature, where law is 'a poor custodian of man's safety'.[41] Moreover, both the first and the second claim argue that enforced reparation is advantageous; they do not show that enforced reparation is good in itself. And that is what Pufendorf needs to show.

In other words, as we have seen in section 3, it would be appropriate to argue that the duty is demanded by commutative justice and then go on to show that it is also in accordance with distributive justice. For that reason, Pufendorf's appeal to distributive justice is not out of place. But the problem is that Pufendorf's argument for the first conclusion is invalid.

However, the problem is not as significant as it seems. In fact, Pufendorf is not guilty of neglecting this important issue; he simply does not explain himself fully. And he does not because, to his mind, the issue did not require explanation. His error seems a large lacuna to us only because we have forgotten the justice that is, at this point, at the forefront of Pufendorf's mind.

For Pufendorf, a person has a right to his bodily integrity even in the state of nature. If someone violates that right, then, as explored in the previous chapter, the victim has less than he ought to have vis-à-vis the violator. This is either because the victim has suffered a wrongful loss or, as we discuss in section 6.2, because the perpetrator has realized a wrongful gain. Hence, an injustice exists that is corrected or repaired—ie eliminated—when the perpetrator surrenders his gain or compensates the victim for her loss.

---

[38] Pufendorf, *Of the Law of Nature and Nations*, III I 2.
[39] Ibid, III I 1.
[40] Ibid.
[41] Ibid, II II 12.

5. Contract

5.1 The Foundations of Contract

Pufendorf's account of the foundations of contract follows what is now a familiar pattern. In line with what we have seen above, he attempts to answer two questions: 'Why are contracts binding?' and 'Why is the institution of contract desirable?' Following Pufendorf, I answer the second question first.

The Desirability of Contract Law In a chapter that is transitional between what we would call the innate rights discussed in chapters 1–3 of Book III of *The Law of Nature and Nations* and the acquired rights examined in chapters 5–9 of that Book, a chapter that examines the character of the division between innate and acquired rights, the categorization of obligations in general and the nature of good faith, Pufendorf remarks that the existence of innate rights alone are insufficient to ensure justice, as

> not all men are so constituted that they are willing to do everything, with which they can help others, out of mere humanity and love, and without assuring themselves of some hope of receiving their equivalent; while it is often the case that the things which can come to us from others are of such a nature that we cannot have the boldness to ask that they be done for us gratis. It is often also not fitting for our person or lot that we be indebted to another for such a kindness, and so in many instances another person is unable to do us a kindness, and we are often unwilling to receive one, unless the other person receives its equivalent from us. Moreover, it often happens that other men do not know how they may serve our interests. Finally, in view of the finite power of man being unable to extend itself to all persons at the same time and with the same force, it is surely reasonable that such actions as are not yet covenanted for by former obligations are bound over to those who, by agreements, have secured for themselves a prior right to them. And so, if mutual offices, the real fruit of humanity, are to be practised more frequently between men, and by a kind of set rule, it was necessary for men themselves to agree among themselves on the mutual rendering of such services as a man could not also be certain of for himself on the mere law of humanity. Therefore, it had to be determined beforehand what one should do for another, and what he should in his turn expect from another, and

demand on his own right. This is, indeed, accomplished by promises and agreements.[42]

Similarly, Pufendorf claims that 'whenever men enter into any agreements, the social nature of man requires that they must be faithfully observed. For if an agreement lacks this guarantee, much the largest part of the advantage which accrues to mankind from the mutual interchange of duties would be lost.'[43] He also maintains that, 'if it were not necessary to keep promises, it would be in no way possible with any confidence to base one's calculations on the assistance of other men', echoing the reliance theory examined in Chapter 1.[44]

The resemblance between Pufendorf's and the modern view is clear, then. In short, it appears that Pufendorf bases the norms of contract law in distributive justice. Again, however, this appearance is misleading.

As Pufendorf tells us, 'It is...a most sacred precept of natural law'—ie of law that precedes the social contract and thus lies outside distributive justice—'and one that governs the grace, manner, and reasonableness of all human life, *That every man keep his given word*, that is, carry out his promises and agreements.'[45] The concerns listed above, then, were thought by Pufendorf to relate to commutative, not distributive, justice.

Moreover, at this point in his discussion, Pufendorf is exploring the desirability of the institution of contract law. He is not examining the reasons contracts are binding. We moderns tend to think that these issues are closely linked, but there is no suggestion of this in Pufendorf. On the contrary, his analysis of the second issue makes no reference to his discussion of the first.

Why are Contracts Binding? The centrepiece of Pufendorf's account of contract is his claim that 'promises and pacts transfer a right to others'.[46] On this view, the question 'Why are contracts binding?' is in a sense a non-question. This is because contracts are agreements that transfer rights, and the transfer of a right is binding by definition. For instance, if I promise to sell you my horse for £1,000 and you

---

[42] Ibid, III IV 1.
[43] Ibid, III IV 2.
[44] Ibid.
[45] Ibid, III IV 3.
[46] Ibid, III V 2. See also Pufendorf, *On the Duty of Man and Citizen*, I 9 7.

agree, I give you a right that I deliver my horse to you and you give me a right that you will pay me £1,000. If one understands what this means, there can be no question about why the contract is binding.

For Pufendorf, there is no great mystery about this. Once one recognizes that legal norms can exist as between individuals, the idea that one person can give a right to another follows as a matter of course.[47] Just as I can give you a portion of my property, I can give you a right that I do something by promising you in a certain way that I will do that thing.[48] Unsurprisingly, the 'certain way' that I must promise in order to transfer a right to you is to make my promise in a way that indicates that I am intending to transfer a right. Following Grotius,[49] Pufendorf calls promises of this kind perfect.[50] And the analysis of this form of promising forms the bulk of Pufendorf's discussion.

5.2 The Nature of Contract

Pufendorf's understanding of the norms that ground contract law have a profound influence on his conception of the nature of contractual obligation. Because he sees contracting as governed by commutative justice and as involving the transfer of right from one person to another (and, typically, from the second back to the first), he identifies contracting as an act by which rights are acquired over people, where the promisor promises another to 'do, allow, or avoid' some action in a way that gives the promisee a right to the performance.[51]

Moreover, the understanding of contracting as involving transfers of rights leads naturally to the idea that certain kinds of responses to breaches of contracts are appropriate. For instance, if I promise to give you my horse but then fail to do so, this must be understood as a violation of the right that you have as against me that I give you my horse. The result is that I have more vis-à-vis you than I ought to have and that you have less vis-à-vis me than you ought to have. Moreover, the value of this injustice is determined by the value of the horse, or more strictly, by the value to you of your receiving the horse. Accordingly, the appropriate response to this violation is to require me to give you my horse or to insist that I put you in a position equivalent to the

---

[47] See also Grotius, *The Jurisprudence of Holland*, vol 1, 294–295; Grotius, *The Law of War and Peace*, II XI–XII.
[48] See, eg Pufendorf, *Of the Law of Nature and Nations*, III V 7.
[49] Grotius, *The Law of War and Peace*, II XI IV.
[50] Pufendorf, *Of the Law of Nature and Nations*, III V 7.
[51] Ibid, III V 4.

one in which you would have been had I given you my horse. We know these responses as specific performance and expectation damages, respectively. We return to this issue in Chapter 12.

5.3 The Interpretation of Contracts

Another consequence of the fact that Pufendorf views contract through the lens of commutative justice is that he understands contracting itself as an interpersonal event. That may seem an almost trivial point until it is realized that a great deal of modern analysis of the law of contract refuses to understand contracting in that way.

One way of bringing this out is to consider discussions of the so-called objective standard as it applies to the formation and interpretation of contracts. The basic idea is that the appropriate method for interpreting a person's utterances[52] is not to examine his subjective intentions but to discover the reasonable appearance of those utterances in the context in which they were made.

For example, if I say 'I will give you my horse for £1,000' and you reply 'Done', then a contract has been formed for the sale of my horse. This is because the utterances made reasonably appear to imply the formation of that contract. And this is so even if I intended by 'my horse' my cow and you intended by 'Done' that you never want to do business with me. Our question is: what is the justification for this approach?

It must now be no surprise that those who have adopted the modern conception struggle with this issue. Various suggestions have been made. Some are hopelessly vague. For instance, writing extra-judicially, Lord Steyn has claimed that 'as a matter of principle, it is not unfair to impute to contracting parties the intention that in the event of a dispute a neutral judge should decide the case applying an objective standard of reasonableness'.[53] The crucial claim here—that the objective standard is fair—is asserted, but not argued for. The vacuity of this position is not coincidental or simply a result of a refusal properly to investigate the issue. It is rather a direct consequence of the general problem we are analysing. As is shown below, Lord Steyn's intuition that the objective standard is fair is correct, but he is unable

---

[52] Strictly, these are speech acts rather than specifically utterances; however, it is more usual for lawyers to concentrate on utterances because these are typical in this context.
[53] Steyn, 'Contract Law: Fufilling the Reasonable Expectation of Honest Men', 433.

to support that intuition because the fairness of that standard is hidden from him by the modern conception.

Other explanations are apparently less vague, but are no better as explanations. The most important theory in this regard is the idea, which goes back to and beyond Lon Fuller and William Perdue,[54] that the point of the objective test is to protect reasonable reliance.[55] The central problem with this view is that it does not explain what it purports to explain. Recall the case above in which I say 'I will sell you my horse for £1,000' where I intend to sell you my cow. As we have seen, the law holds that this is an offer to sell my horse, not my cow. According to the view under examination, this is because that conclusion is necessary to protect your reasonable reliance on my offer should you accept it. And it is certainly true that it is reasonable to rely on my apparent offer to sell you my horse.

But it is frequently reasonable to rely on statements in circumstances where it is clear that no legal obligation is created. For instance, if I am told by someone who is an authority on the economy that the economy will improve in the next year, it is reasonable for me to make some planning decisions on that basis (in fact, it might be quite irrational for me to ignore the information). But this does not mean that I hold any entitlement against the authority. At best, reasonable reliance is a necessary, not sufficient, condition for the existence of the relevant kind of legal obligation. Because of this, reasonable reliance cannot in itself account for the objective standard. The appeal to reasonable reliance must be made consistent with the fact that the law does not always protect that kind of reliance. An appeal to at least some other factor is needed here.[56]

That other factor cannot be provided by reliance theory per se, as the question is about the kinds of reliance that produce obligation. No doubt answers could be provided, however. At this point, the modern theorist is likely to appeal to some policy concern or other, the modern conception's lifeboat for its sinking ship. Considerations such as ease of proof, avoidance of fraud, and commercial certainty, as well as the aforementioned reasonable reliance, are favourites.[57] But again, this is to look in the wrong place.

---

[54] Fuller and Perdue, 'The Reliance Interest in Contract Damages'.
[55] Eg Fridman, 'The Objective Principle and Mistake and Involuntariness in Contract and Restitution', 68–9.
[56] For discussion, see Smith, *Contract Theory*, 80–82.
[57] Chen-Wishart, *Contract Law*, 54–55.

On the other hand, during her investigation of these issues in her student textbook, as an aside that she labels a 'Pause for reflection', Mindy Chen-Wishart opines that:

Making a contract is essentially an exercise in the *communication* of choice, and communication is impossible without objectivity (the context of *conventions* which gives meaning to conduct). Objectivity is indispensable when one seeks to relate to others in any way. We have to suspend our own meaning, enter imaginatively into the other's world and ask: 'What meaning do *they* think they're conveying?' 'What will *they* think I am meaning?' Intention is wholly dependent on manifestations interpreted in a context of shared meaning. The existence and extent of contractual obligations are determined by the signs made, the moves in the language game being played. Any legal concern with undisclosed intention is senseless: it contradicts the very idea of contract as an agreement between parties who convey and receive meaning.[58]

Chen-Wishart's insight does not deserve to be relegated to a 'pause for reflection'. It is central. The searches for the justification of the objective standard that Chen-Wishart examines in the body of her text—ie the famous ones that dominate the modern literature on the topic—are wild goose chases. The truth is much closer to hand. The test for intention in contract law is objective because the test for intention in every communicative context is. The answer to our question, then, is to be found in the interpersonal nature of communication and not in the intra-societal norms of public policy and distributive justice. The modern conception's obsession with the latter is so powerful that it has obscured the former, though on reflection it is desperately obvious.[59]

All the time in our ordinary lives, we are interpreting the utterances of others objectively. It is one of the most pervasive features of human experience—you are doing it now as you read this book. But the moment we turn to law, this everyday event is forgotten and we struggle to find justifications through analysis of public policy or distributive justice for the most perfectly ordinary phenomena. This is the blinding effect of the modern conception.

---

[58] Ibid, 55 (citation omitted).
[59] For a deeper analysis of these issues as they relate to the law of contract, see Beever, 'Agreements, Mistakes, and Contract Formation'; Langille and Ripstein, 'Strictly Speaking, It Went Without Saying'.

On the other hand, the interpersonal nature of communication is front and centre in Pufendorf's theory of contract.[60] As he insists, utterances are and must be interpreted in accordance with their conventional meanings[61]—unless, that is, the utterer indicates otherwise, an indication that must itself conform to conventional meanings. The law of contract is nothing special in this regard. Its objective test is simply a product of the nature of language.[62] However, as Pufendorf also recognizes, different sets of conventions apply in different contexts. General language conventions hold widely, say for the community of speakers of English, but special language conventions hold for particular groups, say lawyers or surgeons. Interpretations of utterances take these contexts into account.[63]

But the approach is not and cannot be *purely* objective, because utterances can constitute agreements only if the parties have and exercise their rational capacities.[64] So, for example, if I program my computer to say 'I will sell you my mouse for £10', that cannot be an offer (by the computer). And it cannot be an offer (by the computer) even if I place the computer in a lifelike android who appears to all to be a human being. Similarly, one cannot form agreements while sleepwalking or while insane, despite being able to make the kinds of utterances that would ordinarily ground agreements.

It is worth observing again the difficulty the law has with these notions. Take, for example, one of English law's leading textbooks on the subject. The example discussed imagines B accepting an offer made by A.

Whether A is actually bound by an acceptance of his apparent offer depends on the state of mind of the alleged offeree (B); to this extent, the test is not purely objective. With regard to B's state of mind, there are three possibilities. First, B actually believes that A intends to be bound: here the objective test is satisfied so that B can hold A to his apparent offer even though A did not, subjectively, have the requisite intention. The general view is that there is no further requirement that A must also be aware of B's state of mind. Secondly, B knows that, in spite of the objective appearance, A does not have the requisite intention: here A is not bound; the objective test does not apply in

[60] Pufendorf, *Of the Law of Nature and Nations*, III V 8; III VI 2; IV I 2–6.
[61] Ibid, IV I 2.
[62] Ibid, IV I 3–5.
[63] Ibid, IV I 6.
[64] Ibid, III VI 3.

favour of B as he knows the truth about A's actual intention. Thirdly, B has simply not formed any view about A's intention, so that B neither believes that A has the requisite intention nor knows that A does not have this intention: this situation has given rise to a conflict of judicial opinion.[65]

The first two cases are, in reality, so simple that they ought to be able to pass without comment. The fact that they cannot points to the confusion generated by the modern view. The first case is entirely ordinary. That A is bound is a consequence of quite unexceptional features of intersubjective communication. If I intend to sell you my cow rather than my horse but that fact is unknown to you, then you can truly say that I offered to sell you my horse. Note also that the irrelevance of A's awareness of B's state of mind is not in the least paradoxical. The second case is also readily explicable: if B knew that A did not have the intention, then A did not communicate to B that he had that intention. If you know that I intended to sell you my cow and not my horse, you cannot correctly say that I offered to sell you my horse.

The third case is also much simpler than presented. A is not bound. This is because B cannot regard himself as accepting an offer from A without the relevant belief. Compare this with the argument presented against the idea that A should be bound.

This latter view no doubt facilitates proof of agreement, but it is hard to see why B should be protected in the situation to which it refers. Where B has no positive belief in A's (apparent) intention to be bound, he cannot be prejudiced by acting in reliance on it; and the purpose of the objective test is simply to protect B from the risk of suffering such prejudice. The test embodies a principle of convenience; it is not based on any inherent superiority of objective over subjective criteria. It is therefore submitted that the objective test should not apply to our third situation since in it B's state of mind is such that there is no risk of his suffering any prejudice as a result of the objective appearance of A's intention.[66]

This is another example of the unnecessary complexity and confusion created by the modern view. Here we see the introduction of notions

---

[65] Peel (ed), *Treitel's The Law of Contract*, 10 (citations omitted).
[66] Ibid, 11 (citations omitted).

of a kind to deal with a problem that was created in the first place by the introduction of notions of that kind.

6. Property

6.1 The Justification of Property Rights

Of the thinkers examined in this book, Pufendorf is the first to present what I call the 'mixed conception' of property. According to this view, the norms of property law are grounded in both commutative and distributive justice.

It is important to note immediately that this is not the view that concerns of commutative and distributive justice aggregate in order to justify private property. On the contrary, as commutative and distributive justice are *separate forms* of justice, the concerns that belong to them cannot aggregate. Rather, Pufendorf's position is that commutative and distributive justice function not together but separately in the justification of property rights. As it were, property needs to get up two steps to get off the ground; commutative justice lifts it up one step and distributive justice up the other. More specifically, commutative justice on its own is capable of establishing only what we might call proto-property rights, but distributive justice opens up a possibility that commutative justice can then utilize in order to create genuine property rights.[67] I examine that theory now. Because it suits modern sensibilities, I begin with the distributive element of Pufendorf's account.

The Social Nature of Property: The System of Property and the Role of Distributive Justice Pufendorf maintains that individuals in the state of nature are at liberty to use all objects, as long as that use does not injure anyone.[68] This is true even if that use causes factual loss to others that does not result in the violation of their rights. In this context, the chief consequence of this position is that there can be no right to property in the state of nature. This is because a regime of property rights is inconsistent with a universal liberty to use objects. A universal liberty

---

[67] See also Grotius, *Commentary on the Law of Prize and Booty*, 226–227 [100']; Grotius, *The Law of War and Peace*, II II II.
[68] Pufendorf, *Of the Law of Nature and Nations*, IV IV 5.

is the same as a universal absence of obligation. But property gives the holder an entitlement to exclude non-owners, and that entitlement is a claim right correlative to obligations in others.

Pufendorf draws attention to this by referring to the social nature of property; to the idea that property involves rights against others.[69] If I originally acquire a piece of property p, then that implies that all others come to have obligations in respect of p that they did not before.[70] In particular, they have an obligation not to use p without my consent. Because all others are bound, Pufendorf categorizes the obligation as social in nature, and maintains that it therefore cannot exist in the (non-social) state of nature.[71] As we see in the following chapter, the basic idea here is expressed more fully by Kant.

Nevertheless, because of these thoughts, Pufendorf maintains that:

Therefore, the proprietorship of things has resulted immediately from the convention of men, either tacit or express. For although after God had made the gift [of objects for people to use], nothing remained to prevent man from appropriating things to himself, yet there was need of some sort of convention if it was to be understood that by such appropriation or seizure the right of others to that thing was excluded.[72]

The full position is this. In the state of nature, people possess innate rights. Moreover, as a universal liberty to use objects exists in the state of nature, individuals are free to take physical possession of objects. However, that possession cannot imply obligations in others beyond those implied by one's innate rights. So, for instance, if I pick up an apple, then you have an obligation not to take or even touch it.[73] But that is because your doing so would violate my bodily integrity. It is not because I have any rights to the apple as such. Hence, when I put the apple down, you are at liberty to take it. To gain rights to the apple per se, it must be possible to create obligations that are social or, as we

---

[69] Ibid, IV IV 3.

[70] Note, then, that the problem concerns acquiring, not having, multital rights in the state of nature. In that state, multital rights exist, eg bodily integrity, but those rights are innate not acquired.

[71] See also Waldron, *The Right to Private Property*, 150.

[72] Pufendorf, *Of the Law of Nature and Nations*, IV IV 4.

[73] This discussion is modelled on that found in Kant, 'The Metaphysics of Morals', 6:247–248.

would say, multital.[74] And that requires a multilateral agreement about the possibility of such obligations. That agreement, of course, is the social contract.

This may make the creation of property rights sound more contingent than Pufendorf intends. It may appear that the above implies that people in the state of nature could, but do not have to, enter a civil condition in which property rights are recognized. But that is not Pufendorf's view. His position is that people in the state of nature have a moral obligation to enter into a society that recognizes property rights, though there is no obligation to create any particular form of property ownership.

And yet there is no precept of natural law whereby all things are commanded to be proper to men in such a way, that every man should be allotted his own separate and distinct portion. Although natural law clearly advised that men should by convention introduce the assignment of such things to individuals, according as it might be of advantage to human society, yet on the condition that it would rest with the judgement of men, whether they wanted all things to be proper or only some, or would hold some things indivisible and leave the rest open to all, yet in such a way that no one might claim them for himself alone. From this it is further understood, that the law of nature approves all conventions which have been introduced about things by men, provided they involve no contradiction or do not overturn society.[75]

In this regard, Pufendorf appeals to the familiar ideas, originating with Aristotle and picked up on by Aquinas (and made in opposition to Plato's communism), that private property prevents quarrels and provides an incentive for industry.[76]

In summary, the role played by distributive justice is that it calls for the formation of a social contract that brings into existence a society (as examined in section 7) and a society in which norms of property ownership are recognized. Without such a contract, property rights cannot exist.

---

[74] This idea is sometimes inaccurately expressed by using the term 'in rem'. A right in rem is simply a right to a thing, a res. Now, it may be characteristic of rights in rem that they are multital, but even if so, rights in rem are not multital in virtue of being in rem.
[75] Pufendorf, *Of the Law of Nature and Nations*, IV IV 4.
[76] Ibid, IV IV 6.

The Interpersonal Nature of Property: Original Acquisition and the Role of Commutative Justice So far, we have examined the social nature of property. As we have seen, property rights are multital and so can be created only in circumstances in which the creation of such rights is possible. That is what we are calling the civil condition. But Pufendorf maintains that property is not entirely social. Though property rights are possible only in a civil condition, their acquisition is otherwise entirely independent of that condition. To put this another way, though distributive justice makes possible the existence of a system of property rights, the acquisition of such rights, though of course made against the background of distributive justice, relies directly only on commutative justice.

Pufendorf describes original acquisition—ie acquisition of something either abandoned or never before owned, as opposed to acquisition through transfer—as follows:

We are said to have occupied a thing, only when we actually take possession of it, and this begins with the joining of body to body immediately or through a proper instrument. Therefore it is the customary thing, that occupancy of movables be effected by the hands, of land by the feet, along with the intention of cultivating it and of establishing boundaries either exact or with some latitude. But merely to have seen a thing, or to know its location, is not held to be sufficient to establish possession.[77]

This is in accordance with well-established legal practices, but the thing to notice is that this formulation pays no attention to distributive justice. The claim is not that original acquisition first requires physical possession because of fairness throughout the community as a whole or any such concern. Rather, Pufendorf's point is concerned with, in his language, dominion: the exerting of control over an object in a way that makes the object one's own.

So, for instance, he argues that wild animals become the property of the trapper 'provided the instruments [ie the traps] are in our power, that is, laid in a place where we have a right [ie at least a liberty] to capture wild animals, and not yet broken by the beast, and provided the game is so securely fastened in them that it cannot get away, at least till such time as we may come to it'.[78] The issue here is the control over the animal, not distributive concerns.

[77] Ibid, IV VI 8.
[78] Ibid, IV VI 9.

In a passage that calls to mind ideas familiar to all American lawyers, Pufendorf extends this position to hunters. When does a hunted animal become the property of the hunter? This is Pufendorf's answer:

> in my opinion the general statement should be that, if an animal has received a mortal wound or been seriously crippled, it cannot be taken by another so long as we keep up the pursuit of it, and provided we have the right to be in that place; while this is not true, in case the wound be not mortal, nor such as seriously to hinder its flight.[79]

Again, the issue is the amount of control that the hunter has over the animal.

The key features of this discussion are the irrelevance of distributive concerns and the, largely implicit, reliance on commutative justice. The idea is that when a pursuer gains a sufficient level of control over an object, that control generates a right in the pursuer correlative to obligations in others. Though, as we saw above, this can occur only in a civil condition that recognizes the creation of multital rights, the norms involved in the creation of each individual such right rely on but do not draw on that recognition. In other words, the creation of specific property rights, appeals directly to commutative justice, even though it relies on a background of distributive justice.

The passage from Pufendorf above is likely to ring bells for American lawyers, because it proved extremely influential in one of American law's most famous cases: *Pierson v Post*.[80] As the headnote appears to have been written by a man with a sense of humour, I repeat it here.

> The declaration stated that *Post*, being in possession of certain dogs and hounds under his command, did, 'upon a certain wild and uninhabited, unpossessed and waste land, called the beach, find and start one of those noxious beasts called a fox,' and whilst there hunting, chasing and pursuing the same with his dogs and hounds, and when in view thereof, *Pierson*, well knowing the fox was so hunted and pursued, did, in the sight of *Post*, to prevent his catching the same, kill and carry it off.[81]

---

[79] Ibid, IV VI 10.
[80] 3 Caines Rep 175 (NY 1805).
[81] Ibid, 175.

Tompkins J, delivering the judgment of the court, considered Pufendorf's views and others of similar kind and concluded that the fox did not belong to Post when Pierson carried it off and hence that Pierson committed no wrong against Post. This was because, as the tradition had it, Post had not achieved a sufficient level of control over the fox to generate a right in him to the fox.

Writing in dissent, however, Livingston J, also a man with a sense of humour, maintained that the case dealt with 'a knotty point, and should have been submitted to the arbitration of sportsmen, without poring over Justinian, Fleta, Bracton, Puffendorf [sic], Locke, Barbeyrac, or Blackstone, all of whom have been cited: they would have had no difficulty in coming to a prompt and correct conclusion'.[82] According to Livingston J, that conclusion was the following:

By the pleadings it is admitted that a fox is a 'wild and noxious beast.' Both parties have regarded him, as the law of nations does a pirate... His depredations on farmers and on barnyards, have not been forgotten; and to put him to death wherever found, is allowed to be meritorious, and of public benefit. Hence it follows, that our decision should have in view the greatest possible encouragement to the destruction of an animal, so cunning and ruthless in his career. But who would keep a pack of hounds; or what gentleman, at the sound of the horn, and at peep of day, would mount his steed, and for hours together, '*sub jove frigido*,' or a vertical sun, pursue the windings of this wily quadruped, if, just as night came on, and his stratagems and strength were nearly exhausted, a saucy intruder, who had not shared in the honors or labors of the chase, were permitted to come in at the death, and bear away in triumph the object of pursuit?[83]

For Tompkins J, the issue was one of commutative justice: whether Post had exerted sufficient control over the fox to generate a right in him to the fox held against Pierson. For Livingston J, on the other hand, the issue was one of distributive justice: how best to organize society so that good ends are achieved for all. With this conception in his head, Livingston J was quite unable to understand the point of the appeal to writers such as Pufendorf. To his mind, the majority were not presenting reasons for their conclusion; they were simply appealing to

---

[82] Ibid, 180.
[83] Ibid, 180–181.

ancient authority. But this authority was of questionable value for the modern world.

Whatever Justinian may have thought of the matter, it must be recollected that his code was compiled many hundred years ago, and it would be very hard indeed, at the distance of so many centuries, not to have a right to establish a rule for ourselves. In his day, we read of no order of men who made it a business, in the language of the declaration in this cause, 'with hounds and dogs to find, start, pursue, hunt, and chase,' these animals, and that, too, without any other motive than the preservation of Roman poultry; if this diversion had been then in fashion, the lawyers who composed his institutes, would have taken care not to pass it by, without suitable encouragement.[84]

The social and economic structure of the Eastern Roman Empire was different to the social and economic structure of contemporary New York. Hence, in order to achieve good outcomes, the legal rules need to be different as well.

Hence, there are two reasons why *Pierson v Post* is useful for our purposes. First, it is an example of the traditional and modern conceptions in conflict. But it is more than this. It is also an exemplar of the way in which that conflict has been resolved. The traditional view has not only lost favour, it has come to be viewed as either empty or unintelligible. Today, as was noted in Chapter 1, this has gone so far that the modern view is frequently attributed even to the traditional thinkers. What is the point of poring over Justinian, Fleta, Bracton, Pufendorf, Locke, Barbeyrac, or Blackstone? This book is intended as an answer to that question.

The Nature of Property Overall To satisfy the modern mind, I began the discussion of property by examining the role of distributive justice and then shifted to commutative justice. However, that is prone to give the reader a false impression. Distributive justice is needed to ground the creation of multital rights, of which property rights are a kind,[85] but it would be wrong to think that distributive justice is foundational or of most importance in our understanding of the nature of private property.

---

[84] Ibid, 181.
[85] Note that, though rights such as the right to bodily integrity are multital, they not created.

As the discussion of Kant's theory in the following chapter reveals more clearly, it is rather better to think of the concerns of distributive justice as presenting only a defeasable barrier to the existence of property.

Perhaps the best way to approach this issue is as follows. As we have seen, original acquisition is impossible in the state of nature, because multital rights cannot be created in that state. We can refer to this as 'the barrier'. Despite its existence, however, the norms that govern original acquisition exist in the state of nature and operate there;[86] it is just that the barrier prevents those norms actually generating property rights. If Pierson had interrupted Post's hunt in the state of nature, then there would, of course, have been no wrong to Post. But imagine now that Post had captured the fox before Pierson carried it off. In those circumstances, it is also true to say that no wrong is committed. But the reason for this is more complicated. It is because, though Post had satisfied the norms for original acquisition of the fox, that acquisition could not carry over into a genuine property right because, in the circumstances in question, no multital rights can be created. Hence, we can truly say that when this Pierson takes the fox that, were the civil condition to be in existence, Pierson would have wronged Post.

Another way of putting this point is to say that the need for the societal recognition of multital rights is an *external* barrier to the existence of property rights—external, that is, to the norms of property itself. The norms of property law are created by commutative justice, but they cannot actually produce property rights in the state of nature, because distributive justice prevents multital rights being created there. This has two interconnected consequences. First, the conceptual analysis of property law refers only to norms of commutative justice. Secondly, if other things were equal, property could be acquired in the state of nature. As we might say, property rights are *latent* in the state of nature. But, as it happens, other things are not equal. Distributive justice demands that property rights cannot be created unless a society has been formed that recognizes the generation of multital rights. Therefore, it is appropriate to say that private property is based on commutative justice, though the concerns of distributive justice are not irrelevant to it.

It is equally important to note just how different this view is to the modern conception. They are almost inversions of each other. Both

---

[86] Pufendorf, *On the Duty of Man and Citizen*, I 12 6.

views recognize that property is a mixture of the social and the interpersonal. But the modern view treats the former as primary and the latter as a kind of systematic fallout of the former. That is, according to the modern view, the foundation of property lies in distributive justice and the interpersonal elements of the law of property are understood to be designed to produce distributively just results, at least in the long term. So, for instance, the modern theorist might note that property can be transferred in accordance with the wills of the parties without any reference to distributive concerns, but she accounts for this rule by alleging (or by alleging that others have believed, or the like) that this rule tends to produce distributively just outcomes (understood as the maximization of welfare or whatever).

According to Pufendorf, on the other hand, it is the interpersonal that is primary and the distributive that is secondary. All the norms of property law are created by commutative justice, but those norms cannot operate to create property rights in the absence of the social contract that recognizes the creation of multital rights, a concern of distributive justice. These views are radically different.

In fact, this difference can be glimpsed in a passage quoted at the beginning of this chapter. Recall Pufendorf's claim that

whenever a person is received into a society an express or tacit agreement is entered into between the society and the member to be received, by which the society undertakes to give him a *pro rata* share of the goods which belong to the society as such, and the member, on his part, promises to undertake to bear his just share of the burdens which make for the preservation of the society as such.[87]

Note here the claim that society undertakes to give a pro rata share of its goods to each member of society. Now if, as the modern conception contends, private property were the creation of the state, then the result would be that property would need to be distributed on a pro rata basis. But there is, of course, no suggestion of this in Pufendorf. The reason for this is that, according to Pufendorf, private property is not the creation of the state. It is therefore not the state's to give. And the state must only provide citizens with a pro rata share of 'the goods which belong to the society as such'.

---

[87] Pufendorf, *Of the Law of Nature and Nations*, I.VII 9.

It must be said that, from the perspective of property law, Pufendorf's theory possesses a clear advantage over the alternative. This is because the law of property, certain partial statutory exceptions aside, ignores distributive concerns. First, the rules do not refer to issues of distributive justice and, secondly, they are oblivious to distributive outcomes. This is why it has taken a great deal of ingenuity on the part of modern theorists to make even plausible the notion that property law is concerned with distributive justice. Now, it is not impossible that the best way to produce distributive justice is to create a system whose rules disregard that form of justice, but Pufendorf's view that property law is simply not concerned with distributive justice is rather more plausible.

Against this, however, the modern theorist is sure to argue that certain features of the law of property cannot be understood without focusing on the distributive. This is because, so it is said, though those features do not refer to distributive justice on their face, analysis reveals that they are motivated by a concern for that form of justice.[88] But this is in reality entirely circular, because the only kind of explanation that this theorist will accept is one that refers to distributive justice. Hence, the only kind of analysis she ever embarks on is a distributive one. Small wonder, then, that she is convinced that these areas of the law are motivated by distributive concerns.

A further point that needs to be broached is that, although Pufendorf insists that property is based directly on commutative and not distributive justice, he accepts that the contribution of distributive justice to the existence of property rights has normative consequences. Because the coming into existence of property rights requires the social contract, those rights can be limited by the content of that contract. In effect, the state is able to place restrictions on the acquisition of property. For instance, it can determine whether certain kinds of animals can be the property of individuals[89] and can limit finder's property rights in treasure.[90]

6.2 The Consequences of Property Rights

Though the implication is fairly obvious, it is worth pointing out that once property rights are established, violations of those rights

---

[88] See, eg, the discussion of the rule against perpetuities in Morris and Barton Leach, *The Rule Against Perpetuities*, 15. The claim made there is that the rule exists because perpetuities are bad for the economy.
[89] Pufendorf, *Of the Law of Nature and Nations*, IV VI 5.
[90] Ibid, IV VI 13.

receive responses of the kind examined in section 3. Compensation for damage to property has no special interest for us in that regard, but of more concern is what is generally known as restitution for wrongs or disgorgement.

To adopt the usual example, imagine that I steal your car and use it as a taxi. Imagine that I thereby make a profit of £2,000 and that you suffer a loss of £500. For the reasons enunciated above, commutative justice demands that I compensate you for your loss. But what about my profit? Must I surrender that? The law's answer to that question is 'Yes', but it has been a notoriously difficult answer to justify. The general response has been to argue that considerations of deterrence provide the sought-for warrant. However, except in some sophisticated economic theories and despite its ubiquity, the suggestion is implausible. For one thing, this remedy often applies to torts of strict liability, where deterrence seems morally inappropriate. For another, the law does not seem to be trying to deter. If the law were trying to deter me from stealing cars and using them as taxis, then why on earth does it insist that I surrender my profit? What sort of a deterrent is that? Why not double damages, or triple, or why not simply kill me? This kind of reference to deterrence is at best the first part of a long explanation that is never presented.

Compare this with Pufendorf's explanation of why a person who profits from an even innocent taking must surrender that profit:

a thing, dominion over which I have lost neither by my consent nor by my misdeed or right of war, still belongs to me, as does also whatever comes of it. Therefore, when it has fallen into the hands of another, and he has profited by its consumption, his good faith, of course, renders him justly immune in person, yet he can on no excuse retain the profit which he has made, when I demand it, since that is a part, as it were, or the fruit still remaining, of a thing that belongs to me.[91]

Again, the modern conception causes us to look in the wrong place. Modern lawyers look for a justification in distributive justice. But the justification is much closer to hand. Because ownership of an object implies a right to the fruits of that object, eg to the profit made by

---

[91] Ibid, IV XIII 6. See also Pufendorf, *On the Duty of Man and Citizen*, I 6 6.

it, the owner is entitled to recover the profits from the converter. We might also say that because (legal) possession of an object entails a right that others do not possess the object without one's consent, when that right is violated, the profits of that violation belong to the owner.

7. The State

Though property is a partial exception, the discussion above examines laws that exist prior to the state. Like Aquinas, Pufendorf holds that the authority of the state is based partly on those laws.[92]

Though laws exist in the state of nature and though—as Pufendorf insists against Hobbes—human beings can generally be expected to respect those laws, Pufendorf accepts that without an efficient enforcement mechanism a sufficient number of individuals will be tempted to violate the law. Hence, there is a need to leave the state of nature and enter a society that possesses the physical power to implement its rules.[93]

Man, then, is an animal with an intense concern for his own preservation, needy by himself, incapable of protection without the help of his fellows, and very well fitted for the mutual provision of benefits. Equally, however, he is at the same time malicious, aggressive, easily provoked and as willing as he is able to inflict harm on others. The conclusion is: in order to be safe, it is necessary for him to be sociable; that is to join forces with men like himself and so conduct himself towards them that they are not given even a plausible excuse for harming him, but rather become willing to preserve and promote his advantages.[94]

Moreover, Pufendorf points out that even those who respect the law in the state of nature are prone to come into conflict, because without an independent judiciary, individuals must act as judges in their own cases.[95]

---

[92] See also Grotius, *Commentary on the Law of Prize and Booty*, 91–2 [40–40']; Grotius, *The Law of War and Peace*, I II I 5.
[93] Pufendorf, *Of the Law of Nature and Nations*, VII I 4, 8–9.
[94] Pufendorf, *On the Duty of Man and Citizen*, I 3 7.
[95] Pufendorf, *Of the Law of Nature and Nations*, VII I 10. In general, see Pufendorf, *On the Duty of Man and Citizen*, II 5.

Pufendorf also maintains that self-realization[96] and industry[97] are possible only in society and that the natural law demands that wrong-doers be punished, an injunction that can be realized completely only in a social condition.[98]

Those considerations involve distributive justice, but we can see that this is a long way from the modern idea that the state and distributive justice are at the basis of all political and legal norms. For Pufendorf, that thought has things almost entirely backwards.

---

[96] Pufendorf, *Of the Law of Nature and Nations*, VII I 1.
[97] Ibid, VII I 7.
[98] Ibid, VII I 11.

8

Kant

This chapter focuses on Kant's late work, the *Rechtslehre*. The title of this work is today usually translated as *Doctrine of Right*. However, for reasons that cannot be presented here, this translation seems to me inappropriate as it obscures the subject matter of Kant's investigation. Instead, I maintain that '*Recht*' in this and in many other contexts must be translated as 'law'. For that reason, I refer not to the *Doctrine of Right* but to the *Doctrine of Law*. I also generally translate '*Recht*' as 'law' in the following.

1. Justice and Law

In order to place Kant's theory in its historical context, two key problems must be confronted. First, we must examine Kant's use of the terminology we have employed in this book. As we will see, Kant' use is different from ours. Secondly, it is important to examine the distinction in Kant between *Recht* and *Gerechtigkeit*, between law and justice. I pursue these issues now.

1.1 Types of Justice

The key passage examining the forms of justice is the following.

A lawful condition is that relation of human beings among one another that contains the conditions under which alone everyone is able to *enjoy* his rights, and the formal condition under which this is possible in accordance with the idea of a will giving laws for everyone is called public justice.

With reference to either the possibility or the actuality or the necessity of possession of objects (the matter of choice) in accordance with laws, public justice can be divided into *protective justice* (*iustitia tutatrix*), *justice in acquiring from one another* (*iustitia commutativa* [commutative justice]), and *distributive justice* [*austeilende Gerechtigkeit*] (*iustitia distributiva*).—In these the law says, *first*, merely what conduct is intrinsically *lawful* in terms of its form (*lex iusti*); *second*, what [objects] are capable of being covered externally by law, in terms of their matter, that is, what way of being in possession is *lawful* (*lex iuridica*); *third*, what is the decision of a court in a particular case in accordance with the given law under which it falls, that is, what is *laid down as law* (*lex iustitiae*).[1]

The first thing to notice about this passage is that, like Pufendorf, Kant restricts commutative justice to contract or exchange. His term is '*wechselseitig erwerbende Gerechtigkeit*', which might be translated literally as the 'justice of reciprocal acquiring'. Also significant is Kant's explication of *austeilende Gerechtigkeit*, a term usually translated as distributive justice. As we can see, however, *austeilende Gerechtigkeit* has nothing to do with distributing benefits and burdens. It is rather focused on 'the decision of a court in a particular case in accordance with the given law under which it falls, that is, what is *laid down as law* (*lex iustitiae*)'.[2] A condition of *austeilende Gerechtigkeit*, then, is a society with public institutions that recognize and enforce people's legal rights. Thus, *austeilende Gerechtigkeit* is the *Gerechtigkeit* (justice) that relates to the way in which *Recht* (law) is *austeilend* (dispensed, administered, dealt out, etc). Accordingly, Kant uses neither 'commutative justice' nor 'distributive justice' as we have been doing. We return to this point in section 1.3.

1.2 *The Relationship between Law and Justice*

What is more, Kant does not treat justice as foundational in the way that his predecessors did. The central passage in this regard is again the one given above. A careful reading of this passage shows, contrary to our modern expectations, that Kant maintains that *Gerechtigkeit*

---

[1] Kant, 'The Metaphysics of Morals', 6:305–306. See also ibid, 6:267, 297, 306, 317, 323.

[2] Ibid, 6:305–306.

(justice) gets its content from *Recht* (law) and not *vice versa*. This is because *Recht* is derived directly from the fundamental moral principle that applies in this context, the Universal Principle of Law (UPL) (examined below), and *Gerechtigkeit* is understood as the area of morality that relates to realizing *Recht* in practice in accordance with public law. Hence, the condition of public justice is the condition in which the law and the rights that people possess receive positive recognition. Similarly, protective justice is that part of public justice that protects what the law determines to be one's property and justice in acquiring from one another is that part of public justice that protects the way in which the law determines property should be acquired and exchanged.

For Kant, then, it is to get things backwards to say that the law is based on justice. This is a genuine departure from the traditional view as we have been exploring it.

1.3 Reconciling the Terminology

The differences noted above are important, but it is also important not to be distracted by terminology. Certainly, the differences point to the fact that Kant's understanding of the foundations of political and legal theory is distinct from his predecessors. We examine Kant's views in this regard shortly. But this is quite consistent with the idea that Kant adheres to the traditional view. That is, despite Kant's definitions, it remains possible that his theory adheres to Figures T1–T3 rather than M1–M3. Most significantly, it remains possible that Kant's theory is grounded in commutative justice as we have defined it in Chapter 4.

As in the previous chapter, then, we use the terms 'commutative justice' and 'distributive justice' in our, rather than Kant's, sense. This is appropriate, because we are tracing the history of ideas, not the history of terminologies.

2. The Foundations of Law

For Kant, all law has its ultimate source in the fundamental moral principle known as the Universal Principle of Law (UPL): 'Any action is *lawful* if it can coexist with everyone's freedom in accordance with a universal law, or if on its maxim the freedom of choice of each can coexist with everyone's freedom in accordance with a universal law.'[3] This is often expressed by saying that the UPL calls for maximum freedom consistent with equal freedom for all.

The immediate consequence of this principle is that actions that interfere with someone's freedom are unlawful unless they themselves prevent violations of freedom (an issue examined below). As Kant puts it, if 'my action or my condition generally can coexist with the freedom of everyone in accordance with a universal law, whoever hinders me in it does me *wrong*; for this hindrance (resistance) cannot coexist with freedom in accordance with a universal law'.[4] Accordingly, the UPL generates a sphere of protected liberty in which individuals must be left alone (unless they choose otherwise, of course).

A further, and also crucial, consequence of the UPL is that it generates what Kant calls the innate right, the right we have simply in virtue of being persons. '*Freedom* (independence from being constrained by another's choice), insofar as it can coexist with the freedom of every other in accordance with a universal law, is the only original right belonging to every man by virtue of his humanity.'[5] Kant also explains that the innate right has three immediate consequences: human beings possess innate equality, have the quality of being their own masters, and are beyond reproach.

Innate equality refers to the 'independence from being bound by others to more than one can in turn bind them'.[6] As we might say, people have equal power vis-à-vis one another. Being one's own master follows from one's independence of others: one is free from the authority of others except in accordance with the rule of law.[7] And finally, being beyond reproach entails that a person has and must be regarded as having done no wrong unless he violates another's rights. Hence, people are by nature innocent and, therefore, cannot be interfered with unless they violate the rights of others.[8]

These considerations lead directly to a right—ie to what we would call a privilege—to coerce others when they threaten the rights of

---

[3] Ibid, 6:230–231.
[4] Ibid.
[5] Ibid, 6:237.
[6] Ibid. These claims must be understood to *exclude* the sovereign. The position of the sovereign is explored in section 6.
[7] Ibid, 6:238.
[8] Ibid.

others. As Kant puts it 'Right is connected with an authorization to use coercion'.[9]

Resistance that counteracts the hindering of an effect promotes this effect and is consistent with it. Now whatever is wrong is a hindrance to freedom in accordance with universal laws. But coercion is a hindrance or resistance to freedom. Therefore, if a certain use of freedom is itself a hindrance to freedom in accordance with universal laws (i.e., wrong), coercion that is opposed to this (as a *hindering of a hindrance to freedom*) is consistent with freedom in accordance with universal laws; that is, it is right. Hence there is connected with right by the principle of contradiction an authorization to coerce someone who infringes upon it.[10]

So if I strike another, that is a hindrance to that person's freedom and is therefore wrong. But if you prevent me from striking another—even if that necessitates striking me—then that is properly characterized, not as a hindrance of freedom, but as a hindering of a hindrance of freedom and is thus not wrong.

It is often thought that a slight of hand is involved in this move. In fact, however, that appearance is the result of deep misunderstanding concerning actions of this kind. Take a simple case. *A* strikes at *B*, provoking *B* to strike back in self-defence. According to a common thought (at least amongst academic philosophers and lawyers), *A*'s and *B*'s actions are per se morally equivalent. Morally speaking, they are actions of the same kind. But *B*'s act is excused or justified because of the circumstances in which it is performed or the way in which it was motivated.[11] Hence, it has been suggested that the central question in this area is: 'How does one provide a theoretically illuminating explanation of why considerations such as self-defence are moral justifications for conduct that would otherwise be immoral?'[12] But no one except philosophers and lawyers think in this way. Generally, people do not think that *A*'s and *B*'s actions are even prima facie morally equivalent.

The problem here is a very deep one. Because (for reasons examined in the third part of this book) we have learnt to think of the law exclusively as something created and imposed on us by the state, we

---

[9] Ibid, 6:231.
[10] Ibid.
[11] Hart, *The Concept of Law*, 179.
[12] Ladenson, 'In Defense of a Hobbesian Conception of Law', 36.

tend to think of legal descriptions of actions as conceptually posterior to their proper moral categorization. Let me explain.

What we need is an answer to the question: why does the law say that *A*'s action was wrongful but *B*'s action was permissible? It is tempting to answer this question by saying that *A*'s action was an assault and an intended battery but *B*'s action was self-defence. But it is generally thought that this answer will not do, because the reference to the legal categories assault, battery, and self-defence render the answer circular. On this view, to say that *A*'s action was an assault and an intended battery is just to say that it was wrongful in a certain way, and to say that *B*'s action was self-defence is just to say that it was permissible because it fell under a certain description. Neither idea actually justifies anything and so provides no answer to our question. We will not have an answer until we know why *A*'s action is classified as an assault and an intended battery and why that makes it wrongful and why *B*'s action is classified as self-defence and why that makes it permissible.

It is also worth noting that these thoughts are encouraged by the structure of the substantive law. Broadly speaking, an action for battery proceeds in four stages. In the first three, the plaintiff must prove that the defendant (i) intentionally; and (ii) directly; (iii) made contact with her body. In the fourth stage, the defendant is permitted to raise any appropriate defences, including the defence of self-defence. This structure can suggest that defences are excuses or justifications. On the face of it, the idea is that a person who successfully relies on the defence of self-defence committed at least a prima facie wrong, but has a reason why she should be exonerated.[13] As it were, *B*'s claim is said to be: 'Yes, what I did was wrong, but you can't blame me for doing it' or 'Yes, what I did was wrong, but it was justified in the circumstances.'

But this way of thinking about the issue is wrongheaded, and Kant's theory helps us to see why. Imagine two people agreeing to shake hands. In these circumstances, these individuals intentionally touch each other, consenting to that touching. Now, the law conceptualizes consent as a defence, but in this situation no one thinks that the parties committed a prima facie wrong that can be excused or justified because of the existence of consent. A person who consensually shakes

---

[13] Again, see Hart, *The Concept of Law*, 179.

another's hand would not defend his action by saying: 'Yes, what I did was wrong, but you can't blame me for doing it' or 'Yes, what I did was wrong, but the circumstances justify it.' On the contrary, because the touching was consensual, no wrong is present. The 'defence' does not provide an excuse or justification; it shows that the action was not in any way wrongful.

The same is true regarding self-defence. Self-defence is not an excuse or justification. A person who strikes another in defence of herself (or others) does not commit a wrong that needs to be excused or justified; she does not commit any wrong at all. This is because legal categories such as assault, battery, and self-defence relate to norms that are independent of the state. Those norms—laws in Kant's terminology—relate to fundamental features of the moral character of our actions.

When *A* aims to strike *B*, he intends to perform an action that will interfere with *B*'s freedom. The performance of that action would be wrongful. And that means that *A* is not at liberty to perform the action. So, when *B* strikes *A* to prevent that action from occurring, she does not prevent *A* doing anything that he is at liberty to do. *B*'s action, then, is not wrongful. Accordingly, *A*'s and *B*'s action are not of the same character differentiated because only *B* has an excuse or justification. They are not of the same character. This is how everyone except some philosophers and lawyers see the issue. A person who kills in self-defence is not seen as an excused or justified wrongdoer.

At this point, it is important to emphasize that the UPL and the innate right are not principles of distributive justice. Kant makes this plain by introducing them long before he examines the state. In other words, the UPL and the innate right apply in the state of nature. It is also clear from the content of these principles that they are not distributive. Rather, they point to moral entitlements that we hold simply in virtue of being (moral) persons. Moreover, those entitlements are held by individuals as individuals and they are held as against all other individuals as individuals. And we hold those rights as against every other individual individually. In other words, the rights have the structure of commutative, not distributive, justice; they correspond to Figure J2 not J1.

With these points in mind, we can examine the innate right in more detail.

3. Bodily Integrity

The first and most important consequence of the innate right and its three corollaries is that it grounds a right to bodily integrity. Clearly, if someone uses or damages my body without my consent, then I have been 'constrained by another's choice'.[14]

Before continuing, it is important to emphasize that the innate right does not prohibit unconsented to damage of another's body because it prohibits unconsented to damage per se. In fact, the innate right is indifferent to damage per se. The right is directly concerned only with freedom. Of course, however, this means that the innate right prohibits unconsented to damage in most cases, but that is because, ordinarily, unconsented to damage of another's body violates that person's freedom. Damage to one's expectations, plans, or economic interests is another matter, however.

From this, it follows that consensual damage is not wrongful (in the absence of positive law to the contrary) and hence does not need to be excused. Also significant is that the innate right can be violated without damage occurring. This is why the torts that deal with intentional invasions of bodily integrity—the torts of trespass to the person—do not require the plaintiff to prove that she suffered any damage. In the language of the law, the torts are actionable per se. For instance, if one person kisses another without that person's consent, then she can be guilty of a battery even though no damage, physical or even emotional, is caused.[15] As far as liability is concerned, the issue is the interference with the plaintiff's freedom, ie with his ability to determine the use of his body for himself, and not with the presence or absence of any factual detriment.[16]

Also worth noting is that the right to bodily integrity stretches beyond the law of battery and the innate right stretches beyond the right to bodily integrity. An example of the first point concerns the tort of assault. An assault occurs if a person creates in another an apprehension of an imminent battery, ie an apprehension that she is about to be touched without her consent. It is therefore natural to think that

---

[14] Kant, 'The Metaphysics of Morals', 6:237. Naturally, as just explained, this follows only if the use or damage was not the result of the prevention of my interfering with someone else's freedom.

[15] *Police v Bannin* [1991] 2 NZLR 237.

[16] This issue can, of course, be relevant for assessing the quantum of damages, but that is a separate issue. That matter has been examined in Chapters 6 and 7.

this tort protects bodily integrity, even though an assault can occur without the plaintiff being touched. This is because it is plausible to think that the right to bodily integrity extends beyond the limits of one's own body, so that, for instance, being put in fear of physical injury constitutes an invasion of that right. An example of the second point involves the law of false imprisonment, which protects freedom of movement. Clearly, that too is an aspect of the innate right. To deprive me of the ability to move around is to constrain me by your choice and violates my innate right.

The next question—the question asked at this point in the previous two chapters—concerns the law's responses to violations of the innate right. Unfortunately, however, that issue cannot be examined here. This is because, curiously, with only the partial exception of punishment,[17] Kant ignores the issue. We cannot be sure why this is. We do know that the production of the *Doctrine of Law* was rushed. It may well be that Kant put the issue aside because he thought that it had been properly dealt with by his predecessors. It may be that that was just not his chosen subject matter.[18] It is impossible to be sure. Accordingly, I ignore the issue also.

4. Contract

Kant's discussion of contract is founded on notions taken from the tradition examined in earlier chapters. It begins with an analysis of the 'possession of another's choice'.[19] This beginning is noteworthy. He does not start by asking: why does the state recognize and enforce contracts? He begins by focusing on a norm that holds as between individuals. For Kant, the essence of contract is not to be found in the idea that it is a system of regulation for the common good, the prevalent modern view, but in the much more common-sense notion that it lies in the interaction between the contracting parties.

Contract, we are told, is about 'possession of another's choice'. Of course, Kant does not mean that one can possess another's choice

---

[17] Kant, 'The Metaphysics of Morals', 6:331–337. And it should be noted here that Kant's examination is of 'the right to punish and to grant clemency', not of the justification and point of punishment.

[18] I owe this observation to Jacob Weinrib.

[19] Kant, 'The Metaphysics of Morals', 6:271.

physically. Rather, the possession is what Kant calls intelligible, a moral or legal possession that he introduces in his discussion of property.[20] In other words, Kant's exploration of contract is based on the idea that contracts transfer rights between the parties, and it attempts to analyse the nature of that transfer.

This is important because, as we saw in section 5 of Chapter 7 and as is examined in detail in Chapter 12, the modern view is entirely different and as a result has difficulty explaining basic features of the law such as the availability of the remedies of expectation damages and specific performance. For Kant, like Pufendorf, these problems simply do not arise. They are pseudo-problems that surface only if we forget about the genuine moral foundations of contract law in commutative justice.

Kant then maintains that contractual rights cannot be acquired originally or as the result of abandonment.[21] This is to say that contract 'can take place only by *transferring*',[22] an idea we have already seen in Pufendorf. Kant adds that in contract the parties form a 'united will'.[23] This means that the effect of contract formation is the simultaneous transfer of rights between the parties. For instance, if you and I agree that I will sell you one of my horses for £1,000, the result is not that I abandon a right to one of my horses that you then acquire and that you abandon a right to some of your money that I then pick up. Rather, when the agreement is formed you gain the right that I give you a horse at the moment that I lose the right to retain it (ie when I gain an obligation to give it to you) and I gain the right that you give me £1,000 at the moment that you lose the right to retain it (ie when you gain an obligation to give £1,000 to me).

There is, of course, much more to be said about Kant's theory. But for our purposes the crucial points have been made. In short, for Kant, contract is a matter of commutative justice, not only in its operation but also in its foundations.

---

[20] Ibid, 6:245.
[21] Ibid, 6:271.
[22] Ibid.
[23] Ibid, 6:272.

5. Property

Kant's theory of property begins with an analysis of 'How to have something external as one's own'.[24] Again, this start is noteworthy. The question he sets out to answer is not 'Why does the state permit the ownership of property?' but 'How can individuals gain legal control of objects?' Again, the focus is on individuals, not on states or communities.

The theory is complicated. Thankfully, however, we need not deal with the details here. As in previous and following chapters, our aim is not to assess the details of the accounts examined, but to explicate the general nature of those accounts and, eventually, to evaluate the kinds of approaches they present.

What is clear is that Kant's position is a mixture of conceptual analysis and normative argument. Though it is often overlooked, the conceptual analysis is important. Unlike his predecessors, Kant spends a great deal of time attempting to elucidate what property actually is. This approach is frequently sneered at today, but that is certainly unjustified. Kant's desire to understand what he is trying to justify before trying to justify it makes perfect sense.

This analysis leaves us with two related definitions of property:

> that outside me is externally mine which it could be a wrong (an infringement upon my freedom which can coexist with the freedom of everyone in accordance with a universal law) to prevent me from using as I please.[25]

> something external is mine if I would be wronged by being disturbed in my use of it even though I am not in possession of it (not holding the object).[26]

These definitions combine to form what is now a familiar understanding of the consequences of property. If I have property in an object, then I am entitled to use the object in any way I choose as long as that use is consistent with the rights of others, and others are under an obligation not to use the object unless I have consented to their doing so.

---

[24] Ibid, 6:245.
[25] Ibid, 6:248–249.
[26] Ibid, 6:249.

Like Pufendorf, Kant presents a theory of original acquisition. The theory consists of three steps.[27] The first is called *apprehension*. This is the taking of physical possession of an object so that the object is under the possessor's physical control. The second step is *giving a sign*. This involves declaring one's physical possession of the object and also indicating that one intends to exclude others from the object. This could mean marking the object or its boundaries or demonstrating physical control of the object. The final step is *appropriation*: 'the act of a general will (in idea) giving an external law through which everyone is bound to agree with my choice'.[28] I examine this further below.

At this point, the key feature of this discussion is the absence of distributive justice. For Kant, property relations arise when individuals act in certain ways with respect to unowned objects, acts which generate obligations in others to respect the actor's rights in the object. It is true that Kant insists that one must give a sign in order to acquire a piece of property, but this does not mean that the norms here are public in the sense that they relate to public law or the state.[29] In fact, Kant does not use the term 'public' in this context. The idea is that, as acquisition generates obligation in others, acquisition must be accompanied by an event that is accessible to those who will come to have the obligations. In that sense, and only in that sense, must giving a sign be public. These issues belong to commutative, not distributive, justice.

But recall Kant's claim that original acquisition requires 'the act of a general will'.[30] What does this mean? It means, as Kant explains elsewhere in the *Doctrine of Law*, that property rights can exist only in the civil condition.[31] This point involves a reference to the state, but as with the analysis of Pufendorf's theory in the previous chapter, that reference is not what it might appear. In other words, Kant's theory is not based on distributive justice; it is what I have called a mixed conception.

Like Pufendorf, Kant maintains that a system of property rights exists in the state of nature. However, also like Pufendorf, Kant maintains that individual property rights cannot come into existence in the state of nature, because their creation requires something that cannot exist in that state. In Chapter 7, we saw that Pufendorf maintains that

---

[27] Ibid, 6:258–259.
[28] Ibid, 6:259.
[29] Against: Byrd and Hruschka, *Kant's Doctrine of Right*, 30–31.
[30] Kant, 'The Metaphysics of Morals', 6:259.
[31] Ibid, 6:255–257, 264–266.

this problem arises from the multital nature of property rights. This is also the problem Kant identifies, though, unlike Pufendorf, Kant puts his finger on the precise nature of this difficulty.

The original acquisition of property creates rights in the owner and obligations in others. But as far as the first two steps of original acquisition are concerned, that form of acquisition is an entirely unilateral activity. And that is a problem. Without some special justification, a unilateral act by one person cannot create obligations in another—let us call this 'the unilateral act problem'.[32] But that special justification cannot exist in the state of nature. Accordingly, property rights cannot exist there.

As in Chapter 7, however, it is important to note that the unilateral act problem does not relate to the foundations of property. Moreover, though the unilateral act problem can be solved only by considerations of distributive justice, that does not mean that property is itself based on distributive justice.

First, as Kant rightly identifies, the unilateral act problem is a problem for commutative, not distributive, justice. The reason a unilateral act cannot create obligations in others is not because the alternative would fail to give people a fair go in life vis-à-vis all others. It is because, in Kant's language, it would violate the principle of being one's own master, a principle that belongs to commutative justice. The problem can be solved only by distributive justice, but that is another matter. Secondly, the idea is that property would exist in the state of nature were it not for the unilateral act problem. This means that the norms of property law are already in place in the state of nature, though no property can exist there (merely) because the unilateral act problem prevents that occurring. In other words, the unilateral act problem is not a problem with the foundations or structure of property law; it is rather a defeasable barrier to the actual acquisition of individual property rights. Kant expresses this by saying that property is provisional but not conclusive in the state of nature.[33]

To summarize, in the state of nature, legal norms that relate to objects exist, those norms divide objects into owned and unowned, and those norms also indicate how unowned objects would become owned, ie would be acquired *were* unilateral acts able to impose obligation. That, however, is impossible. So, though there can be no property

---

[32] Ibid, 6:256. Note that the problem here is the existence of the obligation, not the inability to make use of the object. Compare Sage, 'Original Acquisition and Ulilateralism'.
[33] Kant, 'The Metaphysics of Morals', 6:256–257, 264–266.

rights in the state of nature, a *system* of property rights exists there. Or to put this in the language used in Chapter 7, like Pufendorf, Kant maintains that property rights are latent in the state of nature.

Why, then, do property rights become conclusive in the civil condition? This is perhaps the most difficult aspect of Kant's theory, but perhaps the best strategy is to argue that recognition of property is necessary (not sufficient) to establish a state that respects the UPL and the innate right. Recall that the second of these principles calls for '*Freedom* (independence from being constrained by another's choice), insofar as it can coexist with the freedom of every other in accordance with a universal law'.[34] It is apparent that at least some property is essential in this regard. Individuals with no resources to which they have access as of right are unjustifiably dependent on others. It is important to note that this position is quite compatible with the claims that the need for independence may not justify current property holdings and that property can be used to make individuals dependant on others. Those are separate issues.

6. The State

Kant's theory of the foundations of the state also follows the pattern noticed in earlier chapters. That foundation is not found directly in distributive justice but in the need for a public authority to exist with institutions such as legislatures, courts, police, and so on, so that the freedom demanded by the UPL can be realized.

Kant's argument relies on what has now become known as the republican, as opposed to liberal, conception of freedom.[35] According to this view, freedom is to be understood as the absence of domination. As Philip Pettit explains, 'One agent dominates another if and only if they have a certain power over that other, in particular a power of interference on an arbitrary basis...They have sway over the other, in the old phrase, and the sway is arbitrary.'[36] And domination results in lack of freedom because

the power-victim acts in the relevant area by the leave, explicit or implicit, of the power-bearer; it means that they live at the mercy of that person,

---
[34] Ibid, 6:237.
[35] Skinner, *Liberty Before Liberalism*; Pettit, *Republicanism*.
[36] Pettit, *Republicanism*, 52.

that they are in the position of a dependant or debtor or something of the kind. If there is common knowledge of that implication, as there usually will be, it follows that the power-victim cannot enjoy the psychological status of an equal; they are in the position where fear and deference will be the normal order of the day, not the frankness that goes with intersubjective equality.[37]

Given this account of freedom, it is impossible to be free in the state of nature. This is because, even if others in one's community allow one to live as one chooses, and hence to that extent one is autonomous, that autonomy is in the hands of one's community. In the state of nature, one is unable to insist on even this autonomy as a matter of right. The autonomy exists only if the members of one's community choose to allow it to exist. Even if they do, one does not possess the autonomy demanded by the UPL. Hence, Kant maintains that genuine freedom can exist only in a civil condition that governs through law and that insists that individuals enjoy independence.[38]

Note, as above, that the claim is not that the civil condition guarantees independence or that the civil condition cannot be used to make people dependent. Neither of those claims is true. The idea is merely that the civil condition is a necessary condition for independence.

Though the details are of course different, so far the structure of Kant's theory of the state closely resembles those examined in earlier chapters. But at this point we see a clear difference. For Pufendorf, the chief function of the state is to protect the rights that exist in the state of nature. For Kant, however, the function of the state is to realize the moral imperatives consequent to the UPL. Now certainly, in the state of nature that principle generates private rights such as the right to bodily integrity, as we have seen. And so part of the justification for the state lies in its being a necessary condition for the protection of those rights. But as we have also seen, the UPL cannot be satisfied in the state of nature because people cannot be genuinely free in that condition. Crucially, there is no suggestion that this is only because there is no enforcement mechanism for private rights in the state of nature.

The primary function of the state, recall, is to ensure freedom, ie the absence of domination. As the quotations from Pettit above are

---

[37] Ibid, 63–64.
[38] Kant, 'The Metaphysics of Morals', 6:305–318.

sufficient to reveal, this cannot be a matter merely of recognizing and enforcing a certain set of private rights. Rather, the scope of the injunction incorporates what we understand by political life in general. It relates, for example, to economic, health, environmental, and educational policy.

To take just one example, we can be sure that children will not grow up to enjoy a life free from domination if they are not sufficiently educated. Individuals who lack education will be vulnerable to those who have and they will depend on the good will of others in order to realize even their basic ends. Hence, the UPL calls for all children to receive a level of education sufficient to enable them to live independent lives. But this is not because they have a private right to be educated. There could be no such right. That right must be held against the state.

Moreover, Kant realizes that setting up the state means giving it authority to make law, and that authority has widespread normative consequences. In particular, the state must have authority to make law that interferes with individuals, there being no other way of realizing the demands imposed by the UPL. And Kant recognizes that the state can have authority only if its decisions are binding regardless of their justice.[39]

The reason for this is simple. The claim that the state's laws are binding only if they are just has practical significance only if there is some body with the authority to judge the compatibility of the laws with justice. And that body cannot be part of the state. If it were, then the judgement of this body would not be about the authority but the content of the state's laws (this is what happens in jurisdictions that permit judicial review of legislation, for instance). Accordingly, the body must be the people themselves. But if it is for the people to determine whether the state's laws have authority, then the state has no authority. In other words, that condition is the state of nature in disguise.

In this regard, Kant can be understood to be charting a middle course between theories of the kind proposed by Rousseau and Fichte.[40] All three philosophers held that rights (ie law) exist in the state of nature. But Rousseau maintained that all such rights were

---

[39] Ibid, 313–314.
[40] The *Foundations of Natural Right* was published in 1796 and the *Rechtslehre* in 1797, but it is in any case not important whether Kant was influenced in any way by Fichte.

surrendered in the social contract.[41] Against this, Fichte replied that if that were so then the contract could not be meaningful. As we see Locke stressing in Chapter 10, people enter the social contract in order to have their rights protected, and so it is senseless to think that they surrender those rights in that contract.[42] That is a powerful argument, but Rousseau's position was not unmotivated. He argued that if citizens in the civil condition retained the rights that they possessed in the state of nature, then there would be no body with the legitimate authority to determine disputes about those rights. This is because those rights would be held, inter alia, against any such body; as it were, a person who believes that his pre-social contract rights are being violated but who is told otherwise by a court, by the king, or by whoever is entitled to say: 'But the social contract did not give you authority to violate my rights, and that is what your decision calls for.'[43] But if that is the case, then there is no practical authority. That too is a powerful argument. Kant's solution to this dilemma is to argue with Locke and Fichte that people enter the social contract in order to protect their natural rights, rights that carry over into the civil condition, but also, dealing with the problem noticed by Rousseau, that a consequence of the civil condition is that the sovereign has the authority to abrogate those rights.[44]

In light of the above, we can see that the move from private to public law, or the move from the state of nature to the civil condition, involves a shift from purely commutative to distributive concerns. With respect to education, for instance, we saw that a right to education must be held against the state or community in general. Moreover, in giving content to the right, attention must be paid to the *relative* educational levels of citizens. Imagine, for instance, a society in which almost all received doctoral degrees. In such a community, providing free education to secondary level would probably be insufficient to ensure that children grew up to be independent. Similarly, it is not simply poverty that leaves people open to domination, but also great disparities in wealth. The issue there, then, is the distribution of

---

[41] Rousseau, 'On the Social Contract', I VI 6.
[42] Fichte, *Foundations of Natural Right*, 205. Incidentally, Hobbes gets around this difficulty by denying that the rights exist in the state of nature at all.
[43] Rousseau, 'On the Social Contract', I VI 7.
[44] Of course, this does not imply that the sovereign ought to or is morally permitted to do so. The issue concerns authority, not obligation.

wealth in society. When attention is turned to the civil condition, the UPL relates to all of these issues.

But that does not make the UPL a principle of distributive justice in the sense in which modern thinkers would normally understand that phrase. The UPL has distributive consequences. More accurately, the UPL provides the foundation for distributive justice. But it is not itself a principle *of* distributive justice. On the contrary, it is a principle of commutative justice. For Kant, then, though the forms of justice may be independent qua forms, normatively speaking the commutative is anterior to the distributive.

7. The Modern Conception and Kant's Theory

It is my task in this book to contrast the modern and the traditional views and to show how the former clouds our understanding of political and legal reality. I have been doing this in the previous chapters and continue in the following. But I have also noted that the modern conception so powerfully affects us that we find it difficult to understand the traditional and are often unable even to see it in the works of the traditional thinkers. The best example of this of which I am aware concerns Kant. Accordingly, I examine it now.

Before I begin, however, it is important to say that I am somewhat uncomfortable with the following discussion. This is because I am required to criticize a valuable book. But it is the very value of the book that makes the criticism necessary. The book under consideration, Sharon Byrd and Joachim Hruschka's *Kant's Doctrine of Right*, is one of the best explorations of Kant's theory. One of the reasons for this is that its authors take great care over the theory they examine. For instance, they spend much time placing Kant's terminology and ideas in their historical context. They are most concerned to see the world though Kant's eyes and to communicate that vision to the reader. This is much to be welcomed.

Given that, the following passage in which Byrd and Hruschka outline the structure of their book must come as a shock.

Chapter 1 [of our book] begins with §41 of the *Doctrine of Right*. Section 41 contains the culmination of Kant's theory of private law and prepares for the transition to public law with the postulate of public law in

§42. Because §41 represents the totality of Kant's preceding ideas in the *Doctrine of Right* and maps the chart for moving forward, it is especially difficult to unravel but equally crucial to understand. In Chapter 1 we provide a rough descriptive structure for understanding §41 and thus for understanding the basic system of rights Kant portrays. Section 41 tells us what a juridical state (*rechtlicher Zustand—status iuridicus*) is, and contrasts the juridical state to the non-juridical state or the state of nature. We thus first discuss what a juridical state is for Kant, giving its formal and substantive criteria.[45]

Why, after all the care given to other issues, does the book start by examining section 41? If we are trying to see the world though Kant's eyes, why not start where Kant starts, with section 1?

Byrd and Hruschka's answer is implied in the above. Section 41 deals with what they take to be the foundational issue: the state. But the point is this: if Kant thought that the state was the foundational issue, he would have examined it in section 1, not section 41. More generally, the fact that he explores private law before turning to public law reveals that he thought that order appropriate. The task of the interpreter is to discover why he had that thought. Byrd and Hruschka do not do this. Instead, they force Kant's theory into the confines of the modern conception.

Their desire to make Kant's theory fit the modern view, colours the interpretation Byrd and Hruschka provide. One crucial example of this concerns their presentation of Kant's views regarding private law.

First, they maintain that 'Kant characterizes what he means by public law as follows: "The totality of statutes that need to be announced to the public in order to create a juridical state is *public law*."'[46] They go on to say that:

Initially one might assume Kant is referring only to constitutional law. This assumption, however, overlooks the fact that securing individual rights is the central purpose of the juridical state. Accordingly, all law relating to those rights must also be made public in order to create a juridical state. Kant's notion of public law thus includes private law governing our individual property, contractual, and family rights, constitutional law, public and

---

[45] Byrd and Hruschka, *Kant's Doctrine of Right*, 5.
[46] Ibid, 29. Quotation from Kant, 'The Metaphysics of Morals', 6:311.

administrative law (in the modern sense of public and administrative law). Consequently, if we are in a juridical state, then for Kant *all law* applicable in this state is *public* law.[47]

This argument relies on an assumption. The assumption is that 'The totality of statutes that need to be announced to the public in order to create a juridical state' include ones that relate to private law. To take an example, the idea is that a juridical state protects the right to bodily integrity and so the state must produce a statute that protects that right. That is a matter of public law.

A first problem here concerns the term 'statute'. As this is Kant's term, we should not understand this to be restricted to Acts of the legislature but to include decisions of courts in common law (including *ius commune*) jurisdictions. That is of little concern. The second problem, however, is fundamental. The assumption is false. Its role in the argument relies on a further assumption that belongs to the modern, but not traditional, conception.

A juridical, or at least a just, state will protect rights such as bodily integrity. But it follows from this that the state must pass 'statutes' protecting this right only if all law is the product of the state. That is the modern view, but it is not Kant's. It is not the view of any natural lawyer. Witness also Byrd and Hruschka's claim that 'before a court can use natural law, it has to be drafted (and made binding)'.[48] Here, Byrd and Hruschka reveal their modern (and indeed modern German—the common law and much of the law of the *ius commune* did not need to be drafted to be binding)[49] prejudices. There is no reason to think, and every reason to doubt, that Kant shared this view. In the *Doctrine of Law*, the private law is established before section 41 and there is no suggestion that it requires 'drafting' to be given force. The aspects of the private law discussed in Part I of the *Doctrine of Law* belong to the natural law. They are binding unless contradicted by positive law (see section 6).

Consider also the claim that 'Kant's notion of private law in the non-juridical state is thus different from the modern notion of private law as well'.[50] With reservations to be noted shortly, Byrd and Hruschka take the modern notion to be 'that public law governs the

---

[47] Byrd and Hruschka, *Kant's Doctrine of Right*, 30.
[48] Ibid, 34.
[49] I am aware that Byrd is American. But that only makes the passage stranger.
[50] Byrd and Hruschka, *Kant's Doctrine of Right*, 31.

relationship of private parties to the state, whereas private law governs the relationship of private parties to each other'.[51] According to Byrd and Hruschka, Kant's understanding of private law concerns not this but 'law that does not yet exist in the sense that it has not yet been made public. It is the law we can derive *a priori* from reason, but about which individuals will potentially disagree due to human weakness and being influenced by what they would like to think is right.'[52] But in his discussion of private law, Kant considers precisely what we regard as (elements of) private law—bodily integrity (or at least the innate right), property, contract, etc—and, as we have seen, he does so in a way that concentrates on 'the relationship of private parties to each other'. Here, the modern conception is shrouding Byrd and Hruschka's view of Kant's theory.

Also significant is Byrd and Hruschka's at first astounding claim that 'the distinction between public and private law is not predominant in Anglo-American legal thought'.[53] This may be true of American law, but it is not so of the law of the Commonwealth (ie Australia, Canada, England, and New Zealand). Nevertheless, it seems to me that Byrd and Hruschka are basically right. This is because, though Commonwealth lawyers speak all the time of the distinction between private and public law, they have no idea how to draw that distinction. This is because of their adoption of the modern conception, an issue explored throughout this book but especially in Chapter 12.

Byrd and Hruschka attribute what they label the modern understanding of the distinction between private and public law to German law. But in this they are mistaken. Their ascription of the notion to German law is fine. The mistake is in thinking that it is the *modern* view. It is not modern; it is traditional. And it survives most vividly in German law because, as we see in Chapter 9, much to its credit, that law was the last major legal system to be influenced by the modern view.

[51] Ibid, 29.
[52] Ibid, 31.
[53] Ibid, 29.

PART III:

Forgetting

In the first two parts of this book, we examined the growth and establishment of the traditional view. We are about to set off on a new path. Part III starts by exploring a new beginning in the understanding of political and legal reality. It is a beginning that quite self-consciously attempts to raze the tradition to the ground in order to construct an entirely new model. That beginning is the most powerful statement of the modern view.[1]

This statement is so powerful, so overwhelming, that although some of the theorists subject to it attempted to claw their way back to the tradition, they were unable to do so. We examine one of those theorists also.

The progenitor of this model—I am, of course, talking of Hobbes—was a man of extraordinary ability. However, that alone does not explain the impact of his theory. On the contrary, the ground was prepared for it by historical events that shifted attention from individuals to the state.[2] These events were, unsurprisingly, ones that concerned the state. But it was also crucial that they concerned the concerns individuals had for the state. I take two examples to explain this idea.

The Thirty Years' War (1618–1648) in the Holy Roman Empire and the Eighty Years' War (1568–1648) between Spain and the Dutch Republic were ended by the Peace of Westphalia, a series of treaties between the warring parties. The wars had been fought for many

---

[1] The claim is not that it is the first statement of the modern view. Hobbes' theory is chosen, not because no antecedents to it can be found, but because those antecedents are not as important as Hobbes' theory.

[2] Of course, these historical events affected Hobbes and the production of his theory also.

of the usual bad reasons, but religion was to the forefront, specifically the clash between Catholicism and Protestantism. The main plank in the solution to this problem was the recognition of principle set out in the Peace of Augsburg of 1555, which dictated that each ruler or *Fürst* had the right to determine the religion of his territory (as long as he chose Catholicism, Lutheranism, or Calvinism). The peace also recognized some limited freedom of religion for individuals in states, but it is important not to see that through modern eyes. The concern was not generally understood as one for the liberty of the individuals concerned but for respect for the religion itself. In other words, the idea was not that people should be able to follow their own beliefs, but that the persecution of people of one faith would insult the religion of the *Fürsten* of that faith, and so had to be prevented.

This is usefully compared with the so-called Glorious Revolution that occurred in England in 1688. This revolution was also concerned with religion, but its cause and resolution were rather different. The problem that led to the Glorious Revolution was not a religious dispute between sovereigns. It was that the King, James II, had a religion of which the populace disapproved (he was Catholic). The result was that James was replaced by William III and Mary II as joint monarchs—both of whom were Protestants (though William was of the Dutch Reformed Church and hence a non-conformist)—and, through the Bill of Rights Act 1689 and Act of Settlement 1701, any future Catholic monarchs were prevented.

The difference to which I want to draw attention is the place of citizens in the latter events. The difference can be expressed in this way. The Peace of Westphalia was about subjects in the sense that it created rights and obligations in those subjects. But it was not made by considering the interests of those people. The war was fought between princes who had not learnt to deal with religious pluralism. The Glorious Revolution, on the other hand, was about subjects in a much broader sense. It was about James' subjects' refusal to accept their King's modernization programme.[3] The interests of the subjects were forced on the sovereign and the settlement necessarily reflected those interests.

This difference reflects a shift in thinking, of course. The shift can be expressed as follows. The Peace of Westphalia represents the idea

---

[3] At least, this is so on the interpretation provided by Pincus, *1688*.

that politics affects subjects but is not necessarily the business of subjects. The Glorious Revolution represents the idea that politics both affects and is very certainly the business of subjects.[4]

Of course, that view was not new in 1688. Nor was it rejected by the traditional thinkers examined in Part II of this book. What is significant about the modern view is not what it discovered—in this context, it did not discover anything—but what it forgot.

The interest in the relationship between the individual and the state is found in many works. It is found in Plato, Aristotle, Cicero, Aquinas, Pufendorf, and Kant for example. But in those thinkers, with the partial exception of Plato, that interest went hand in hand with an interest in the relationship between individuals as individuals. In the hands of modern philosophers, however, the first interest became a mania, while the second interest was forgotten.

Modern political philosophy is dominated by isms: anarchism, capitalism, collectivism, colonialism, communism, communitarianism, conservatism, democratism, egalitarianism, fascism, federalism, liberalism, libertarianism, Marxism, nationalism, republicanism, socialism, totalitarianism, utilitarianism, and so on. All of these are concerned with the state and its relationship to individuals. This is even true of the modern sense of the term 'individualism'. There is no commutative justice-ism. The war between these isms have driven the commutative from our minds. This part of this book is an examination of some of the leading figures in the victorious party in that war.

---

[4] Somewhat ironically, this view is promoted even by Hobbes. It is evident in his idea of the social contract, that everyone must 'sign'. It is most evident in the fact that *Leviathan* is, though not literally, addressed to everyone. It attempts to explain to everyone why they have political obligations. This is entirely compatible with Hobbes' authoritarianism. As it were, Hobbes' position is that subjects have no business getting into (day-to-day) politics, but it is their business to ask why that is not their business.

9
Hobbes

1. Biographical Background

Hobbes was born in 1588 and his most famous works of political philosophy, '*De Cive*' and *Leviathan*, were published in 1642 and 1651, respectively. Those publication dates are portentous: they mark the beginning and end of the English Civil War.[1] Though Hobbes' philosophy can stand on its own, it is hardly surprising that the war and the events that led up to it had an enormous effect on his thought. What is more, understanding this effect helps us to explain the form of Hobbes' theory and the enormous impact that it had, especially in England.

The English Civil War had four main causes: conflict between the power of the King and the power of Parliament, religion, finance, and economics. Our concern, however, is not with the actual causes of the war, about which we need not speculate further, but with the reasons for which the participants fought, ie their conscious motivations. This is because Hobbes' theory was written in part as a response to those motivations. In that regard, the first two causes of the war were more significant than the others.[2]

It will help if we begin with the second. In a country that remembered the turmoil created by the Reformation and in which anti-Catholic paranoia remained widespread, Charles I's marriage to

---

[1] My apologies to the Scots, Irish, and Welsh: in order to keep the following manageable, I examine the Civil War only from the English perspective.

[2] Though some fought for the principle as we now know it, 'No taxation without representation', this was understood to relate to the first cause rather than to the third.

the French and Catholic Henrietta-Marie de Bourbon in 1625 was not welcomed. The concern was twofold: that Charles' descendants, and thus his heir, would be raised as a Catholic and that the marriage revealed Charles' own religious predilections. Also significant in this regard was Charles' support for and enforcement of so-called High Anglicanism, a theology and sacramental practice that seemed to many English Protestants 'dangerously' close to Catholicism. To people who thought this way, opposition to the King, or at least to his religious policies, seemed to be a religious and moral duty.

Also of great significance was the clash between the King and the Parliament. In order to understand this conflict, it is of course important to see it through contemporary eyes. In particular, it would be a mistake to think of the conflict as a struggle between two powerful and coordinate governmental bodies, the one seeking to extend its power vis-à-vis the other. It is better understood as an attempt by Parliament to gain real governmental power.

Before the Civil War, the main constitutional role of Parliament was to approve the raising of new forms of taxation. It was not generally to pass laws for the governing of the Kingdom. But many regarded that as unsatisfactory and saw an opportunity to expand Parliament's role. Aware that the King's finances were in poor shape, Members of the House of Commons, such as John Pym, took their opportunity to present the King with demands, and the Long Parliament began to pass what we would now call laws, ie Acts of Parliament.

This point is of great significance, because it shows that the Parliament of this period demanded more than mere reform. It rather insisted on a change to the contemporary political system, effectively demoting the monarchy from its pre-eminent to a coordinate position. Also crucial is the fact that Parliament made these demands as of right. In other words, in our language, the argument was not that it was a good idea to give Parliament more power, but rather that Parliament had a right to that power. To put this another way, Parliament claimed an absolute entitlement to a coordinate position with the monarchy, derived either from natural law or from the agreements of previous monarchs about which they, the Parliamentarians, held themselves to be competent judges.[3] Many thought that the violation of this right justified revolution. The tension reached such a point that the two

---

[3] See, eg The Petition of Right 1628.

sides began to assemble armies, and when they met in 1642, the Civil War broke out.

The Civil War is usually divided into three main phases, or individual civil wars. The first lasted from 1642 until 1646. It was brought to an end by the defeat of the Royalists at the Battles of Naseby and Langport in June and July of 1645 and the subsequent flight of Charles to Scots forces in Nottinghamshire in 1646. Those forces handed Charles back to the English and he was imprisoned.

At that stage, most Parliamentarians had no desire to replace Charles, only to influence his government. But in the light of on-going Royalist opposition, growing divisions within the Parliamentarian faction and the support of the Scots, Charles decided to roll the dice one more time: the second civil war. However, royalist and Scots forces were defeated at the Battle of Preston in 1648 and the King was recaptured.

Infuriated by his actions, the leaders of the Parliamentarian army insisted that Charles be removed from the throne. He was charged with treason and convicted by a High Court of Justice as a 'tyrant, traitor, murderer and public enemy'. He was executed on 30 January 1649.

Note the idea that Charles was guilty of treason. To us today, that might seem nothing more than an excuse, a 'trumped up charge', to have Charles killed. But it was more than that. It was sincerely believed that Charles had committed treason because he had violated the rights mentioned above, rights about which people other than the King were held to be competent judges.

The third civil war was fought between 1650 and 1652, in which the Royalists were led by Charles I's son, the future Charles II. The Royalist cause was effectively defeated at Worcester on 3 September 1651, though Charles managed to escape to France.

It is not hard to imagine that the Civil War had an enormous impact on English society.[4] Those who remember the twentieth century do not need to be told of the devastation caused by war. But what is also significant is that, as the war continued, English society seemed in increasing danger of complete collapse. Perhaps the most significant movements in this regard were the levellers and the diggers.

---

[4] Let alone that of others involved. It has been estimated, for instance, that while England lost 3.7 per cent of its population, Ireland lost a staggering 30 per cent.

The levellers were especially active between the first and second civil war. It cannot be said that they held a coherent political programme, but central to the movement were the ideas of popular sovereignty, wide (or at least extended) suffrage, equality before the law, and religious freedom. This was enough for them then to be branded (and even remembered today) as radicals. Importantly for our purposes, the levellers supported their ideas by appeal to notions of natural rights, thought to derive directly from God and so to be superior to any political authority.

The diggers, as Protestant Christian agrarian communists, were even more radical. Believing that God had given English land to the English people, they argued that private property was a violation of God's law and set up communes in various parts of England, most famously at St George's Hill in Weybridge, Surrey.

Due to the power of vested interests, these movements failed. But the central feature of them is that they took the rebels at their word: there was a higher law, they agreed, higher than the command of the king or of anybody claiming sovereignty. They just disagreed about the content of that law.

Hobbes' greatest philosophical achievement—and it is genuinely great, as evidenced by the fact that many have still to learn it—was that he saw that this attitude destroyed the possibility of government. Many rejected the *content* of the diggers', levellers', or others' views. But only Hobbes saw that the problem lay in the form and not in the specific content of the rival theories. Any view that posits law (or any sort of moral norms) about which the people are to judge and upon which the power of the sovereign depends is inconsistent with the existence of the civil condition. More succinctly, the idea of a higher law, where this is understood to mean that individuals have obligations that they must act on and that trump the authority of the state, is consistent only with the state of nature.

The point can be put simply. If it is up to the people to determine whether the sovereign's rule is legitimate (because of the natural law or whatever), then the so-called sovereign has no authority. This is because, in such circumstances, one has an obligation to obey the sovereign only when one believes that one should. That is the state of nature in disguise. On this view, authority ultimately lies with the people.[5]

---

[5] In section 6 of Chapter 8, we examined Kant's alternative to Hobbes' account, an alternative that takes the problem Hobbes notices fully into account.

For Hobbes, then, the ultimate cause of the English Civil War was the idea of a higher law. What is more, Hobbes thought that peace would prove impossible until that idea had been destroyed. One question we might ask, then, is how this idea came to be held. Why did people in the seventeenth century believe that they possessed ultimate authority?

The answer is that they always believed this. Something changed that produced the Civil War because of the belief, but that thing was not the creation of the belief. The short story is this. Before the seventeenth century, the theory known as the divine right of kings was widely held, at least as a matter of popular belief. According to this view, as the standard formulations have it, the authority of the king is derived directly from God. Hence, the king's subjects must obey the king's commands, because that is commanded by God.

We can immediately see a crucial flaw in this theory, though no one saw things this way before Hobbes. According to it, there is a sense in which kings have absolute authority, but also a sense in which they have no authority at all. They have absolute authority in the sense that, God being the quiet type, the ability of the king to do as he wills could not be challenged. As we might say, for practical purposes the king has complete authority. But he has no theoretical authority, his position being entirely dependent on the will of God. It might help to think of the matter in this way. Assuming that kings have a divine right, when my king tells me to do x, why should I do x? According to the theory under examination, the answer is because God told me to obey the king. On this view, at the level of theory, God has all the authority, the king has none.

As long as people accepted the divine right of kings, the tension between the theory and its practice remained at the theoretical level. But that tension was a time bomb, set to go off at the moment the theory and the practice separated. And that happened in England during and after the Reformation, coming to a head in the seventeenth century.[6]

As noted above, many of Charles' opponents, especially the Puritans, believed that the king was forcing High Anglicanism on them, a form of worship they regarded as heretical. One can immediately see

---

[6] It also went off during the Reformation in England and elsewhere. But, for the reasons explored in outline in the introduction to this part of the book and below, it did not have the effects that it did in seventeenth-century England.

the tension this would have generated even in those who accepted Charles' divine right. The idea was that God gave Charles the rightful authority to govern, and so the citizen had an obligation to obey Charles' commands, but Charles commanded something contrary to the law of God and hence the citizen had an obligation not to obey that command. The traditional response to such difficulties, usually traced to William of Ockham, maintained that, while an individual's ultimate obligation was to God, she nevertheless must always obey the commands of the sovereign, even when they violate the commands of God, because the individual who obeys the command of the sovereign in such circumstances does not violate the command of God. This is because, while the sovereign infringes God's command by requiring his subjects to violate it, the individual merely 'passively obeys' the sovereign's command.[7] The difficulties surrounding the succession of James I, Charles' father, to the throne after Elizabeth I had died without an heir and the almost hysterical anti-Catholic atmosphere meant that this view lost its appeal. The citizens of England remained sure that they must obey God's command but, they thought, surely God could not be commanding 'Papist heresy'.

When citizens of other European countries experienced similar difficulties, they tended to move to a state that would accommodate their religious views. Good examples are the movements of Protestant Salzburgers to Prussia in 1732[8] and the relocation of the Huguenots from France to countries such as England, Switzerland, and the Netherlands. Some English migration occurred also. But there was a crucial difference. The Protestants in Salzburg and France were a minority in countries governed by and largely populated by Catholics. Hence, even if they felt that they should resist their rulers, they recognized that that would have been pointless. In consequence, emigration seemed to be the only genuine option. In England, on the other hand, the Protestants constituted a significant majority. Accordingly, the idea that obeying God's commands meant resistance was far more tempting.

But for the reasons that we have seen, that temptation almost destroyed England. With the benefit of hindsight, the problem is clear: everyone thought that they should do what God commands,

---

[7] Ockham, *A Letter to the Friars Minor and Other Writings*, 72.
[8] Clark, *Iron Kingdom*, ch 5. In this chapter, Clark also examines the interesting tension in Prussia between its Lutheran population and Calvinist monarchs.

but everyone disagreed about what God was commanding. Charles thought God commanded High Anglicanism and his own rule above the law. Some Parliamentarians thought on the contrary that God commanded Puritanism and parliamentary government. The Levellers thought that God commanded popular sovereignty; the Diggers that He commanded communism. No amount of appealing to the need to obey God's command could settle this. On the contrary, the appeal served only to push division into conflict.

The collapse in English society was caused, inter alia, by a collapse in its understanding of political authority. Hobbes' task, then, was to provide a new account of that authority, an account designed to show that the sovereign—be that one individual or an assembly—has genuine authority. I examine that theory below.

Before I turn to that topic, it is important to bring out the second consequence of this history. The first is the one we have been examining: the historical lesson that the idea of a higher law is incompatible with political authority. The second consequence is much harder for us to see, because it corresponds with our modern view.

If Hobbes' task is to provide a new account of political authority that enables people to live in peace, then the task is to provide an account of the proper relationship between the individual and the state. In the context of civil war, it is hardly surprising that that would be the focus. The focus is entirely consistent with the idea that politico-legal norms exist as between individuals *inter se*. But in the context of civil war, it is also unsurprising if that fact were forgotten. It is rather likely that such politico-legal norms would be neglected and that, if the focus was maintained, the existence of those norms would be forgotten. That is the story of modern political and legal theory. I begin to tell it now.

2. Hobbes' Political Theory

As discussed above, Hobbes' task in *Leviathan* is to provide a genuine account of political authority. For the reasons we have seen, this account cannot appeal to citizens' recognition of moral claims that they might be disposed to dispute. Instead, the account must be based on something citizens must accept. Hobbes' ingenuous response is to base political authority on citizens' self-interest. He does so by arguing that citizens cannot lead even remotely worthwhile lives unless the sovereign possesses authority. That argument starts by imagining life without sovereign authority; that is, by imagining life in the state of nature.

2.1 Life in the State of Nature

Hobbes begins by pointing to the 'natural equality' of human beings.[9] By this, he means to draw attention to the fact that human beings are of roughly equal physical power and pose roughly equal danger to each other. As Hobbes puts it, 'the weakest has strength enough to kill the strongest, either by secret machination, or by confederacy with others, that are in the same danger with himself'.[10] This is important, because it reveals that no one in the state of nature can be or feel secure.

Hobbes then argues that this natural equality produces diffidence or fear.[11] The idea is this: imagining that you and I are in the state of nature, I realize that my plans to achieve my ends might come into conflict with your plans to achieve your ends, and that our natural equality entails that this conflict poses a danger to me and my ability to live my life as I choose.

The result of this, Hobbes maintains, is a condition of war.[12] This is not the crude claim it first appears to be. It is not that human nature is aggressive and so people in the state of nature will necessarily fight. The claim is rather that the state of nature has a 'logic' to it that pushes its inhabitants into conflict. That 'logic' is the following.

I know that you pose a danger to me. And I also know that the only way to remove that danger is to kill you. It does not follow from this that I will kill you or even that I will want to kill you. But the problem is that I also know that you know that I am a danger to you and that you know that the only way to remove that danger is to kill me. So, not only do I have a reason to kill you, I recognize that you have a reason to kill me. What is more, I also know that if I kill you, then you will not be able to avenge your death—ie if I kill you, then I will remove a danger to me without creating a new danger. And I also know that if you kill me, I will not be able to avenge my death—ie

[9] Hobbes, *Leviathan*, XIII 1.
[10] Ibid.
[11] Ibid, XIII 3.
[12] Ibid, XIII 4.

if you kill me, then you remove the danger to you without creating any new danger. And the problem now is that it seems that reason demands that I kill you and that you kill me. I have a reason to kill you because you are dangerous to me, and you are dangerous to me not only because you threaten the realization of my ends, but also because you recognize that I am dangerous to you, giving you a reason to kill me. The same argument applies, of course, to you.

According to Alan Ryan, Hobbes' point can be illustrated by reference to recent experience.

> The logic of fear is something with which humanity has become extremely familiar during the past fifty years [ie during the Cold War]. It is the logic of interaction between two persons or two societies who can each annihilate the other, and neither of whom possesses second-strike capacity, that is, the ability to revenge himself on the other post mortem. Two nuclear powers who can wipe out the other side's nuclear forces if they strike first and therefore cannot revenge themselves on the other side if they do not strike first would be the post-World War II illustration of Hobbes' theory. The point to notice is that the horrors of the situation do not hinge on either party's wishing to attack the other. People in this situation are driven to attack one another by the logic of the situation, no matter what their motives. Thus, I look at you and know that you can kill me if you have to; I know that you must have asked the question whether you have to. Do you have to?[13]

In fact, however, though this example is helpful, there is a crucial disanalogy here. In reality, both sides in the Cold War possessed massive second-strike capacity. This is why the military strategy surrounding the use of nuclear weapons became known as the doctrine of mutually assured destruction (MAD). The idea behind that doctrine was that if the USA had launched an attack on the USSR, then that would have guaranteed the destruction of the USSR; but, before being destroyed, the USSR would have been able to launch enough of its own weapons—ie 'ante-mortem'—so that the USA would be destroyed also. Hence, destruction is mutually assured.

In fact, however, this scenario was probably too 'optimistic'. In reality, even a successful pre-emptive strike—ie a strike that would prevent retaliation—would have had to have been so large that the fallout

---

[13] Ryan, 'Hobbes's Political Philosophy', 220.

would probably have destroyed the human race. In that way, MAD was really mad. And this means that, even if one's enemy had no second-strike potential, it would not be in one's self-interest to attack.

Accordingly, the Cold War does not provide a good illustration of Hobbes' theory. If the USA had attacked the USSR, then it—the USA—would have been destroyed. But if I kill you in the state of nature, typically you will not be able to act before your death to ensure my death. So I have a reason to kill you that the USA did not have to destroy the USSR. A better analogy for the state of nature than the Cold War would be Europe on the eve of the First World War, given the beliefs of the antagonistic powers (ie that the war would be short and that rapid mobilization would provide significant advantage).

In consequence, the point that Hobbes is making is this: even if we assume that human nature is generally benevolent, the conditions of the state of nature engender conflict. In that state, even good people are *driven* to attack each other.[14]

Later, Hobbes also adds glory to his list of the causes of conflict in the state of nature. This is the desire of human beings to be well thought of by others or, more powerfully, not to be badly thought of by others.[15] He then nicely summarizes his position:

in the nature of man, we find three principal causes of quarrel. First, competition; secondly, diffidence; thirdly, glory.

The first, maketh men invade for gain; the second, for safety; and the third, for reputation. The first use violence, to make themselves masters of other men's persons, wives, children, and cattle; the second, to defend them; the third, for trifles, as a word, a smile, a different opinion, and any other sign of undervalue, either direct in their persons, or by reflection in their kindred, their friends, their nation, their profession, or their name.[16]

The problem with the state of nature, then, is clear. It is a state in which human beings lack security. But the problem is also deeper

---

[14] For this reason, we should find the criticisms of this view made by, for instance, Pufendorf to be unconvincing. Pufendorf, *Of the Law of Nature and Nations*, II II 7–9 appeals to the Bible as evidence for the claim that the state of nature is peaceful and argues that people enter the civil condition in the spirit of cooperation. Pufendorf's argument is that people in the state of nature have a sense of morality that prevents them acting as Hobbes predicts. But that cannot defeat Hobbes' argument, which alleges that the state of nature is such that even morally good agents will be pushed into conflict with each other.
[15] Hobbes, *Leviathan*, XIII 5.
[16] Ibid, XIII 6–7.

than this. Because of the lack of security, there can be little incentive to industry in the state of nature.[17] Hence, Hobbes famously concludes that in the state of nature there can be

no culture of the earth; no navigation, nor use of the commodities that may be imported by sea; no commodious building; no instruments of moving, and removing such things as require much force; no knowledge of the face of the earth; no account of time; no arts; no letters; no society; and which is worst of all, continual fear, and danger of violent death; and the life of man, solitary, poor, nasty, brutish, and short.[18]

2.2 Rights, Liberties, Laws, and Justice in the State of Nature

A modern reader coming to *Leviathan* for the first time is likely to expect that Hobbes will now go on to argue that, as life in the state of nature is so awful, it is in individuals' self-interest to recognize the existence of a public authority capable of putting an end to the 'logic' of the state of nature. And this may even be Hobbes' view (more on this later); but it is not what he actually says. Instead, at this point, Hobbes begins to talk about concepts such as rights, natural laws, and justice. We need to examine these ideas now.

The first important claim that Hobbes makes in this regard is that nothing can be unjust in the state of nature. As we have seen and will see again, this idea was rejected by many of Hobbes' predecessors and successors. But both the idea and its rejection are much more complicated than they at first appear to be.

On the face of it, Hobbes' claim is that no moral obligations exist in the state of nature that prohibit behaviour towards others we are inclined to describe as unjust, such as striking or killing. Accordingly, the opposition to this view is usually taken to hold, and occasionally does hold, that such moral prohibitions exist. But the claim is not this, and the reply is seldom this one.

In order to understand Hobbes' position, we must come to terms with his use of the words 'just' and 'unjust'. This is what he tells us:

The notions of right and wrong, justice and injustice have there [ie in the state of nature] no place. Where there is no common power, there is no law:

[17] Ibid, XIII 9.
[18] Ibid.

where no law, no injustice. Force, and fraud, are in war the two cardinal virtues. Justice, and injustice are none of the faculties neither of the body, nor mind. If they were, they might be in a man that were alone in the world, as well as his senses, and passions. They are qualities, that relate to men in society, not in solitude.[19]

It is evident that the argument of this passage is semantic rather than normative. It is not that before the sovereign there were no moral norms corresponding to what we have been calling justice. It is that terms such as 'right' and 'wrong' and 'justice' and 'injustice' refer, not to such norms, but only to norms created in civil conditions. In other words, Hobbes simply *defines* the relevant terms to refer to normative consequences of the decisions of the sovereign.

Because of this, Hobbes' insistence that nothing is unjust (or just) in the state of nature does not deny that moral norms we identify as belonging to justice exist in that state. His position with respect to those norms is determined by his wider moral theory and not by his definitions of 'justice' and the like.

Similarly, the implication of this view that no law can be unjust does not imply that no law can be unjust in our sense. In fact, Hobbes makes a crucial distinction between justice and equity, between just and equitable laws,[20] and between good and just laws.[21] So, it is quite consistent with Hobbes' theory to imagine the existence of what the tradition would call an unjust law. At this point, the difference is merely terminological. Hobbes would insist that such a law is properly characterized as just but inequitable or bad, because 'justice' is defined so that it takes its content from the commands of the sovereign.

Accordingly, when Hobbes' maintains that the sovereign cannot rule unjustly, this does not mean that he cannot rule unjustly in our sense of the term. Hobbes accepts that sovereigns can rule inequitably and badly. The claim is a mere tautology: that the commands of the sovereign cannot be in violation of the commands of the sovereign.

Hobbes then introduces the idea of the right of nature.[22] The first thing to say about this right is that it is what we call a liberty, ie the absence of a contrary duty.[23] Given that and given Hobbes' claim that

---

[19] Ibid, XIII 13. See also ibid, XV 3.
[20] Ibid, XV 2, XVIII 6, XXVI 7.
[21] Ibid, XXX 20–30.
[22] Ibid, XIV 1.
[23] Ibid, XIV 2. See Hohfeld, *Fundamental Legal Conceptions*.

there is no justice or injustice and no right and wrong in the state of nature, it comes as no surprise that rights in this sense exist in that state. But Hobbes draws particular attention to a certain right: the right to defend oneself, 'the liberty each man hath, to use his own power, as he will himself, for the preservation of his own nature; that is to say, of his own life; and consequently, of doing any thing, which in his own judgment, and reason, he shall conceive to be the aptest means thereunto'.[24]

In itself, the right of nature is of comparatively little importance. It becomes significant because Hobbes transposes it into the basis of his first law of nature. As he defines that concept:

A LAW OF NATURE, (*lex naturalis,*) is a precept, or general rule, found out by reason, by which a man is forbidden to do, that, which is destructive of his life, or taketh away the means of preserving the same; and to omit, that, by which he thinketh it may be best preserved.[25]

Notice here the shift from the idea that one is at *liberty* to preserve one's life to the view that one is *obligated* to do so. This shift is to some extent elided by the fact that Hobbes refers to the first as a right. But there is a gulf between these two claims, and Hobbes does not tell us how to traverse it.

This difficulty relates to a deep interpretive controversy over the proper reading of Hobbes' theory. I do not propose to enter into this debate. For one thing, the issue cannot here receive the attention it deserves. For another, our interest is more in Hobbes' impact than on the details of his theory. The strategy I propose is to adopt an interpretation that minimizes Hobbes' commitments and thus presents his theory in as strong a form as possible. More concretely, in the following I interpret the laws of nature simply as demands of prudence. On this view, the foundation of the laws of nature, elucidated above, is not read as a moral principle but simply as a demand of prudence. This does not rule out the idea that it might also be a moral principle. That possibility is simply overlooked.

If prudence is the ground of the laws of nature, then it is easy to see why they have the form Hobbes attributes to them. Consider the first: '*that every man, ought to endeavour peace, as far as he has hope of obtaining*

---

[24] Hobbes, *Leviathan*, XIV 1.
[25] Ibid, XIV 3.

it; and when he cannot obtain it, that he may seek, and use, all helps, and advantages of war'.[26] The first part of this law states that people must endeavour to escape the 'logic' of the civil condition if they can; the second maintains that if they cannot, people must attempt to avoid the consequences of that 'logic'. The other natural laws Hobbes mentions are ways of achieving or cementing the realization of the first half of this first law.

A feature of Hobbes' account is his claim that in the state of nature 'every man has a right to every thing; even to one another's body'.[27] In the light of the above, we can see that this means (i) that individuals are under no duties towards others, including no duties to respect their bodily integrity or the like; and (ii) that individuals have an obligation (of prudence) to invade these interests when that is a good means of preserving their own life.

Before we consider the second, and crucial, natural law, it is important also to consider the distinction Hobbes draws between natural and civil laws. Natural law is defined above. Civil law, on the other hand, consists of 'those rules, which the commonwealth hath commanded…, by word, writing, or other sufficient sign of the will, to make use of for the distinction of right, and wrong; that is to say, of what is contrary, and what is not contrary to the rule'.[28] As we might now say, civil law is positive law. Moreover, Hobbes maintains that natural laws 'are not properly laws, but qualities that dispose men to peace, and obedience'.[29] For this reason, when not accompanied by 'nature' or 'natural', I will henceforth use the term 'law' to refer only to civil laws.

2.3 The Social Contract

The second law of nature is '*that a man be willing, when others are so too, as far-forth, as for peace, and defence of himself he shall think it necessary, to lay down this right to all things; and be contented with so much liberty against other men, as he would allow other men against himself*'.[30] This right to all things is the liberty noted above, 'to every thing; even to one another's body'.[31] Hobbes maintains that if others will reciprocate, one must

[26] Ibid, XIV 4.
[27] Ibid.
[28] Ibid, XXVI 3.
[29] Ibid, XXVI 8.
[30] Ibid, XIV 5.
[31] Ibid, XIV 4.

surrender this right, not by simply renouncing it, but by transferring it to a person or body, thereby giving that person or body the authority to create laws that destroy the 'logic' of the state of nature.[32]

But how does this transfer take place? As Hobbes explains, it occurs though the mechanism of the social contract.[33] This is a hypothetical event in which individuals surrender their right of nature in return for the surrender of the same right in others, and transfer that right to a person or body known as the sovereign.

It is a crucial feature of Hobbes' account that the sovereign is not a party to the social contract.[34] As we would say, that contract is between the subjects to gift authority to the sovereign. Many of Hobbes' successors have thought this a fatal flaw in Hobbes' theory;[35] it is anything but. As Hobbes realizes, if the sovereign is party to the contract, then his position with respect to the terms of the contract is on a par with that of the other parties. And this implies the denial of the authority of the sovereign.

Hobbes expresses the idea by asking this question: if the sovereign is party to the contract and a citizen alleges that the sovereign has breached the contract, who is to judge?[36] Philosophers have tended to brush this point aside, but it is fundamental. Who is to decide whether the sovereign is violating the contract? If the answer is the sovereign, then the sovereign is not bound by the contract. If the answer is the citizen, then the citizen is not bound. And if the answer is someone else, then that person is the real sovereign. Let me explain.

It is important to remember that we are talking about authority and not about obligation per se. The issue, then, is not what some person should do, but *who gets to decide* what people should do. And in that light, Hobbes' position is entirely compelling. The claim that the sovereign is party to the contract just means that it is not up to the sovereign to determine the ambit of his own authority; that in disputes as to the extent of the sovereign's authority, it is not the sovereign who gets to decide. But if that is so, then someone else must have that ability. If that person is an individual or body other than the sovereign,

---

[32] Ibid, XIV 7.
[33] Ibid, XIV 9.
[34] Ibid, XVII–XVIII.
[35] Eg Locke, *Two Treatises of Government*, s 93: 'This is to think, that men are so foolish, that they take care to avoid what mischiefs may be done them by pole-cats, or foxes; but are content, nay, think is safety, to be devoured by lions.'
[36] Hobbes, *Leviathan*, XVIII 4.

then that person gets to determine the ambit of the (apparent) sovereign's authority. In other words, that person is the real sovereign. But if, as we will see Locke contends, each individual citizen is able to decide whether the sovereign has violated his authority, then they are sovereign. Locke may have approved of the sound of that claim but, as Hobbes realizes, a community of that kind is a state of nature. If I get to decide this matter, then the practical implication is that I must obey the sovereign only if I believe that the sovereign is acting within his authority. If so, then the sovereign has no authority. And note that, though my belief might be false, if I am the judge, then what matters is whether I have the belief and not whether the belief is true.

It may also help to think of the matter in this way. If A and B enter into a contract, then A and B gain obligations vis-à-vis one another. This is true even if no person exists who is competent to judge this matter, ie even if A and B must judge the content of the contract for themselves. Accordingly, as far as obligation is concerned, there is no difficulty with the idea that the sovereign can be part of the contract. But our concern is not with obligation but with authority. And authority (or at least political authority) is the power to determine obligation. It is about having the right to decide what obligations people hold. Hence, in the circumstances imagined, while A and B owe obligations to each other, neither can possess authority because neither gets to decide what the obligations of the other are (ie neither's reading of the contract is authoritative).

Nor is it adequate to argue, as Locke effectively does, that the social contract gives limited authority to the sovereign. The analogy with this view is that the contract between A and B determines that A gets to decide on B's obligations unless x occurs. But who gets to decide if x has occurred? If the answer is B, then A has no real authority. If the answer is A, then the unless clause is meaningless. Authority is all or nothing.[37]

In consequence, Hobbes maintains that, though the sovereign *should* govern according to equity, his authority does not depend on his doing so.[38] Or to put the point from the perspective of the citizen: the citizen may well believe, and be correct in believing, that the sovereign is governing inequitably, but she nevertheless has an overriding obligation

---

[37] Ibid, XX 18.
[38] Hobbes, '*De Cive*', XIII; Hobbes, *Leviathan*, XXX 1; Hobbes, *Dialogue*, 15, 18–19, 28.

to obey the commands of the sovereign. As we saw in section 1, the alternative is collapse into anarchy.

That is the essence of Hobbes' theory. There are, of course, questions that one can ask about it. Moreover, Hobbes reaches many further conclusions with which one may disagree. But investigating those issues is not our task here. Rather, our goal is to understand the impact of this theory on the way in which politics and law is viewed. In order to do this, I examine some of the most important consequences of the theory, some drawn explicitly by Hobbes, but some only implicit in his account.

3. The Implications of Hobbes' Theory

3.1 *Justice*

As we saw in section 2.2 above, Hobbes' defines 'justice' in an idiosyncratic fashion. But he also explores the conceptions of justice held by his predecessors. In particular, he examines the distinction between commutative and distributive justice.

First, like Pufendorf (who followed him) but unlike Aquinas, Hobbes defines commutative justice as the justice involved in contracting.[39] Moreover, unlike either Pufendorf or Aquinas, he insists that this justice is determined entirely by the wills of the parties. In other words, he rejects the concept of the *laesio enormous*.[40] On the other hand, Hobbes identifies distributive justice with equity.

On the face of it, this robs both forms of justice of any significance. Commutative justice is simply giving to people what they have bargained for and distributive justice is just equity, which as we have seen is peripheral to Hobbes' theory. In fact, however, neither conclusion is warranted. The first, and most important, is examined in section 4, as it points to a deep problem with Hobbes' account. The second is explored here.

Hobbes' claim that distributive justice belongs to equity means that it has no role to play in the theory presented in *Leviathan*. But it must be remembered that that theory is an account of the *authority* of the sovereign. It is not a description of how the sovereign *should* govern,

---

[39] Hobbes, *Leviathan*, XV 14.
[40] Ibid.

an issue that receives only the most cursory attention in *Leviathan*.[41] Despite this, Hobbes is clear that the sovereign *should* rule according to equity,[42] a claim that implies that he should rule according to distributive justice. These obligations are genuine, but they are not generated by the social contract. That view, then, appears to produce agreement with Figure M1. In company with Plato, then, Hobbes stands at the head of the modern view.

3.2 *Justice and Law*

As we saw in section 2.2 above, Hobbes maintains that justice gains its content from the law. With the exception of Kant's view, this is a reversal of the traditional conception. But, as stressed in section 2.2, much turns on Hobbes' use of terminology. Hobbes' simply defines justice so that it gets its content from law. Is there, then, a real difference in this regard between Hobbes and the traditional thinkers?

According to the traditional view, law gets its content from justice, either directly or because it was created by a body set up in accordance with the demands of justice. To what extent can Hobbes accommodate this view? First, he would agree that law is created by a body set up in accordance with the demands of justice, ie, in his language, set up in accordance with the demands of equity. I have presented an interpretation of Hobbes' view that relies on prudence rather than morality. A consequence of that view is that sovereign authority does not rely on morality. And I have argued that this idea is central to Hobbes' project. But that is perfectly consistent with the notion that sovereign authority is demanded by morality; the point is just that that authority does not rely on that demand.

What is more, Hobbes also accepts that law can be given content by justice ('equity') directly. This may come as a surprise, as Hobbes is usually characterized as a hard legal positivist. But Hobbes is quite clear that both the law of nature and equity are binding on judges. Accordingly, in the absence of positive law to the contrary, judges must follow the natural law and equity.[43] We have examined the natural law above, but in order fully to comprehend Hobbes' account, it is necessary now to examine equity.

---

[41] Ibid, XXX 21–30.
[42] Ibid, XXX 1; Hobbes, '*De Cive*', XIII; Hobbes, *Dialogue*, 15, 18–19, 28.
[43] Hobbes, *Leviathan*, XXI 7, XXVI 7, 17, 24, 26.

For Hobbes, as we saw in section 3.1 above, equity and distributive justice are identical. But what do these terms mean? This is what Hobbes tells us:

And distributive justice, the justice of an arbitrator; that is to say, the act of defining what is just. Wherein, (being trusted by them that make him arbitrator,) if he perform his trust, he is said to distribute to every man his own: and his is indeed just distribution, and may be called (though improperly) distributive justice; but more properly equity; which also is a law of nature...[44]

This is anything but transparent. However, things are a little clearer in, 'De Cive'.

it is commanded by the law of nature, *that every man in dividing right to others, show himself equal to either party*. By the foregoing law we are forbidden to assume more right by nature to ourselves, than we grant to others. We may take less if we will; for that sometimes is an argument of modesty. But if at any time matter of right be to be divided by us unto others, we are forbidden by this law to favour one more or less than another. For he that by favouring one before another observes not this natural equality, reproaches him whom he thus undervalues; but it is declared above, that a reproach is against the laws of nature.[45]

Clear now is the focus on what we know as distributive justice. For Hobbes, then, 'distributive justice' has the same meaning as it does for us,[46] and equity too is defined in terms of distributive justice. Consequently, we can conclude that the equity binding on judges is distributive justice.

The first key point to notice is that commutative justice in our sense of the term is missing from this account. With the one hidden exception examined in section 4, the idea that individuals might owe each other politico-legal obligations *inter se* in advance of legislation is absent from Hobbes' theory. The second key point is that this absence is in no way argued for. Hobbes presents no argument to show that

---

[44] Ibid, XV 15.
[45] Hobbes, '*De Cive*', III 15.
[46] Though the content of the theory of distributive justice may be different. See ibid, III 6.

such obligations cannot exist. Nor is the non-existence of those obligations a consequence of any position for which Hobbes argues. For instance, the idea that norms of commutative justice are binding on judges is easily compatible with his theory. He could himself have argued that commutative justice (as we understand it) is part of equity. At a theoretical level, what prevents him from doing this is the mere fact that he *defines* equity in terms of distributive justice. At the practical level, what prevents him from doing this is the fact that, focused on contemporary political events, the norms in question are not in his mind. They are not argued against and rejected. They are simply forgotten.

A crucial consequence of this is a shift in the rhetorical focus of philosophical enquiry. For instance, when the traditionalist asked herself why courts recognize a right to bodily integrity, she set about answering this question by looking for norms that govern the interactions between individuals and deducing from those norms the state's motivation to enforce them. In other words, she argued that the right is grounded in commutative justice, which the state has an obligation to enforce. But when those under the influence of Hobbes' viewpoint ask the same question, they look first to the state. Their first question is: 'Why is the state doing this?' Now, they *could* answer that question by reference to commutative justice, but the shift in focus from individuals to the state has elided that option; that is, it seems to the modern thinker, in the grip of Hobbes' general outlook, that the answer to the question 'Why is the state doing this?' must be on the level of the question. It seems that, as the question is about the state, the answer must also be about the state. Or to put it another way, as the question is about a body that represents all of us taken together, the answer seems to have to refer to all of us taken together. The answer must be found in distributive justice. But these thoughts are entirely mistaken.

We revisit this idea below, but for now the crucial point is that Hobbes' theory refocused the minds of political and legal theorists. The traditionalists were concerned with the whole of political life: with the relations between individuals *inter se*, with the state, and with international relations (though I have ignored the last of these in this book). After Hobbes, however, the focus was almost entirely on the state. This is evident even from the titles of the relevant works. The great works of Grotius, Pufendorf, Kant, Fichte, and Hegel are entitled *The Law of War and Peace*,[47] *On the Law of Nature and Nations*, *The Doctrine of Law*, *The Foundations of Natural Law*, and *Elements of the Philosophy of Law*, respectively. But the central works of Hobbes, Locke, and Bentham are entitled '*De Cive*' ('The Citizen') and *Leviathan* (ie the state), *Two Treatises of Government*, and *The Principles of Morals and Legislation*, respectively. Consider also more recently Robert Nozick's *Anarchy, State, and Utopia*. The shift of focus to the state is plain to see. Even more telling is John Rawls' *A Theory of Justice*. Though this work apparently refers to justice in total, it immediately defines justice as 'the first virtue of *social institutions*'.[48] Of course, Rawls is entitled to define his subject matter as he pleases, but it tells us a great deal about the shift in focus from Grotius to Rawls that the latter can title a book concerned only with distributive justice *A Theory of Justice*.

As historians of political philosophy, this shift ought to strike us as seismic. It is political philosophy's Copernican revolution. Instead, however, because we have forgotten the justice about which the traditionalists were speaking, we fail even to see it.

Leviathan is the seminal work in the history of modern political philosophy. There are two reasons for this. In conjunction with Hobbes' other writings, it is the first book that understands and responds to the problem of political authority. And it entirely changed the way in which English-speaking philosophers thought about political and legal reality. Like van Gogh paintings, Hobbes' theory made people see the world in a different way.

But that analogy is also revealing in another respect. After seeing a van Gogh wheat field, it is difficult to see wheat fields in the same way again. But that does not mean that there was anything wrong with how one saw them in the first place. In fact, the idea is quite consistent with the possibility that one now sees them less well than one did before. And this, I suggest, is true of Hobbes. He taught us to see the political and legal world differently, but worse. The power of his theory has blinded us to more accurate views of that world. And we have become so accustomed to our partial sight, that it is only with great effort and after much squinting that we are able to open our eyes.

---

[47] To the modern mind, this is about only conflicts between *states*, but Grotius' work concerns also conflicts between individuals.

[48] Rawls, *A Theory of Justice*, 3 (emphasis added).

3.3 Bodily Integrity, Contract, and Property

Given what has been said above, it is unsurprising to find Hobbes maintaining that the rules of contract and property law, and the very existence of property, are created by the sovereign in the civil condition.[49] The same must be true of the right to bodily integrity.

But it is again important to note that Hobbes *could have* thought that the sovereign ought to have recognized these rights due to commutative justice as we are using that term. The shift in focus, however, again obscures this option. The relevant question appears only to be 'What purpose does the recognition of these rights serve for all of us taken together?' In other words, the issue seems necessarily to be one of distributive justice.[50] But it is not.

3.4 Private and Public Law

I have titled this subsection 'Private and Public Law' rather than 'Public and Private Law' for a reason, even though the latter sounds more natural. Why does it sound more natural? After all, 'r' comes before 'u' in the alphabet. The answer is that, however unconsciously, we English speakers have become used to thinking of public law as conceptually more fundamental than private law. As we have seen, that view was not shared by the traditionalists. It was invented by Hobbes.

In line with the arguments I have presented above, Hobbes could have maintained that areas of the law such as tort, contract, property, and unjust enrichment have their moral foundations in commutative justice as we use that term. But he does not do this. What he does is far more radical.

First, Hobbes maintains that, from a philosopher's perspective at any rate, the crucial division in law is not between private and public, but between the distributive and the penal.[51] Distributive laws are those that determine the rights of individuals. Penal laws are those that punish individuals for violating the rights given by the distributive laws. And that division is intended to be exhaustive. In consequence, Hobbes leaves no room for a distinction between crimes and other legal wrongs such as torts or breaches of contract.[52] It follows from

---

[49] Hobbes, '*De Cive*', VI 15; Hobbes, *Leviathan*, XIII 13, XVIII 10, XXIV 10.
[50] Hobbes, *Leviathan*, XXIV 5.
[51] Hobbes, '*De Cive*', XIV 6–7; Hobbes, *Leviathan*, XXVI 38.
[52] Hobbes, '*De Cive*', XIV 6–7; Hobbes, *Leviathan*, XXVII 2, XXVIII 1, 7.

this position that the private law must be understood as the criminal law is understood. But it is also of great significance that the understanding of the criminal law changes too.

In Chapter 4, we glimpsed in Aristotle's theory the idea that many of the rights protected by the criminal law are grounded in commutative justice. But *Leviathan's* shift from the individual to the state occludes this. As above, the question now seems only to be about the state or about all of us taken together. This is reflected in Hobbes' definition of all law as either distributive, ie as distributing rights throughout a community, or penal, ie as punishing violations of distributive law. On this view, all law has its ultimate moral foundation in distributive justice.[53]

On the Hobbesian model, the right to bodily integrity—whether recognized in tort or in the criminal law—is based on distributive justice. When the criminal law responds to a violation of that right, it does so in order to punish the violator of the distributive law. Exactly the same is true when tort law responds to that violation. The criminal law and the law of tort have the same conceptual structure and the same general function. They simply perform that function in different ways.

Along with the shift in focus from the individual to the state, then, we see a parallel shift in attention from private to public law. For the traditional thinkers, private law lay at the foundation of the political system. For Hobbes and his followers, it is little more than an afterthought, easily ignored by philosophers. We have arrived at M3. As we see in Chapters 11 and 12, this view has had a large impact on the way in which private law is viewed today.

3.5 Conclusion

I have been emphasizing two features of Hobbes' theory: the shift from private to public and the fact that this shift was suggested by the form but not necessitated by Hobbes' theory. The crucial consequence of this is that there is no argument in Hobbes against the traditional view. That view is simply dropped for Hobbes' new beginning. It was the first stage in our forgetting.

---

[53] Of course, as has been emphasized, this is not the source of the law's authority.

4. The Social Contract, Self-Interest, and Commutative Justice

I end our examination of Hobbes' account by exploring a difficulty not only for that theory but for the whole modern view that it invented.

As we have seen, Hobbes maintains that the authority of the sovereign derives from the social contract. But what is the normative status of that contract? In other words, what exactly changes when citizens, as it were, sign the contract?

It may appear that I have given the answer already: they surrender their natural right to the sovereign and agree to abide by his laws in order to achieve peace. But that answer is not complete. What is the nature of that surrender? What does it change?

The first thing that must be said is that the surrender is not of anything material. It is the surrender of authority, of a norm. Now, if authority were material, then the surrender in itself would be sufficient to establish Hobbes' position. If one literally *gave* the sovereign authority by agreeing to the social contract, then the sovereign would literally *have* authority. But authority is not like this. For the social contract to work, it must show that the surrender of authority in some way *binds* the individual, ie that it creates a norm that the individual is bound to respect. But how does that happen?

Though this problem is frequently ignored in the secondary literature, it seems to have exercised Hobbes. As we have seen, his second law of nature maintains that individuals in the state of nature must give up their natural freedom in return for the same surrender from others. This is elucidated in sections 5 and 6 of chapter XIV of *Leviathan*. In section 9 of that chapter, he introduces the idea of the social contract and examines the nature of contracting and surrounding issues in sections 10–33. But in section 1 of chapter XV he introduces his third law of nature.

FROM that law of nature, by which we are obliged to transfer to another, such rights, as being retained, hinder the peace of mankind, there followeth a third; which is this, that men perform their covenants made: without which, covenants are in vain, and but empty words; and the right of all men to all things remaining, we are still in the condition of war.[54]

---

[54] Hobbes, *Leviathan*, XV 1.

At first, this must seem odd. Hobbes has already argued that one must enter the social contract and that that contract transfers one's natural right to the sovereign. What is the point, then, of arguing for the additional law that one must keep one's contracts? Is this third natural law really additional to what has come before?

The answer to that question is 'Yes'. And it is an answer that few apart from Hobbes himself have seen. The point is this. Though this area is controversial, as noted above, the first two laws of nature appear to derive entirely from consideration of self-interest. They are dictates of prudence. But the third law is not. It does not follow from the fact that it is prudent to enter into the social contract in order to escape the state of nature that it is prudent to keep one's contractual promise. In fact, it may not be prudent to keep one's promise. Because of this, the move from the second to the third law must involve a shift from self-interest to morality.[55] And it is because of this shift that the third law is needed. The first and second laws are prudential, but the third is moral.

In order to see this, it is necessary to understand why the third law cannot be prudential. Let us consider the contrary position for the sake of argument. If the third law were merely prudential, then it would have to be the case that violating it would be inconsistent with self-interest. The idea must be that, if we do not keep the promise we made when we entered the social contract, then we will end up back in the state of nature. But that idea is false. It is plausible to think that people will not leave the state of nature unless everyone, or nearly everyone, agrees to form the social contract. It is perhaps even right to say that people must promise sincerely. If that is right, then prudence demands that individuals in the state of nature sincerely promise to surrender their natural right and obey the sovereign. But that is quite different from saying that prudence demands that individuals keep their sincerely made promises when the transition to the civil condition has been achieved. On the contrary, prudence makes that demand only if one's breaking of one's promise *will* lead others to do so and hence *will* lead to the collapse of the civil condition. But that thought is highly implausible. This, of course, is a version of the free rider problem.

---

[55] Cf Diggs, *The Unlawfulnesse of Subjects*, 123; Diggs, *An Answer to a Printed Book*, 9. This latter book was published anonymously, but it appears to have been written by members of the Tew Circle, with whose work Hobbes was familiar.

Consider again Hobbes' claim 'that men perform their covenants made: without which, covenants are in vain, and but empty words'.[56] That claim is literally true only if 'men' refers to all or many men. But that is not the question. The third law states not that people in general must keep their promises, but that each and every one of us must do so. Alternatively, the appeal is to the kind of thought, 'But imagine if everyone did that.' But without reference to morality, thoughts of that kind are irrelevant, as not everyone will do that.

In his earlier work, Hobbes had argued that breach of contract involved a contradiction.

> The breach or violation of covenant, is that which men call INJURY, consisting in some action or omission, which is therefore called UNJUST. For it is action or omission, without *jus*, or right; which was transferred or relinquished before. There is a great similitude between that we call injury, or injustice in the actions and conversations of men in the world, and that which is called *absurd* in the arguments and disputations of the Schools. For as he, that is driven to contradict an assertion by him before maintained, is said to be reduced to an absurdity; so he that through passion doth, or omitteth that which before by covenant he promised not to do, or not to omit, is said to commit injustice. And there is in every breach of covenant a contradiction properly so called; for he that covenanteth, willeth to do, or omit, in the time to come; and he that doth any action, willeth it in that present, which is part of the future time, contained in the covenant: and therefore he that violateth a covenant, willeth the doing and the not doing of the same thing, at the same time; which is a plain contradiction.[57]

But again, the point here is not obvious. What would it prove to show that the party in breach is in contradiction?

Again, a connection must be made with morality here. Hobbes' arguments are, broadly speaking, Kantian. Hobbes' rhetorical genius is revealed in the fact that his formulation is almost perfectly ambiguous between the prudential and the moral readings of his theory, but only the second can support his position.

What is more, Hobbes' argues that unperformed contracts do not obligate in the state of nature. This is because, as in that state there is no guarantee that the other party will perform, there can be no

---

[56] Hobbes, *Leviathan*, XV 1. See also Hobbes, '*De Cive*', II 22, III 1–3, VI 20.
[57] Hobbes, 'Human Nature', XVI 2.

obligation, Hobbes alleges, on one to perform.[58] From our perspective, the chief feature of this argument is that it operates on the assumption that contracts create obligations per se, it is just that in the state of nature further considerations undermine that obligation. Again, then, we see Hobbes' account of contract covertly introducing moral notions into his general theory.

For our purposes, the chief consequence of this observation is not that Hobbes is unable to present an amoral account of sovereign authority; it concerns rather the nature of the morality upon which the account relies. The first thing to notice is that the moral norm in question is prior to the state. Again, Hobbes' presentation beautifully elides this point.

In separating the discussion of the social contract from that of the bindingness of contracts, ie in separating the second law of nature and its consequences from the third, Hobbes appears able to ground the authority of the sovereign before he establishes that contracts are binding. Because of this, he is able to give the impression—though he does not actually say—that contracts are binding because the sovereign says that they are. But this is an obfustication. The social contract is not merely a speech act in which people say that they will do such and such, generating no obligation. The social contract is what *binds* people to obey the sovereign. Without this, Hobbes' theory could not ground sovereign *authority*. This in turn means that the norm that makes contracts binding is and must be prior to the authority of the sovereign. It is this norm that generates the sovereign's authority. It is prior to the state.[59]

What is more, the norm in question belongs to commutative, not distributive, justice, even as Hobbes defines the former term. It is a norm that relates to the justice of contracting. More significantly, it is a norm that operates as between individuals in the state of nature. It cannot belong to distributive justice. Though Hobbes' theory presents a new beginning in political thought, it is not able entirely to escape the tradition.

Now, the claim is not that the above represents Hobbes' position. It may do, but it seems to me that, given the material that we have to hand, the evidence suggests that it does not. The point, however, is that Hobbes is committed to the existence of commutative justice and

[58] Hobbes, 'De Cive', II 11; Hobbes, *Leviathan*, XIV 18.
[59] Cf Searle, *Making the Social World*, 62, 133–134.

to the notion that it grounds all politico-legal obligation, even if he did not realize it.

This problem leads to a second. If the state of nature contains a norm against breaching one's agreements, then it seems entirely implausible to think that this is the only norm in existence. It is surely bizarre to argue that natural rights exist in the state of nature but that they demand only that people keep their contracts, while leaving them free to kill and maim each other.[60] If the state of nature contains a norm that demands that one keep one's contracts, then it surely also contains norms insisting that one not interfere with the bodily integrity of others, for instance. In other words, it is unclear why one would accept Hobbes' commitments without also being prepared to accept the traditional view more generally.

5. Conclusion

Hobbes' theory is a work of remarkable brilliance. But it was also an error. It rejects the tradition without any justification at all. Moreover, as we have just seen, it fails to escape the tradition, as the idea of the social contract, and hence of the foundational political value, must rely on commutative justice. For that reason also, the theory collapses back into the tradition. The new beginning, though a work of extraordinary genius, was a massive mistake.

6. Montesquieu

Though Hobbes' first influence was in England, it quickly spread to the Continent. It can be seen in the writings of figures such as Montesquieu and Rousseau. Although many of these thinkers were reacting against Hobbes, the imprint on them of the general structure of Hobbes' theory is unmistakable. It is also significant that the works of these authors were produced at a time when French society was shifting its focus more and more to issues of politics and the state. Montesquieu published *The Spirit of the Laws* in 1748 and Rousseau published the *Discourse on the*

---

[60] Cf Hume, 'Of the Original Contract', 468.

Origin Inequality in 1754 and *The Social Contract* in 1762. The French Revolution broke out in 1789. The following is the briefest examination of the first of these theories.

For our purposes, the chief feature of Montesquieu's account is the point of view from which he chooses to analyse the law. At the beginning of the work, he tells us that his task is not to study 'laws but the spirit of the laws'.[61] And as he explains, 'this spirit consists in the various relations that laws may have with various things'.[62] In other words, his is an attempt to understand, not law, but the effects of law. The book is a long investigation of those laws that suit particular kinds of political systems. The aim of the book, then, is to study law from the perspective of the state's goals. As Montesquieu admits, this means that he does not examine law for its own sake at all. 'I have had to follow the natural order of laws less than that of these relations and of these things.'[63] And as he says in his title, his study is not of laws but of the spirit of the laws.

Montesquieu's approach has been so completely swallowed by modern legal analysis that it is now ubiquitous, and as a result it can be hard to see that such analysis is not analysis of law as such. Because of this, modern readers tend to find Montesquieu's apology hard to fathom. He saw that he was not examining law as such, but we do not. His investigation is certainly worthwhile, but it is not, as we tend to think it, legal analysis proper. It is rather a parallel discipline to the study of law qua law.

He saw something else that we do not. His approach departed from the tradition. That view examined law—specifically private law—in part because it held that the foundations of the state were to be found there. Montesquieu did not reject this idea, but chose to focus on a different issue. Nevertheless, Montesquieu recognized that it was revolutionary to study law, all law, through the lens of the state's goals. That approach reversed the traditional methodology.

Montesquieu's focus on the spirit of the laws also leads him to declare that he will ignore the traditional divide between public and private law.[64] But it is truer to say that he ignores the private law completely. For instance, in his examination of 'the laws in relation to

[61] Montesquieu, *The Spirit of the Laws*, 1.3.16.
[62] Ibid.
[63] Ibid.
[64] Ibid.

commerce', he explores the impact of trade on the life of the nation, but not even one commercial law is examined.[65]

In this regard, it is not clear that *The Spirit of the Laws* can be regarded as an examination of law at all. At most, it can be said to be an analysis of law only if it is accepted that the sole appropriate viewpoint from which to understand law is the societal. That is the modern view, but it was invented by Hobbes.

Montesquieu's neglect of the private law allowed him to say some obviously false—though now widely accepted—things about law. For instance, he maintained that 'Laws should be so appropriate to the people for whom they are made that it is very unlikely that the laws of one nation can suit another.'[66] But this, as we should know, is wrong. It is incompatible with the spread of Western private law around the world, sometimes involuntarily but often voluntarily by adoption of the common law or codes based on the French *Code Civil* or the German *Bürgerliches Gesetzbuch*. Of course, different cultures interpret these documents in somewhat different ways, but even with respect to diverse cultures the commonality is much more significant than the differences.[67]

Montesquieu also maintained that law must relate

to the way of life of the peoples, be they ploughmen, hunters, or herdsmen; they should relate to the degree of liberty that the constitution can sustain, to the religion of the inhabitants, their inclinations, their wealth, their number, their commerce, their mores and their manners; finally the laws are related to one another, to their origin, to the purpose of the legislator, and to the order of things on which they are established.[68]

Similarly, again anticipating the modern view, he wrote that 'Laws must relate to the nature and the principle of the government that is established or that one wants to establish, whether those laws form it as do political laws, or maintain it, as do civil laws.'[69]

---

[65] Ibid, Books 20–22.

[66] Ibid, 1.3.12.

[67] The work of the legal historian, Alan Watson, is especially important in this regard. See eg Watson, *The Evolution of Western Private Law: Expanded Edition*; Watson, *Legal History and a Common Law for Europe*.

[68] Montesquieu, *The Spirit of the Laws*, 1.3.14.

[69] Ibid, 1.3.13.

But these claims are flatly inconsistent with the facts. Any student of the laws of Imperial Rome must be struck by how similar they are to our own, not of course in their detail, but in their general structure. It is for this reason that students of the common law were frequently introduced to the fundamental conceptions of that law by studying the Roman. In general, the private law of all Western legal systems bears—in structure, not in detail—a remarkable similarity, no matter whether those systems were democracies, monarchies, or dictatorships. This is because that law is not about 'the way of life of the peoples'. It is about only two kinds of relationship and three kinds of event. The relationships are about our relationship to things (the law of property) and our relationship with other individuals (the law of obligations). The events are one individual harming another (tort), one individual benefiting another (unjust enrichment), and two individuals getting together (contract). That is it.

7. Germany

In the West, the influence of the modern view came last to Germany. This is something about which Germans ought to be proud. But it has come. Some of this was inevitable. In particular, German philosophers were no more successful at insulating themselves from international developments than others have been (or should be). After Hegel, the Germans quickly became infatuated by the political isms listed in the introduction to this part of the book, and of course they invented many of them. In law, however, there seem to be three main reasons for the death of the traditional view.

The civil law has been blest with the attention of the Western world's most distinguished theorists of the substantive law. However, many of these theorists focused on the Roman law rather than the indigenous laws of the various European states.[70] As a result, when the *ius commune* was replaced by civil codes, studies associated with Roman law came to be seen as merely historical and as no longer relevant to the study of the modern law. Reinhard Zimmermann has documented the decline in the perceived importance of legal history over the period of codification,[71] and there has also been a similar

---

[70] This is true also of the natural lawyers, though they sought to reform Roman law.
[71] Zimmermann, *Roman Law, Contemporary Law, European Law*, lecture 1.

decline in the perceived importance of the legal theory associated with this period.

In the absence of legal theory, it is perhaps natural to think that European private law is based on distributive justice, as it is—at least nominally—contained in statutory codes promulgated by the state. The inference seems clear: as it was the state that passed the civil code, the code must reflect the state's justice, ie distributive justice. But that is another non sequitur. It is quite possible that the state chose to implement a code designed to achieve commutative justice. This is particularly plausible when one remembers that the civil codes were largely designed to preserve the law and its values as they existed before codification.[72] And certainly, no lawyer of the *ius commune* would or could have accepted the idea that the law emanated from the state. It would have seemed rather the other way around. So, despite the apparent paradox, it is likely to be the case that if one wants to understand the state's statute (ie the civil code), one must ignore the state's justice (ie distributive justice) and see instead that the state wanted the code to reflect commutative justice.

When asked a difficult legal question, the common lawyer, if she is a modern, thinks either of cases or statutes and, if she is a traditionalist, ponders principles and ideas. But the German lawyer reaches for his copy of the BGB, a statute. In such a climate, it is no wonder that the traditional view is forgotten.

The third reason is undoubtedly the disaster for Germans and the world known as the Third Reich and, in particular, the (eventual[73]) desire after the defeat of the Nazis to put aside traditional thoughts about law, thoughts believed to be essentially conservative, nationalistic, and militaristic—'Prussian', in a word. The German nation's desire for a new beginning is understandable, indeed admirable, but its past contained more value that it was prepared to accept—even, or perhaps even especially, that of Prussia.[74]

---

[72] For discussion, see Gordley, 'Myths of the French Civil Code'; Zimmermann, *Roman Law, Contemporary Law, European Law*, 3–4.
[73] See Müller, *Hitler's Justice: The Courts of the Third Reich*.
[74] For a brilliant account, see Clark, *Iron Kingdom*.

10

Locke

1. Biographical Background

Locke was born in 1632 and his most important work of political philosophy, the *Two Treatises of Government*, was published in 1689. That date, however, is not significant. It appears that Locke was writing the *Treatises* in the period 1678–1681, the time of the so-called Exclusion Crisis.[1]

In 1673, James, the brother and presumptive heir of Charles II, refused to take the oath demanded by the Test Act, thereby revealing that he was a Catholic. In a land where anti-Catholic sentiment had been stirred to the point of hysteria due to the Popish Plot—a Catholic conspiracy to kill Charles fabricated by Titus Oates—the revelation was inflammatory. Apart from the religious concerns, opponents of that faith were convinced that Catholicism was inexorably tied to autocracy.[2]

In response to James' revelations, the Earl of Shaftesbury, founder of the Whig movement and not coincidentally Locke's patron, introduced into Parliament the Exclusion Bill, designed to prevent James taking the throne. Whatever else they are, Locke's *Treatises* were intended to support this movement.

---

[1] Laslett, '*Two Treatises of Government* and the Revolution of 1688'.
[2] As it was in the hands of James II, influenced as he was by Louis XIV's modernization programme. Pincus, *1688*.

It is worth stressing the seriousness with which the Whig movement took the issue. So opposed to Catholicism were the Whigs that every November, on the anniversary of Elizabeth I's accession to the throne, they conducted large processions in London in which they burnt an effigy of the Pope. Locke was himself implicated in the Rye House Plot, a conspiracy to assassinate Charles and James, though historians have found little evidence to support the idea that Locke was involved. Nevertheless, he was forced to flee to the Netherlands in 1683, not returning until after the Glorious Revolution in 1688.

The consequence of this is unsurprising. Like Hobbes', Locke's chief focus was the state. Accordingly, all of the issues discussed in the *Treatises* are approached from the perspective of government. They are two treatises *of government*.

But we must not overstate the similarities between Hobbes and Locke. In particular, given Locke's hostility to absolute government, his theory had to part company with many of Hobbes' most fundamental commitments. And the way in which it does this is of great significance for us.

As we will see, despite Locke's antipathy to Hobbes, his theory is greatly influenced by his predecessor's. This is most evident in its adoption of the social contract methodology and its use of the concept of consent. But Locke tries to avoid Hobbes' conclusions by building rights into the state of nature, so that individuals have rights before the civil condition is formed. This, as we see in more detail below, is an attempt to marry the modern and the traditional models. But as we also see, it is a failure. It can account neither for the state's authority nor for the existence of the rights so crucial to Locke's argument for limited government. This is because, though he is clearly influenced by the tradition, he has forgotten the understanding of justice upon which the tradition was based.

2. The State of Nature

The fundamental difference between Locke and Hobbes comes out immediately in Locke's description of the state of nature. As we saw in the previous chapter, Hobbes maintains that the state of nature is void of law, rights, wrongs, justice, and injustice. For Locke, however, that view could not be more wrong.

Locke agrees with Hobbes that the state of nature is a condition in which individuals possess 'perfect freedom to order their actions, and dispose of their possessions and persons, as they think fit...without asking leave, or depending upon the will of any other man', but Locke maintains that this liberty exists only 'within the bounds of the law of nature.'[3] Moreover, the law of nature in Locke is a far more powerful idea than it is in Hobbes. In particular, it is a moral concept with important normative consequences. As Locke puts it, 'The state of nature has a law of nature to govern it, which obliges every one: and reason, which is that law, teaches all mankind, who will but consult it, that being all equal and independent, no one ought to harm another in his life, health, liberty, or possessions.'[4] This is clearly no mere appeal to self-interest.

The foundation of the law of nature is examined in section 4. For the moment, we proceed on the assumption that it exists and that it establishes rights to life, health, liberty, and possessions.

For Locke, two crucial consequences follow from the existence of the natural law. First, individuals in the state of nature are entitled—ie have a specific legal permission—to restrain others from violating the law.[5] One would be permitted to prevent a person striking another, for instance. Secondly, individuals in the state of nature are entitled to punish those who violate the law.[6] One would be permitted to punish a person who struck another, for example. In general, then, the state of nature is a state of law.

Despite this, Locke agrees with Hobbes that all is not well in the state of nature. But again, the analysis of the problem is different. For Hobbes, as we saw in Chapter 9, the problem is that the 'logic' of the state of nature drives people into conflict and thus prevents them living worthwhile lives. That argument is amoral. But Locke's reasoning is quite different. For him, the problem is that the rights possessed by individuals in the state of nature receive inadequate protection, even though individuals are entitled to enforce them. The problem is obvious. Individuals frequently lack the physical power and the will to enforce the law. This argument is moral. Hence, though both

---

[3] Locke, *Two Treatises of Government*, II 4.
[4] Ibid, II 6.
[5] Ibid, II 7.
[6] Ibid.

Hobbes and Locke appeal to the need for security, their appeals are importantly different.

Moreover, Locke also maintains that the state of nature is problematic because of the rights that it contains. The problem here is that, in that condition, it must be for each individual to determine the ambit of her own rights, there being no neutral body to decide disputes. And this leads to unavoidable conflict and the undermining of those rights.

In consequence, then, Locke maintains that individuals are under an obligation to leave the state of nature and form societies with public authorities capable of enforcing the natural law by protecting natural rights and dealing with the inevitable disputes that arise concerning them.[7]

In order to fulfil its purpose, then, the created society must be the ultimate authority on the use of coercion. In order to respond to the problem just presented, the state must have the ultimate power to determine disputes and to enforce its resolutions. This means that, in transferring from the state of nature to the civil condition, individuals must surrender to the sovereign their natural right to protect, enforce, and punish those who violate the natural law.[8]

The creation of the sovereign and the surrender to him of that right is achieved through the social contract. I examine that notion now.

3. The Social Contract

3.1 The Fact of Consent

The differences between Hobbes' and Locke's approaches encountered above carry over to their theories of the social contract. As discussed in Chapter 9, at least on the face of it, Hobbes' account of the social contract is based entirely on self-interest. But Locke's is clearly not. His view is again overtly moral. His appeal to contract is designed to show that the sovereign's authority to govern rests entirely on the consent of the governed.

This generates a problem for Locke that Hobbes did not have—or at least did not have so obviously. If sovereign authority requires consent,

---

[7] Ibid, II 87, 123, 128–130.
[8] Ibid, II 87–89, 99.

then it seems that there is no sovereign authority because, apart from a few exceptions, as a matter of fact citizens have not consented to the authority of their sovereigns. To put the point somewhat differently, Locke's theory seems a poor account of political authority, as it sets necessary conditions for that authority that could be met only in the most unusual circumstances.

Locke is well aware of this difficulty, however. To respond to it, he presents his notorious theory of tacit consent. It is worth examining this argument in detail.

And to this I say, that every man, that hath any possessions, or enjoyment, of any part of the dominions of any government, doth thereby give his tacit consent, and is as far forth obliged to obedience to the laws of that government, during such enjoyment, as any one under it; whether this his possession be of land, to him and his heirs for ever, or a lodging only for a week; or whether it be barely traveling freely on the highway; and in effect, it reaches as far as the very being of any one within the territories of that government.[9]

There are two ways of interpreting these claims. The first takes the notion of tacit consent literally. It reads Locke as holding that a person who performs an activity of the kind mentioned thereby literally consents to the authority of the sovereign. On this view, tacit consent is real consent that is *implied* from behaviour. Let me explain.

Imagine that you ask me if I would like to come to dinner. Ordinarily, I would indicate my desire to do so by saying something such as, 'Thanks very much, I would love to come.' But I might do the same thing by picking up my wallet, putting on my jacket and walking out the door with a large smile on my face. Here, I communicate my desire by behaving in a certain way. We might say that my consent to accompanying you to dinner is express in the first case and tacit in the sense of being implicit in the second.

This reading preserves the moral force of consent, but it means that Locke's argument relies on a factual claim that is implausible. Collecting my wallet and jacket and walking out the door might indicate consent to going to dinner, but walking down the highway is not even implicit consent to the authority of the sovereign. This can be tested simply. If you ask me whether I consented to going to your

[9] Ibid, II 119; see also II 110.

house for dinner, my response would be 'Of course I did.' But if you ask me after my return from one of my evening walks whether I consented to the authority of the sovereign, I would be bemused.

The basic point, of course, is that consent is necessarily intentional. It is an intentional act that must be communicated. In other words, it is a speech act. When I left my room, I intended to consent to come to dinner and communicated that to you by my action. But while walking down the highway could be viewed as a form of communication, it cannot reasonably be thought to communicate consent to sovereign authority when the relevant intention is in all but the most bizarre circumstances completely absent.

Another reading of Locke's claims is available, however. This second interpretation is built on the observation that Locke talks about having and enjoying possessions and rights. On this view, Locke's argument centres on the *benefit* that individuals gain from the existence of the state, such as the enjoyment of the use of the highways.[10] This position is based on factual claims that are entirely plausible—I do gain a benefit by walking down the highway, for example—but the moral point is lost. Benefit is not consent. On this reading, tacit consent is not consent. Consequently, this interpretation takes us far from the theory Locke seems to present in the second of the *Treatises*.

Now, one might argue that, despite all the references to consent, Locke really intended to rely on benefit or that, though Locke did not so intend, his theory can be revised and improved by replacing the argument from consent with one from benefit. But that strategy too is fraught with difficulty.

The first thing to notice about it is that this argument is not contractual but is based on the principle of unjust enrichment. The argument is not 'You owe an obligation to the state because you consented to its authority' but 'You owe an obligation to the state because the state benefits you.' And when the analogy with the law of unjust enrichment is revealed, it can be seen that the theory collapses. For one thing, a benefit can generate an obligation only if it is freely accepted,[11] but this is seldom the case with respect to the benefits received from the state. If my walking on the highway commits me, then how am I to

---

[10] For a similar reading of Locke's theory of property, see Waldron, *The Right to Private Property*, 152–153, 170.

[11] The claim is that there cannot be obligation without free acceptance, not that free acceptance is sufficient to ground obligation. Again, there is a parallel with law here. If *A* provides a benefit for *B* that *B* has not requested but accepts, must *B* pay *A* for the benefit?

avoid committing myself?[12] For another, it is generally recognized that unjust enrichment generates an obligation only when the benefit can be returned. If it cannot be returned, then there is no obligation. In law, this is known as the defence of change of position. Finally, the obligation generated by the principle of unjust enrichment is only to return the enrichment. If I mistakenly pay £1,000 into your bank account, then you gain an obligation to pay £1,000 to me. But you do not gain an obligation to obey my commands in general. The authority of the state cannot be justified by appeal to unjust enrichment.

Also significant is the fact that abandoning consent for the principle of unjust enrichment would undermine Locke's argument for limited government. As we see shortly, Locke maintains that the limited nature of the consent given in the social contract limits the power of government; but that argument cannot run on the position under examination.

3.2 Limited Sovereign Authority

As we have seen, Locke maintains that we enter the civil condition in order to protect and enforce the rights that we possess in the state of nature. Therefore, he maintains, the authority to which we consent is only the authority to protect and enforce those rights.[13] A government that coerced in other ways would act outside its authority, Locke maintains. From these ideas, Locke concludes that sovereignty is fiduciary and that citizens retain the legitimate power to remove the sovereign if he acts unjustly.[14]

This is the second great problem with Locke's theory. It is presented as a theory of the (limited) authority of the sovereign, but in attempting to limit that authority, Locke destroys it. This issue was discussed in section 2.3 of Chapter 9, but it will be useful to examine a specific issue here, a case of a kind that was at the forefront of Locke's mind.

Though some have answered 'Yes' (see eg Birks, *Introduction to the Law of Restitution*, ch 8) others have answered 'No' (see Grantham and Rickett, *Enrichment and Restitution in New Zealand*, 243–257). Cf *Lumbers v W Cook Builders Pty Ltd (In liq)* [2008] HCA 27, [2008] 232 CLR 635. In any case, no legal theorist would argue that there was an obligation in the circumstances relevant to the state, even on the dubious assumption that the state ought to be treated as a private person in this regard.

[12] Cf Ripstein, *Force and Freedom: Kant's Legal and Political Philosophy*, ch 8.
[13] Locke, *Two Treatises of Government*, II 90, 135–142.
[14] Ibid, II 149, 203–204.

Imagine a dispute between *A* and *B* over the ownership of a particular object, *p*. Assume also that in fact *A* owns *p*. And remember that we are entitled to say that *A* owes *p* in advance of any authoritative ruling to that effect, by a court for instance, because of the existence of a natural law that demands respect for life, health, liberty, and possessions. If we thought that ownership and the like depended on authoritative rulings, then Locke's claim that natural rights limit the authority of the sovereign would come to nothing.

In the state of nature, as we saw, the dispute between *A* and *B* cannot be settled. Because of the absence of a public authority, each party must decide for himself whether he owns *p*. And the problem is that they both think that they do. The point of moving to the civil condition is to enable disputes of this kind to be settled.

Imagine now, then, that we are in the civil condition and that *A* and *B* take their dispute to a court. Locke's position is the following: (i) the court has the authority to determine *A v B*; but (ii) its authority is constrained by the natural law so that it lacks the authority to decide inconsistently with that law.[15] The problem is that (i) and (ii) are inconsistent.

Imagine that the court deals with the dispute in a careful and conscientious fashion but nevertheless finds for *B*. This, according to Locke, is not within its authority. It is a violation of the natural law. In these circumstances, *A* must be entitled to say, 'You have decided for *B*, but you are wrong, *p* is mine', because the claim is correct.[16] And that means that the court has no authority to determine the dispute between *A* and *B*.

The point can also be expressed in terms of the distinction between obligation and authority introduced in section 2.3 of Chapter 9. Obligation is about what one should do, while authority is about who gets to decide what one should do. A person has authority over another only if she is able to determine the other's obligations. But this is precisely what Locke denies the sovereign. At least in many important areas, he insists that the natural law and not the sovereign gets to decide what an individual's obligations are. But the natural law does not literally decide anything. It is not a decision-maker. In the end,

---

[15] In fact, Locke seems thoroughly confused about this. See eg ibid, II 91.
[16] Ibid, II 138.

then, it must be for the individual to decide.[17] And that means that the individual has authority, not the sovereign. But if that is so, then we are still in the state of nature. In attempting to limit the authority of the sovereign, Locke never gets to the sovereign. He is unable to escape the state of nature.

The comparison with Hobbes' view is stark and not at all to Locke's credit. Of special significance is Locke's attempt to deal with the problem generated by the idea of a higher law, examined in the previous chapter. Recall that this problem had a theoretical and a practical side. The theoretical side is that the idea of a higher law in the sense defined in that chapter is inconsistent with the idea of sovereign authority. The practical problem is that belief in a higher law tends to promote revolution. Locke's answer to the difficulty ignores the theoretical side of the problem entirely.[18] That is unsurprising given that any acknowledgement of the problem would destroy his theory. He responds to the practical problem by suggesting that his view would not result in anarchy because at least most individuals can be trusted to do the right thing as in the end they must 'answer... to the supreme judge of all men'.[19]

This view reflects Locke's extraordinary notion that the demands of morality are all but entirely transparent.[20] Hence, as Shirley Letwin points out,[21] when one of Locke's friends prodded him to produce a work demonstrating the truths of ethics, Locke responded that such was not necessary as 'the Gospel contains so perfect a body of ethics, that reason may be excused from that inquiry, since she may find man's duty clearer and easier in revelation, than in herself'.[22] For this reason, politics, for Locke, is understood to be the study of the best way to achieve what everyone knows ought to be done.[23]

---

[17] Ibid, II 149, 203–204, 224–226, 240. See also Jeremy Waldron's claim that, on Locke's view, 'An owner is not entitled to decide to allow his goods to perish uselessly in his possession', but that 'what counts as use and what counts as useless destruction is for the owner to decide': Waldron, *The Right to Private Property*, 161. If this is indeed Locke's view, and I agree that it is, then it evinces a poor understanding of the reality of authority.

[18] Locke, *Two Treatises of Government*, II 149, 203–204, 224–226, 240.

[19] Ibid, II 21.

[20] Compare Kant, 'Groundwork of the Metaphysics of Morals', 4:403–405.

[21] Letwin, *On the History of the Idea of Law*, 114.

[22] Locke, 'Some Familiar Letters Between Mr. Locke and Several of His Friends', 377.

[23] See also Letwin, *On the History of the Idea of Law*, 124.

This suggests the frankly bizarre notion that the English Civil War would have been averted had people taken their moral and religious obligations *more* seriously. It must be said that in this regard Locke entirely loses touch with reality. And it is for this reason that, at the end of the day, his theory lacks a coherent account of authority.

In conclusion, it is worth noting that despite Locke's apparent influence on Western political systems, his theory is in this regard deceased. There is no reflection of it in our systems, none of which allow citizens to escape sovereign authority by asserting a sincere claim that the actions of the sovereign have overstepped its authority. In particular, the concept of judicial review of legislation, as exercised by courts such as the Supreme Courts of Canada and the United States, is not Lockean. The authority of the court is an aspect of the authority of the sovereign. In practice, like Hobbes we too recognize that authority is all or nothing. As Hobbes recommended, we give all that authority to the sovereign though, as Hobbes advised against, we also accept the existence of divided sovereigns.

3.3 *The Moral Significance of Consent*

A further problem for Locke, one that he does not examine, concerns the significance of consent. As we have seen, he maintains that sovereign authority is legitimate only if it has been consented to. But why is this? What is the moral significance of consent? The question must also be asked from the other direction. As we saw in section 3.2, Locke holds that individuals are entitled to rebel if the sovereign governs unjustly. But he does not think that citizens can simply, for whatever reason, withdraw their consent and thus render sovereign authority illegitimate with respect to them. But why not?

The general point here is that while consent may justify action that would otherwise be illegitimate, it does not in and of itself generate commitments. For instance, if I consent to your entry into my house, that does not mean that I cannot require you to leave.[24] Accordingly, it seems to follow that consent to sovereign authority can be removed for any reason whatsoever.

The answer to this point is, of course, that one not merely consented but contracted, and one has an obligation to keep one's contracts. Or

---

[24] It does mean, however, that I come under obligations to you that I would not otherwise have. See Beever, *Rediscovering the Law of Negligence*, 321–335.

to put the point from the other side, one contracted and contracts generate rights in others. Specifically, the social contract gives rise to an obligation in citizens to obey the sovereign and produces rights in the sovereign to be obeyed. But what is the justification for that answer?

Of course, the justification cannot refer to the sovereign. The justification is the ultimate justification of sovereign authority. Nor can it lie in distributive justice; there is no suggestion of this idea in Locke. The obligation must rather be a matter of commutative justice.

Now, this is not what Locke says. He provides no justification at all. But that is no surprise. As we are about to discuss in more detail, Locke relies on commutative justice, but he lacks the concept of that form of justice and so cannot justify his reliance on it, or even articulate the nature of it. Commutative justice is present in Locke's theory, but it was absent from Locke's mind. As we see now, this explains some of the most serious lacunas in Locke's account.

4. Rights in the State of Nature

4.1 Bodily Integrity

As we saw above, Locke maintains that individuals possess rights in the state of nature.[25] These are rights that others not harm one's 'life, health, liberty, or possessions'.[26] Clearly, this implies a right to bodily integrity and also, with the addition of further arguments examined below, property rights. But what is less apparent is the origin of these rights. What is the justification for the claim that these rights exist in the state of nature?

Locke's first answer is that the rights arise from the fact that all are 'equal and independent',[27] but this argument will not do. If Locke intends that individuals are morally equal and morally ought to be independent, then the claim relies on an argument that he does not supply. If he intends only that individuals are roughly equal in power, talent, and the like, and are equally able to exist without the aid of others, then the argument does not support the conclusion. Moreover, an objection to both views, equality per se could establish only that

---

[25] Locke, *Two Treatises of Government*, II 4.
[26] Ibid, II 6.
[27] Ibid.

individuals must have equal rights. It cannot determine that they possess the list of rights Locke enunciates.[28]

He then argues that natural rights follow from the fact that people are 'all the workmanship of one omnipotent, and infinitely wise maker'.[29] This is meant to show that, as we are God's property, we must abide by his wishes. But what is missing is any evidence to suggest that God wishes us to have the rights Locke catalogues. This, of course, is for the reason we have seen earlier: Locke thinks that the commands of God are entirely transparent and so require no argument. But this view cannot be accepted. Locke then falls back on the argument examined and rejected in the previous paragraph: the idea that equality generates the natural rights. In consequence, then, it has to be said that Locke offers no real argument for the existence of natural rights.[30]

Why is this? One response, the one most famously taken by Bentham, rejects the idea that there can be any natural rights. But even if that were conceded, it would not explain the absence of even a bad argument.

I suggest that the problem is this. Locke's natural rights exist prior to existence of the polity and do not rely on distributive concerns. Accordingly, they must be based on commutative justice. As we saw in the second part of this book, that idea was nothing new. It was, in fact, the standard view adopted by the traditional thinkers. But those thinkers articulated that view in accordance with an understanding of justice that Locke lacked the conceptual tools to articulate. In short, he lacked the concept of commutative justice. Accordingly, though he is groping towards it in the passages examined above, he never finds it, and hence his theory is left without a foundation.

---

[28] Hence, the idea might generate the need for the reciprocity that Locke claims, but it does not do more than this. Ibid, II 5.

[29] Ibid, II 6.

[30] See also the claim that, although Locke's commitment to natural law theory entails that all rights ought to receive rational, as opposed to merely theological, foundation, 'It does seem to me that parts of Locke's political philosophy are difficult to restate in secular terms. His argument for the juridical equality of persons...and his account of the inalienability and imprescriptibility of certain human rights...are the most prominent examples. Moreover, these positions are so fundamental to Locke's political philosophy that they give the whole thing an undeniably theological [and non-rational] flavour': Waldron, *The Right to Private Property*, 142.

To put this another way, Locke needs an argument to demonstrate the existence of rights that hold as between individuals in the state of nature; all he has, however, is a theory of the state.

4.2 Property

The fifth chapter of the second of the *Treatises* is crucial. In it, Locke tries to demonstrate that rights to property exist in the state of nature.[31] In this regard, Locke has, and recognizes that he has, two problems. First, he must show that individuals have some entitlement to property and how that entitlement arises. Secondly, he must show that there is nothing unfair in the nature of property acquisition. Locke's recognition of these two problems is notable in itself, as few modern theorists recognize a distinction between these ideas. I examine them in turn.

The first argument found in Locke (the 'use argument') is also found in many other writers. It is based on the idea that people are entitled to use objects.

God, who hath given the world to men in common, hath also given them reason to make use of it to the best advantage of life, and convenience. The earth, and all that is therein, is given to men for the support and comfort of their being. And...being given for the use of men, there must of necessity be a means to appropriate them some way or other, before they can be of any use, or at all beneficial to any particular man. The fruit, or venison, which nourishes the wild Indian, who knows no enclosure, and is still a tenant in common, must be his, and so his, i. e. a part of him, that another can no longer have any right to it, before it can do him any good for the support of his life.[32]

This argument is fallacious. It relies on conflating liberties and claim rights. The use of objects requires the former not the latter, but property is a claim right. For this reason, it is not obvious that Locke's Indian must own fruit or venison.[33]

---

[31] Here I side with ibid, 137–138 and against Tully, *A Discourse on Property*. A related argument was also attempted by Locke's contemporaries, Hale, *Treatise of the Nature of Lawes*, 36–37; Cumberland, *De legibus naturæ disquisitio philosophica*, 337–338; Baxter, *The Second Part of the Nonconformists Plea for Peace*, 54; Tyrrell, *Patriarcha non monarcha*, 108–114.

[32] Locke, *Two Treatises of Government*, II 26.

[33] See also Waldron, *The Right to Private Property*, 169.

The more famous and more important argument is presented in the following section (the 'labour argument').

> Though the earth, and all inferior creatures, be common to all men, yet every man has a property in his own person: this no body has any right to but himself. The labour of his body, and the work of his hands, we may say, are properly his. Whatsoever, then he removes out of the state that nature hath provided, and left it in, he hath mixed his labour with, and joined to it something that is his own, and thereby makes it his property. It being by him removed from the common state nature hath placed it in, it hath by this labour something annexed to it, that excludes the common right of other men: for this labour being the unquestionable property of the labourer, no man but he can have a right to what that is once joined to, at least where there is enough, and as good, left in common for others.[34]

This argument can be expressed in the simplest terms:

             (1)   I own my person.[35]
Hence,   (2)   I own my labour.
Therefore, (3)   I own the things upon which I labour.

But this just helps to reveal the argument's weakness. Simply, (3) does not follow from (2). At best, (2) generates an entitlement to receive the benefit of one's labour. Again, this is a feature of the principle of unjust enrichment and it has nothing to do with property.

The difficulty here carries over from that encountered in our examination of the natural rights above. If we knew why we own our persons, then we would know why we own our labour, and that might reveal, or at least give us some reason to think, that we own the things upon which we labour. But all of these arguments, *which relate to commutative justice*, are missing.

However, it is sometimes thought that Locke's theory can be improved by replacing the labour argument as presented with the idea that genuine respect for persons requires the existence of property rights. For instance, John Simmons has argued that Locke's idea is really that people need property in order to lead independent and

---

[34] Locke, *Two Treatises of Government*, II 27.
[35] As Waldron, *The Right to Private Property*, 178 insists, the right is to the person and not to the body.

self-governing lives.³⁶ Alternatively, according to CB Macpherson, Locke proposed a theory of property accumulation restricted only by the following (in the end he thought irrelevant) three principles: one may only appropriate as much as one can use before it spoils (the 'spoliation argument'); one must leave 'enough and as good' for others (the 'enough and as good argument'); and one may only appropriate property through one's own labour.³⁷

Different though they are, these theories both fail to notice what is essential to Locke's view. The labour argument is different from the others, as it relates to commutative, not distributive, justice. Of course, Locke is unable to say this. In the light of the above, however, the point becomes transparent. The point of the labour argument is not to show that property acquisition is fair vis-à-vis all other members of one's community. It is designed to show how one person can gain an entitlement to an object such that other persons acquire an obligation owed directly to the labourer to respect that labourer's possession. In that light, the point of the argument is clear. In labouring on an object, 'something [is] annexed to it, that excludes the common right of other men'.³⁸ The idea, then, is that an individual's right to his body in the state of nature generates a right to the things upon which he labours. It is clear that that is the structure the argument is meant to have, though the argument is itself absent. And it is also noteworthy that this understanding of the argument was shared by Kant, whose commitment to the traditional view permitted him to see it. To Locke's claim that labour annexes something to an object, Kant replied that

since there corresponds to a right on one side a duty on the other, [Locke must think that] an external thing always remains under obligation to the first possessor even though it has left his hands; that, because it is already under obligation to him, it rejects anyone else who pretends to be the possessor of it. So he would think of my right as if it were a guardian spirit accompanying the thing, always pointing me out to whoever else wanted to take possession of it and protecting it against any incursions by them.³⁹

Simmons' suggestion, then, though powerful, misses Locke's focus. Simmons' concern relates to distributive, not commutative, justice.

---

³⁶ Eg Simmons, *On The Edge of Anarchy*.
³⁷ Macpherson, *The Political Theory of Possessive Individualism*.
³⁸ Locke, *Two Treatises of Government*, II 27.
³⁹ Kant, 'The Metaphysics of Morals', 6:260–261. See also ibid, 6:241.

The argument presented by Simmons perhaps shows why property rights should be created by the sovereign in the civil condition if they do not already exist, but it cannot show what Locke is trying to show: that property rights exist in the state of nature. Macpherson too wrongly interprets the labour argument as a restriction on the acquisition of property, a concern of distributive justice. But it is quite the reverse. It is intended as the explanation of the acquisition of property rights, upon which restrictions may or may not be placed for reasons of distributive justice.[40]

This is why Locke introduces the spoliation argument by saying:

It will perhaps be objected to this [ie to the labour argument], that if gathering the acorns, or other fruits of the earth, &c. makes a right to them, then any one may engross as much as he will. To which I answer, Not so. The same law of nature, that does by this means give us property, does also bound that property too.[41]

The objection considered here is based on distributive justice. The form of the argument is as follows:

Postulation: The conclusion of the argument from commutative justice cannot be accepted, because it has unjust distributive consequences.

Reply: In fact, those consequences do not obtain.

This is not the assertion of a further requirement or restriction. It is an attempt to demonstrate that the argument from (what we know as) commutative justice does not face an objection founded in distributive justice.[42]

The 'enough and as good' argument must be interpreted in the same way.[43] This is raised specifically in relation to the ownership of land. This is what Locke first tells us:

But the chief matter of property being now not the fruits of the earth, and the beasts that subsist on it, but the earth itself; as that which takes in and carries with it all the rest; I think it is plain, that property in that too is

---

[40] See also Waldron, *The Right to Private Property*, 171.
[41] Locke, *Two Treatises of Government*, II 31.
[42] See also Waldron, *The Right to Private Property*, 207–209.
[43] Ibid, 209–18.

acquired as the former. As much land as a man tills, plants, improves, cultivates, and can use the product of, so much is his property. He by his labour does, as it were, enclose it from the common.[44]

This to say that acquisition of land follows the labour argument.

Locke then introduces what some have taken to be a further restriction on acquisition: consent.[45] 'Nor will it invalidate his right, to say every body else has an equal title to it; and therefore he cannot appropriate, he cannot enclose, without the consent of all his fellow-commoners, all mankind.'[46] But this does not assert that consent is required for acquisition. It asserts the opposite: that the previous claim cannot be asserted (the semi-colon is misleading here). The 'therefore' must be part of the argument being rejected, it cannot precede a conclusion drawn from the rejection of an argument. To put this more fully, it would follow from the fact that everyone has equal title to property that the consent of everyone would be required in order for an individual to acquire—that is the position being rejected—but it would not follow from the rejection of the idea that everyone has equal title to property that the consent of everyone would be required in order for an individual to acquire. This is confirmed in the remainder of the section in which Locke proceeds with the labour argument and ignores the supposed need for consent. 'He that in obedience to this command of God [to labour], subdued, tilled and sowed any part of it, thereby annexed to it something that was his property, which another had no title to, nor could without injury take from him.'[47]

Locke then implicitly considers an objection parallel to the one examined in connection with the spoliation argument above: that the acquisition of land based on labour alone would be distributively unjust. His response is of the same kind; he simply denies that any distributive injustice is generated. 'Nor was this appropriation of any parcel of land, by improving it, any prejudice to any other man, since there was still enough, and as good left; and more than the yet unprovided could use.'[48] In other words, the acquisition of land is Pareto efficient.

It is important to stress again that, like the spoliation argument, the 'enough and as good' argument is not intended as a justification of

---

[44] Locke, *Two Treatises of Government*, II 32.
[45] Tully, *A Discourse on Property*; Tully, *Locke in Context*.
[46] Locke, *Two Treatises of Government*, II 32.
[47] Ibid. See also Waldron, *The Right to Private Property*, 152–153.
[48] Locke, *Two Treatises of Government*, II 32. See also Waldron, *The Right to Private Property*, 170.

property. That justification lies wholly in the use and labour arguments, arguments based on what we understand to be commutative justice. Like the spoliation argument, the 'enough and as good' argument is intended to defeat objections to the use and labour arguments that arise in distributive justice. In short, they are attempts to show that the consequences of commutative justice are not distributively unjust.

In summary, then, the justification for property is found entirely in the use and labour arguments, arguments that we recognize as belonging to commutative justice. The spoliation and 'enough and as good' arguments are not part of the justification of property. They are replies to the objection that, though property is justified by commutative justice, the institution of property nevertheless should not be permitted because it is distributively unjust.

Accordingly we can see that Locke's theory of property shares a similar structure to Aquinas', Pufendorf's, and Kant's. All theories separately employ arguments based on commutative and distributive justice. The difference is that Locke cannot present or understand himself as doing so.

We can see, then, that Locke's interpreters find it difficult to understand his theory, and misunderstand his purposes, because they have forgotten what he has forgotten but is groping towards: that there are two forms of justice, independent of and coequal with each other. Though the difficulties with Locke's theory hardly evaporate when their relation to commutative justice is revealed, it at least becomes evident why Locke's arguments take the form that they do and his strategy becomes apparent.

But in the light of this discussion, it is also clear that part of the problem here is Locke's own. Simply, though he seems dimly aware of and utilizes arguments of commutative justice, he is unable to articulate these properly. This is because, writing after the collapse of the traditional conception in England, he lacked the conceptual tools necessary to elucidate his ideas. In short, he had lost the tools that belong to the analysis of commutative justice. Most obviously, he used arguments of commutative justice, but the term 'commutative justice' is to be found nowhere in his arguments. Locke was groping for the tradition, but was unable to find it.

It is also worth noting that Locke's replies to the objections based on distributive justice are unconvincing. His reply to the spoliation argument maintains either that acquisition in accordance with the labour argument *entails* that spoliation will not occur or covertly imports a new moral argument limiting property acquisition based on the idea that God did not give us dominion of objects in order that they be wasted. The first view, which I think is Locke's, turns on the meaning of spoliation. According to this position, if an object is laboured on, then it is used and hence not spoiled. In other words, the passage 'As much as any one can make use of to any advantage of life before it spoils, so much he may by his labour fix a property in'[49] is a factual statement and not the postulation of a moral principle. The problem with the view, however, is that labour must be given so wide an interpretation—so as to include investment, for example—that the claim in the end comes to nothing.[50] On the alternative view, the problem is more obvious: we are missing the new moral argument.

The 'enough and as good' argument is similarly flawed. Though Locke argues convincingly that the existence of private property increases the wealth of all,[51] this argument is not sufficient to establish his conclusion. Locke may well be right that 'a king of a large and fruitful territory [in America in the eighteenth century], feeds, lodges, and is clad worse than a day-labourer in England',[52] but one may nevertheless rationally prefer to be the former, as only he is able to lead an independent and self-governing life. It is to be noted that this point too would have been understood by the traditional thinkers to reflect commutative rather than distributive justice.

5. Locke's Theory and the Private Law

I have claimed that in the second of his two *Treatises*, Locke was groping for the tradition that he was unable to find. Evidence of this is also found in his attitude to private law. As we have seen, he holds that private rights exist in the state of nature: rights to bodily integrity, to property and to the performance of contracts. But as we have also seen, he is unable to justify these rights. And as I now show, he is unable properly to account for the appropriate responses to the violations of these rights.

---

[49] Locke, *Two Treatises of Government*, II 31.
[50] Or at least almost nothing. See Waldron, *The Right to Private Property*, 208.
[51] Locke, *Two Treatises of Government*, II 37–45.
[52] Ibid, II 41.

As we know, according to the traditional theorists, the appropriate response is reparation. And again, Locke shares this view.[53] But we see once again that Locke is unable to account for his own thesis.

In section 2, we saw that Locke maintains that individuals in the state of nature are entitled to punish those who violate others' natural rights.[54] He also holds that victims of wrongdoing have a right to reparation. When a wrong is committed,

> there is commonly injury done to some person or other, and some other man receives damage by his transgression: in which case he who hath received any damage, has, besides the right of punishment common to him with other men, a particular right to seek reparation from him that has done it.[55]

That sounds perfectly plausible, but we are missing what we need yet again: a justification for the claim.

Moreover, like Aquinas, Locke goes on to say that while magistrates are entitled to 'remit the punishment of criminal offences by his own authority, but yet cannot remit the satisfaction due to any private man for the damage he has received. That, he who has suffered the damage has a right to demand in his own name, and he alone can remit.'[56] In the light of what has been said, it is easy to understand these ideas. Punishment for crimes is based on distributive justice (more is said about this notion in Chapter 11) and so the magistrate may, if the public interest so demands, remit punishment. But reparation is based on commutative justice, and so the public interest is irrelevant, the issue being solely between the parties. But again Locke lacks the tools to express this.

As a result, and despite the fact that he distinguishes the justice of punishment and reparation as just observed, his 'argument' for reparation is nothing more than a loose analogy drawn between punishment and reparation. Once again, it is commutative justice that is missing.

---

[53] Ibid, II 11.
[54] Ibid, II 7.
[55] Ibid, II 10.
[56] Ibid, II 11.

11

The Utilitarians

Unlike the previous chapters, this one deals with a movement rather than a person. This is appropriate for two reasons. First, the movement is characterized by a considerable degree of intellectual harmony. Of course, the thinkers examined here disagree on some issues, sometimes important ones, but they all share the same general understanding of the nature of morality and its connection with politics and law. Secondly, the movement has been extremely influential as a movement. And, as is to some extent revealed in the following, its influence over modern thinkers is difficult to overestimate, even over those who claim to reject the movement. This influence is most clearly seen in the way in which utilitarianism fortifies the modern conception of political and legal philosophy. If it was Hobbes who shattered the traditional view, it was the utilitarians who cemented over the rubble.

1. Biographical Background

The biographical background of the three thinkers I examine in this chapter, Jeremy Bentham (1748–1832), John Stuart Mill (1806–1873), and Henry Sidgwick (1838–1900), is less important than it is for Hobbes or Locke. Of most significance is the way in which they saw their theory and the contribution they hoped it would make.

In short, the utilitarians were reformers. They were men struck by the many injustices of their age. They saw these injustices as having their source in outmoded views of moral and social correctness—in particular, doctrines of natural rights and the law itself—and wanted to replace these ideas with a more rational and impartial approach based on the good of all.

Because of this, the concerns of the utilitarians were not the same as Hobbes' or Locke's. While the older theorists focused on questions about the justification of the state, the utilitarians concentrated on asking how the state—presuming that it is per se just—should treat its citizens. In other words, their focus was on obligation, rather than authority.

But for us, the similarities between the views are nevertheless highly significant. Just like Hobbes and Locke, the utilitarians concentrated on the public rather than the private, on distributive rather than commutative justice. If they attended to private law at all, then, it was through that lens. The question for them was: what does this law do for the good of all?

2. The Principle of Utility and the Death of Commutative Justice

2.1 *Justice and Utilitarianism*

At the heart of utilitarianism stands the principle of utility, in Bentham's words, 'that principle which approves or disapproves of every action whatsoever, according to the tendency which it appears to have to augment or diminish the happiness of the party whose interest is in question'.[1] Accepting this formulation, Mill defined utilitarianism as 'The creed which accepts as the foundation of morals, Utility, or the Greatest Happiness Principle, [that] holds that actions are right in proportion as they tend to promote happiness, wrong as they tend to produce the reverse of happiness'.[2]

The crucial feature of this position is its monism. For the utilitarian, there is ultimately only one moral question: 'Does this (action, policy, thought, whatever) maximize utility?' This question has obvious application to the individual. If I want to know which of two options I ought to choose and only my own happiness is at stake, then I ought to choose the option that maximizes my happiness. It also clearly applies to society. If I need to choose between two

---

[1] Bentham, *The Principles of Morals and Legislation*, I 2.
[2] Mill, 'Utilitarianism', 2.2.

options and the happiness of others will be affected (as it almost always will), then I must choose the option that maximizes happiness for all (including me).

Utilitarians regard this monism as unproblematic, despite the fact that the Principle of Utility ranges over two apparently distinct normative spheres: the individual and society. This is because, as Bentham explains, society is just a collection of individuals and hence the interests of society are simply the interests of the individuals that constitute it.[3] For Bentham, then, once this point is recognized it can be seen that a concern with the well-being of society *is* a concern with the well-being of individuals.

The structure of this position is most clearly brought out by Mill's attempt to justify the Principle of Utility. Though Mill accepts that the principle cannot be given a strict proof,[4] he maintains that it can nevertheless be given an 'empirical' foundation.[5] His argument is that happiness is the only thing that we desire for its own sake. While we desire many other things, he insists, they are all desired as means to happiness.[6] While this argument is almost certainly not sound, it is instructive to accept it *arguendo* but ask what it is meant to prove. On reflection, the conclusion of the argument is that individuals desire only happiness as an end in itself. This is *perhaps* a justification for philosophical hedonism (ie the theory that happiness is the only intrinsic good, a view Mill also held in some form); but it does not argue for the Principle of Utility. More fully, Mill contends that you, I, and everyone else want only happiness for itself, but this is not nearly sufficient to show that right action maximizes happiness for all.

Mill's position relies on two crucial unstated premises. The first and most obvious (and perhaps partly overt[7]) premise is that, *ceteris paribus*, if one wants something, then one ought to have it. This is how we can get from the 'is' that Mill argues for (that people want happiness) to the 'ought' that he needs (that people ought to be happy). Let us concede that also.

---

[3] Bentham, *The Principles of Morals and Legislation*, I 4–5.
[4] Mill, 'Utilitarianism', 1.5, 4.1.
[5] Ibid, 4.10.
[6] Ibid, 4.3–10.
[7] Ibid, 4.1–3.

The second premise is that it is permissible to generalize these claims across persons. The idea is that the following argument is valid.

(1) Considering me alone: my happiness ought to be maximized.
(2) Considering you alone: your happiness ought to be maximized.
Hence, (3) considering you and I together (and no one else): our happiness ought to be maximized.
And (4) considering everybody (ie without any constraint on our focus): the happiness of everyone ought to be maximized.

The inferences from (2) on have been famously doubted—we examine perhaps the most influential criticism below. But it is instructive to pursue these ideas to their conclusions.

The first point to note is that we have apparently produced an interpersonal morality (3). We began with two personal claims—(1) that my happiness ought to be maximized and (2) that your happiness ought to be maximized—and we aggregated these to produce the interpersonal claim (3) that our happiness ought to be maximized. Hence, utilitarianism provides an account of 'commutative justice'. It also provides a theory of distributive justice (4). It is possible, then, to say that utilitarianism preserves the Aristotelian separation between commutative and distributive justice.

But that is hardly something to excite us. As the argument demonstrates, commutative justice on this view is entirely reducible to the distributive. Accordingly, for the utilitarian, commutative justice is redundant. It is, as we can see, the first step in the generalization from the individual to society, but there is no particular reason to stop there.

Though this is sufficiently obvious, it can also be brought out by considering the following cases, where 'commutative justice' is interpreted in line with the argument above. On this view, while we can ask what commutative justice would demand in a dispute between two individuals, this is the same as asking what distributive justice would demand were those people living in a two-person society. More importantly, though asking what commutative justice requires with respect to a certain dispute is intelligible, that form of justice is without practical consequence. This is because, if (as is almost always the case) the interests of third parties are at stake, then utilitarianism demands that those interests be taken into account equally with those of the parties themselves; or, on the other hand (as is perhaps never the case), if the interests of no third parties are at stake, then utilitarianism holds that only the interests of the parties should be taken into account, but as only those interests are relevant this is of no consequence. To put this another way, according to utilitarianism, if commutative justice demands a course of action inconsistent with distributive justice, then commutative justice should be ignored and distributive justice followed; but if commutative justice and distributive justice agree, then they can both be followed. But this is the same as saying that distributive justice should always be followed. Commutative justice is entirely redundant.

For this reason, commutative justice or interpersonal morality does not feature in utilitarianism. According to Bentham, for instance, 'The general object which *all* laws have, or ought to have, in common, is to augment the total happiness of the community.'[8] Commutative justice is entirely off the radar. For this reason, though Bentham recognizes that it is commonly thought that wrongs can be done to particular individuals—eg when I strike you this seems to be wrong specifically to you—he maintains that this thought is the result of inadequate reflection. In fact, Bentham tells us, the wrong is social. That is, the wrong is committed against everyone. The victim is a victim, says Bentham, not because she suffers a personal wrong, but because she personally suffered from the wrong;[9] in other words, because she suffered loss. So if I strike you, that is wrong because it violates a rule[10] determined in accordance with distributive justice. Hence, my action wrongs everyone. Of course, however, you are *the* victim of the wrong. But this means, not that I committed a wrong against you that I did not commit against anyone else, but that the wrong that I committed against the world caused only you to suffer loss.

Despite the influence of the modern conception of political philosophy, I expect that the reader will find this position to be quite unintuitive. If I strike you, it seems right to say that I commit a wrong specifically against you, even if I also commit a wrong against the world. It is noteworthy, then, that Mill felt the need to respond to this very issue.

It is no objection against this doctrine to say, that when we feel our sentiment of justice outraged, we are not thinking of society at large, or of any collective interest, but only of the individual case. It is common enough

---

[8] Bentham, *The Principles of Morals and Legislation*, XIII 1 (emphasis added).
[9] Ibid, XII 3–4.
[10] Or perhaps only a rule of thumb.

certainly, though the reverse of commendable, to feel resentment merely because we have suffered pain; but a person whose resentment is really a moral feeling, that is, who considers whether an act is blamable before he allows himself to resent it—such a person, though he may not say expressly to himself that he is standing up for the interest of society, certainly does feel that he is asserting a rule which is for the benefit of others as well as for his own. If he is not feeling this—if he is regarding the act solely as it affects him individually—he is not consciously just; he is not concerning himself about the justice of his actions.[11]

This, which seems so reasonable in its context, cannot have that appearance now. As Mill asserts, it is axiomatic that moral feelings must have morality as their object. But it is mere bluster to assert that it is axiomatic that all morality is reducible to distributive justice and that moral feelings must have distributive justice as their object.

Given the redundancy of commutative justice on this model, it is instructive to see what utilitarians made of the history of commutative justice theory. Unfortunately, they give it little attention. The most significant treatment is found in the work of Sidgwick.

After discussing the view (that he rejects) that evil should be inflicted on wrongdoers even if it leads to no good, Sidgwick claims that 'This, then, is one element of what Aristotle calls Corrective Justice, which is embodied in criminal law. It must not be confounded with the principle of Reparation, on which legal awards of damages are based.'[12] I do not think that this should be read to imply that reparation is not based on what we are calling commutative justice. Rather, the 'it' that must not be confounded with the principle of reparation is not commutative justice per se, but *that part* of commutative justice which (allegedly) demands that wrongdoers suffer evil even if no good comes of it. Commutative justice is also relevant to reparation (though Sidgwick has no interest in commutative justice in that context).

That said, the key thing to notice about this account is that, for Sidgwick, commutative or corrective justice is concerned with correcting injustices that are, and must be, defined independently. For Sidgwick, they must be defined by the principle of utility and hence by distributive justice. The result of this, as we examine in section 6, is that the theory of reparation collapses into the theory of punishment.

---

[11] Mill, 'Utilitarianism', 5.23.
[12] Sidgwick, *The Methods of Ethics*, III V 5.6.

2.2 Rawls' Criticism of Utilitarian Justice

Famously, John Rawls rejects the argument (1)–(4) examined above. This is because, as he puts it, 'This view of social cooperation is the consequence of extending to society the principle of choice for one man, and then, to make this extension work, conflating all persons into one through the imaginative acts of the impartial sympathetic spectator. Utilitarianism does not take seriously the distinction between persons.'[13] In other words, the inference from (1) and (2) to (4) is invalid.

We need not examine Rawls' arguments in this regard in detail. Ours is not an investigation of the content of distributive justice. It suffices to say that the general thrust of the argument is that, while individuals do not have morally independent elements that must be considered separately, societies do. So, while choosing to sacrifice my head to my stomach by taking another glass of wine need not raise any moral difficulty, sacrificing you for me does.

The crucial point for our purposes, however, is that Rawls questions only the inference from (1) and (2) to (4). (3) is entirely ignored. But it should not be. If (1) plus (2) does not equal (4) *because* that inference ignores the distinction between persons, then the inference from (1) and (2) to (3) is also invalid. And if that is so, then there is no reason to think that (3) is reducible to (4). This possibility Rawls simply overlooks, and he does so because the dominance of the modern conception means that he never gives the issue even a first thought.

3. The Foundation of Rights

In light of the above, it comes as no surprise that utilitarians hold that our rights are also grounded on the Principle of Utility and are therefore aspects of distributive justice as we are using the term. As Mill says, 'To have a right...is, I conceive, to have something which society ought to defend me in the possession of. If the objector goes on to ask, why it ought? I can give him no other reason than general utility.'[14] That is Mill's short answer. His longer answer refers to his also famous Harm Principle. I examine it now.

---

[13] Rawls, *A Theory of Justice*, 24.
[14] Mill, 'Utilitarianism', 5.26. See also Sidgwick, *The Methods of Ethics*, III V 1.5.

The Harm Principle is, Mill tells us, a 'very simple principle, as entitled to govern absolutely the dealings of society with the individual in the way of compulsion and control, whether the means used be physical force in the form of legal penalties, or the moral coercion of public opinion'.[15] It states that

> the sole end for which mankind are warranted, individually or collectively in interfering with the liberty of action of any of their number, is self-protection. That the only purpose for which power can be rightfully exercised over any member of a civilized community, against his will, is to prevent harm to others.[16]

This principle is itself, Mill thinks, justified by the Principle of Utility.[17]

A feature of the principle is that it is intended to cover all exercises of power over an individual, whether that occurs through law or otherwise by the state or by other individuals. A second feature is that it postulates a necessary, not sufficient, justification for interference. That is, Mill's view is that one is entitled to interfere with a person *only* to prevent that person harming another. But it must also be borne in mind that the interference itself will be harmful, and so it is justified only if it minimizes harm to others.[18]

One upshot of these points is that certain forms of interference are appropriate in a wider range of circumstances than other forms. For instance, the interference of social pressure can be considerable,[19] but it is usually less harmful than interference by law. Accordingly, there are many circumstances in which interference of the first but not the second kind is warranted. To think of this from the other side of the equation, we are entitled to be protected from some harm by the law, but from other harm only by social pressure. For Mill, rights are defined in accordance with the former. Our rights correspond to our entitlement to be protected from some harm through law. This view entails that all our rights are determined by distributive justice. It is an example of Figure M3.

---

[15] Mill, 'On Liberty', 1.11.
[16] Ibid.
[17] Ibid, 1.13.
[18] Ibid.
[19] Ibid, especially ch 3.

For the utilitarians, then, the rights that we have examined earlier in this book—the rights to bodily integrity, to the performance of contacts, and to property—are ultimately founded on distributive justice.

4. Responses to Violations of Rights

Because utilitarians hold that all rights have their source in the Principle of Utility, because they maintain that all actions must cohere with this principle, and because that principle is distributive in character, the utilitarians hold that all of the law's responses to rights' violations have the same basic character. The rights are based in distributive justice, the law protects them because of their basis in distributive justice, and the law responds to their violation in order to defend or produce distributive justice in various ways. As the discussion in section 2.1 revealed, one could also say that the law responds in order to achieve 'corrective' or 'commutative justice', as those terms were defined in that section.

Because of this, the utilitarians understand legal responses to rights violations as impositions of *penalties* for wrongdoing.[20] The response is a sanction imposed by the state, ultimately for reasons of distributive justice.

Two crucial problems follow from this view. I examine the first now and the second in the following section of this chapter.

The first problem is apparent on its face: with the exception of exemplary or punitive damages,[21] the private law seems unconcerned with punishment. This is most clearly seen in the fact that damage awards are not calculated to reflect the culpability of the defendant. I illustrate this with the use of some examples.

If I drive negligently and crash into you, damaging your car to the tune of £1,000, then I will have to pay you £1,000 to compensate you for your loss. This is so regardless of the degree of my culpability.[22]

---

[20] Mill, 'Utilitarianism', 5.14, 24; Sidgwick, *The Methods of Ethics*, III V 1.5.

[21] For an analysis of these relevant to this discussion, see Beever, 'Justice and Punishment in Tort'. As I argue there, the availability of these damages at common law is itself an error caused by the modern conception.

[22] Note that if I intend to crash into your car, then the damages may increase, but that does not show that they do so out of a desire to punish. See Beever, 'The Structure of Aggravated and Exemplary Damages', 88–94.

It makes no difference whether I was looking on the back seat for a CD or only momentarily distracted by my squabbling children. What is more, I may be liable even were I entirely inculpable. If I take your umbrella from an umbrella stand in the reasonable belief that it is mine, then I commit the tort of conversion and am potentially liable to you. But this cannot be because I was culpable: I was not. It cannot be right, then, to think that these legal responses are punitive.

The poverty of the utilitarian view is most starkly revealed by considering cases of unjust enrichment. If you pay money into my bank account in the mistaken belief that you owed it to me, I come under an obligation to return it to you. But this is not because I have done anything wrong. Again, it cannot be right to think of these responses as punitive.[23]

The position adopted by the utilitarians is remarkable. Only an incredible failure of analysis would lead theorists as intelligent as Bentham, Mill, and Sidgwick to claim that all legal responses are punitive. The idea is as flatly inconsistent with the facts as any claim could be. But it is important to note that the utilitarians are driven to this view by their general approach. As is stressed in the following chapter, this failure is the result of the forgetting of commutative justice.

5. Understanding the Private Law

The second problem that follows from defining all rights in terms of distributive justice is that it becomes impossible to understand the role of the private law. Because they have no general interest in the substantive law, Mill and Sidgwick fail to notice the difficulty that this causes. But the problem was noticed by and greatly troubled Bentham. It is highly instructive to examine his attempt to deal with it.

As we have seen, Bentham maintains that the function of law is to promote happiness in the community in general. It does so mainly by preventing acts that would produce disutility or, as Bentham expresses it, mischief.[24] It achieves this goal by punishing in order to deter

---

[23] It is tempting to respond that the wrong in these cases is not acting to return the money. But that is of no help. If it is wrongful not to return the money, that is because of the obligation to return the money. But what is the explanation of that obligation? It cannot be that the obligation is imposed to punish.

[24] Bentham, *The Principles of Morals and Legislation*, XIII 1, XIV 1.

the wrongdoer and others from committing offences.[25] It is entirely unsurprising that Bentham adopts this view given his general account of justice. As we have seen, first order rules of law are designed to promote distributive justice, and the response to violations of those laws is designed to preserve or regain distributive justice (though that might be called 'corrective' or 'commutative' justice).

For Bentham, therefore, compensation, too, is part of retributive justice. In perhaps the most obscure passage from *The Principles of Morals and Legislation*, Bentham claims with respect to compensation that 'This property of punishment, if it be *vindictive* compensation that is in view, will, with little variation, be in proportion to the quantity: if *lucrative,* it is the peculiar and characteristic property of pecuniary punishment.'[26] This appears to mean the following. First, wrongdoers should be required to pay compensation when that would deter them and others from committing offences (vindictive compensation). Secondly, if the wrongdoer's act was aimed to realize monetary gain, then the requirement to pay compensation is particularly appropriate, because it takes away the very thing that the wrongdoer was trying to gain, thus clearly teaching the wrongdoer that wrongdoing does not pay (lucrative compensation). On either view, compensation is conceptualized as a form of punishment.

As Bentham notices, this entails that the criminal law and tort law possess exactly the same normative structure. Both respond to violations of laws set up in accordance with distributive justice and both respond to those violations with punitive measures.

It is not surprising, then, to find Bentham beginning his discussion of the separation between public and private law by claiming that 'Between these two branches..., it is evident enough, there cannot but be a very intimate connection; so intimate is it indeed, that the limits between them are by no means easy to mark out.'[27] In fact, in the first edition of his book, Bentham found the limits impossible to mark out. Consequently, the book ended with the lame suggestion that the distinction between private and criminal law is 'The most intricate distinction of all',[28] an only just tacit admission of failure.

---

[25] Ibid, XIV 3–6.
[26] Ibid, XV 21.
[27] Ibid, XVII 1.
[28] Ibid, XVII 29.

For us, this must seem astonishing. What was absolutely plain to the traditional theorists is totally obscure for Bentham. In the last chapter of *The Principles of Morals and Legislation*, Bentham sets himself an entirely ordinary question that, he then realized, he did not have the theoretical resources to answer.

This is not the end of the matter, however. Bentham returned to the question nine years later to provide an answer perfectly consistent with, in fact suggested by, his theory of law and justice, and yet totally implausible.

This position relies on the distinction Bentham draws between imperative, punitive, and expository laws. An imperative law demands that people do or refrain from doing certain things. A punitive law dictates certain consequences for the violation of an imperative law. To use Bentham's example, the law 'Do not steal' is imperative, and the law 'Those who steal shall be hanged' is punitive.[29] But Bentham notices that these laws are meaningless unless a definition of stealing is provided. He notes that the contemporary definition is '*the taking of a thing which is another's, by one who has no* TITLE *so to do, and is conscious of his having none*'.[30] But this definition is in turn unhelpful unless the nature of title is explained. That is the job of expository laws.[31]

Now, it is plain that the private law contains all three of Bentham's laws,[32] but Bentham maintains that we must put this fact aside in our analysis of the law. In fact, Bentham insists that the distinction between private and criminal law, *rightly understood*, cannot be found in the positive law, because, due to its casuistical development, that law is thoroughly confused. Instead, a large rethink of the law is required. For Bentham, this implies that private law properly understood is concerned only with the expository. On this view, then, the role of the criminal law is to define our rights in general terms and how the violation of those rights will be dealt with, while the function of the private law is to fill in the definitions of our rights given by the criminal law.

Although this, or some similar, reconceptualization of the law is demanded by Bentham's theory, it is entirely radical. It would mean that not only the law of tort, but also that part of the law of contract

---

[29] Ibid, XVII 21n1 6.
[30] Ibid, XVII 21n1 10.
[31] Ibid.
[32] That is, if we assume with Bentham that tort is in fact punitive.

that deals with (not merely responds to) breach of contract would belong to the criminal law.[33] And I have no idea what to say about the law of unjust enrichment, except that it was surely in part the dominance of this kind of thinking that explains the arrival so late of unjust enrichment to the common law. Bentham's is a reconceptualization that would shatter the common lawyer's understanding of her subject.

But what is more important is that it is a reconceptualization that surely ought not be made. What sort of confusion has led to the quite absurd idea that the only way to justify the requirement to compensate people for their injuries is to argue that the requirement is appropriately punitive? We know the answer. The confusion is the modern conception.

---

[33] See also Sidgwick, *The Methods of Ethics*, III V 7.4, who claims that breach of contract calls for a penalty.

PART IV:
Implications

We have witnessed the discovery and forgetting of the traditional view. In this final part of the book, I examine some of the implications of that forgetting. Chapter 12 shows that it has left us unable to understand even the most basic features of our law, resulting in the academic floundering we know as policy analysis. Chapter 13 reveals that the forgetting has also seriously damaged our understanding of the political: of the foundations of our politico-legal obligations, of the nature of justice, and of the relationship between law and politics.

Of course, I cannot examine all implications, or even a significant number of them. Instead, I concentrate on those I consider to be the most important and revealing. In general, my task is to demonstrate the following two claims.

First, we have ideas and practices that appear to be perfectly ordinary. Despite this, however, they turn out to be extremely problematic given the modern conception. In consequence, those captured by that conception either present complex and convoluted—and frankly rather implausible—accounts of those phenomena or argue that the ideas and practices should be rejected. But these very same ideas and practices turn out to be readily explicable on the traditional view. Accordingly, we discover that, though the traditional view appears so foreign when expressed as a theory, we in fact think in terms of it routinely. Consequently, we have not only forgotten what our predecessors knew, we have forgotten what we ourselves know. More precisely, our theory is deeply out of touch with our reality.

Secondly, as a result of the first point, we come to see that extremely important political considerations, considerations that we experience in our ordinary lives and express in ordinary language, cannot be captured in the vocabulary of modern political discourse. As a result, modern societies find themselves unable properly to acknowledge, respect, and protect those political considerations.

12

Legal Analysis

This chapter explores the impact of the modern conception on our understanding of the law. The basic thesis is that the modern conception is an enormous obstacle standing in the way of our understanding of our own law. It prevents us from coming to terms with even the most basic features of that law and sends us on wild goose chases for justifications of legal phenomena that serve only to distance us further from that law.

The basic strategy of the argument is the following. First, we examine certain foundational features of the law's structure. These are concepts and ideas that are largely taken for granted by practising and academic lawyers alike. Secondly, I then show that these features must appear to be problematic in the light of the modern conception. They appear both hard to explain and to justify. Moreover, we will see that the explanations and justifications provided by proponents of the modern view stand a long way from their subject matter. In other words, these explanations and justifications utilize concepts quite different from the ones found in the law. They attempt to explain and justify the law, as it were, from a great distance. The third step in the argument is to show that these features of the law that seem so problematic on the modern conception are readily explicable and justifiable on the traditional view. What is more, the traditional view stands very close to its subject matter. It justifies the concepts found in the law, not by appeal to a range of alternative concepts, but by reference to those concepts themselves.

This enquiry is not new to us. With respect to the relationship between injury and loss in tort, the objective standard in contract law, the issue of remedies in that law, the acquisition of property and disgorgement for wrongdoing, these steps have been conducted in previous chapters. Some of these issues are also examined in more detail below.

It is important to state at the outset that the claim is not that adopting the traditional outlook will make all the problems surrounding our understanding of the law evaporate. Of course, that is not the case. The law is complex, life more so, and thus understanding the law and its application will at times be extremely difficult. The point, however, is that the modern view struggles even to *begin* to understand the *basic* nature of the law. Things start hard and get increasingly more difficult. According to the traditional view, on the other hand, the basic structure of the law is readily comprehensible, though naturally, as investigation becomes more detailed, comprehension requires more effort. The traditional view, then, is not a panacea for misunderstanding of the law. Rather, adopting it removes the obstacle to our understanding that is the modern conception.

Also, again entirely naturally, theorists of the traditional view will disagree among themselves, as do theorists of the modern view. They may even disagree with some of what I say here. But the difference is that the traditional theorists have a common and sufficiently perspicuous frame of reference that means that their debates about the law share a focus; modern theorists, on the other hand, often have so little in common that it is far from clear that they engage with each other at all. It is one thing to dispute the requirements of fairness between the parties in a particular circumstance; it is another to examine the social desirability of the possible outcomes and the means to those outcomes in that situation. In the latter case, unless the disputants discuss the foundations of their political preferences—and they seldom do—the 'debate' is sure to be intractable.

1. The Nature of Our Legal Rights

Perhaps the most fundamental issue that arises in this context concerns our understanding of the rights and obligations found in the private law. That law is said to operate *in personam*, a fact regarded as an elementary feature of legal analysis. However, it seems to be increasingly difficult for commentators to understand what this means.

This issue is perhaps best illustrated by considering the famous decision of the New York Court of Appeal in *Palsgraf v Long Island*

Railroad Co.[1] This judgment is especially useful because the court was almost evenly divided between proponents of the modern and traditional views.

1.1 Palsgraf v Long Island Railroad Co

Palsgraf is one of the leading decisions in the law of negligence. In order to facilitate our investigation of the case, it will help briefly to lay out the structure of this area of the law. It consists of the following five stages, which correspond to five questions.[2]

(1) *The standard of care*—Did the defendant act in a way that produced an unreasonable level of risk; ie, was the defendant negligent?
(2) *The duty of care*—Was the defendant under an obligation to this particular plaintiff to avoid injuring that person?
(3) *Remoteness, legal, or proximate causation*—Was the plaintiff's injury of a kind for which the defendant was responsible?
(4) *Factual causation or cause-in-fact*—Did the defendant's negligent action cause the plaintiff's injury?
(5) *The defences*—These are divided into a number of separate issues that correspond to their own questions. The most important are:

   Contributory negligence—Was the plaintiff's injury caused in part by her own negligence?
   And
   Voluntary assumption of risk—Did the plaintiff consent to the risk or the activity that resulted in her injury?

As the defences are not relevant here, they are ignored in the following.

A defendant will be liable if (1)–(4) and no relevant defences are established. That is, ignoring the defences, (1)–(4) are each necessary and are jointly sufficient conditions for liability.

The Modern Conception In *Palsgraf*, employees of the defendant, for whom the defendant was responsible,[3] pushed a man onto a moving

---

[1] 162 NE 99 (NY 1928). For the same result, though the case is much less interesting, see *Bourhill v Young* [1943] AC 92 (HL).
[2] The third and fourth stages are often combined into one,—'causation',—but that need not bother us here.
[3] This feature of this case is known as vicarious liability. Unsurprisingly, modern theorists insist that it has its origin in distributive justice. That, however, is not the case. The best analysis of vicarious liability with which I am familiar is Stevens, *Torts and Rights*, 257–274.

train. The man was carrying a package wrapped in newspaper. Nothing indicated that it contained anything out of the ordinary. The actions of the defendant's employees dislodged this package. It fell to the ground. It contained fireworks. They exploded. The explosion caused scales far down the platform to fall onto the plaintiff, resulting in personal injury.

The question for the court was: could the plaintiff recover for her injuries from the defendant? More specifically, the question was: was the defendant liable to the plaintiff in the tort of negligence? All accepted that it was negligent to push a man onto a moving train. All accepted that the plaintiff was not placed at a reasonably foreseeable risk of injury.

Recall what the modern theorists tell us. They claim that all legal responses have the same basic character: they are penal. The utilitarians further maintain that legal wrongs are wrongs done to the world. And they say that if we single out a particular person as *the* victim of a wrong, that is not because she is somehow the solitary victim of the wrong, but because she uniquely suffers loss as the result of the wrong committed against the world. In *Palsgraf*, this view was powerfully presented by Andrews J.

His Honour first asked: why were the defendant's employees' actions wrongful? His answer was that they created an unacceptable risk of injury to some person. In other words, the actions were wrongful because they were negligent (to someone). And in line with the modern view, Andrews J took this to demonstrate that those actions were wrongful in themselves, ie that they wronged everyone.

Should we drive down Broadway at a reckless speed, we are negligent whether we strike an approaching car or miss it by an inch. The act itself is wrongful. It is a wrong not only to those who happen to be within the radius of danger but to all who might have been there—a wrong to the public at large. Such is the language of the street.[4]

The language of the street is the language of the modern conception.

Moreover, Andrews J maintained that the aim of the law is to protect society as a whole, rather than to protect particular persons.

For a different view, also consistent with commutative justice, see Neyers, 'A Theory of Vicarious Liability'.

[4] *Palsgraf v Long Island Railroad Co* 162 NE 99 (NY 1928) 102.

'Due care is a duty imposed on each one of us to protect society from unnecessary danger, not to protect A, B or C alone.'[5] Therefore, when the defendant's employees created an unreasonable risk to the man boarding the train, they wronged everyone. This, of course, entails that they wronged the plaintiff. Hence, given that she was injured by their wrongdoing—ie given that the plaintiff was a victim of the defendant's employees' wrongdoing—on the face of it the plaintiff ought to be able to recover.

The proposition is this. Every one owes to the world at large the duty of refraining from those acts that may unreasonably threaten the safety of others. Such an act occurs. Not only is he wronged to whom harm might reasonably be expected to result, but he also who is in fact injured, even if he be outside what would generally be thought the danger zone.[6]

Therefore, in the language of the law, the plaintiff was owed a duty of care by the defendant.

This approach, as we have seen, follows the modern view. Moreover, it seems to be entirely principled. It generates its conclusions by applying a valid conception of wrongdoing, a conception with which we are entirely familiar. It follows, as Andrews J tells us, the 'language of the street'. But, as we now discuss, despite its undoubted appeal, it generates very significant difficulties.

Recall Andrews J's view. The defendant was liable to the plaintiff because his employees (for whom he was responsible) created an unreasonable risk of injury to someone, and hence performed an action that wronged the world. The plaintiff, of course, was part of the world and so was owed a duty of care. That is, she was a person who the defendant's employees had a duty to protect from harm. Hence, because she was injured, she was entitled to recover from the defendant. If this is right, then it follows that *anyone* injured by the defendant's employees' actions could recover, no matter what their circumstances. And when that is generalized, it follows that a person who commits a negligent act is liable to anybody who can causally trace any injury she suffers to that act. And that simply cannot be right.

Imagine the following scene from the turn of the previous century set in a small town in northern Austria. A man called Hans Patschert is

---
[5] Ibid.
[6] Ibid, 103.

out riding his bicycle. Not looking where he is going, he crashes into a woman by the name of Klara Pölzl, injuring her slightly. Seeing this, another man, Alois Hitler, rushes to Klara's aid. If the accident had not occurred, we can be sure that Klara and Alois would never have met. As it is, however, they fall in love, marry, and have six children. The fourth of these, Adolf, proves to be a difficult child. Can we say, then, that Hans can be sued for all of the destruction Adolf causes?

In fact, there are two ways of taking this point. Unsurprisingly, they relate to the modern and traditional views. I examine them below. For the moment, it suffices that the impossibility of the liability regime outlined above is intuitively obvious.

Accordingly, though Andrews J's position can seem entirely reasonable, it is remarkable that it would have disastrous consequences were it allowed to stand on its own. Moreover, Andrews J was aware of this. He was aware that other notions needed to be introduced in order to limit liability. This is why he tells us that the 'right to recover damages rests [also] on additional considerations'.[7]

What are these 'additional considerations'? Andrews J linked them to what lawyers know as proximate causation, legal causation, or remoteness. The precise nature of this need not concern us here; what is important is what Andrews J says about it:

A cause, but not the proximate cause. What we do mean by the word 'proximate' is, that because of convenience, of public policy, of a rough sense of justice, the law arbitrarily declines to trace a series of events beyond a certain point. This is not logic. It is practical politics... We may regret that the line was drawn just where it was, but drawn somewhere it had to be.[8]

'It is all a question of expediency', he later claims.[9]

The picture, then, is this. Andrews J's enquiry travels through three stages.[10] First, he asks whether the defendant committed a wrong. In this context, that is determined by asking whether the

---

[7] Ibid.

[8] Ibid, 103–104.

[9] Ibid, 104. The policy is arbitrary, not because it is chosen for no good reason, but because the choice of any particular policy is not related to wrongdoing or negligence. Hence, it is arbitrary from the perspective of the enquiry into negligence.

[10] Factual causation and defences are two others, but they need not be discussed here.

defendant was negligent, ie whether he (or those for whom he was responsible) created an unreasonable risk of injury to someone. Secondly, if the answer to the first question is in the affirmative, then it follows that everyone in the world was wronged. That stage is, of course, totally redundant. This approach creates the unacceptable conclusion that anyone who suffers loss as the result of the defendant's wrongdoing can recover. Hence, in order to keep liability in check, a third stage of the enquiry that imposes restraints on liability must be added.

Accordingly, in *Palsgraf*, Andrews J defined and applied the stages of the negligence enquiry as follows.

(1) *The standard of care*—Did the defendant act in a way that produced an unreasonable level of risk; ie, was the defendant negligent? Yes.
(2) *The duty of care*—Was the defendant under an obligation to this particular plaintiff to avoid injuring that person? Yes—the duty of care is owed to the whole world.
(3) *Remoteness, legal or proximate causation*—Was the plaintiff's injury of a kind for which the defendant is responsible? Yes—convenience *et al* was in favour of the plaintiff in these circumstances.
(4) *Factual causation or cause-in-fact*—Did the defendant's negligent action cause the plaintiff's injury? Yes.

Three features of this approach need to be emphasized because they are inherited by the modern law. The first is the need to control what appears in principle to be an out-of-control or, as lawyers like to put it, indeterminate liability.[11] As we see in section 1.2, though there are slight differences between Andrews J's and the modern approach, in this regard they are essentially the same. The second point is that, as Andrews J is honest enough to admit, his approach introduces arbitrariness into the enquiry. Today, this is usually either lamely denied or excused on the purported ground that 'there is no alternative'. The third point concerns the nature of those arbitrary restrictions. They are based on 'convenience,...public policy,...a rough sense of justice,...practical politics [and]...expediency'.[12] Of course, we know what this means. It means, broadly speaking, the court's sense of distributive justice.

---

[11] We owe this expression to the judgment of Cardozo CJ in *Ultramares Corp v Touche* 174 NE 441 (NY 1931) 444. For an analysis of that judgment, see Beever, *Rediscovering the Law of Negligence*, 234–237.
[12] *Palsgraf v Long Island Railroad Co* 162 NE 99 (NY 1928) 103–104.

The Modern Conception of the Rejection of the Modern Conception In the light of the difficulties enunciated above, it is less remarkable than it would otherwise be that Andrews J's view lost. Before I examine why it lost, however, I first explore why it is generally thought today that it lost.

Recall the problem. Andrew J's approach to the first two stages of the negligence enquiry would generate indeterminate liability and so it cannot stand on its own. Recall also the example I used to illustrate this difficulty. Hans cannot be liable for all the destruction caused during the Second World War. But why not?

The modern answer is that such would be impractical and unfair, both in this case and in general. In this case, the problem is of course that Hans cannot pay for all the destruction. He is not wealthy enough. Moreover, requiring him even to begin would destroy him financially, which would be unfair, given that many others were also responsible for the destruction. In general, the issue is that indeterminate liability would produce a flood of litigation, overwhelming the courts (the floodgates argument), and would be inefficient. These are, of course, as are all related arguments, concerns of distributive justice.[13]

Now, in *Palsgraf*, the majority of the New York Court of Appeal ruled that the defendant owed the plaintiff no duty of care. This is because, they said, the plaintiff was not put at a reasonably foreseeable risk of injury by the defendant's employees' negligence. Consequently, unlike Andrews J, they gave a negative answer to question (2). But why was this and what does this imply?

To the modern mind, the answer to the second question is that the majority thought that Andrews J's concerns 'of convenience, of public policy, of a rough sense of justice, [of] practical politics [and]...expediency'[14] ought to be examined at stage (2) rather than at stage (3) of the enquiry. That, as we see in section 1.2, is also the modern approach.

But it is surely clear that this is a debate without any importance. If they are to be explored, it does not make any difference where these issues are to be explored. And it is important to see that moving the concerns from stage (3) to stage (2) does precisely nothing to explain

---

[13] See eg *Canadian National Railway Co v Norsk Pacific Steamship Co Ltd* [1992] 1 SCR 1021, 1137.
[14] *Palsgraf v Long Island Railroad Co* 162 NE 99 (NY 1928) 103–104.

the different conclusions reached by the majority and the dissent in *Palsgraf*.

So why did the majority say that the defendant owed the plaintiff no duty of care? According to the modern view, it was because the judges thought that a convenient and expedient way of avoiding indeterminate liability was to institute a rule according to which a plaintiff could succeed only against a defendant who placed her at reasonably foreseeable risk.

As a result of this, modern lawyers—and perhaps now also jurisdictions—are split along the lines drawn in *Palsgraf*. Those who support what they take to be the majority's position argue that policies such as floodgates and economic efficiency support restricting recovery to those placed at reasonably foreseeable risk, while those who support the dissent's more 'flexible' and 'generous' approach reject that rule. Given these thoughts, the former are often labelled 'conservatives', while the latter label themselves 'liberals'. In the United States, it seems that the 'liberal' position may soon achieve victory.[15]

The Traditional View Let us return to poor Hans. We have agreed that he should not be liable. But the reasons offered above are not the ones that matter. Though they are not completely irrelevant, they are about as useful in explaining the limits of Hans' liability as the observation that love reduces transactions costs with respect to sex is useful in explaining my love for my wife[16]—ie not completely useless but pretty close.

Why was Hans negligent? It was because he rode his bicycle in a way that posed a risk of injury to pedestrians. He was not negligent for creating a risk of, for example, the 'Blitz' on London or the siege of Stalingrad. One might have said to him, 'Be careful, you might, hit someone', but it would have been absurd to have said 'Be careful, you might cause London to be bombed and one-and-a-half million people to die at Stalingrad.' Similarly, one might have said, 'Be careful, you might hit Klara or her mother Johanna.' But it would have been crazy to have said 'Be careful, you might injure someone in London or Tsaritsyn (Stalingrad).' Accordingly, though Hans was at fault and caused the Second World War, he was not at fault for causing the war.

---

[15] For an important discussion, see Goldberg and Zipursky, 'The *Restatement (Third)* and the Place of Duty in Negligence'.

[16] Compare Posner, *Economic Analysis of the Law*, 342.

For this reason, he cannot be liable in the law of negligence, based as it is on fault, for those consequences of his action.

These points are, of course, obvious. But what is remarkable is that they are lost on modern legal analysis. They are lost because, though they are obvious, when we turn from 'casual' reflection to 'serious' analysis, we drop those of our intuitions that match the traditional view and pick up the modern conception. That conception then causes us to say quite incredible things, such as that the reason Hans is not liable for the Second World War is that adopting that kind of approach would lead to a flood of claims that would overwhelm the courts. If we instead rediscover our ordinary intuitions and take them seriously, it is possible to make much greater sense of the phenomena at hand. In particular, if we do this, Cardozo CJ's judgment in *Palsgraf* will appear entirely different to that represented above.

Why were the defendant's employees negligent in *Palsgraf*? They were negligent because they tried to push a man onto a moving train. And why is that negligent? Because he might be injured, his property damaged, and so on. But is it negligent to push a man onto a moving train because a woman standing at the other end of the platform might by injured? Not unless there was reason to believe that, for instance, the man was carrying something that might fall out of his hands and explode. That is what in fact happened, but the defendant's employees had no reason to believe that the man was carrying any such thing.

In other words, the defendant's employees were negligent to the man they pushed on the train, but they were not negligent to the plaintiff. They were not sufficiently careful of the man, but they were not at all careless of the safety of the plaintiff. One could meaningfully have said to them as they were acting 'Don't push that man, you might injure him', but the command 'Don't push that man, you might injure that woman standing at the other end of the platform' would have seemed senseless. Accordingly, it is plausible to think that the man, but not the plaintiff, was wronged by the defendant's employees.

Note that the view enunciated here is perfectly consistent with Andrews J's claims. I have not denied that the plaintiff in *Palsgraf* was wronged. The claim is that she was wronged in one way but not in another. She was wronged in the way that everyone was wronged, according to the language of the street. But she was nevertheless not wronged in the way that the owner of the package was uniquely wronged, according to the language of the traditional conception.

There are two different types of wrongdoing here—to be analysed in more detail in a moment. Andrews J focused on the first but, as we are about to see, Cardozo CJ based his decision on the second. For Cardozo CJ, the defendant's employees did not wrong the plaintiff in the relevant sense.

As I have argued, Cardozo CJ—perhaps the greatest tort judge of all time—first pointed out that, while the defendant's employees may have been negligent to the man boarding the train, they were not negligent to the plaintiff.

The conduct of the defendant's guard, if a wrong in its relation to the holder of the package, was not a wrong in its relation to the plaintiff, standing far away. Relatively to her it was not negligence at all. Nothing in the situation gave notice that the falling package had in it the potency of peril to persons thus removed.[17]

A defendant is said to be negligent (ie he falls below the standard of care) if he creates a risk that a reasonable person would not create. In English law, the question is whether the defendant created an unreasonable risk.[18] An unreasonable risk of what? An unreasonable risk of injury to another person. The risk, then, is relational: 'risk imports relation'.[19] In *Palsgraf*, the defendant's employees were negligent because they placed the owner of the package at risk of suffering personal injury and property damage. But they were not negligent for creating a risk of scales falling on the plaintiff. The defendant's employees did create such a risk, but, as that risk was not reasonably foreseeable, they did not act unreasonably in creating that risk.

Accordingly, as Cardozo CJ argued, the defendant's employees were not negligent to the plaintiff. Hence, the plaintiff was not wronged by the defendant's employees (in the sense relevant in tort law). If the plaintiff was not wronged, then she could not have had a cause of action. To have held otherwise would have been to allow the plaintiff to sue for the wrong done to another, to have allowed her to sue

---

[17] *Palsgraf v Long Island Railroad Co* 162 NE 99 (NY 1928) 99.
[18] *Bolton v Stone* [1951] AC 850 (HL); *Overseas Tankship (UK) Ltd v Morts Dock & Engineering Co Ltd (The Wagon Mound, No 2)* [1967] AC 617 (PC).
[19] *Palsgraf v Long Island Railroad Co* 162 NE 99 (NY 1928) 100.

for the wrong done to the owner of the package.[20] But in tort, 'The plaintiff sues in her own right for a wrong personal to her, and not as the vicarious beneficiary of a breach of duty to another.'[21]

Negligence, like risk, is thus a term of relation. Negligence in the abstract, apart from things related, is surely not a tort, if indeed it is understandable at all... Negligence is not a tort unless it results in the commission of a wrong, and the commission of a wrong imports the violation of a right, in this case, we are told, the right to be protected against interference with one's bodily security. But bodily security is protected, not against all forms of interference or aggression, but only against some. One who seeks redress at law does not make out a cause of action by showing without more that there has been damage to his person. If the harm was not willful, he must show that the act as to him had possibilities of danger so many and apparent as to entitle him to be protected against the doing of it though the harm was unintended. Affront to personality is still the keynote of the wrong... The victim does not sue derivatively, or by right of subrogation, to vindicate an interest invaded in the person of another. Thus to view his cause of action is to ignore the fundamental difference between tort and crime... He sues for breach of a duty owing to himself.[22]

According to Cardozo CJ, then, as the plaintiff was not placed at a reasonably foreseeable risk by the defendant's employees' acts, she was not owed a duty of care. Therefore, she had no cause of action.

Cardozo CJ's is a brilliant judgment. But that should not prevent us from seeing that a judge who instinctively thought in terms of the traditional view would find it comparatively trite. Cardozo CJ's judgment is a work of genius, not because of the ingenuity of his argument, but because of his rediscovery of a very simple principle in the face of much pressure to forget it. It is worth emphasizing just how simple both this principle and its application to the case are: the defendant's employee's actions may have constituted a commutative injustice to the owner of the package, but not to the plaintiff; hence, there can be no liability.

---

[20] This assumes that a wrong was done to the owner of the package, but even this is unclear. It was at least arguable that the defendant's employees were acting reasonably to prevent injury to that person. Ibid, 99.
[21] Ibid, 100.
[22] Ibid, 101.

It is a mark of how blinding the modern conception is that distinguished commentators have not been able even to understand this most basic idea. William Prosser, for instance, claimed that both Cardozo CJ and Andrews J 'beg the question shamelessly, stating dogmatic propositions without reason or explanation.'[23] With respect to Cardozo CJ's judgment, the problem is rather that Prosser cannot understand the reasons Cardozo CJ offered.

1.2 The Modern Conception and the Modern Approach to the Law

As indicated above, the modern approach to the law of negligence is a close relative of Andrews J's position in *Palsgraf*. It relies heavily on 'convenience,... public policy,... a rough sense of justice,... practical politics [and]... expediency',[24] what is now referred to by the umbrella label, 'policy'.

Recall the five stages of the negligence enquiry listed at the beginning of this section. The modern view understands (1), the standard of care, to correspond to a general principle that underlies the law of negligence: the principle that one is responsible for the consequences of one's negligence. But, as we saw above, that principle alone generates indeterminate liability. Hence, there is a need to introduce other concepts in order to restrict liability within sensible limits. On the modern view, that is the point of (2)–(5).[25] To use the contemporary jargon, they are *control mechanisms*, designed to limit potential liability.

This view, for example, is found in David Ibbetson's claim that without the control mechanisms there would be nothing 'to restrain the urge to move from the proposition that a person has suffered loss from the negligence of another to the conception that the loss ought to be compensated'.[26] In other words, the general principle alone generates indeterminate liability and so control mechanisms must be instituted. The view is also neatly captured by Stephen Todd's description of the role of the duty of care enquiry.

The duty requirement exists because the potential scope of negligence as a basis for legal liability is virtually unlimited. On its face 'negligence' looks

---

[23] Prosser, 'Palsgraf Revisited', 7.
[24] *Palsgraf v Long Island Railroad Co* 162 NE 99 (NY 1928) 103–104.
[25] In fact, (4) is problematic in this regard. It may be better to regard (4) as part of the general principle than as an exception. The point is not decisive, however.
[26] Ibbetson, 'How the Romans did for Us: Ancient Roots of the Tort of Negligence', 488.

only to the quality of the defendant's conduct and not to factors such as the likely or possible number of plaintiffs, the likelihood that loss would be caused, the nature and extent of particular loss and the circumstances in which the loss came to be inflicted. Thus the courts have had to devise principles to delimit the boundaries of liability. To this end they have instituted a requirement in every case of foreseeability of damage to the person bringing the action, and have also taken account of these other factors in deciding whether, for reasons of policy, liability ought to be especially restricted or denied altogether. The language of duty provides the formula for expressing these conclusions of policy. It operates as a 'control device' or filter through which any particular claim must pass. It is apparent, then, that the function of the duty of care is not so much to identify cases where liability is imposed as to identify those where it is not.[27]

Witness also John Fleming's claim that:

Negligence is a matter of risk, that is of recognisable danger of harm. This immediately raised the question 'Risk to whom?' and 'Risk of what?'

For the purpose of dealing with these questions, the courts have evolved a number of artificial concepts, like 'duty of care' and 'remoteness of damage', which are concerned with the basic problems of what harms are included within the scope of the unreasonable risk created by the defendant, and what interest the law deems worthy of protection against negligent harm in consonance with current notions of policy.[28]

And WVH Roger's assertion that:

A general liability for carelessly causing harm to others would, at least as things are perceived by the courts, be too onerous for a practical system of law...Duty is the primary control device which allows the courts to keep liability for negligence within what they regard as acceptable limits...[29]

And finally, the claim in *Prosser and Keeton on Torts* that duty 'is only an expression of the sum total of those considerations of policy which lead the law to say that the plaintiff is entitled to protection'.[30]

---

[27] Todd, 'Negligence: The Duty of Care', section 4.1 (citation omitted), quotation from *Smith v Littlewoods Organisation Ltd* [1987] 1 AC 241 (HL), 280.
[28] Fleming, *The Law of Torts*, 115.
[29] Rogers, *Winfield and Jolowicz on Tort*, 152. See also Cane, *The Anatomy of Tort Law*, 10.
[30] Keeton and others, *Prosser and Keeton on the Law of Torts*, 358.

Hence, the dominant understanding of the law of negligence is, or is very similar to, the following. A general principle of liability exists, according to which a person is liable for the consequences of her negligence. However, a list of exceptions to this principle also exists that limit liability beyond that called for by the general principle. In fact, it would be possible to teach the law of negligence according to the modern conception by teaching the general principle in the first class and then spending the rest of the course detailing the exceptions. Perhaps some courses are taught in that way.

1.3 The Traditional View and the Traditional Approach to the Law

But this is not how things appear on the traditional view. Both views agree that the point of (1) is to determine whether the defendant created an unreasonable risk and was therefore negligent. But on the traditional view, (2) follows from (1). This is because, through the eyes of commutative justice, the creation of an unreasonable risk by a defendant can be a wrong to a particular plaintiff only if that risk was a risk to that person. That is what the great cases of *Palsgraf* and *Donoghue v Stevenson*[31] are all about.[32]

Similarly, (3) also follows from (1). A risk is unreasonable only if it threatens a certain kind of injury or injuries. Accordingly, if the plaintiff suffers injury of a different kind, the defendant was not negligent for creating the risk of that injury and the plaintiff was not wronged by the defendant.

Take, for example, the facts presented in *Doughty v Turner Manufacturing Co Ltd*.[33] One of the defendant's employees, for whom the defendant was responsible, negligently knocked an asbestos and cement cover into a cauldron containing a sodium cyanide solution at 800 degrees Celsius. This caused a small splash that injured no one. However, after one or two minutes, an explosion occurred that expelled some of the solution from the cauldron, burning the plaintiff. Tests later discovered that the materials from which the covers were made undergo a chemical reaction at high temperature that produces water. This water would turn to steam and, coming into contact with a liquid at high temperature, would cause an explosion, such as the

---

[31] *M'Alister (or Donoghue) (Pauper) v Stevenson* [1932] AC 562 (HL Sc).
[32] See also *Bourhill v Young* [1943] AC 92 (HL).
[33] [1964] 1 QB 518 (CA).

one that injured the plaintiff in *Doughty*. At the time of the accident, however, that was unforeseeable.

It was admitted that the defendant's employee was negligent. He should have been more careful not to knock the cover into the cauldron. But the plaintiff failed. According to the modern view, then, this must have been because the judges' sense of public policy required that result: perhaps the judges felt a need to protect industry from ruinous liability. The truth, however, is quite different.

According to Diplock LJ:

> The... risk [of a splash] was well-known (that was foreseeable) at the time of the accident; but it did not happen. It was the second risk [of the explosion] which happened and caused the plaintiff damage by burning. The crucial finding by the learned judge... was that this was not a risk of which the defendants at the time of the accident knew, or ought to have known. This finding, which was justified by the evidence and has not been assailed in this appeal, would appear to lead logically to the conclusion that in causing, or failing to prevent, the immersion of the cover in the liquid, the defendants, by their servants, were in breach of no duty of care owed to the plaintiff, for this was not an act or omission which they could reasonably foresee was likely to cause him damage.[34]

The defendant's employee was negligent for creating a risk of a splash. Hence, had the plaintiff been injured by a splash, the defendant would have been liable. But the defendant's employee was not negligent for creating the risk of an explosion and hence was not negligent for creating the risk of the injury that the plaintiff in fact suffered. Therefore, no matter how unethical the defendant's employee's behaviour, and no matter how distributively unjust the result, the plaintiff suffered no commutative injustice and had no cause of action. The plaintiff was damaged but not injured in the legal sense, or to put it more precisely, the loss to the plaintiff was not the result of a violation of the plaintiff's rights by the defendant. This has nothing to do with public policy.[35]

The next stage in the negligence enquiry, (4), is also internal to the traditional view. The defendant can be liable to the plaintiff only if the plaintiff was injured by the defendant. The defences, (5), fit this

---

[34] Ibid, 530.
[35] For a more detailed analysis, see Beever, *Rediscovering the Law of Negligence*, 135–137.

model also. A plaintiff who consented to the defendant's action cannot have been wronged by it. And if the plaintiff was herself negligent and that negligence contributed to her injury, then commutative justice demands that she bear her fair share of the loss.[36] (Related issues are also examined in sections 2, 3.1 and 3.3.)

Here we see that the traditional view has a ready explanation for the concepts that we find in the law. What is more, those explanations utilize those concepts themselves. On the modern view, the law of negligence is a problematic creature, which requires constant tending by policy arguments that are quite unrelated to its general principle. But on the traditional view, once that view is taken seriously, that law is in its general structure almost self-evident.[37]

2. The Objective Standard of Care

In Chapter 7, we examined the objective standard as it applies to contract. Here we examine it as it applies in tort, in particular in the law of negligence.

This area of the law judges the defendant's behaviour in accordance with an objective standard.[38] Moreover, though the standard is sometimes adjusted, it remains objective.[39] In the case of child defendants, the standard is sometimes that of a child of like age, intelligence, and experience;[40] in the case of medical professionals, the standard is of an ordinary medical professional of the relevant kind;[41] and so on. The key feature of the law in this regard is its refusal to judge the defendant's behaviour in the light of the defendant's personal capacities, talents, disabilities, etc. Why is this?

---

[36] A full analysis of this ideas can be found in ibid, chs 3–4, 10, 12–13.

[37] As noted in the introduction to this chapter, this does not imply that understanding the law is a simple matter or that disagreement between traditional thinkers is impossible.

[38] *Vaughan v Menlove* (1837) 3 Hodges 51, 132 ER 490; *Restatement (Third) of Torts: Physical and Emotional Harm*, s 3.

[39] *Restatement (Third) of Torts: Physical and Emotional Harm*, s 3d. Against: *McErlean v Sarel* (1987) 42 DLR (4th) 577 (Ont CA), [53].

[40] *McHale v Watson* (1966) 115 CLR 199 (HCA). *Restatement (Third) of Torts: Physical and Emotional Harm*, s 10.

[41] *Bolam v Friern Hospital Management Committee* [1957] 1 WLR 582 (QBD); *Bolitho v City and Hackney HA* [1988] AC 232 (HL); *Restatement (Third) of Torts: Physical and Emotional Harm*, s 12.

Proponents of the modern view have responded in one of two ways. They have argued either that the negligence standard is justified on grounds of economic efficiency [42] or they have produced accounts of responsibility designed to generate the necessary objectivity.[43] The answer, however, is much closer to hand.

For a traditional theorist, the issue is what is demanded by commutative justice in these contexts. The question is not one about the plaintiff or the defendant in isolation. Hence, the question is not whether the plaintiff has suffered an unjustified loss (a question that is likely to lead to the postulation of strict liability). Nor is the question whether the defendant has committed a personal moral failing (a question likely to lead to the postulation of a subjective, fault-based standard). The question is rather what is fair as between the parties.[44]

Take, for instance, the foundational case of *Vaughan v Menlove*.[45] The defendant built his rick of hay next to the plaintiff's barn. The rick caught fire, which spread to and destroyed the barn. On appeal, the defendant accepted that a reasonable man would have known of the risk of fire and would have built the rick elsewhere, but argued that his remarkable stupidity meant that he could not have been expected to have been aware of this risk.

The court rejected the relevance of this claim. It maintained that the question was not what could have been expected of the defendant but what could have been expected of 'a man of ordinary prudence'.[46] Hence, the view was not that the defendant was personally responsible for what he did. Rather, the view was that, although the defendant may not have been personally responsible, he was nevertheless rightly held liable, because fairness as between himself and the plaintiff demanded that result. This is the best way in which to understand Oliver Wendell Holmes' famous claim that:

If...a man is born hasty and awkward, is always having accidents and hurting himself or his neighbors, no doubt his congenital defects will be allowed for in the courts of Heaven, but his slips are no less troublesome

---

[42] See most famously *United States v Carroll Towing* 159 F 2d 169 (US 1947).

[43] See eg Honoré, *Responsibility and Fault*; Raz, 'Responsibility and the Negligence Standard'. For my response to the former, see Beever, 'Corrective Justice and Personal Responsibility in Tort Law'.

[44] Weinrib, *The Idea of Private Law*, 63–66.

[45] (1837) 3 Hodges 51, 132 ER 490.

[46] Ibid, 493.

to his neighbors than if they sprang from guilty neglect. His neighbors accordingly require him, at his proper peril, to come up to their standard, and the courts which they establish decline to take his personal equation into account.[47]

The clumsy man is not personally morally responsible for his clumsiness. Hence, his 'personal equation' is allowed for in the courts of heaven. This, presumably, is because his victims can be miraculously cured there, and thus their injuries can be ignored. But on this earth, that cannot happen. And though the man is not personally responsible for his clumsiness, nor are the victims of his behaviour so responsible. The law must determine who is to bear the loss. Consequently, it is necessary to adopt an approach that fairly represents the interests of both parties. According to the traditional view and to the commutative justice upon which it relies, that is the role of the objective standard. By setting an impersonal, general standard, the law judges the interaction by focusing neither on the plaintiff nor on the defendant in isolation, but on a standard designed to do justice as between them.[48]

This is also why the standard of care is adjusted. If the relationship between the parties is that of a doctor and patient, then the level of care that the latter is entitled to expect from the former is that of the ordinary reasonable doctor. Likewise, if the defendant is a child and the parties are playing with each other, then the fact that the child is a child is relevant to the relationship between the parties and ought to be taken into account.[49] But if one is struck by a child driving a vehicle, then the fact that the child is a child is not relevant to the relationship between the parties and should be ignored.[50] On this view, the objective standard is not an approach that requires justification from external moral or economic considerations. It is *itself* a moral principle. It is a principle of commutative justice. Only the modern conception prevents us from seeing this.

---

[47] Holmes, *The Common Law*, 108. Cf Honoré, *Responsibility and Fault*, 24. The claim is not that Holmes himself so understood this passage. He appears to have thought of it as supporting an argument based in distributive justice.

[48] For this view in detail, see Beever, *Rediscovering the Law of Negligence*, ch 3.

[49] See, eg *McHale v Watson* (1966) 115 CLR 199 (HCA). That case, however, is wrongly decided on the facts. For discussion, see Beever, *Rediscovering the Law of Negligence*, 87–96.

[50] Eg *McErlean v Sarel* (1987) 42 DLR (4th) 577 (Ont CA).

3. Injuries and Damage: The Role of Loss

3.1 Tort

Somewhat ironically, in *Leviathan* Hobbes claims that 'irrational creatures cannot distinguish between *injury*, and *damage*'.[51] By this he means that only the irrational cannot see the difference between being wronged and being caused loss. This irrationality is deeply embedded in the modern view of law and it has its origin in the modern conception.

In Chapter 11, we saw that proponents of the modern view hold that if obligations are imposed on people for reasons of justice, then it follows that violations of those obligations wrong the world. As Bentham tells us, a particular person is *the* victim of a wrong, not because she was wronged uniquely, but only because she uniquely suffered loss as a result of a wrong to everyone. This view promotes the idea that the concept of loss must play a leading role in determining issues of liability. Hence, we have the idea that 'at a very general level...we may say that tort is concerned with the allocation of responsibility for losses',[52] a claim that the vast majority of tort lawyers would accept without question. Next to the one examined in section 1, this misunderstanding is perhaps the most pernicious to our understanding of the law.

Take this example. Imagine that your friend Peter intended to give you a book as a birthday present. Before he could give it to you, however, I destroyed it. This causes you loss.[53] As a result of my action, you are worse off than you would have been had I not acted. Here I have committed a wrong and caused you loss. Hence, on the modern view, you are a victim of my wrong. Surely, then, you can sue me for your loss. In fact, however, though exceptions exist, the general rule is that you cannot sue me.[54] Only Peter can sue. Why is this?

This question is regarded as probably the most difficult and contentious question to face the modern law. In recent times, debate has

---

[51] Hobbes, *Leviathan*, XVII 11.
[52] Rogers, *Winfield and Jolowicz on Tort*, 2.
[53] In case one is inclined to dispute this, imagine that the book was owed to you.
[54] See, eg *Robins Dry Dock & Repair Co v Flint* 275 US 303 (US 1927); *East River Steamship Corp v Transamerica Delaval Inc* 476 US 858 (US 1986); *Spartan Steel & Alloys Ltd v Martin & Co (Contractors) Ltd* [1973] QB 27 (CA); *Murphy v Brentwood District Council* [1991] 1 AC 398 (HL).

raged in this area, with a plethora of public policy arguments being used to support every conceivable position.[55] But on the traditional view, the law's general position is straightforward. You did not own the book; Peter did. Hence, only Peter had a right in the book that he held against me. For that reason, only Peter can sue me. In destroying the book, I commit a commutative injustice only against him. This problem—the so-called problem of economic loss—is a mere pseudo-problem created by the modern conception.[56]

But, one might point out, there is no blanket rule against the recovery of economic loss. For instance, if you damage the car that I use as a taxi, ordinarily I can recover from you not only the cost of repair, but the loss of the profits that I would have made had I been able to use the taxi. But Pufendorf had dealt with this issue long ago:

in determining the amount of damage, it should be observed that under that heading comes not merely the thing belonging to us or owed us which is damaged, destroyed, or frustrated, but the fruits as well which come from it, whether they have already been received—in which case they may already be estimated as separate items—or are only hoped for, provided the owner might have received them...; although the expenses, necessary to secure such fruits or profits, should be deducted, lest we become more rich at another's cost... For example, whoever burns a man's house must not merely rebuild it, but also make good the rent which would have come from it in the meantime.[57]

These losses are consequences of the defendant's violation of the plaintiff's rights.[58]

Consider also Mill's Harm Principle in this context. Recall that, according to this view, interference with a person is justified only in order to prevent harm to others in a way that minimizes overall harm. The first problem with this theory is that it depends on an account of harm that Mill fails to provide.

---

[55] For one influential statement of the modern view, see James, 'Limitations on Liability for Economic Loss Caused by Negligence'.

[56] For a more detailed analysis, see Benson, 'Economic Loss'; Brown, 'Still Crazy'; Beever, *Rediscovering the Law of Negligence*, chs 7–8. And for a general critique of the loss-based approach in favour of one based on rights, see both that work and Stevens, *Torts and Rights*.

[57] Pufendorf, *Of the Law of Nature and Nations*, III I 3. For discussion of consequential economic loss, see Beever, *Rediscovering the Law of Negligence*, 246–250.

[58] Other examples are examined in Beever, *Rediscovering the Law of Negligence*, chs 6–9.

This generates all sorts of difficulties. For instance, Mill opposes the enforcement of the traditional restriction of activity on the Sabbath on the ground that that activity does not cause harm to others. To demonstrate this, he maintains that the traditionalists have 'a belief that God not only abominates the act of the misbeliever, but will not hold us guiltless if we leave him unmolested'.[59] But that point undermines his position. The traditionalists do believe that they will be harmed if they permit others to engage in certain activities on the Sabbath. They, ie those who permit the activity, might burn in hell for eternity. Similarly, Mill maintains that indecency should be prohibited, but he does not explain why it is harmful.[60] And he maintains that parents should be required to see that their children are educated, but does not argue that the failure to be educated is a harm (rather than the failure to be given a deserved benefit).[61] In other words, Mill's theory trades on an account of harm that it does not supply.

But let us put that problem aside. The second problem, of more relevance here, is that Mill's approach makes it difficult to understand the law's responses. The general problem is this. Imagine that driving negligently I lose control of my vehicle, crashing into and damaging yours. In these circumstances, the law holds that I have an obligation to compensate you for your loss. But how can that be justified according to the Harm Principle? Of course, the accident harmed you and so was in violation of the Harm Principle. But requiring me to pay you is also a harm (it is an interference with my liberty and causes me loss), and so can be justified only if it minimizes harm overall. Does it?

The common answer is that it does because it deters future acts of the kind that I performed and hence minimizes harm in the long run. But that answer is beset with a number of well-known difficulties.[62] The most important are the following four. These related points are that, while deterrence might explain why the defendant must pay damages, deterrence is inconsistent with the fact that (1) these damages equal the plaintiff's loss (and/or, in appropriate cases, the defendant's gain); (2) there must be a plaintiff who has suffered loss; (3) there must be a defendant who has committed a wrong; and (4) only a plaintiff

---

[59] Mill, 'On Liberty', 4.22.
[60] Ibid, 5.8.
[61] Ibid, 5.16.
[62] Eg Coleman, *The Practice of Principle*, 3–63; Stone, 'The Significance of Doing and Suffering'; Weinrib, *The Idea of Private Law*, 39–42.

(ie a wronged person) can bring the action against the defendant (ie the wrongdoer).

The first point is that deterrence does not seem to be the goal of the law, despite the routine claim to the contrary, as the law's responses (at least in all but exceptional cases) ignore deterrence. In our example, for instance, I will have to pay you for your loss. The court will not estimate an amount needed effectively to deter people from careless driving. The second point is that a plaintiff, a victim, must bring a cause of action, but this rule is senseless if deterrence is the goal. For instance, if I drive through a red light fortunately injuring no one, then I commit no tort. But this is surely the kind of action that ought to be deterred. The basic point here is that deterrence focuses entirely on the defendant, and so tort law's linking of a defendant with a plaintiff seems entirely arbitrary.

The third point is that tort law insists that liability fall only on wrongdoers. But deterrence has no place for this requirement. On the deterrence rationale, liability should be occasioned whenever it would deter future wrongdoing. Punishing some innocent actions will help achieve that goal—for instance, by providing an example. On the other hand, tort law requires that liability fall on all those who wrongfully injure another. But deterrence dictates only that liability fall when it would deter future wrongdoing. Hence, if the defendant has wrongfully injured the plaintiff but the imposition of liability would not deter future wrongdoing—because the circumstances are unique, because others are unlikely to repeat the defendant's behaviour, or because the facts of the case are not widely known, etc—then a system of deterrence would impose no liability. Tort law is not such a system. Finally, fourthly, a system based on deterrence would not insist that only the victim of a wrong can take action against the wrongdoer. In general, it is no more of a deterrent to know that if I perform an action I will have to pay damages to one person rather than to another.

Now, the claim is not that answers to these problems are impossible.[63] The point is more fundamental. Let us return to our example: I drive negligently and damage your car. I must pay for your loss. Why? It ought to be obvious that the answer to this question does not depend on deterrence or any such concern. The reason is that the

---

[63] For an attempt to provide some answers, see Kaplow and Shavell, *Fairness Versus Welfare*.

loss you suffered is a result of the wrong that I committed against you. That is enough to justify liability. It is only the modern view, and in particular our commitment to principles such as the Harm Principle, that makes theorists think that this answer is insufficient.

To return to the kind of example discussed in the Introduction to this book, if my son smashes one of his brother's toys, we make him do something to 'compensate' his brother. But that is not because we are trying to deter him from further wrongful acts (though it does deter him, we are aware of this, and we regard it as a positive by-product of our actions). It is because, without even thinking of distributive issues, we feel that his brother deserves it. Moreover, when my son asks why he has to give his brother his new toy car, for instance, we tell him 'Because you smashed your brother's car'. Though he might not like it, he does not find this remotely difficult to understand.

But, as I have noted, modern theorists do. Hence, we find John Gardner asking: 'Why isn't this impulse to "disgorge" [or compensate] just irrational crying over spilt milk on both sides?'[64] For Gardner, 'To provide the missing link here an account of the symbolic or expressive force of actions of reparation and restitution is required.'[65] How have we come to this?

Gardner's view is not Mill's. But the structure of their views is the same. For both Mill and Gardner, a wrong is an event. Hence, for both, the response to the wrong can only be a response to something that has already happened. As the response also interferes with the defendant, it appears also to be wrong and so in need of justification. But as we saw in Chapters 6 and 7, the commission of a commutative injustice creates a wrongful state of affairs. The wrong is that the defendant has more than he should have vis-à-vis the plaintiff. That wrong exists until it is repaired. Hence, the repair is seen as the undoing, correction, or repair of the wrong.

In fact, Gardner's analogy is more apt than he realizes. After the commission of a commutative injustice, the milk is spilt. It has not gone away. It is lying on the floor and needs to be cleaned up. The response is the cleaning up. No appeal to 'the symbolic or expressive force of actions of reparation and restitution is required'.

[64] Gardner, 'The Purity and Priority of Private Law', 474.
[65] Ibid.

3.2 Contract

The approaches to contract law examined in the second part of this book are usefully compared with the modern approach, outlined in Chapter 1. When a contract is breached, the standard response is for a court to award expectation damages or (less frequently) specific performance—that is, to require the defendant to pay the plaintiff a sum sufficient to put the plaintiff in the position in which he would have been had the contract been performed or, more simply, to require the defendant to perform the contract.[66] But as we saw, Lon Fuller and William Perdue argue that these responses have no natural place in the law. With particular reference to expectation damages, they claim:

This seems on the face of things a queer kind of 'compensation'. We can, to be sure, make the term 'compensation' seem appropriate by saying that the defendant's breach 'deprived' the plaintiff of the expectancy. But this is in essence only a metaphorical statement of the effect of the legal rule. In actuality the loss which the plaintiff suffers (deprivation of the expectancy) is not a datum of nature but the reflection of a normative order. It appears as a 'loss' only by reference to an unstated *ought*. Consequently, when the law gauges damages by the value of the promised performance it is not merely measuring a quantum, but is seeking an end, however vaguely conceived this end may be.[67]

It is certainly true that a breach of contract is (at least ordinarily) 'not a datum of nature but the reflection of a normative order'. If I renege on my promise to give you my horse, the consequence of this (ordinarily) is that I fail to benefit you but not that I make you worse off. Of course, I make you worse off than you would have been had I performed but, as Fuller and Perdue point out, that can be conceptualized as a loss only with the addition of the thought that I ought to have performed. With that, the traditional thinkers would have had no issue. But they would have been astounded by the claim that this ought is understood by the law only vaguely. And they would have been equally bemused to see where Fuller and Perdue sought to discover it: in distributive justice.[68]

---

[66] In civilian systems, the default award is specific performance rather than damages, a position that has been strengthened in Germany recently. For discussion, see Zimmermann, 'Remedies for Non-Performance'.

[67] Fuller and Perdue, 'The Reliance Interest in Contract Damages', 53.

[68] Ibid.

Consider again Mindy Chen-Wishart's summary of the significance of Fuller and Perdue's theory, from the perspective of 80 years of reflection.

[T]o enforce a promise is essentially to compel the promisor to benefit the promisee. Fuller and Perdue famously observed that expectation damages represents a 'queer kind of compensation' since it gives the promisee something he never had. As such, it seems to contradict the foundational principle of modern liberalism, the 'harm principle', according to which the state should only interfere with individual liberty to *prevent harm* to another.[69]

Of course, the traditionalists might say, it seems queer if that is where you are looking. For one thing, the Harm Principle defines harm in an amoral sense. In other words, harm on this conception is (or is meant to be) entirely a matter of fact. This thought renders the very real harm that the promisee suffers, the violation of his rights, invisible. Moreover, the harm principle, as the purported 'principle of modern liberalism', ie of (at least one aspect of) distributive justice, distracts from the solution to what is again only a pseudo-problem. The issue is not the appropriate rules governing the structure of society and the possible violation of them by the promisor; it is rather the fact that the promisor gave the promisee a right that the promisor then breached. The point of the legal response is simply to respect that right.

In other words, the problem at the heart of the modern conception of contract law is a problem of the modern conception's own invention.[70] It is, as I have said, a pseudo-problem that arises from forgetting the nature of justice.

Also worth considering is the question: why are contracts binding at all? According to the modern view, the promisee fails to realize a promised benefit when the promisor fails to perform. But that does not mean that the person is harmed. Because of this, Mill and Sidgwick attempt to explain the binding nature of contract by appealing to the reasonable expectations of the parties.[71] The idea is that contracts are binding because of the need to protect the parties'

---

[69] Chen-Wishart, *Contract Law*, 22

[70] See also Gordley, 'A Perennial Misstep'; Benson, 'The Expectation and Reliance Interests'.

[71] Mill, 'Utilitarianism', 5.8, 36; Sidgwick, *The Methods of Ethics*, III VI 6.3; IV III 4.7–8.

reliance interests. This view generates notorious problems. The following are the four most important.

First, because the theory of reasonable expectations is concerned with expectations, it focuses on the parties' declarations, rather than intentions. In short, the issue is not what the parties agreed to but what it would be reasonable for them to expect.[72] And because of this, the theory is committed to denying that contracts are formed through agreement.[73] On this view, agreement is simply irrelevant to contract formation.[74] As is vividly revealed in the judgment of Fagan CJ in the South African case *George v Fairmead (pty) Ltd*, this view shatters the distinction between contract and tort.

As I read the decisions, our Courts, in applying the test [to determine the existence of a contract], have taken into account the fact that there is another party involved and have considered his position. They have, in effect, said: Has the first party—the one who is trying to resile—*been to blame* in the sense that by his conduct he has led the other party, as a reasonable man, to believe that he was binding himself?[75]

It is important not to underestimate this difficulty. The problem is not that the distinction between tort and contract is less neat and tidy than once believed.[76] Rather, it is that contract has disappeared as a separate legal subject, swallowed by the law of tort. Fagan CJ is speaking of negligence, rather than of agreement. If the theory correctly describes contract formation, then there are no legal obligations that arise from actual agreement. But that is strange indeed. Surely, agreement is not something to which the law should be blind.[77]

---

[72] See, however, the discussion of interpretation in Chapter 7.

[73] See, eg Atiyah, *The Rise and Fall of Freedom of Contract*, 771–778; Collins, *The Law of Contract*, 206–207; Fuller and Perdue, 'The Reliance Interest in Contract Damages'; Gilmore, *The Death of Contract*, 65–76; Pound, *Jurisprudence*, v 4, 457. See also Zimmermann, *The Law of Obligations*, 597 n 52. The problem is also diagnosed by Simester and Chan, 'Inducing Breach of Contract: One Tort or Two?', 142–143.

[74] Hence, the view to which the theory is committed is not 'Contracts are formed when there is no agreement'. It is rather 'Agreement is irrelevant to contracting'.

[75] [1958] 2 SA 465 (emphasis added). See also *National Carriers Ltd v Panalpina (Northern) Ltd* [1981] AC 675 (HL) (Lord Wilberforce); Gilmore, *The Death of Contract*, ch 4.

[76] In any case, this neatness is an illusion. See Beever, *Rediscovering the Law of Negligence*, 311–315.

[77] Again, the point is not that no obligations arise *when* people agree. According to the theory here examined, contracts may be formed when people agree, but not because they agree; agreement is irrelevant. Note also that it is not to the point that the rules of contract law may differ from those of tort law.

The second problem with the theory of reasonable expectations flows from the first: it severs contract formation from free will. According to the theory, contractual obligation does not arise because of free agreement; rather, contractual liability is imposed to protect reasonable expectations.[78] Hence, contract law is seen as an imposition on freedom rather than the realization thereof.[79]

The third problem with the theory of reasonable expectations is that, if contractual obligation is imposed to protect reasonable expectations, then it is unclear why it is not unilaterally revocable. Why cannot either party rescind its promise before the other party's detrimental reliance has occurred? As long as the rescission is clear to the other party, there is no reliance interest to protect.[80]

Fourthly, it is simply untrue that the common law imposes contractual obligation when such would be required to protect reasonable expectations; the common law requires an external manifestation *of agreement*.[81] Accordingly, an offer cannot be made by one who is sleep talking, no matter how awake that person appears and hence how reasonable the induced reliance.[82] Offers and acceptances must be volitional. (Recall the example of the android from section 5.3 of Chapter 7.) Moreover, if *A* overhears a conversation between *B* and *C* on a matter about which *B* is an expert, then *A*'s reliance on *B*'s statements is not unreasonable. In fact, it may be unreasonable, perhaps quite irrational, for *A* not to rely.[83] But *A*'s reasonable reliance would

---

[78] See n 73.

[79] Zimmermann, *The Law of Obligations*, 584.

[80] Of course, the party intending to perform may have already suffered reliance losses, including opportunity costs, but those can be compensated for without imposing liability for expectation. Gordley, 'A Perennial Misstep'.

[81] Smith, *Contract Theory*, 173–176.

[82] It is possible to explain this by suggesting that, for instance, the words emanating from the mouth of the sleep talker cannot be taken as a declaration of the sleep talker. Of course this is correct, but it is correct only because of the connection between declaration and will, a connection severed by the theory explored here. It is perhaps not surprising that no authority on this point is to be found. But it is trite that one cannot be liable in negligence unless one has acted voluntarily, despite the fact that negligence is not personal fault but the failure to live up to the standard of the ordinary reasonable person. See, eg, *Waugh v Allan* [1964] 2 Lloyd's Rep 1 (HL); *Buckley and The Toronto Transportation Commission v Smith Transport Ltd* [1946] OR 798 (Ont CA). Similarly, it is generally accepted that one cannot be liable in torts of strict liability, such as trespass to land, unless one acted volitionally. It would be most odd if one could not be found to have acted negligently or to have committed a tort of strict liability in circumstances in which one could be held to have made or accepted an offer.

[83] Of course, we may think it unreasonable to allow *A* to sue *B* for detrimental reliance, but that is another matter entirely. See Beever, *Rediscovering the Law of Negligence*, 280–281.

be far from sufficient to conclude that a contract existed between *A* and *B*. In fact, the notion of *reasonable* reliance, as it operates in this context, appears covertly to rely on the rejection of the theory of reasonable expectations: reliance is reasonable only if the party relying had good reason to believe that the other party *actually agreed* to that reliance and the other party was acting *volitionally*.

Now, it must be acknowledged that defences of the theory could be provided. But the point is that these conclusions are so fundamentally at odds with the intuitive understanding of contract law that, even in the face of these defences, other things being equal an alternative to the theory under consideration should be preferred if a plausible view can be found. And we have already found one.

In contract, the promisor gives the promisee a right. If the contract is breached, then that right is violated. The violation of this right is a commutative injustice that requires reparation. The right is a right to have the contract performed. Hence, the remedy consists of requiring the contract to be performed or demanding that the defendant put the plaintiff in the position in which he would have been had the contract been performed. The difficulties listed above are pseudo-problems. We do not need the theory of reasonable expectations.

3.3 Misfeasance and Nonfeasance

As if the problems above were not difficult enough, the modern view collapses when faced with the law's distinction between misfeasance and nonfeasance and, in particular, its ruling that there can be no liability for the latter. The most stark and compelling example of this rule is that, outside certain special categories, the common law imposes no duty to rescue. So, to take the standard example, if I am standing on a wharf when I see a child fall into the water and begin to drown, I have no duty to rescue that child. I am entitled to stand and watch the child drown. Even if I could rescue the child simply by kicking into the water a lifebuoy that happens to be lying at my feet, I cannot be liable for failing to do so. What could possibly justify so extraordinary a rule?

Various suggestions have been made.[84] In *Stovin v Wise*, Lord Hoffmann summarized these into three categories: political, moral,

---

[84] For discussion, see eg Bender, 'A Lawyer's Primer on Feminist Theory and Tort', 33–38; Epstein, 'A Theory of Strict Liability', 197–201; Ripstein, 'Three Duties to Rescue'; Weinrib,

and economic.[85] Put shortly, the argument is that liability for failing to conduct a rescue would interfere with freedom (political), would arbitrarily single out individual defendants for liability who were no more to blame than anyone else for not conducting the rescue (moral), and would be inefficient (economic). Perhaps these arguments generally have weight, but they are hardly compelling when applied to the case under discussion.[86] If these are the best arguments going, then one ought to be under a duty to rescue the child in our example.

According to Jane Stapleton, the law at this point adopts a position of extreme libertarianism in its preference for freedom of action over the interests of the child.[87] But this claim must be read in conjunction with the fact that Stapleton also maintains that the protection of the vulnerable lies at the heart of the law of tort.[88] To put this another way, the law is extremely libertarian, but at the same time communitarian at heart. Here, we see the modern understanding of the law attempting, not to steer a course between Scylla and Charybdis, but rather to steer at both at the same time, the contradiction being the only thing keeping it from going down.

The non-existence of a duty to rescue is not easily explicable in terms of policy. If it is true that the law is concerned to promote the kinds of policies that we have discussed, then it appears inconceivable that it would not impose a duty to conduct easy rescues, at least in certain cases. The fact that continental systems do impose such duties in both civil law and, with the exceptions only of Finland and Sweden, in criminal law, is further evidence that the common law is not responding to the kinds of concerns often thought to drive it.[89] In fact, the absence of a duty to rescue points away from the modern approaches altogether.

And again we can see that this, on the face of it perplexing feature of the law, is readily explicable on the traditional view. If the child is not

---

'The Case for a Duty to Rescue'; Weinrib, 'Legal Formalism: On the Immanent Rationality of Law', 977–978.

[85] [1996] AC 823 (HL), 930–931.

[86] For an analysis of the moral argument, see Weinrib, 'The Case for a Duty to Rescue'. For reasons of the kind discussed below, Weinrib now holds that a duty to rescue cannot be supported at common law. See, eg Weinrib, 'Legal Formalism: On the Immanent Rationality of Law', 977–978.

[87] Stapleton, 'Duty of Care Factors: A Selection from the Judicial Menus', 73–74.

[88] See Stapleton, 'The Golden Thread at the Heart of Tort Law: Protection of the Vulnerable'.

[89] For a summary of the continental positions, see Smits, *The Good Samaritan in European Private Law*, 2–11.

mine, then she has no right against me that I rescue her. My failure to do so may be reprehensible, but it does not injure her. Certainly, she suffers loss, but only 'irrational creatures cannot distinguish between *injury*, and *damage*'.[90]

4. The Common Law and the Traditional View

I have argued that the modern conception leads us to misunderstand our law. But if the modern conception is our conception, then how can it lead to a misunderstanding of *our* law? Why would our law be structured inconsistently with our conception? At its most general, there are two answers to this question.

First, the law deals with situations in which commutative, not distributive, justice is appropriate. For instance, when one person complains that another violated her bodily integrity or failed to perform a contract, that is a complaint about commutation—about 'those things that belong to our intercourse with other men', about the failure to 'Render to each one his right'.[91] The complaint is not about distribution. Even having forgotten commutative justice as theory, then, the intuitively right result to these cases is likely to accord with that form of justice. For this reason, the fundamental structure of the private law remains based on commutative justice.

But that is not the only reason. The fundamental structure of the private law is based on commutative justice also because those who created that law consciously did so in terms of commutative justice. The traditional view survived longer in law than in philosophy and founders of our law were traditionalists.

For instance, Sir Edward Coke distinguished criminal from private law by remarking that, unlike the latter, the former 'concerneth the safety of his majestie, the quiet of the common-wealth, and the life, honour, fame, liberty, blood, wife, and posteritie of the party accused besides the forfeiture of his lands, goods, and all that he hath'.[92] In other words, *unlike the private law*, the commands of the criminal law are instituted in accordance with the interests of society as a whole

---

[90] For a comprehensive discussion of the duties involved here, see Ripstein, 'Three Duties to Rescue'. As Ripstein explains, there is room for a legal duty to rescue.
[91] Aquinas, *Summa theologica*, SS 58 1 a.
[92] Coke, *The Institutes of the Laws of England*, Part III intro para 2.

(distributive justice) and the response to the violation of those rules is punishment. Similarly, Sir Mathew Hale defined the private law in terms of rights persons possess in and of themselves or in respect to things, and defined these rights before turning to discuss the state.[93] Hence, those rights could only be ones of commutative justice.

Perhaps the clearest example of the influence of the traditional view, however, is seen in Sir William Blackstone.

Wrongs are divisible into two sorts of species: *private wrongs* and *public wrongs*. The former are an infringement or privation of civil rights belonging to individuals considered as individuals; and are thereupon frequently termed *civil injuries*: the latter are a breach and violation of public rights and duties, which affect the whole community, considered as a community; and are distinguished by the harsher appellation of *crimes* and *misdemeanours*.[94]

This adopts the distinction between commutative justice on the one hand and distributive justice on the other, and defines tort law in terms of the former and criminal law in terms of the latter.

Because of this, our forgetting of commutative justice means that we find it difficult even to understand what parts of our law are about. Consider, for instance, PH Winfield's attempt to define the difference between tort law and criminal law. According to Winfield, the two areas of law are distinguished by the fact that they deliver different sanctions: punishment for a crime, damages for a tort.[95] This immediately raises the problem of the availability of exemplary or punitive damages in tort, but Winfield attempts to avoid this problem by defining punishment as that 'which, when once liability to it has been decreed, is not avoidable by any act of the party offending'.[96] This distinguishes 'punishment' from exemplary damages, because the victim can decline to insist on receiving the latter in response to some action of the wrongdoer, but cannot rescue the defendant from 'punishment' once decreed by a court. This definition of 'punishment' is obviously strategic. It is no part of our ordinary understanding of punishment, but is rather designed to exclude exemplary damages from the

---

[93] Hale, *The History of the Common Law of England; and, an Analysis of the Civil Part of the Law*, II 1.
[94] Blackstone, *Commentaries on the Laws of England*, vol 1, III i.
[95] Winfield, *The Province of the Law of Tort*, 201.
[96] Ibid, 200.

definition simply in order to avoid the problem encountered above. As such, it could not possibly reveal anything substantive about the distinction between tort and crime. Moreover, while the fact that the victim has more power in tort than in criminal law does point to an important difference between those laws, Winfield does nothing to reveal it. Finally, even putting the problem of exemplary damages aside, the mere observation that tort law deals out damages while criminal law responds with 'punishment' tells us little of interest. What we need to know is *why* those areas of the law respond in that way.[97] In short, Winfield inherits Bentham's inability to understand the nature of private law and its distinction from the public.

Interestingly, in developing his account, Winfield explores Blackstone's view and reproduces the passage from Blackstone quoted above.[98] However, while Winfield develops Blackstone's comments concerning punishment, he ignores the central feature of Blackstone's analysis: the notion that the private law deals with 'civil rights belonging to individuals considered as individuals,' while the criminal law polices 'public rights and duties, which affect the whole community, considered as a community'. Apparently, Winfield has no use for these ideas. Why not? His commitment to the modern view meant that even he does not understand them.

Instead, Winfield maintains that 'the law of tort is based upon a general principle that all harm to another person is presumptively unlawful.'[99] Against this, Winfield notices that not all acts that cause harm to others are actionable, but responds that 'To say that all unjustifiable harm is actionable is a totally different thing from saying that all harm is actionable.'[100] In other words, if *A* harms *B* and does not have to compensate *B*, this must be because *A*'s action was justified by something that warrants an exception being made to the general principle of liability. I examined this view in section 1.

As a result, introductory chapters in tort textbooks are not what one might expect them to be. In accordance with common practice, the authors of these texts usually feel the need to provide some definition of their subject matter, but are forced to admit that they are unable to provide anything genuinely satisfactory.[101] That is, of course,

---

[97] See also Rogers, *Winfield and Jolowicz on Tort*, 1, 6–7.
[98] Winfield, *The Province of the Law of Tort*, 193.
[99] Ibid, 36.
[100] Ibid, 37.
[101] Eg Rogers, *Winfield and Jolowicz on Tort*, 1.

unsurprising. No one who sees the world through the eyes of the modern conception will be able properly to understand the law. But what is genuinely remarkable is that our acknowledged inability to produce even poor definitions of tort law has not led us to see that there is something very wrong indeed with our understanding of that law. Our inability to define the law in even a rough way reveals that we cannot know what the law is about. If we understood it, we would be able to define it.

5. Conclusion

Our acceptance of the modern conception has made it almost impossible for us to understand our law. Nowhere is this more evident than in the modern law of negligence. Though there is disagreement around the edges, the vast majority of modern lawyers accept that the law of negligence plays a vital role and ought to be preserved. How, then, is it possible for an academic as deservedly distinguished as David Ibbetson to write 'That the tort of negligence is in a mess goes almost without saying'?[102] How can it be that we think an area of the law that we believe to be largely justified is a mess? The answer, the only possible answer, is that we do not know why the law is justified. We feel its justification without being able to articulate it, hence it seems a mess. The justification that it needs is beyond our current comprehension. In this book, I have argued that that is because we have buried the necessary forms of justification under the modern conception. This book, then, is another exercise in normative archaeology.[103]

As recently as 1932, Lord Atkin said:

The British law has always necessarily ingrained in it moral teaching in this sense: that it lays down standards of honesty and plain dealing *between man and man*... If he swears to his neighbour, he is not to disappoint him. In other words, he is to keep his contracts. He is not to injure his neighbour by word. That is to say, he is not to libel or slander him... He is not to injure his neighbour by acts of negligence; and that certainly covers a very large field of the law. I doubt whether the whole law of tort could not be

---

[102] Ibbetson, 'How the Romans did for Us: Ancient Roots of the Tort of Negligence', 475.
[103] Cf Beever, *Rediscovering the Law of Negligence*, 29.

comprised in the golden maxim to *do unto your neighbour as you would that he should do unto you.*[104]

Due to the dominance of the modern conception, few modern lawyers will read this passage as it was intended to be read. It is not a discussion of public policy.

But it is not only the law that we misunderstand. In the following chapters I show that we also misconceive the political world and, most fundamentally, ourselves.

---

[104] Lord Atkin, 'Law as an Educational Subject', 30 (emphasis added).

13

Political Philosophy

We now turn our attention to the political world. As in the previous chapter, the argument is that the modern conception distorts our understanding. This is revealed by showing that the modern view is capable of explaining ordinary features of this world with difficulty at best, while these same features are readily explicable on the traditional view.

Of course, the discussion is not comprehensive. It focuses on four key areas: the foundations of political obligation, the modern treatment of justice, the relationship between politics and commutative justice, and the connection between law and politics. The analysis is once again closely linked with the law. That is as it must be. If the thesis of this book is correct, law lies at the foundations of politics and it is in the intersection of the two worlds that the greatest difficulties will be found and the most important discoveries made.

1. The Foundations of Political Obligation

The second part of this book examined the view that political obligation is grounded on a set of rights and obligations that hold between individuals *inter se*. That, as we have also seen, is not the modern view. Due mainly to Hobbes and influenced by theorists such as the utilitarians and John Rawls, we have become used to the idea that all of our rights and duties are an aspect of or are posterior to political obligation. As Hobbes would have put it, they are found in the social contract or are created by the sovereign appointed by that contract. As

Rawls would have it, they are a product of the agreement formed in the original position or of the body that governs in accordance with that agreement. But despite our unfamiliarity with the traditional view expressed as such, when we drop our modern guard, we often think as the traditionalists did.

This can be seen in two ways. First, when we are not thinking as theorists, we reflexively adopt understandings of political phenomena that fit the traditional view. Secondly, when acting as theorists, we base our views on assumptions that belong to the traditional view and are inconsistent with the modern.

Take, for instance, our common notions of property. As we saw in Chapter 1, the modern view holds that property is grounded in distributive justice. But that is a peculiarly theoretical perspective. It is much more common to think that the role of distributive justice is not to ground property rights but only to justify redistributing them.

The best example of this concerns income tax. Usually, this tax is deducted from our salary before we receive it, taken to pay for public goods. Of course, most people are reluctant to see this money go, but they also accept that this form of taxation is at least in its general outline justified by distributive justice. Nevertheless, people think that it is *their money* that is taken, even if they think that the taking is entirely justified.

This attitude is inconsistent with the modern view. As the income is taxed in accordance with distributive justice, it cannot be distributive justice that makes us think that the income is ours. Why, then, do we have that view?

The answer is that we regard the money as ours because our employers agreed to pay it to us in return for our labour. In other words, we believe that the money is ours because of the relationship that we have with our employer, and that is a matter of commutative justice. The money is ours because there is a form of justice that operates as between ourselves and our employers that indicates that we should get the money, but we are deprived of some of that money, because of justice within the community as a whole. Intuitively, then, we regard property—not in the strictly legal sense but in the sense of belonging—as based on commutative, not distributive, justice. This becomes difficult to understand only after one has internalized the misguided assumptions of the modern conception.

Consider also the following scenario. As has been mentioned a number of times in this book, if you pay me £1,000 in the mistaken belief that you owed me a debt, then I will owe an obligation to pay you £1,000. Now, for convenience, imagine that you paid £1,000 into a bank account that had a zero balance. At law, the position is that I own the £1,000 (strictly that I have a chose in action worth £1,000) but owe you an obligation to pay £1,000. In other words, the £1,000 is mine. But we seldom think that way. If my wife sees a bank statement and asks me 'Is this money ours?', unless I am a pedantic lawyer (I am only sometimes!), I will say 'No'.

This is not because distributive justice requires me to return the money. Distributive justice may or may not require that of me. It is because, as between you and me, you ought to have the money, a matter of commutative justice. Again, then, we can see that our sense of property or belonging is grounded on commutative, not distributive, justice.

Commutative justice is a feature of our understanding of the world. We just do not understand that we understand the world that way.

We have already seen that the modern view is built on silent assumptions that belong to the traditional. Examples of this were examined in previous chapters. We saw, for instance, that Hobbes' social contract argument requires the notion that contracts are binding, which entails that contractual obligation cannot be a product of sovereign authority but must rather be based on notions of commutative justice. We also saw that this problem with Hobbes' account is frequently overlooked. It is overlooked because somewhere at the back of our minds sits the traditional view, making us think that individuals in the state of nature are bound when they form their agreement. Without that thought, our response to Hobbes' postulation of the formation of the social contract would be: 'So what does that prove?' The modern view can appear plausible to us only because we unconsciously hold to the traditional.

Recall also from Chapter 1 the discussion of Rawls' theory. As we saw, Rawls maintains that a principle of equality governs interactions between people in the original position. '[T]he parties in the original position are equal. That is, all have the same rights in the procedure for choosing principles; each can make proposals, submit reasons for their acceptance, and so on.'[1] In the light of the above and of the fact that this principle holds prior to the formation of the social contract, we can see that, contra Rawls, this is a principle of commutative, not

---

[1] Rawls, *A Theory of Justice*, 17.

distributive, justice. What is more, the principle does not only govern the way in which debate in the original position proceeds. It directly generates rights and duties, most importantly including the right to bodily integrity and the obligation to perform contractual promises. A social contract that violated these rights would be void, not because no such contract would be generated by rational and reasonable people deliberating from behind a veil of ignorance (though perhaps it would not), but because it would violate the norms presupposed by the social contract.

Recall also Locke's view that individuals possess rights to bodily integrity, property, and contract in the state of nature and that the social contract is formed out of the need to protect those rights. Though Locke is unable to state it, this is a view founded on commutative justice. As the structure of Locke's theory makes plain, natural rights are held by individuals against each other *inter se*, which is why they exist in the state of nature. When the civil condition comes into being then, it is not a legal *tabula rasa*.

Another instructive example concerns the modern understanding of the Magna Carta, which many take to be the foundational document of the United Kingdom. As we are told:

Though it's been transformed somewhat, the Magna Carta that was signed in 1215 still forms the legal foundation of Great Britain today. Together with the Bill of Rights in the year 1791, it also became the basis for all the laws of the United States. The US Constitution draws to a large extent on the Magna Carta. And it wouldn't be an exaggeration to say that the Magna Carta provided the basis for every declaration that created the conditions for increased civil liberties and rights—at first, on the British isle, and later, on the European continent.[2]

But what was the Magna Carta? It was an agreement, a contract, reached between King John and his barons. (Later versions were agreements made by later kings.) And the fact that the Magna Carta represents an agreement is absolutely fundamental to our understanding of it. It is because John and later kings agreed to be bound by it that it has the status that it does. As I have discussed in more detail elsewhere,[3]

---

[2] 'The Great Charter of Freedoms: Magna Carta—June 15, 1215', *Deutsche Welle*, 19/04/2010 <http://www.dw-world.de/dw/article/1,4621342,00.html>.

[3] Beever, 'Our Most Fundamental Rights'.

this means that the Magna Carta cannot be foundational. On the contrary, its significance is based entirely on the idea that individuals are bound by their agreements, a matter of commutative justice.

We can summarize this argument by saying that the idea that our fundamental politico-legal obligations are owed to other individuals as such is both the most familiar and exotic notion in modern life.

Are the norms that we have discussed political? Not in the sense in which that term is used here. They apply to, but are prior to, the community and the state. Hence, one wishing to insist on a right not to be harmed does not need to appeal to decisions of the legislature or the like, but can appeal directly to this foundational norm. If these norms are not political, what are they? The short answer is that they are legal.

Not intending to be even remotely controversial, in his discussion of the connection between law and disagreement, Jeremy Waldron remarks that 'law is the offspring of politics'.[4] Indeed, this claim is not now controversial: the vast majority of theorists in philosophy, politics, and law would accept it without question. But it is nevertheless wrong. Some law is the offspring of politics, but some law is politics' foundation.

Again, much depends on definition. One could define 'law' to mean certain decisions of political bodies or the like. But that is not how we use the term in ordinary discourse, or even ordinary lawyer's discourse. There, we use 'law' to refer to statues, cases, and the like, but also to general legal principles.[5] And these principles are, or at least can be, instances of what Rawls calls our natural duties.

2. The Distortion of Justice

As noted in Chapter 4, the fundamental misunderstanding of commutative or corrective justice is the thought that it is concerned only with correcting injustices, a result of confusing the name of a concept

---

[4] Waldron, 'Kant's Legal Positivism', 1538.

[5] Eg the Neighbour Principle: 'You must take reasonable care to avoid acts or omissions which you can reasonably foresee would be likely to injure your neighbour. Who, then, in law is my neighbour? The answer seems to be—persons who are so closely and directly affected by my act that I ought reasonably to have them in contemplation as being so affected when I am directing my mind to the acts or omissions which are called in question.' *M'Alister (or Donoghue) (Pauper) v Stevenson* [1932] AC 562 (HL Sc), 580.

for the concept itself. This misunderstanding has led to the further mistake of thinking that commutative justice is able to operate only on the basis of norms grounded in distributive justice.

A high-profile statement of this view can be found in the judgment of the High Court of Australia in *Harriton v Stevens*.[6] In that case, the plaintiff's mother had contracted rubella when she was pregnant with the plaintiff. She was negligently informed that the disease posed no risk to her foetus. Had she correctly been advised that her foetus was at serious risk of deformity, she would have had the pregnancy terminated. As it was, however, her child was born with 'catastrophic disabilities', including blindness, deafness, mental retardation, and spasticity.[7] The child claimed damages for 'wrongful life', a claim that rests on the notion that she ought not to have been born. It was alleged that corrective justice demanded that she succeed.

In response, Crennan J replied:

Aristotelian notions of 'corrective justice', *requiring somebody who has harmed another without justification to indemnify that other*, and 'distributive justice', requiring calculation of benefits and losses and burdens in society, were referred to by Lord Steyn in *McFarlane v Tayside Health Board*,[8] for the purpose of explicating the dynamic interrelationship between differing values, which values need to be considered when faced with a novel claim in negligence... However, there remains a problem in Aristotle's analysis, relevant to this submission. In emphasising 'corrective justice', even as added to by his consideration of 'distributive justice', Aristotle left unexplored the dependence of 'correction' on the prior establishment of principles. As Finnis puts it, '"[c]orrection" and "restitution" are notions parasitic on some prior determination of what is to count as a crime, a tort, a binding agreement, etc. The values of fairness, coherence, and the corporate welfare of the community or community expectations... are not considered singly, in isolation from each other or from relevant matters, particularly the doctrines and well-established principles determining what constitutes negligence.'

[Hence,] a need for 'corrective justice' alone could never be determinative of a novel claim in negligence.[9]

---

[6] (2006) HCA 15, (2006) 226 CLR 52.
[7] Ibid, [20].
[8] [2000] 2 AC 59 (HL Sc).
[9] *Harriton v Stevens* (2006) HCA 15, (2006) 226 CLR 52, [274]–[275] (emphasis added, citations omitted). Quotation from Finnis, *Natural Law and Natural Rights*, 178–179.

On this view, corrective or commutative justice is interpreted merely as the demand that wrongs be corrected. This view completely denudes commutative justice of its positive content. Moreover, none of the theorists examined in the second part of this book would have accepted that all physical injuries constitute damage in the eyes of commutative justice. This is most clear in Pufendorf, who insists that a wrong in the eyes of commutative justice is a violation of a right. It is also implied by Kant's principle of being beyond reproach. For all of the thinkers, these rights are determined in accordance with commutative justice, which generates rights and obligations that people owe to each other as individuals. Thus, it is possible to conclude that commutative justice 'requires somebody who has harmed another without justification to indemnify the other'[10] only if we forget what commutative justice meant to those who discovered and developed it and adopt instead the definition provided by Sidgwick.

Moreover, Pufendorf would have insisted that the plaintiff in *Harriton v Stevens* could not recover. This is because she had no right not to have been born, a conclusion based entirely on commutative justice. Crennan J's comments demonstrate a failure to come to terms with the tradition to which commutative justice theory belongs.

The same mistake is found in John Gardner's denial that norms of the kind 'finders keepers' and 'surrenderers losers' could belong to commutative justice.[11] Gardner insists that these norms must be based on distributive justice, because that form of justice 'answers the geometric question of whether and why things should be allocated among people *full stop*, not the arithmetic question of whether and why things should be allocated *back* from one person to another.'[12] Clear here is the assumption that commutative justice must be concerned solely with correction,[13] the error of thinking that all arithmetic is subtraction.

Likewise, with respect to 'surrenderers losers', Gardner maintains that:

A second way for things to be justly allocated... is for them to be voluntarily sold or gifted by those who justly acquired them... All of this... belongs

---

[10] *McFarlane v Tayside Area Health Board* [2000] 2 AC 59 (HL Sc), 82.
[11] Gardner, 'What is Tort Law For? Part I', 11–14.
[12] Ibid, 12.
[13] Cf ibid, 12 n 28.

to the theory of distributive justice. It is all about allocation *tout court*. 'Surrenders losers' never gives us a ground for allocating anything back.[14]

But this is clearly not how the traditional thinkers saw it. For them, the law of sale and gift lay squarely within the realm of commutative justice.

What is noticeable about these positions is that they present *as obvious* claims deeply at odds with the traditional view. Indeed, it seems that these claims are thought to be so obvious that they do not need to be argued for.

Also significant is the level of implausibility Gardner is prepared to attribute to the positions he rejects. His claim is that commutative justice cannot ground any primary rights or norms, because it is concerned only with giving back. His complaint is that his opponents fail to see this. But how could they possibly fail to see that? Is it not more likely that they operated with a different conception of commutative justice that does not generate this difficulty, a possibility that Gardner spends no time examining? The problem here, again, is the dominance of the modern view. It closes the modern mind to alternative possibilities, presenting as obvious what is at least highly doubtful.

The fundamental misunderstanding under discussion here is buried very deeply in Gardner's approach. It infects his definition of justice per se. 'Norms of justice are moral norms of a distinctive type', he tells us. 'They are norms for tackling *allocative* moral questions, questions about who is to get how much of what.'[15]

This definition virtually guarantees that commutative justice will be misunderstood. Allocation is a concept that meshes at least reasonably well with distributive justice, ie with distributing/allocating benefits and burdens, but it sits comfortably only with the rectificatory element of commutative justice.

Helpfully, Gardner himself illustrates the problems that this approach generates when he considers the relationship between justice and torture. First, he tells us that 'allocative questions', and hence questions of justice, 'are forced upon us only when people make competing claims to assignable goods'.[16] Consequently, issues of justice are not raised when dealing with unlimited goods. This leads Gardner to conclude

[14] Ibid, 13.
[15] Ibid, 6.
[16] Ibid.

that the right not to be tortured cannot not lie in justice, as 'in principle there is an unlimited amount of non-torture to go round, so there need be no competition for it'.[17] This prompts Gardner to say:

> If...we say of someone who was tortured by the secret police that her treatment was unjust, she might well say, if her moral sensitivity has been left intact, that this misses the point and marginalizes her grievance. She is not complaining that she was the wrong person to be picked out for torture, that she was a victim of some kind of misallocation by the secret police, that she of all people should not have been tortured. She is complaining that torture should not have been used at all, against anyone. Her complaint is one of barbarity, never mind any incidental injustices involved in it.[18]

The passage 'if her moral sensitivity has been left intact' is interesting. What role is it meant to play? I ask this question because the complaint of those who have been tortured is almost uniformly precisely that they have been treated unjustly.[19] The claim of those who campaign on behalf of torture victims is the same. Is the suggestion that we are to think of all of these people as having lost their moral sensitivity?

The claim that it is wrong to think that victims of torture have been treated unjustly or that such is only incidental is absurd. The position is revealed to be even more implausible when one realizes that it is further committed to denying that slavery, genocide, murder, theft, rape, and so on and on are unjust, as there is an unlimited supply of non-slavery, non-genocide, etc, to go around. But it is important to see that this absurdity is not a feature of these conclusions alone. Gardner is forced to these conclusions by his definition of justice. Because he holds that justice is concerned with allocation, the right to torture cannot be a demand of justice as, he correctly points out, there is no moral issue concerning the *allocation* of torture. There is an infinite amount of non-torture to go around.

But when one's theory generates so incredible a set of conclusions, the appropriate response is not to announce them as the obvious truth and condemn all other theories inconsistent with them as obviously false.

---

[17] Ibid.
[18] Ibid. See also ibid, 46.
[19] Of course, other claims are or might also be made, but it must be stressed that Gardner's assertion is that torture is not contrary to justice, not that torture is also contrary to other values. The latter claim is, of course, correct.

The appropriate response is to re-examine the argument that led to so strange a result. The definition of justice under examination is wrong. It is only even prima facie adequate as a definition of distributive justice.

It is to be noted that Gardner's definition of justice has no pedigree. Aristotle does not define justice in terms of allocation. On the contrary, he tells us that justice is about lawfulness and fairness and that injustice is about unlawfulness, unfairness, and overreaching.[20] Similarly, Aquinas maintains that 'justice consists of those things that belong to our intercourse with other men...Hence the act of justice in relation to its proper matter and object is indicated in the words, "Rendering to each one his right."'[21] These are much more helpful and accurate definitions, and they clearly encompass the prohibition on torture. It is at least in part their focus on commutative justice that prevents Aristotle and Aquinas delineating justice in the unacceptably narrow fashion of some modern theorists.

The occluding of commutative justice is perhaps even more clearly, if less dramatically, seen in this analysis of the forms of justice as they operate in the law of tort:

> corrective justice provides the structure of tort law within which distributive justice operates. As a result, tort law might be judged, all things considered, to be a distributively unfair way of dealing with harm even if it was judged distributively just *as between doers and sufferers of harm*. This contrast could be captured by distinguishing between distributive justice in a global sense and principles of distributive justice that are 'local' to tort law.[22]

On this view, 'local distributive justice' is the distributive justice that operates as between two individuals taken as such. But distributive justice does not so operate.

First, as was discussed in section 3 of Chapter 6, the distinction between commutative and distributive justice is found in the forms of those concepts. That form relates to types of analysis, not to the number of parties involved. As discussed, if P_1 performs an action that wrongs P_2, P_3, and P_4, it cannot be assumed that the wrong is a distributive injustice just because more than two parties are implicated.

---

[20] Aristotle, *Nicomachean Ethics*, 1129a–b.
[21] Aquinas, *Summa theologica*, SS 58 1 a.
[22] Cane, 'Distributive Justice and Tort Law', 413. See also Gardner, 'What is Tort Law For? Part I', 12–13.

Similarly, if a norm requires a transaction between only P_1 and P_2, that does not prove that the norm is one of commutative justice merely because there are only two parties present. Hence, 'local distributive justice' is not problematic because it focuses on two parties.

The problem is that the passage alleges that 'local distributive justice' can trump 'global distributive justice'. If that is so, then 'local distributive justice' cannot be an aspect of distributive justice. 'Local distributive justice' is an oxymoron.

Take our four-person society again. Here, it is possible to imagine that distributive justice would call for a transfer between P_1 and P_2 on the assumption that P_3 and P_4 did not exist where that transfer would not be called for when distributive justice is applied to the whole society. But that is of no significance. If as a matter of distributive justice the transfer should not be made considering P_1, P_2, P_3, and P_4, then as a matter of distributive justice it should not be made. That it should be made *were* P_1 and P_2 the sole members of the society is of only counterfactual relevance.

To put this another way, the claim that 'local distributive justice' as between P_1 and P_2 demands x is to claim that distributive justice *would* require x were P_1 and P_2 the sole inhabitants of society. But as P_1 and P_2 are not the sole inhabitants of society, the point is irrelevant. The appeal to 'local distributive justice', ie to what distributive justice would recommend were the world different, is obscurantist.

In that light, we can see that if 'local distributive justice' is to play the role assigned to it, then it cannot be distributive justice at all. It must be commutative justice. And here we can again see the modern view unconsciously attempting to claw its way back to the traditional.

3. Liberalism, Totalitarianism, and Commutative Justice

As is well known, Roman law recognized property in human beings and indeed devoted considerable energy to describing the legal relationships that arose between individuals in respect of this property. Today, of course, slavery is regarded as an abomination and no modern legal system condones it. In that regard, we see the Roman law as unjust. None of that is new. But it is important to see that this injustice is both commutative and distributive.

Imagine that A throws a sharp object in a public place and that the object strikes and injures B.[23] Under our law, A will have an action against B.[24] But under Roman law, if B was C's slave, then C and not B would have an action against A. This is certainly unjust, but not only because of distributive concerns. The inability of B to sue A under Roman law is an injustice as between A and B. Slavery, then, is commutatively and distributively unjust.

Accordingly, the move from the Roman to the modern law discloses an improvement from the perspectives of commutative and distributive justice. The former improvement is not political in the sense of the term used here.

We can see, then, that the concerns of commutative justice can operate in parallel with those of distributive justice. They often do so. (This is perhaps one of the reasons that the former form of justice has been so easily forgotten.) Institutions such as slavery have their commutative and distributive aspects, both of which may be objectionable. It follows from this that opposition to slavery is likely to involve appeals to both forms of justice. Moreover, it is also very likely that the great movements in the history of political philosophy and the theories associated with them have this dual aspect. But it is also likely, given the forgetting of commutative justice exposed in this book, that those movements are not properly understood, as the commutative aspect of them will be ignored, or at best downplayed and misunderstood. As we see now, this has indeed occurred.

Perhaps the major theme of the twentieth century is its political conflicts. Foremost amongst these has been the conflict between two political ideologies: totalitarianism and liberalism. But what precisely are these?

What is totalitarianism? What are totalitarian movements out to achieve? According to *The Oxford Dictionary of Philosophy*, totalitarianism is 'The principle of government according to which all institutional and private arrangements are subject to control by the state. There are thus no autonomous associations, nor is there any principled or legally recognized private/public distinction.'[25] This is a very helpful definition because, in the light of what has gone before, it hints at its own limitations.

---

[23] Birks and McLeod (eds), *Justinian's Institutes* I 4.3.4.
[24] In New Zealand, however, the action, which still exists in principle, is barred by s 317 of the Accident Compensation Act 2001.
[25] Blackburn, *The Oxford Dictionary of Philosophy*.

Consider Karl Dietrich Bracher's analysis of the appeal of National Socialism in Weimar Germany.

Ideologically, it rested on the duality of nationalism (toward the outside) and anti-parliamentarianism (within). Economically it was rooted in that 'middle-class panic' in which the fight against the decline of economic, social, and national prestige was easily transposed to the realm of chauvinism and imperialism. Psychologically, the 'movement' profited in no small measure from the generation problem and the romantic protest mood of the youth. Above all, there loomed an ideology of unity, in which the heterogeneity of the social ties and interests of the ideology's supporters, the antagonisms of the petty-bourgeoisie, small landowners, dissatisfied intellectuals, and nationalist adventurers, were to be welded into a mystical community and the suppressed aggression turned toward the outside.[26]

This passage reveals what I will call the two faces of totalitarianism. First, totalitarianism is a theory about the appropriate relationship between the individual and the state. In short, it holds that the individual ought to be entirely subordinated to the state. Hence, totalitarianism is a 'principle of government' that demands 'control by the state' and rejects any 'private/public distinction'. That is a political theory. But it is also only half of the story. Totalitarianism is also a theory about the appropriate relationship between individuals. It holds that individuals ought to be merged into each other legally, morally, socially, and psychologically. This is an interpersonal theory.

This interpersonal, Romantic aspect of totalitarianism featured very strongly in the totalitarian movements of the twentieth century. It can also be seen, not coincidentally wrapped up with consideration of the first face of totalitarianism, in the following passages, the first from the speeches of Joseph Goebbels, the second from the writings of Che Guevara.

The revolution we have made is a total one. It has encompassed every area of public life and fundamentally restructured them all. It has completely changed and reshaped people's relationship to each other, to the state, and questions of existence. [It has brought about] the transformation of the German nation into one people.

---

[26] Bracher, *The German Dictatorship*, 186.

On 30 January [with the coming to power of the Nazis] the era of individualism finally died... The individual will be replaced by the community of the people.[27]

Individualism as such, as the isolated action of a person alone in a social environment, must disappear in Cuba. Individualism tomorrow should be the proper utilization of the whole individual, to the absolute benefit of the community.[28]

It is still necessary to deepen conscious participation, individual and collective, in all the structures of management and production, and to link this to the idea of the need for technical and ideological education, so that the individual will realize that these processes are closely interdependent and their advancement is parallel. In this way the individual will reach total consciousness as a social being, which is equivalent to the full realization as a human creature, once the chains of alienation are broken...

A person begins to become free from thinking of the annoying fact that one needs to work to satisfy one's animal needs. Individuals start to see themselves reflected in their work and to understand their full stature as human beings through the object created, through the work accomplished. Work no longer entails surrendering a part of one's being in the form of labor power sold, which no longer belongs to the individual, but becomes an expression of oneself, a contribution to the common life in which one is reflected, the fulfillment of one's social duty.[29]

It is notable that the dominance of the modern conception has meant that we theorists have tended to downplay or ignore what I am calling the second face of totalitarianism, despite the fact that it was perhaps the primary reason for its appeal. Of even more significance is that the modern conception has blinded us to the second face of totalitarianism's great rival, liberalism.

The Oxford Dictionary of Philosophy defines liberalism as a 'political ideology centred upon the individual..., thought of as possessing rights against the government, including rights of due process under the law, equality of respect, freedom of expression and action, and freedom from religious and ideological constraint'. In other words, liberalism

---

[27] Quoted in Evans, *The Third Reich in Power*, 120.
[28] Guevara, 'Speech to Medical Students and Health Workers', 115.
[29] Guevara, 'Socialism and Man in Cuba', 220.

is a theory about the appropriate relationship between the individual and the state, which holds that the state ought to be subordinated to the individual. That is a political theory. But that is only one of liberalism's faces. Liberalism is also concerned with the appropriate relationship between individuals, maintaining that individuals ought to be able to insist on legal, moral, social, and psychological independence from each other. That is an interpersonal theory.

In other words, liberalism is committed to a certain view of both distributive and commutative justice. It is political and interpersonal.

This position has the, at first unintuitive, consequence that liberalism is not *only* a theory of politics. But that ought not to surprise us. If liberalism is the position that individual liberty ought to be upheld and politics is concerned with the 'practice of government or administration... The science or study of government and the state', then liberalism cannot be entirely political, as there is more to individual liberty than that concerned with government and the state. Liberalism is a theory of politics, but it is more than that.

It is important to stress that our concern is with concepts and not labels. One may choose to define 'liberalism' so that it has only the first face identified above. Alternatively, one may define 'politics' so that it encompasses the interpersonal (in which case, it would be synonymous with the politico-legal). But the point is that any theory properly concerned with the freedom of the individual, any 'ideology centred upon the individual', must be concerned both with the power of the state over individuals and the independence of individuals from each other. Hence, the claim is this. To the extent to which the movement that labels itself 'liberalism' has ignored the interpersonal, it provides an incomplete account of liberty at best. And to the extent to which that movement propounds views inconsistent with interpersonal freedom, it is not genuinely liberal at all.[30]

Though this is not the place to explore the issue, my view is that all leading liberal theories (egalitarian, libertarian, etc) are subject to criticism that flows from these observations. In general, egalitarian theories fail to give proper respect to interpersonal liberty while libertarian views fail sufficiently to acknowledge the need to protect interpersonal independence. The one partial exception is Mill, who at least recognizes liberalism's second face in insisting that the Harm

---

[30] The claim is that a genuine liberal must be concerned with commutative justice. It is not that anyone concerned with commutative justice is a liberal. That claim is, of course, false.

Principle applies to all action, including the behaviour of government and interpersonal interactions.[31] As we have seen, however, the problem with Mill's view is that, while it recognizes the existence of a norm that protects both forms of liberty, it wrongly holds that the source of that norm lies solely in the social and distributive.

4. Law and Politics

This section examines a central issue concerning the relationship between law and politics. The issue can be expressed shortly. How can the law-making power of judges be reconciled with modern, democratic political theory? The question is of no small moment. But it receives remarkably little attention from modern political and legal theorists.[32]

4.1 The Modern Conception

Political systems can be divided into the democratic and the non-democratic. The former can in turn be divided into systems of representative and direct democracy. Under the latter, political power is expressed directly; under the former, through elected representatives. Thus, representative democracy 'implies the transmission of the people's authority to elected representatives...Periodic elections make for both the establishment and authorisation of governments, and their chastening through the threat of rejection at the polls.'[33]

In the following, I concentrate only on representative democracy. This is because it is the system of most significance to the vast majority of the readers of this book. What is more, though I suggest below that the modern view of law is in tension with representative democracy, the tension between the former and direct democracy is significantly greater and more obvious. Given that, the key point to make is that, according to the theory of representative democracy, individuals possess political power only because they receive a mandate from the people. Given that a number of wars have been fought for this value,

---

[31] Mill, 'On Liberty', 1.11.
[32] There are, of course, exceptions. See, eg Golding, *Legal Reasoning, Legal Theory and Rights*; Levi, *An Introduction to Legal Reasoning*; Strauss, *The Living Constitution*; and most especially Dworkin, *Taking Rights Seriously*; Dworkin, *Law's Empire*. Much of this work, however, is concerned with special problems that arise from the Constitution of the United States.
[33] Maddox, 'Representative Government'.

it can safely be said that it is a central commitment of at least Western political systems.

Another distinction must be made at this point, a distinction between those who have political power because they represent us and those who have that power because it has been delegated to them by those who represent us. Examples of the latter include city councillors (to whose council authority is delegated) and administrative officials (to whose office power is delegated). As these examples indicate, delegation of power can itself take two general forms. It can set up a system in which individuals act as representatives of the people or as representatives of the delegating power. Local councils are an example of the first. Their power comes entirely from the legislature, but they act as representatives of and are accountable to the people who elect them. For our purposes, these cases can be ignored. Administrative officials are an example of the second. They are not representatives of or accountable to the people. On the contrary, they are accountable (usually) to the legislature. A classic example of this is the accountability of the executive to Parliament in parliamentary democracies (though, of course, in practice the executive regards itself as accountable also—or too often only—to the people).[34]

All this can be summarized by saying that, according to the theory of representative democracy, political power is to be held only by those who represent the people or who are accountable to those who represent the people.

Given that, it is immediately clear that judges do not represent the people.[35] The most obvious point is that they are unelected. Nor are they accountable to the public. On the contrary, they are appointed to their positions for 'life' (ie at least until a late retirement age) and are protected from the kinds of scrutiny that when applied to politicians is thought not only appropriate but essential to democracy.[36] Nor are judges accountable to those who represent the people. They do not have to undergo scrutiny before parliamentary or congressional committees or the like. Their tenure is not subject to review by

---

[34] For an extended discussion of this matter, see Tomkins, *Public Law*.
[35] The sometime election of judges in the United States is generally regarded, even sometimes in the US itself, as aberrational.
[36] Newspapers, for instance, would be roundly condemned if they published criticism of individual judges that even approaches that which is routine of individual politicians. Moreover, it is very likely that the judges themselves would not protect such speech from defamation actions as they would speech directed at politicians.

the legislature or executive. Though they can be impeached, this can occur only in the most unusual circumstances through extraordinary procedures. In short, it is easier by orders of magnitude to remove a government than it is to remove a judge.

The special conditions under which judges operate are the result, not of historical accident, but of deliberate planning. It is thought to be an essential concomitant of justice that judges be independent in these ways, a notion captured in the idea of the separation of powers. Such is the modern conception of political legitimacy. How does this relate to the modern conception of law?

As all are told, the common law is a system of precedents found in the decided cases. That system, of course, contains gaps in the sense that issues arise for which there is no standing precedent. When such issues come to court, judges must fill these gaps. But what exactly is going on when this happens?

There are three modern answers. One is presented by Jeremy Bentham, one by Ronald Dworkin, the third is given by almost everyone else. Dworkin is discussed in a moment. I begin with Bentham.

According to Bentham, judges should not fill any gaps. Instead, the common law ought to be replaced by a comprehensive code able to answer any question that might arise.[37] Though I have encountered some residual enthusiasm for this view amongst political scientists and philosophers, no one with any experience of the law thinks it even remotely realistic.[38]

The view held by the vast majority of modern lawyers flows from an almost irresistible line of reasoning. Consequently, it is often thought to be the result of plain good sense. This has tended to obscure the difficulties that the view generates, according to the notion that highly counterintuitive conclusions cannot follow from that which seems obvious. The problem with this notion is that it is wrong. It is, in fact, entirely inconsistent with the history of Western philosophy, which could be viewed as the result of the deeply counterintuitive conclusions thrown up by taking deeply intuitive notions to their logical conclusions.

The line of reasoning is as follows. First, gaps in the law exist. Hence, those gaps cannot be filled by appealing to the law alone.

---

[37] Bentham, *The Principles of Morals and Legislation*, concluding note, para 21–22.

[38] For a sustained argument to this effect, an argument that reveals just how strange Bentham's view is, see Lieberman, *The Province of Legislation Determined*.

Thus, they can be filled only by appeal to non-legal, political values. These values fall under the umbrella term 'policy'. Hence, we have the idea that judges fill gaps in the law by legislating: by making new law in terms of their sense of what is best for the community, of distributive justice.

Here we can see the clash with the theory of representative democracy. According to that view, recall, political power is to be held only by those who represent the people or who are accountable to those who represent the people. But on the modern view of law, judges neither represent the people nor are accountable to those who represent the people, and yet possess political power. This is a very significant problem. It shows a deep inconsistency between our understandings of politics and law. It is absolutely fundamental.

What is more, two further problems need to be added. The first is that judicial law-making is retrospective in effect. In other words, when a court creates a new law, that law applies not only in the future, but also to the instant case and into the past. We think that the legislature should make such laws only in the most exceptional circumstances, if at all,[39] so what could justify the routine law-making of this kind on the part of judges?

The second problem is that judges generally lack the expertise necessary to make the relevant kinds of decisions. As I have explored this matter in detail elsewhere, it suffices to say that, with few exceptions, judges are not social policy experts. How, then, can it be appropriate for them to make social policy decisions?[40]

In this light, it is useful to examine Hobbes' analysis of the law-making power of judges. Hobbes argues that judges have a mandate to legislate delegated to them by the king.[41] Because the king cannot govern all matters, he appoints others to govern for him in certain

---

[39] Certain exceptions to this exist however, eg with respect to taxation, where retrospective legislation is generally accepted. But these exceptions rest on special justifications not applicable to the common law in total. And the most important point, of course, is that though special exceptions hold with respect to legislation, retrospectivity is entirely routine in the common law.

[40] See, eg Beever, *Rediscovering the Law of Negligence*, 172–173. Nolan and Robertson, 'Rights and Private Law', 22–23 are kind enough to describe this as a strong attack on the modern, policy-based understanding of the law. I should say, however, that I regard it as of much less significance than the other claims made here and in *Rediscovering*. It is, however, unsurprising that this argument has made the most impact, given that it is directly translatable into the language of public policy and the modern conception (ie 'it is bad policy to allow judges to do this') as the other arguments are not.

[41] Hobbes, *Leviathan*, XIII 7, XXVI 23.

areas. Some of these individuals are judges, who have the authority both to apply the law and to legislate within certain parameters.

Naturally, this view is unpalatable today. The monarch no longer possesses any legislative power that she is able to delegate. Nor is judges' power a consequence of what remains of a greatly shrunk royal prerogative. The constitutional changes that have produced these states of affairs are a direct result of the theory of representative democracy. Hobbes' theory will no longer do. What, then, could possibly justify the legislative power of our judges?

The argument that nothing does has been led in recent times by Dworkin. For our purposes, this has been unfortunate. This is not because Dworkin has misused the argument as such. Rather, the problem is that Dworkin has tied this criticism to a theory of law that many have been reluctant to accept. In conjunction with the fact that the view Dworkin attacks seems to be a piece of common sense, this this has led to the appearance that one can answer the criticism at least in part by rejecting Dworkin's general theory. As a result, responses to Dworkin's criticism often fail adequately to address the force that it possesses quite independently of his other views.

Consider, for instance, the following riposte.

It is difficult to know quite what to make of [the] argument [that judicial law making is problematic], in particular in a legal system like that of the United Kingdom, where even following the passage of the Human Rights Act 1998 judges are regarded as having fairly limited ability to develop the law. Positivists, in general, simply do not share Dworkin's concerns about the democratic legitimacy of judges developing the law where the law is unsettled or the application of the rules would work significant injustice. The positivist would say that where, as in most common law countries at least, judges have the power to make law in this gap-filling, interstitial way, everyone both recognises that judges have this power and accepts it as an ineradicable part of the system, since it would be inconvenient, to say the least, to have to send all cases of unsettled law back to the legislature for 'democratic' resolution. Disallowing judges from resolving disputes where the law was not perfectly clear would also undoubtedly cause a great deal of injustice, on the principle that justice delayed is justice denied.[42]

---

[42] Penner, *McCoubrey & White's Textbook on Jurisprudence*, 125. See also Stapleton, 'The Golden Thread', who takes it for granted that the—in fact counter-majoritarian—tendencies of the High Court of Australia should be encouraged. See also the exchange between Thomas, 'Fairness and Certainty in Adjudication: Formalism v. Substantialism'; Allan, 'The

This dismissal of Dworkin's position is breath taking.

On this picture, ultimate legislative power resides with the legislature, though, for the reasons presented, some of this power is 'delegated' to judges. This, then, is what we might have expected given the argument of this book: an updated version of Hobbes' account. While it may have been felt sufficient to defend positivism from Dworkin's attacks, it does not answer the criticisms examined above.

First, it is not plausible to suggest that the law-making power of judges is in any sense delegated from the legislature. Not only has no act of delegation occurred, the picture is inconsistent with our understanding of these branches of government. Judges are neither representatives of the people nor accountable to those who represent the people. Nor does the response deal with the problems of retrospectivity or lack of expertise.

The passage supports the legislative power of judges by pointing out that such power is limited and by claiming that it is recognized and accepted by everyone. It is said to be recognized and accepted by everyone because there is no alternative given the system that we have (because it is 'an ineradicable part of the system') and because the alternatives to the system we have are unpalatable because inconvenient and unjust. I examine these claims in turn.

It is certainly true that judicial law-making power is limited. This seems to defend such power, because the existence of limits is often thought to lend support to an activity. For instance, one might argue that noisy activities in a residential area should be permitted (only) if they are time-restricted. However, though limits seem to provide justification, that is an illusion.

First, the appeal to a limit assumes that there is an independent justification for the activity in question. Without that, the appeal would be entirely without force. Murder would not be justified by imposing a limit on it. Secondly, the appeal assumes that the activity is problematic per se. No one would attempt to justify kindness by limiting it. The point of the limit is to reduce the negative aspects of activity while leaving at least many of the positive ones in place, so that the activity can be justified. The limit itself does no justificatory work.

Translating these points to the case at hand, we can see that two conclusions follow. First, the fact that judicial law-making is limited

---

Invisible Hand in Justice Thomas's Philosophy of Law'; Thomas, 'The "Invisible Hand" Prompts a Response'.

tacitly acknowledges that it is problematic. Secondly, even limited judicial law-making can be justified only if (*not*: if) an argument in favour of judicial law-making as such can be found. Can it? That question brings us to the other points made in the passage under examination.

The claim that the modern of view of judicial law-making is accepted by everyone is meant to show that the activity is democratically acceptable. But the claim is false. The practice in question is not accepted by the general public. The claim, remember, is not that the public accepts the rather bland idea that judges change the law, but that the public is comfortable with the fact that judges legislate, ie that they change the law in accordance with their sense of best policy. That is clearly not widely accepted. Rightly or wrongly, it is what the public call judicial activism and it is widely condemned. Moreover, even if the claim were true, the conclusion would not follow from it. Even if everyone accepted the legislative power of judges, that would not make that power consistent with democracy. It would show only that people did not care about democracy or did not understand its requirements.

The next claim is that our system of adjudication is committed to judicial legislation. This might mean only that judges in our system in fact legislate. That may be so, but no justification is to be found here. On the other hand, the claim might be that judges in any system like ours must legislate. The only support for that position is found in the next argument.

That argument is that alternatives to the current system are inconvenient and unjust. We can immediately see that this argument must be rejected, because it relies on the implausible notion that the common law is to be preferred to its alternatives because of its *efficiency*.

One way to detect this problem is to notice that the argument attempts to bind us in a false dichotomy. We are asked to compare two systems: the current practice of the common law and one identical but for the fact that all gap-filling were done by the legislature. Naturally, the latter would be less efficient than the status quo. But it is also just as clear that the latter is not the only alternative. A different system would be for the legislature to appoint a panel of experts, accountable to the legislature, entrusted with making law in the necessary areas. This panel could receive questions from judges concerning gaps in the law, questions that could be referred at any time whether raised in a case or not. Moreover, these questions could be examined concurrently with court processes, as the issue to be decided by the panel would be concerned not with any specific parties but with society in general. None of this would be at all difficult and it would likely be far more efficient in the long run than the current practice as well as, accepting the modern conception, more rational. For example, the members of the panel could be appointed because they had the relevant social policy expertise. The decisions of the body could also be examined on a regular basis by select committees of Parliament, a Congressional committee, or the like. And those decisions could be of prospective force only.

This suggestion fits rather neatly with one of the most powerful trends of the twentieth century. In many areas of life, rule in accordance with law enforceable by the ordinary courts has been replaced by rule in accordance with the commands of administrative bodies. This has been done primarily for reasons of efficiency.[43] In that light, it cannot be claimed that judicial law-making must be preferred because it is more efficient than the alternatives. It is not.

I am not suggesting that a system such as the one outlined above is attractive. On the contrary, it is repellent. But it is not repellent because it would be inefficient. It is repellent because it would be unjust (for reasons other than inefficiency). But if that is right, then it must follow that justice requires judges to have the power that they do, despite the fact that that power seems undemocratic and cannot be justified on grounds of efficiency. How could that be possible?

Before we answer this question, it is also relevant to discuss the view, often articulated by judges, that law-making is best done by reference to a concrete dispute and not by abstract reflection.[44] This may seem to lend support to the modern view, but the way to test that claim is to imagine the same advice given to a legislator. No one would suggest that legislators should act only on the basis of concrete disputes or that, when they do so, they should formulate their response by focusing on the character of that particular dispute. In fact, then, this concern too points to a significant difference between legislation and judicial law-making. It indicates that the latter is much more closely tied (in private law) to the parties' dispute and less to public policy than often suggested. It intimates, in short, an unconscious acknowledgement that we are in the realm of commutative justice.

---

[43] For an analysis of and lament for this process, see Dicey, *The Law of the Constitution*, lv-lxi; Hayek, *The Road to Serfdom*, ch 6; Hayek, *The Constitution of Liberty*, ch 16.

[44] For an interesting discussion of this issue, see *Couch v AG (No 2)* [2010] NZSC 27, [2010] 3 NZLR 149, [33], [35]–[41], [47]–[49], [77]–[83].

Recall the line of reasoning that led to the mainstream, modern view: gaps in the law exist, those gaps cannot be filled by appealing to the law alone, they can be filled only by appeal to non-legal, political values. Dworkin's strategy is to turn this line of reasoning on its head. His argument is that law and politics are intertwined, that apparent gaps in the law can be filled by appealing to values that are both political and legal and hence that no gaps in the law really exist.[45] For this reason, as Shirley Letwin has pointed out, Dworkin's theory involves the most radical denial of the rule of law.[46] For this reason, I submit that it is the wrong answer to our question and I will say nothing more about it here.

4.2 The Traditional Conception

Consider the line of reasoning again: gaps in the law exist, those gaps cannot be filled by appealing to the law alone, they can be filled only by appeal to non-legal, political values. The traditional alternative to this view can be expressed in two different ways. The traditional thinker would say: gaps in the law do not exist, apparent gaps can be filled by appealing to the law alone, by appeal to legal, non-political values. They are able to say this because they use 'law' to refer to what we are calling the politico-legal norms that underlie the legal system. Because we are unused to that terminology, it is best to express the idea a different way. Gaps in the (positive) law exist, they cannot be filled by appeal to the (positive) law alone, but they can be filled by appeal to non-political values. These values, of course, are those that belong to commutative justice.

Recall the following passage discussed in Chapter 1.

If B wants to argue that A violated her rights in acting in some way,... one has to take into account considerations of public policy in determining whether B had a right that A not act in the way he did. For example, suppose that B argues: 'A said something offensive to me and that upset me a great deal. I have an ongoing right that A not do anything that might offend me, so A violated my rights in acting as he did.' In determining whether B has such a right against A, it [is] obvious that one has to take into account the impact on freedom of speech that recognising the existence of such a

---

[45] These arguments are found primarily in Dworkin, *Taking Rights Seriously*; Dworkin, *Law's Empire*.
[46] Letwin, *On the History of the Idea of Law*, 276, 301.

right would have, and that the adverse effect that recognising a 'right not to be offended' would have on freedom of speech is one of the most obvious reasons why no such right is recognised in English law.[47]

Hopefully, it is now clear that this view is mistaken. The question, we are told, is: does the plaintiff have a right not to be offended by the defendant? We are also told that this question must be answered by reference to public policy, taking into account issues such as freedom of speech. But the question actually asked cannot be answered in that way. Once we turn to public policy, the question becomes, not 'Does the plaintiff have a right not to be offended by the defendant?', but 'Would it be right for people in general to have rights not to be offended that they hold against people in general?' That is a quite different question and answering it is not a precondition for answering the original question.

The original question can be answered by reference to the individual parties. One can ask whether it would be just as between them for the plaintiff to have a right as against the defendant not to be offended. Answering that question might also require a consideration of freedom of speech, but the issue here would be the value to the defendant of the defendant's freedom of speech and the significance of that value vis-à-vis the plaintiff.

Now, one might reasonably ask, how exactly would the latter approach resolve the question? But it is not the task of this book to give an answer. The task has been to show that answers that take this form are possible. Aquinas may have answered it differently from Pufendorf, Pufendorf differently from Kant, and others who I have not considered may give yet different answers—just as different answers would be given by theorists arguing on the basis of distributive justice. The point is that answers of this kind can be given. Or to put this another way, I will have achieved my goal if the reader asks this question herself.

For now, the significant point is that, on the picture elucidated above, when a court fills the gaps in the positive law, its law-making need not be political. It need not make a decision about what is best for society as a whole. Rather, it is able to determine how the gap should be filled by considering justice as between the parties.

---

[47] McBride and Bagshaw, *Tort Law*, xix (citation omitted).

It may help to illustrate these points through the use of another example. The plaintiff in *Donoghue v Stevenson*[48] was injured by a product negligently manufactured by the defendant. The law at the time indicated that the manufacturer of the article could not be liable.[49] In what is surely the most celebrated case of the twentieth century, the plaintiff contested the existing rules, succeeding in the House of Lords. The question that faced the court can be put in these terms. If A manufactures a product, does so negligently because that product poses a foreseeable risk of a certain kind r, B uses that product (in accordance with the purpose for which it was manufactured) and is injured as a result of the materialization of r, should A be liable to B? Surely we have not come so far that we can no longer see that there is an obvious answer to this question that does not appeal to public policy or the like. The answer is the one given by the House of Lords. A's action is unjust as between the parties and hence A is liable to B.

But, one might object, the rule to this affect was introduced only in *Donoghue v Stevenson*, only, that is, in 1932. Or, if one is American, it was propounded in *MacPherson v Buick Motor Co*,[50] only in 1916. In England, and indeed in Scotland,[51] the great impediment to the recognition of this rule was the decision of the Court of Exchequer in *Winterbottom v Wright*.[52] In that case, in analogous circumstances, the court held that the plaintiff could not recover.

The facts as alleged in the objection are true. But what do those facts prove? How do they constitute an objection to the position advanced here? The answer is that they do not. The issue under discussion is whether disputes of the kind in question can be settled by considering commutative justice. It is irrelevant that those considering commutative justice might disagree. Moreover, it may well be that the attitudes that influenced the outcomes of the cases above have changed over time, but that hardly proves that they belong to distributive justice. With respect to our specific case, the issue is whether it can be said that A ought to be liable to B considering only the relationship between A

---

[48] *M'Alister (or Donoghue) (Pauper) v Stevenson* [1932] AC 562 (HL Sc). For convenience, I ignore the fact that this was an appeal from a strike-out application.
[49] Eg *Mullen v A G Barr & Co Ltd* 1929 SLT 341 (IH).
[50] 111 NE 1050 (NY 1916).
[51] See, eg the references to *Winterbottom v Wright* in *Mullen v A G Barr & Co Ltd* 1929 SLT 341 (IH).
[52] (1842) 10 M & W 109, 152 ER 402.

and *B*. The issue is not whether everyone throughout the history of the world would have agreed with our answer.

However, it is worth noticing that the reasons given for denying liability in *Winterbottom v Wright* were not ones of commutative justice. Rather, the court denied the plaintiff's claim because it felt that liability would undermine the socially beneficial effects of the law of contract and would produce a precedent that would, when applied to other cases, result in what lawyers now call indeterminate liability. In other words, the concerns were ones of distributive justice.[53]

The position advanced here, then, is that when judges make law, they need not engage with the political. It is important to say that this is not the claim that judicial decisions lack political consequences. A good case to illustrate this point is *Paris v Stepney Borough Council*.[54]

The plaintiff employee of the defendants was blind in one eye. He was injured when he struck a U-bolt with a hammer, dislodging a shard of metal that entered his right eye, causing complete blindness. He argued that the defendants were negligent in failing to provide him with safety glasses. At the relevant stage, his argument was not that all employees should have been provided with safety glasses. It was that, given that he was already blind in one eye, the defendants should have taken into account the seriousness of the injury if the other eye was damaged and supplied him with glasses. The House of Lords agreed. Lord Normand said:

The test is what precautions would the ordinary reasonable and prudent man take. The relevant considerations include all those facts which could affect the conduct of a reasonable and prudent man and his decision on the precautions to be taken. Would a reasonable and prudent man be influenced, not only by the greater or less probability of an accident occurring, but also by the gravity of the consequences if an accident does occur? ... The court's task of deciding what precautions a reasonable and prudent man would take in the circumstances of a particular case may not be easy. Nevertheless the judgment of the reasonable and prudent man should be allowed its common everyday scope, and it should not be restrained from considering

---

[53] For my analysis of this case, with most of which I still agree, see Beever, *Rediscovering the Law of Negligence*, 115–118. And for my analysis of the first appearance of 'indeterminate liability' in Cardozo CJ's judgment in *Ultramares Corp v Touche* 174 NE 441 (NY 1931), see Beever, *Rediscovering the Law of Negligence*, 234–237.

[54] [1951] AC 367 (HL).

the foreseeable consequences of an accident and their seriousness for the person to whom the duty of care is owed.[55]

All of this is concerned with justice as between the parties.

However, the decision has been criticized on the ground that it

not only inhibited the recruitment of persons with monocular vision, but also severely retarded the placing in employment of other persons who had suffered loss of a limb or some other bodily function. Apart from the unfortunate effect this had on the normal rehabilitation processes, the point of issue here is that in plant after plant, and company after company, lengthy, extensive and continuing discussions were held to try to assess the effect of this judgment on particular applications for employment. These assessments contributed nothing to productivity nor to the reduction of injury.[56]

It is telling that this criticism was made in an article entitled '*Legislation and Injury Control*' (my emphasis).

If the criticism is sound, then *Paris v Stepney Borough Council* made for bad politics. But it may nevertheless have been good law. I have argued elsewhere that it was the right decision as between the parties,[57] a claim entirely consistent with the view that it had undesirable political consequences. When the court made it, it did not engage in politics, though of course it made a decision with political consequences. The desirability of those consequences is for political agents—and not courts—to determine.

On this view, then, we need not regard the common law and democracy as being in inevitable tension. We need not see judges as usurping political power or the judiciary as an essentially counter-democratic institution. This is a view that allows for a genuine separation of powers.

It is perhaps necessary to say that judges make value judgements when they make new law (or even when they apply old law). That is unavoidable. And of course it remains the case that those value judgements are made by unelected and unaccountable individuals. There is a problem here, but it is not the one noticed above.

We elect political representatives because it is their job to represent our interests in fora that consider the interests of the community. We

---

[55] Ibid, 380–381.
[56] Wigglesworth, 'Legislation and Injury Control', 193.
[57] Beever, *Rediscovering the Law of Negligence*, 92–93.

do so (hopefully) to ensure that the government's plan for achieving distributive justice does justice to us. But we do not go to court for these reasons. We go to court to have our rights vindicated. In private law, we go to have justice done as between us and our opponent. For that reason, it would be inappropriate to have our disputes decided by people who are placed under the same pressures as our political representatives. They ought not to be pushed towards the community's interests, public policy, or distributive justice.[58] They ought to be focused on us, on what justice as between us requires, on commutative justice.

The problem mentioned above, then, is not that judges are unelected and unaccountable; it is that they are individual people with their particular experiences and prejudices rather than infallible ciphers for commutative justice. But that problem is presented to us, not by the design of our institutions, but because it is endemic to the human condition. It is the same problem presented to us by the fact that politicians are not infallible with respect to distributive justice. In law, the best that can be done is to ensure that disputes of the relevant kind are heard by those experienced, and therefore with expertise, in dealing with disagreements between individuals by focusing on those disagreements (rather than translating them into the community's concerns); who learn to remove their subjective outlook, as far as that is possible, though a submerging of their personality into the impersonality of the law represented by the history of case law; to have their decisions criticized by an academy likewise focused; and, at the end of the day, to have the possibility of error corrected by the legislature.

That is what the common law looked like. But it does not look like that now. Moreover, with respect to the kind of legislative 'correction' just mentioned, it is important that it take the form of a dialogue rather than a directive. That is, the legislature ought to recognize that, though it has superior law-making power, judges have superior expertise with respect to commutative justice. Hence, though the legislature may occasionally be called on to remove obstacles to the achievement of commutative justice,[59] it must be convinced that it is right to act and it usually ought to act only with considerable judicial and academic support. Again, this is in sharp contrast to what occurs

---

[58] Against: Bentham, 'Draught for the Organization of Judicial Establishments', 316–317.

[59] As I believe occurred with respect to the various statutes dealing with contributory negligence. See Beever, *Rediscovering the Law of Negligence*, 341–345.

today, as Australia's recent legal reform demonstrates, the atmosphere of which is here neatly captured by Justice Peter Underwood.

[I]t appears there is no need to refer anything to a review panel. Indeed, it appears that there is no need even to study [an objected to] development in the common law. It is sufficient if there is a perception that a common law development might cause a financial problem or some other problem for there to be legislative action to remove that development and deny others in the situation of the respondents a remedy that the law has decided is their entitlement.

This is a very dangerous development, not only for [the approach set out in *Donoghue v Stevenson*], but also for all other aspects of the common law. It will become uncertain. No one will know whether a particular aspect of the common law will or will not fall under the legislative knife; a knife wielded in accordance with the political beliefs of the party that happens to be in power from time to time. Historically, legislative incursions into the common law have been restrained and largely remedial. Recently, all that has changed. Legislation is enacted instantaneously and as an immediate response to perceived, but untested, economic factors. More likely than not the legislation will vary from jurisdiction to jurisdiction so that the common law of the country will be fragmented. In effect, there is every danger of the judicial development being subject to the unnecessary superior and instantaneous editing of the legislature.[60]

My only addition is that this is surely what we ought to have expected. The legislators regard themselves as replacing law based on the political preferences of judges with law based on the political preferences of the legislature. All they have done is to believe the modern conception.

5. Conclusion

This chapter has argued that the modern conception blinds us to important features of the politico-legal realm. We fail to understand the foundation of political authority, the nature of justice, the character of movements such as liberalism and totalitarianism, and the relationship between law and politics. It is worth asking ourselves: what is the impact of all this forgetting on our lives?

---

[60] Underwood, 'Is Ms Donoghue's Snail in Mortal Peril?', 60 (citation omitted).

14

Conclusion

The focus of this book has been conceptual. It has charted the rise and fall of an idea and pursued the fall into various conceptual difficulties that face the modern legal and political thinker. I would be remiss, however, were I to leave the reader with the impression that the consequences of the fall are deleterious only to our comprehension. On the contrary. It is one half of justice that we have forgotten. The consequence must surely be that, to a significant extent at least, our societies are less respectful of that form of justice than they ought to be, as it is difficult to respect something that you have forgotten.

The examination of this issue is pressing. But it cannot be undertaken here. It requires another investigation of this kind. Suffice it for the moment to say this.

According to one of the most influential analysts of law in the twentieth century, that law, and here specifically the law of negligence, 'in origin contemplating only interpersonal justice, eventually also opened itself to a consideration of personal needs, distributive justice and stricter liability. This transformation has been rapidly gaining pace since the individualistic fault dogma began to give ground to the mid-20th century quest for social security.'[1] There is only a small similarity between this and the following claim, but it is a similarity worth pondering. 'On 30 January [with the coming to power of the Nazis] the era of individualism finally died... The individual will be replaced by the community of the people.'[2]

---

[1] Fleming, *The Law of Torts*, 114.
[2] Joseph Goebbels, quoted in Evans, *The Third Reich in Power*, 120.

We are no fascists. But we must ask whether our forgetting of commutative justice has led us to ignore the importance of interpersonal freedom, to overplay the needs of the community vis-à-vis the autonomy of the individual, and to overemphasize the importance of the state and overestimate its ability to facilitate justice. Increasingly, many on both the left and the right are giving positive answers to those questions.

Most fundamentally, however, the dominance of the modern conception has distorted our view of ourselves. When we speak of public discourse, we talk almost as if we were creatures who relate to other individuals only via the state and its concerns. This encourages us to forget who we are. Again, then, though we mean something somewhat different by them, we can repeat Goebbels' words: 'The revolution we have made is a total one. It has encompassed every area of public life and fundamentally restructured them all. It has completely changed and reshaped people's relationship to each other, to the state, and questions of existence.'[3] According to the Stanford Encyclopaedia of Philosophy, for instance, marriage is 'the institution regulating sex, reproduction, and family life'.[4] Tell that to my wife. Thankfully, we still think that marriage is, in the happily old-fashioned words of the *OED*, 'the relation between persons married to each other'.

---

[3] Joseph Goebbels, quoted ibid.
[4] Brake, 'Marriage and Domestic Partnership'.

Bibliography

Allan, James, 'The Invisible Hand in Justice Thomas's Philosophy of Law', [1999] *New Zealand Law Review* 213
Aquinas, Thomas, *Summa theologica*, English Dominicans (tr), (New York: Benziger Bros, 1947)
Aristotle, *The Politics*, in Everson, Stephen (ed), *The Politics and The Constitution of Athens* (Cambridge: Cambridge University Press, 1996)
———, *Nicomachean Ethics*, Irwin, Terence (tr), (Indianapolis, IN: Hackett, 1999)
———, *The Art of Rhetoric*, Lawson-Tancred, HC (tr), (London: Penguin, 2004)
Atiyah, PS, *The Rise and Fall of Freedom of Contract* (Oxford: Oxford University Press, 1979)
Baxter, Richard, *The Second Part of the Nonconformists Plea for Peace* (London: 1680)
Beever, Allan, 'The Structure of Aggravated and Exemplary Damages', (2003) 23 *Oxford Journal of Legal Studies* 87
———, *Rediscovering the Law of Negligence* (Oxford: Hart, 2007)
———, 'Corrective Justice and Personal Responsibility in Tort Law', (2008) 28 *Oxford Journal of Legal Studies* 475
———, 'Justice and Punishment in Tort: A Comparative Theoretical Analysis' in Rickett, Charles (ed), *Justifying Private Law Remedies* (Oxford: Hart, 2008)
———, 'Agreements, Mistakes, and Contract Formation', (2009) 20 *King's Law Journal* 21
———, 'Our Most Fundamental Rights' in Robertson, Andrew and Nolan, Donal (eds), *Rights and Private Law* (Oxford: Hart, 2011)
Bender, Leslie, 'A Lawyer's Primer on Feminist Theory and Tort', (1988) 38 *Journal of Legal Education* 3
Benson, Peter, 'The Basis for Excluding Liability for Economic Loss in Tort Law' in Owen, David (ed), *Philosophical Foundations of Tort Law* (Oxford: Oxford University Press, 1995)
———, 'The Expectation and Reliance Interests in Contract Theory: A Reply to Fuller and Perdue', [2001] *Issues in Legal Scholarship*, article 5, http://www.bepress.com/ils/iss1/art5
Bentham, Jeremy, 'Bentham's Draught for the Organization of Judicial Establishments Compared with that of the National Assembly, with a Comment on the Same' in Bowring, John (ed), *The Works of Jeremy Bentham* (Edinburgh: William Tait, 1843)

Bentham, Jeremy, *The Principles of Morals and Legislation* (Amherst, NY: Prometheus Books, 1988)

Birks, Peter, *Introduction to the Law of Restitution* (2nd edn, Oxford: Clarendon Press, 1989)

—— and McLeod, Grant, *Justinian's Institutes* (London: Duckworth, 1987)

Blackburn, Simon, *The Oxford Dictionary of Philosophy* (2nd revised edn, Oxford: Oxford University Press, 2008)

Blackstone, William, *Commentaries on the Laws of England, vol 1* (Dublin: Cavendish, 1766)

Bracher, Karl Dietrich, *The German Dictatorship: The Origins, Structure and Consequences of National Socialism* (Harmondsworth: Penguin University Books, 1970)

Brake, Elizabeth, 'Marriage and Domestic Partnership' (2009) *Stanford Encyclopaedia of Philosophy* <http://plato.stanford.edu/entries/marriage/>

Brown, Russell, 'Still Crazy After All These Years: *Anns, Cooper v.* Hobart and Pure Economic Loss', (2003) 36 *University of British Columbia Law Review* 159

Byrd, B Sharon and Hruschka, Joachim, *Kant's Doctrine of Right: A Commentary* (New York: Cambridge University Press, 2010)

Cane, Peter, *The Anatomy of Tort Law* (Oxford: Hart Publishing, 1997)

——, 'Distributive Justice and Tort Law', [2001] *New Zealand Law Review* 401

Chen-Wishart, Mindy, *Contract Law* (2nd edn, Oxford: Oxford University Press, 2008)

Cicero, 'The Laws' in *The Republic and The Laws* (Oxford: Oxford University Press, 2008)

——, 'The Republic' in *The Republic and The Laws* (Oxford: Oxford University Press, 2008)

Clark, Christopher, *Iron Kingdom: The Rise and Downfall of Prussia 1600–1947* (London: Penguin, 2007)

Coke, Edward, *The Institutes of the Laws of England* (London: W Clarke, 1817)

Coleman, Jules, *The Practice of Principle* (Oxford: Oxford University Press, 2001)

Collins, Hugh, *The Law of Contract* (3rd edn, London: Butterworths, 1997)

Cumberland, Richard, *De legibus naturæ disquisitio philosophica: in qua earum forma, summa capita, ordo, promulgatio, & obligatio è rerum natura investigantur: quinetiam elementa philosophiæ Hobbianæ c ùm moralis tum civilis considerantur & refutantur* (London: E Flesher, 1672)

Deakin, Simon, Johnston, Angus, and Markesinis, Basil, *Markesinis and Deakin's Tort Law* (6th edn, Oxford: Clarendon Press, 2008)

Dicey, AV, *Introduction to the Study of the Law of the Constitution* (8th edn, Indianapolis: Liberty Fund, 1982)

Diggs, Duddley, *An Answer to a Printed Book, Intituled, Observations upon some of His Maiesties Late Answers and Expresses* (Oxford: Leonard Lichfield, 1642)

——, *The Unlawfulnesse of Subjects, Taking up Armes against their Soveraigne, in What Case Soever: Together with an Answer to all Objections Scattered in their Severall Bookes, and a Proofe that not Withstanding such Resistance as they Plead for were not Damnable, yet the Present waree Made upon the King is so, Because those Cases, in which only Some Men have Dared to Excuse it, are Evidently not now, His Majesty Fighting onely to Preserve Himselfe, and the Rights of the Subjects* (np, 1644)

Dobbs, Dan B, *Torts and Compensation Personal Accountability and Social Responsibility for Injury* (2nd edn, Los Angeles: West Group, 1993)

Dworkin, Ronald, *Taking Rights Seriously* (Cambridge, Mass: Harvard University Press, 1977)

———, *Law's Empire* (Cambridge, Mass: Belknap, 1986)

———, 'What is Equality? Part III: The Place of Liberty', (1987) 73 *Iowa Law Review* 1

Epstein, Richard A, 'A Theory of Strict Liability', (1973) 2 *The Journal of Legal Studies* 151

Evans, Richard J, *The Third Reich in Power 1933–1939: How the Nazis Won Over the Hearts and Minds of a Nation* (London: Penguin, 2006)

Fichte, JG, *Foundations of Natural Right*, Baur, Michael (tr), (Cambridge: Cambridge University Press, 2000)

Finnis, John, *Natural Law and Natural Rights* (Oxford: Clarendon Press, 1980)

———, *Aquinas* (Oxford: Oxford University Press, 2004)

Fleming, John, *The Law of Torts* (9th edn, Sydney: LBC Information Services, 1998)

Fridman, Daniel, 'The Objective Principle and Mistake and Involuntariness in Contract and Restitution', (2003) 119 *Law Quarterly Review* 68

Fuller, Lon L and Perdue, William R, 'The Reliance Interest in Contract Damages', (1936) 46 *Yale Law Journal* 52

Gardner, John, 'The Purity and Priority of Private Law', (1996) 46 *University of Toronto Law Journal* 459

———, 'What is Tort Law For? Part I: The Place of Corrective Justice', (2011) 30 *Law and Philosophy* 1

Gerhardt, Volker, 'Refusing Sovereign Power—The Relation between Philosophy and Politics in the Modern Age ' in Ameriks, Karl and Höffe, Otfried (eds), *Kant's Moral and Legal Philosophy* (Cambridge: Cambridge University Press, 2009)

Gilmore, Grant, *The Death of Contract* (Columbus, Ohio: Ohio State University Press, 1974)

Goldberg, John CP and Zipursky, Benjamin C, 'The *Restatement (Third)* and the Place of Duty in Negligence', (2001) 54 *Vanderbilt Law Review* 657

Golding, Martin P, *Legal Reasoning, Legal Theory and Rights* (Burlington, VT: Aldershot, 1984)

Gordley, James, 'Myths of the French Civil Code', (1994) 42 *American Journal of Comparative Law* 459

———, 'A Perennial Misstep: From Cajetan to Fuller and Perdue to "Efficient Breach"', [2001] *Issues in Legal Scholarship*, article 5, http://www.bepress.com/ils/iss1/art4

Gordley, James, *Foundations of Private Law: Property, Tort, Contract, Unjust Enrichment* (Oxford: Oxford University Press, 2006)

Grantham, Ross and Rickett, Charles, *Enrichment and Restitution in New Zealand* (Oxford: Hart Publishing, 2000)

Grotius, Hugo, *The Law of War and Peace*, Kelsey, Francis W (tr), (Oxford: Clarendon Press, 1925)

———, *The Jurisprudence of Holland, vol 1*, Lee, RW (tr), (Oxford: Clarendon Press, 1926)

———, *Commentary on the Law of Prize and Booty*, Williams, Gwladys L (tr), (Oxford: Clarendon Press, 1950)

Guevara, Ernesto, 'Socialism and Man in Cuba' in Deutschmann, David (ed), *Che Guevara Reader* (Melbourne: Ocean Press, 2003)

———, 'Speech to Medical Students and Health Workers' in Deutschmann, David (ed), *Che Guevara Reader* (Melbourne: Ocean Press, 2003)

Hale, Matthew, *The History of the Common Law of England; and, an Analysis of the Civil Part of the Law* (London: Henry Butterworth, 1820)

———, *Treatise of the Nature of Lawes in General and Touching the Law of Nature* (unpublished manuscript, British Library MS Hargrave 485, nd)

Hart, HLA, *The Concept of Law* (2nd edn, Oxford: Oxford University Press, 1994)

Hayek, FA, *The Constitution of Liberty* (Abingdon: Routledge Classics, 2006)

———, *The Road to Serfdom, Text and Documents: The Definitive Edition* (Chicago: University of Chicago Press, 2007)

Hobbes, Thomas, *A Dialogue between a Philosopher and a Student of the Common Laws of England* (Chicago: University of Chicago Press, 1971)

———, *Leviathan* (Oxford: Oxford University Press, 1996)

———, 'The Citizen (*De Cive*)' in Gert, Bernard (ed), *Man and Citizen (De Homine and De Cive)* (Indianapolis: Hackett, 1998)

———, 'Human Nature' in Gaskin, JCA (ed), *Human Nature and De Corpore Politico* (Oxford: Oxford University Press, 1999)

Hohfeld, Wesley Newcomb, *Fundamental Legal Conceptions as Applied in Judicial Reasoning* (Dartmouth: Ashgate, 2001)

Holmes, Oliver W, *The Common Law* (New York: Dover Publications, 1881)

Honoré, Tony, *Responsibility and Fault* (Oxford: Hart, 1999)

Hume, David, 'Of the Original Contract' in Miller, EF (ed), *Essays, Moral, Political, and Literary* (Indianapolis: Liberty Classics, 1985)

Ibbetson, David J, 'How the Romans did for Us: Ancient Roots of the Tort of Negligence', (2003) 26 *University of New South Wales Law Journal* 475

James, Fleming, 'Limitations on Liability for Economic Loss Caused by Negligence', (1972) 25 *Vanderbilt Law Review* 43

Kant, Immanuel, 'Groundwork of the Metaphysics of Morals' in Gregor, Mary (ed), *Practical Philosophy* (Cambridge: Cambridge University Press, 1996)

———, 'The Metaphysics of Morals' in Gregor, Mary (ed), *Practical Philosophy* (Cambridge: Cambridge University Press, 1996)

——, 'On the Common Saying: That May be Correct in Theory, but It Is of No Use in Practice' in Gregor, Mary (ed), *Practical Philosophy* (Cambridge: Cambridge University Press, 1996)

——, 'Toward Perpetual Peace' in Gregor, Mary (ed), *Practical Philosophy* (Cambridge: Cambridge University Press, 1996)

Kaplow, Louis and Shavell, Steven, *Fairness Versus Welfare* (Cambridge, MA: Harvard University Press, 2002)

Keeton, W Page, Dobbs, Dan B, Keeton, Robert E, and Owen, David G, *Prosser and Keeton on the Law of Torts* (5th edn, St Paul, Minn: West Group, 1984)

Ladenson, R, 'In Defense of a Hobbesian Conception of Law' in Raz, Joseph (ed), *Authority* (Oxford: Blackwell, 1990)

Langille, Brian and Ripstein, Arthur, 'Strictly Speaking, It Went Without Saying', (1996) 2 *Legal Theory* 63

Laslett, Peter, '*Two Treatises of Government* and the Revolution of 1688' *Two Treatises of Government* (Cambridge: Cambridge University Press, 1988)

Letwin, Shirley Robin, *On the History of the Idea of Law* (Cambridge: Cambridge University Press, 2005)

Levi, Edward, *An Introduction to Legal Reasoning* (Chicago: University of Chicago Press, 1949)

Lewis, V Bradley, 'Reason Striving to Become Law: Nature and Law in Plato's *Laws*', (2009) 54 *American Journal of Jurisprudence* 67

Lieberman, David, *The Province of Legislation Determined: Legal Theory in Eighteenth Century Britain* (New York: Cambridge University Press, 1989)

Locke, John, 'Some Familiar Letters Between Mr. Locke and Several of His Friends', *The Works of John Locke*, (11th edn, London: Davison, 1812)

——, *Two Treatises of Government and a Letter Concerning Toleration* (Stilwell, KS: Digireads.com, 2005)

Lord Atkin, 'Law as an Educational Subject', [1932] *Journal of the Society of Public Teachers of Law* 27

Macpherson, CB, *The Political Theory of Possessive Individualism: Hobbes to Locke* (Oxford: Clarendon Press, 1962)

Maddox, Graham, 'Representative Government' in Coper, Michael, Blackshield, Tony, and Williams, George (eds), *The Oxford Companion to the High Court of Australia* (Oxford: Oxford University Press, 2007)

Marx, Karl, 'The Eighteenth Brumaire of Louis Bonaparte' in Tucker, Robert C (ed), *The Marx-Engles Reader* (2nd edn, Princeton, NJ: Princeton University Press, 1978)

McBride, Nicholas J and Bagshaw, Roderick, *Tort Law* (3nd edn, Harlow: Pearson Education Ltd, 2008)

Mill, John Stuart, '*On Liberty*' *The Basic Writings of John Stuart Mill: On Liberty, The Subjection of Women and Utilitarianism* (New York: Classic Books America, 2009)

——, '*Utilitarianism*' *The Basic Writings of John Stuart Mill: On Liberty, The Subjection of Women and Utilitarianism* (New York: Classic Books America, 2009)

Montesquieu, Charles de Secondat, *The Spirit of the Laws*, Cohler, Anne M, Miller, Basia Carolyn, and Stone, Harold Samuel (trs), (Cambridge: Cambridge University Press, 1989)

Morris, JHC and Barton Leach, W, *The Rule Against Perpetuities* (2nd edn, London: Stevens & Sons Ltd, 1962)

Müller, Ingo, *Hitler's Justice: The Courts of the Third Reich*, Lucas Schneider, Deborah (tr), (Boston: Harvard University Press, 1991)

Neyers, Jason W, 'A Theory of Vicarious Liability', (2005) 43 *Alberta Law Review* 287

Nolan, Donal and Robertson, Andrew, 'Rights and Private Law' in Robertson, Andrew and Nolan, Donal (eds), *Rights and Private Law* (Oxford: Hart, 2011)

Nozick, Robert, *Anarchy, State, and Utopia* (Oxford: Blackwell, 1975)

Ockham, William of, *A Letter to the Friars Minor and Other Writings* (Cambridge: Cambridge University Press, 1995)

Orrego, Cristóbal, 'H.L.A. Hart's Understanding of Classical Natural Law Theory', (2004) 24 *Oxford Journal of Legal Studies* 287

Peel, Edwin (ed), *Treitel's The Law of Contract* (12th edn, London: Sweet & Maxwell, 2003)

Penner, JE, *McCoubrey & White's Textbook on Jurisprudence* (4th edn, Oxford: Oxford University Press, 2008)

Pettit, Philip, *Republicanism: A Theory of Freedom and Government* (Oxford: Clarendon Press, 1997)

Pincus, Steve, *1688: The First Modern Revolution* (New Haven: Yale University Press, 2009)

Plato, *The Laws*, Saunders, Trevor J (tr), (London: Penguin Classics, 2004)

Plato, *The Republic*, Lee, Desmond (tr), (London: Penguin Books, 2007)

Popper, Karl, *The Open Society and its Enemies* (London: Routledge, 2003)

Posner, Richard A, *Economic Analysis of the Law* (8th edn, New York: Aspen Publishers, 2010)

Pound, Roscoe, *Jurisprudence* (St Paul, Minn: West Publishing Co, 1959)

Prosser, William L, 'Palsgraf Revisited', (1953) 52 *Michigan Law Review* 1

Pufendorf, Samuel, *De statu imperii Germanici* (Genevae: Apud Petrum Columensium, 1667)

———, *Of the Law of Nature and Nations*, Oldfather, HC and Oldfather, WA (trs), (Oxford: Clarendon Press, 1934)

———, *On the Duty of Man and Citizen According to Natural Law*, Silverthorne, Michael (tr), (Cambridge: Cambridge University Press, 2006)

Rawls, John, *Political Liberalism* (New York: Columbia University Press, 1993)

———, *A Theory of Justice: Revised Edition* (Cambridge, Mass: Belknap, 1999)

———, *Justice as Fairness: A Restatement* (Cambridge, Mass: Belknap, 2001)

Raz, Joseph, 'Responsibility and the Negligence Standard', (2010) 30 *Oxford Journal of Legal Studies* 1

Restatement (Third) of Torts: Physical and Emotional Harm (3rd edn, St Paul, Minn: American Law Institute Publishers, 2010)
Ripstein, Arthur, 'Three Duties to Rescue: Moral, Civil, and Criminal', (2000) 19 *Law and Philosophy* 751
———, 'The Division of Responsibility and the Law of Tort', (2003–2004) 72 *Fordham Law Review* 1811
———, *Force and Freedom: Kant's Legal and Political Philosophy* (Boston, MA: Harvard University Press, 2009)
Rogers, WVH, *Winfield and Jolowicz on Tort* (16th edn, London: Sweet & Maxwell, 2002)
———, *Winfield and Jolowicz on Tort* (18th edn, London: Sweet & Maxwell, 2010)
Rousseau, Jean-Jaques, 'On the Social Contract' in Cress, Donald A (ed), *The Basic Political Writings* (Indianapolis: Hackett, 1987)
Ryan, Alan, 'Hobbes's Political Philosophy' in Sorrell, Tom (ed), *The Cambridge Companion to Hobbes* (Cambridge: Cambridge University Press, 1996)
Sage, NW, 'Original Acquisition and Unilateralism: Kant, Hegel, and Corrective Justice', (2012) 25 *Canadian Journal of Law and Jurisprudence* 119
Saunders, Trevor J, 'Introduction' *The Laws* (London: Penguin, 2004)
Searle, John R, *Making the Social World: The Structure of Human Civilization* (New York: Oxford University Press, 2010)
Seneca, *De clementia*, Braund, Susanna (tr), (Oxford: Oxford University Press, 2009)
Sidgwick, Henry, *The Methods of Ethics* (7th edn, London: Macmillan & Co, 1907)
Simester, AP and Chan, Winnie, 'Inducing Breach of Contract: One Tort or Two?', [2004] *Cambridge Law Journal* 132
Simmons, A John, *On the Edge of Anarchy: Locke, Consent, and the Limits of Society* (Princeton, NJ: Princeton University Press, 1993)
Skinner, Quentin, *Liberty Before Liberalism* (Cambridge: Cambridge University Press, 1998)
———, 'The Idea of the State: A Genealogy' (2010) *The State of the State* <http://itunes.apple.com/us/itunes-u/the-state-of-the-state/id381703022>
Smith, Stephen A, *Contract Theory* (Oxford: Clarendon Press, 2004)
Smits, Jan M, *The Good Samaritan in European Private Law: On the Perils of Principles without a Programme and a Programme for the Future* (Deventer: Kluwer, 2000)
Stapleton, Jane, 'Duty of Care Factors: A Selection from the Judicial Menus' in Cane, Peter and Stapleton, Jane (eds), *The Law of Obligations: Essays in Celebration of John Fleming* (Oxford: Clarendon Press, 1998)
———, 'The Golden Thread at the Heart of Tort Law: Protection of the Vulnerable', (2003) 24 *Australian Bar Review* 135
Stevens, Robert, *Torts and Rights* (Oxford: Oxford University Press, 2007)
Steyn, Lord, 'Contract Law: Fufilling the Reasonable Expectation of Honest Men', (1997) 113 *Law Quarterly Review* 433
Stone, Martin, 'The Significance of Doing and Suffering' in Postema, Gerald J (ed), *Philosophy and the Law of Torts* (Cambridge: Cambridge University Press, 2001)

Strauss, David A, *The Living Constitution* (New York: Oxford University Press, 2010)

Thomas, EW, 'Fairness and Certainty in Adjudication: Formalism v. Substantialism', (1999) 9 *Otago Law Review* 459

———, 'The 'Invisible Hand' Prompts a Response', [1999] *New Zealand Law Review* 227

Todd, Stephen, 'Negligence: The Duty of Care' in Todd, Stephen (ed), *The Law of Torts in New Zealand* (3rd edn, Wellington: Brookers, 2001)

Tomkins, Adam, *Public Law* (Oxford: Oxford University Press, 2003)

Tuck, Richard, *Natural Rights Theories: Their Origin and Development* (Cambridge: Cambridge University Press, 1979)

Tully, James, *A Discourse on Property, John Locke and his Adversaries* (Cambridge: Cambridge University Press, 1980)

———, *An Approach to Political Philosophy: Locke in Context* (Cambridge: Cambridge University Press, 1993)

Tyrrell, James, *Patriarcha non monarcha: Being Observations on a Late Treatise and Divers other Miscellanies, Published under the Name of Sir Robert Filmer, Baronet: in which the Falseness of those Opinions that would make Monarchy Jure divino are Laid Open, and the True Principles of Government and Property (especially in our Kingdom) Asserted; by a Lover of Truth and of his Country* (London: Richard Janeway, 1681)

Underwood, Peter, 'Is Ms Donoghue's Snail in Mortal Peril?', (2004) 12 *Torts Law Journal* 39

Waldron, Jeremy, 'Kant's Legal Positivism', (1995–1996) 109 *Harvard Law Review* 1535

———, *The Right to Private Property* (Oxford: Clarendon Press, 1998)

Watson, Alan (ed), *The Digest of Justinian* (Philadelphia: University of Pennsylvania Press, 1985)

———, *The Evolution of Western Private Law: Expanded Edition* (Baltimore: The John Hopkins University Press, 2001)

———, *Legal History and a Common Law for Europe* (Stockholm: Institutet för Rättshistorisk Forskning, 2001)

Weinrib, Ernest J, 'The Case for a Duty to Rescue', (1980) 90 *Yale Law Journal* 247

———, 'Legal Formalism: On the Immanent Rationality of Law', (1988) 97 *Yale Law Journal* 949

———, *The Idea of Private Law* (Cambridge, Mass: Harvard University Press, 1995)

Wigglesworth, EC, 'Legislation and Injury Control', (1978) 18 *Medical Science and Law* 191

Winfield, PH, *The Province of the Law of Tort* (Cambridge: Cambridge University Press, 1931)

Zimmermann, Reinhard, *The Law of Obligations: Roman Foundations of the Civilian Tradition* (Oxford: Oxford University Press, 1996)

———, *Roman Law, Contemporary Law, European Law: The Civilian Tradition Today* (Oxford: Oxford University Press, 2001)

———, 'Remedies for Non-Performance: The Revised German Law of Obligations, Viewed Against the Background of the Principles of European Contract Law', (2002) 6 *Edinburgh Law Review* 271

Index

adjudication 115–116
Ashby v White 127–128
Aquinas, St Thomas
  bodily integrity 106–108
  Catholicism 99–100
  commutative justice 101–105
  courts, role of 115–116
  crime 108
  distributive justice 101–102
  end of law 103–105
  harm 100–101
  justice as virtue 106
  natural law 100
  property 110–114
  rectification 102, 108–110
  state 114–116
Aristotle
  biography 61–63
  corrective justice 67–79
  crime 86–88
  distributive justice 64–74
  legislation 82
  natural law 84–85
  priority of law over politics 81–85
  private law 85–88
  Pythagoras' theory of justice 77–78
  rectification 73–74, 76, 79, 86
  revenge 87
Atkin, Lord 276–277
Augustine, St 9–10

Bagshaw, Roderick 26–27, 301–302
Bentham, Jeremy
  biography 227–228
  common law 295
  criminal law 237–239
  injury 236–239, 262
  private law 236–239
  punishment 236–239
  rectification 236–239
  wrongdoing, the nature of 231
  see also utilitarianism
Blackstone, Sir William 274–275
bodily integrity 106–108, 125–126, 157–158, 196, 217–219
Bracher, Karl Dietrich 290
Byrd, Sharon 167–170

Chen-Wishart, Mindy 28, 134, 268
Cicero
  biography 90–91
  democracy 92–93
  priority of law over politics 93–94
  private law 93–94
  rule of law 91–94
  republicanism 92–93
Coke, Sir Edward 273–274
common law 295–297
commutative justice 20, 67–69, 73–79, 80, 101–105, 119–123, 150–151, 191, 193–194, 201–202, 217–226, 228–229, 232, 284
consent 155–156, 210–213, 216–217, 223
contract 27–29, 129–137, 158–159, 196
  breach of contract 131–132, 267–268
  commutative justice 20
  distributive justice 28–29, 64–67
  Harm Principle 28–29, 268
  objective standard of interpretation 132–137
  reasonable expectations, theory of 268–271

contract *(continued)*
  reliance theory of 133, 268–271
  corrective justice *see* commutative justice
  as aspect of distributive justice 69–74, 282–288
crime 86–88, 108, 196–197, 237–239

democracy 83, 92–93, 293–294
  and judge made law 293–307
deterrence 147
Diggers, the 178, 181
distributive justice 28–29, 45–46, 50–53, 101–102, 119, 150–151, 191–193, 219–225, 228–229
divine right of kings 178
Dobbs, Dan 104
Donoghue v Stevenson 257, 307
Doughty v Turner Manufacturing 257–258
Dworkin, Ronald 297, 301

Eighty Years' War 171–173
English Civil War 6, 175–181
equity 186, 190–193

Fichte, JG 165–166, 194–195
Fleming, John 308
Foucault, Michel 2
Fuller, Lon 28–29, 133, 267–268

Gardner, John 266, 284–287
George v Fairmead (Pty) Ltd 269
German law and legal scholarship 170, 205–206
Glorious Revolution 172–173
Goebbels, Joseph 290–291, 308–309
Gordley, James 69–70
Grotius, Hugo 194–195
Guevara, Ernesto 'Che' 290–291

Hale, Sir Mathew 274
  harm *see* injury
Harm Principle 28–29, 234–235, 263–266, 268, 292–293
Harriton v Stevens 283–284
Hart, HLA 9–10
Hegel, GWF 194–195

Hobbes, Thomas 6
  biography 175–181
  bodily integrity 196
  civil law 188
  common law 296–297
  commutative justice 122, 191, 193–194, 201–202
  contract 196
  crime 196–197
  distributive justice 191–193
  equity 186, 190–193
  influence on political philosophy 195
  injury 262
  justice 185–187
  natural law 186–189, 192, 198–202
  political authority 178–181, 189–190
  priority of politics over law 194–197
  priority of public over private law 196–197
  private law 196–197
  property 196
  social contract argument 181–191, 198–202, 280
Holmes, Oliver Wendell 260–261
Holy Roman Empire 96–98
Hruschka, Joachim 167–170

injury 100–101, 126–127, 157–158, 235–239, 246, 262, 284

James, William 99

Kant, Immanuel
  bodily integrity 157–158
  commutative justice 150–151
  consent 155–156
  contract 158–159
  distributive justice 150–151
  end of law 151–152
  injury 157–158, 284
  original acquisition 161–163
  priority of law over justice 151–152
  priority of law over politics 151–152, 156, 167–170
  property 160–163, 221
  republicanism 163–167

self-defence and the defence of others 153–156
state, the 163–167

laesio enormis 78, 191
legal positivism 2
Letwin, Shirley 215, 301
Levellers, the 178, 181
liberalism 291–293
Locke, John
  biography 207–208
  bodily integrity 217–219
  commutative justice 217–226
  consent 210–213, 216–217, 223
  distributive justice 219–225
  natural rights 208–210, 213–226, 281
  political authority 213–216
  private law 225–226
  property 219–225
  rectification 226
  social contract argument 210–217

McBride, Neil 26–27, 301–302
Macpherson, CB 221–222
Macpherson v Buick Motor Co 303
Magna Carta 281–282
marriage 309
Mill, John Stuart
  basis of the principle of utility 229–230
  biography 227–228
  Harm Principle 234–235, 263–266, 292–293
  reasonable expectations, theory of 268–271
  rights, theory of 233–235
  wrongdoing, the nature of 231–232
  see also utilitarianism
misfeasance and nonfeasance 271–273
Montesquieu, Charles-Louis De Secondat 202–205

negligence, law of 245–259
  objective standard of care 259–261, 304–305
  see also tort

Nozick, Robert 195

original acquisition 140–143, 161–163

Palsgraf v Long Island Railroad 244–259
Paris v Stepney Borough Council 304–305
Perdue, William 28–29, 133, 267–268
Pettit, Philip 163–164
Pierson v Post 141–143
Plato
  authoritarianism 43
  biography 37–39, 55
  distributive justice 45–46, 50–53
  education 40–43
  philosopher kings 42–43
  priority of politics over law 59–60
  private law 44, 47–53
  problem of political power 39–43, 58–60
  property 52–53
  punishment 47–49
  rectification 49–52
  relationship between *The Republic* and *The Laws* 54–60
  relationship with modern philosophy 45–46, 50
  rule of law 57–60
political authority 178–181, 189–190, 213–216
Popper, Karl 39
priority of law over politics 6–7, 81–85, 93–94, 98, 123–124, 151–152, 156, 167–170, 203, 282
priority of politics over law 6–7, 21, 59–60, 194–197
priority of public over private law 196–197
private law 20–21, 44, 47–53, 85–88, 93–94, 196–197, 225–226, 236–239
  adjudication 273, 306
  in personam nature of 244–259
  legislative intervention 306–307
  priority over public law 6–7
  see also contract law, negligence, tort law, unjust enrichment

property 19, 22, 52–53, 101–114, 137–148, 160–163, 196, 219–225, 279–280
  mixed conception of 137–146, 160–163
Pufendorf, Samuel
  bodily integrity 125–126
  breach of contract 131–132
  commutative justice 119–123
  contract 129–137
  disgorgement 146–148, 263
  distributive justice 119
  end of law 123–125
  influence of Hobbes 95, 122
  injury 126–127, 284
  interpretation of Aristotle 121–122
  justice, definitions of 118–123
  objective standard of interpretation in contract 132–137
  original acquisition 140–143
  priority of law over politics 123–124
  property 137–148
  rectification 126–128
  state, the 148–149
punishment 47–49, 236–239, 246
Prussia 97–98, 206

Rawls, John
  natural duties 15, 31–33, 282
  nature of political philosophy 14–21, 29–33, 195
  priority of politics over law 21, 195
  private law 20–21
  social contract argument 16–20, 29–31, 280–281
  utilitarianism, rejection of 233
reasonable expectations, theory of 268–271
rectification 49–52, 73–74, 76, 79, 86, 102, 108–110, 126–128, 226, 235–239, 246
republicanism 92–93, 163–167
Rousseau, Jean-Jacques 165–166, 202–203
rule of law 57–60, 91–94
Ryan, Alan 183

Saunders, Trevor 55–56
scholasticism 99
self-defence and the defence of others 153–156
Seneca 91
Sidgwick, Henry
  biography 227–228
  commutative (corrective) justice 232, 284
  reasonable expectations, theory of 268–271
  see also utilitarianism
Simmons, John 220–222
slavery 288–289
social contract argument 16–20, 29–31, 181–191, 198–202, 210–217, 280–281
Stapleton, Jane 272
state, the 114–116, 148–149, 163–167
Steyn, Lord 132–133

Thirty Years' War 171–173
tort law 22–27
  compensation 24–25
  commutative justice 273–276
  definition of 274–276
  deterrence 23–24, 264–266
  disgorgement 146–148, 263
  distributive justice 25–27
  economic loss 262–263
  Harm Principle 263–266
  injury 262–266, 273
  loss 262–266
  misfeasance and nonfeasance 271–273
  policy 26–27
  rectification 262–266
  see also negligence
torture 285–287
totalitarianism 289–291

Ulpian 91
Underwood, Peter 307
unjust enrichment 212–213, 220, 236, 239
utilitarianism
  basis of the principle of utility 229–230